HOW TO CREATE
INCREDIBLE
EDIBLES

HOW TO CREATE
INCREDIBLE
EDIBLES:

An Illustrated Guide to
Imaginative Food Presentation

by
FLORRIE PAUL

LECTURER – INSTRUCTOR

IN THE ART OF "KITCHEN KRAFT"©

FOR THE HOUSEWIFE AND CATERER

NORMAN PUBLISHING CO.
21 ALMROTH DRIVE, WAYNE, N. J. 07470

Library of Congress Cataloging in Publication Data

Paul, Florrie
    How to create incredible edibles.

    1.   Cookery (Garnishes)   I.   Title.
TX652.P34   641.5   75-11526

Reprinted in 1982   ISBN 0-9601788-1-3

Reprinted in 1979 under title: *How to Create Incredible Edibles: An illustrated Guide to Imaginative Food Presentation,* by Norman Publishing Co., Wayne, N. J.
ISBN 0-9601788-1-3

Copyright © 1975 by Florrie Paul

Published in 1975 under title: *How to Create Incredible Edibles: An illustrated Guide to Imaginative Food Preparation,* by Frederick Fell Publishers Inc., New York, N.Y.
ISBN 0-8119-0244-7

For information address:

Norman Publishing Co.
21 Almroth Drive
Wayne, N.J. 07470

Manufactured in the United States of America.

DEDICATION

It is what we do today that makes our happy memories for
tomorrow . . . and so when people gather today and talk about
legacies and materialistic things to bequeath, my mind wanders.

It wanders back through the years to the warm comforting
feeling of waking to the aroma of yeast bread baking early on
Friday morning for the Sabbath. My taste buds aroused by the
taste of hot coffee cake from the old black coal stove that no
commercial bakery has yet to match; (perhaps, because the
memories with it are not for sale). The pride in wearing a
"home made dress" Grandma made especially for me; the simmering of a big cauldron holding the "Soup de Jour" made with
leftover inexpensive meat bones from the corner butcher. My
memory tingles once again with the excitement of my cousins
arriving with their parents for Sunday dinner or holiday meals.
In those days it was not just the gathering of the clan for funerals
and weddings, or, if the family left is big enough, "The Cousins
Club Monthly Meeting" that we find so prevalent nowadays in
our fast-moving modern society.

My Grandmother passed on much too soon and far too suddenly, leaving behind only *this* "legacy of memories". Of

course, it was not drawn up in a formal will by a lawyer. An immigrant of little means, how she would have laughed at the thought, for her only "worldly possession" was an antiquated foot treadle sewing machine. So, bequeathed to a child of ten, were only the rich memories of a truly beautiful woman of 51 years. There were no recipes written down, no secrets given to such a young grandchild, always underfoot in her kitchen but . . . a legacy was nonetheless passed on. A heritage of drive and motivation to equal her culinary accomplishments and a spirit that was almost contagious to all for her enthusiasm for life.

I, too, wish to "leave an estate" to my children and to all of your children through YOU! Not houses, furs or diamonds for I haven't that many . . . but rather, as I look back over the years of homemade movies . . . birthdays in our house are never recalled by *what* the gifts were but rather the fun in preparing for the special occasion. It was my daughter, ecstatic with glee . . . "Mommy, you made me a bride-doll cake" . . . "Ma, can I have a turtle cake this year for the kids in school?" . . . or with the advent of Summer, the Hawaiian watermelon outrigger for the backyard Luau party. . . . Very often a request for a chef doll centerpiece was the first I knew I was sponsoring the barbecue party for the Cub Scout troop.

My lecture audiences often ask what schools I enrolled in to learn this culinary art . . . there was never any formal tutoring . . . merely the school of experience and fun-filled days fooling around in my own kitchen, of getting to weddings and catered affairs early to see the work of highly skilled chefs. It is then *this* "legacy of memories" I wish to share with you, your friends and guests. In this time of Woman's Lib I am "way out of it," as my college daughter would be the first to say, but then she's younger . . . if I burned my bra at 46 years old I'd look like a mess, and besides I need all the help and support I can get. But then, where else could one find a job with so much power and such reward? What business firm would hire an inexperienced woman of 23 and give her the almighty power to shape and mold the life of other human beings given unto her only by the virtue of birth?

If I were to thank all the people that have passed through and touched upon my life and so contributed to *my* book of memories I would sound very much like the award winning actress on "Oscar Night". Simply then, much thanks to my Mom and Dad, family and friends who were such willing guinea pigs at my dinner and party tables, my students and lecture audiences for their applause and encouragement in getting this book going; a very special salute for bravery to my poor husband, Norman, who had to cut my first meatball dinner with a cleaver (and swore it was delicious) and to my children, Diane, Steven and Douglas, who many times had to barbecue hot dogs and prepare their own dinners because Mom was busy demonstrating and teaching all you other girls how to "Create Incredible Edibles."

FLORRIE PAUL

11

INTRODUCTION

"Creating incredible edibles" . . . the art of food sculpture . . . an impressive title for a book that simply shows you how food can be fun. But then, it's almost as impressive as the introduction usually accorded me on my round of demonstration-lectures. . . . "and here she is, food sculptress and lecturer: Florrie Paul, Domestic Engineer." Don't let that title of domestic engineer over-impress you either, for you too have the same "degree". . . . Mrs. Summa Cum Laude. Domestic Engineer is just a nice way of saying, "I'm just a housewife." Just a housewife? Don't you believe it! The men in this country have the greatest earning power in the world . . . but ladies, we as "housewives" control the biggest purchasing power in the world. Stop and think about it . . . we prove it week in and week out! Whatever our men manage to earn, we manage to spend! I know, for I meet you buying shoes and clothes for the kids; I bump into you at the supermarket, walking up and down the aisles mumbling to yourself about the rising cost of food. I'd like to share some thoughts and ideas with you to show you how some simple food sculpture tricks can really "Create Incredible Edibles." The Art of Food Sculpture is merely presenting food to the table with a bit of a creative flair. This simple rule will keep making *your* table the Talk of the Town!

Actually it's as easy as learning your A B C 's.

A. Appeal . . . to the eye as well as the appetite; make it tasty, then make it look pretty and it will automatically be appetizing!

B. Balance . . . of diet, forms and textures, e.g. if your dinner is chicken breasts smothered in mushroom sauce, then for heaven's sake don't team it that night with mashed potatoes and white asparagus. The table you present then is low in height, with no variation in form and texture, and is colorless. Therefore your whole plate looks "flat," consequently you've already lost the first "A." Suggestion: instead, southern fry or bake your chicken breasts in bread or corn flake crumbs (texture), put your sweet potatoes through a pastry tube decoratively onto canned pineapple slices and serve fresh green beans almondine with a little cranberry sauce to the side. Yummy to the tummy as well as to the eye. You've just earned yourself an "A."

C. Color contrasts . . . even if it's a simple plate of fresh garden vegetables you're serving, place your green peppers next to the red cherry tomatoes, alongside the black jumbo olives rather than tomato slices next to carrot slices. Note that we used color contrast in the simple chicken plate we just presented above.

You've done so well I'm going to award you a "letter" for your apron! Its a capital "D" . . . design . . . and your production will always be dramatic. Put your sweet potatoes into an orange cup, or serve your fresh pineapple in the form of a peacock; instead of the usual silver tray or serving plate, have your hand fruit tumbling onto the tray from a beautiful wicker cornucopia intermixed with fresh nuts and preserved fruits (dried apricots, dates, prunes, etc.).

Rule 1: *It's not what you have, but what you do with it that counts* . . . but then your mother has been telling you that since you reached 15. You've heard of metal craft, copper craft, jewelry craft . . . now lets have some fun with "Kitchen Kraft." The only craft where nothing is wasted—where you can *eat* all your mistakes. Food sculpture is the art of presenting food in a creative manner . . . presenting a beautiful table. One eats with his eyes long before a morsel of food touches his lips.

Rule 2: *It doesn't have to be expensive to be elegant!* e.g.: start with two cans of tuna fish and a couple of hard cooked eggs, add to this some fresh garden vegetables and, lo and behold, it's a floral arrangement. Your edible centerpiece looks like a wicker (tuna) basket, bordered with tempting egg salad, and topped brim full with vegetable flowers. (see chapter 8) You now have a delicious, inexpensive and nutritious luncheon menu that will provide your guests with plenty of table conversation to start off a pleasant afternoon.

Rule 3: *A carpenter is as good as his tools!* A pineapple knife is not the same as a grapefruit knife . . . as a coping saw would not do the same job as a hacksaw. There are tricks and ways to make life easier in the kitchen, so let me share some with you now.

If the blade of a knife or kitchen implement is straight, utilize it only to make a straight cut; if it is curved such as a grapefruit or pineapple knife, use it correctly to loosen the meat along the curve of the rind shell of the pineapple, melon or grapefruit. Always keep your tools sharpened. Purchase good kitchen implements for they will be more economical in the long run than replacing the 98¢ melon baller over, again and again. Personally, I only use a double-ended baller with razor sharp bevelled edges, and a riveted wooden handle which gives me two different sized balls. I prefer the strength and durability of the stainless steel 7″ blade of a professional serrater, although you could manage in some cases with an 89¢ potato crinkler available in the local supermarket. There is more latitude in working with the French imported lemon stripper (actually a bar instrument) because its small, sharp stainless steel opening works equally well on the rinds of melons, oranges, lemons, turnips and cucumbers and also on the delicate crown cap of mushrooms and radishes. The strength of this stripper also can be utilized on the sometimes very rough rino skin of the watermelon, and the tuberous roots of the beet and hard-cored carrot. (See chapter 7 on vegetable flowers. See chapter on tools for descriptions, pictures, and usages.)

Rule 4: *Because a kitchen tool has a name does not mean it has a limit!* . . . therefore don't limit your mind, use your ingenuity. Because we call it a grapefruit spoon doesn't mean its only use is to release the meat pulp of a grapefruit. The perfect examples of this very rule are the cheese rose we create with the use of the grapefruit spoon, and the making of a viking cucumber relish dish where we also put to use the grapefruit knife. (See chapter 6 & 7: cheese rose and cucumber relish dish). A grapefruit spoon is fantastic in cleaning out tomatoes and peppers to prepare them as shells for stuffing. Set your table with a grapefruit spoon when serving cantalope halves or melon sections as an entree. It makes for much easier "spooning" than the usual dessert spoon.

I use the professional serrater not only to tenderize meat and cut the potatoes it was designed for, but to slice canapé breads, melons, carrots, celery, bulk meats and cheeses, etc. (See appropriate chapters on same). If you don't already own and recognize some of the instruments depicted on the next few pages go to your local houseware store or nearest bar-restaurant supply house. However, before you do even that, first go to your own kitchen drawer and reach deep into the back. Don't be surprised if you find you've actually owned it all along, perhaps had not found much use for it, and allocated it to the dark recesses of the nearest junk drawer. If you still have no luck, since I merchandize all my food sculpture tools, write to me personally at 21 Almroth Drive, Wayne, New Jersey 07470, and I will make arrangements to mail it to you. After collecting kitchen gadgets for 20 some odd years, if I don't already have it, at least I know what it's about and where it's at!

So now put down the book and put on the apron! Food Sculpture is simply the use of good instruments, this book with some terrific ideas of food presentation, some guide lines and practice, practice, practice!!! So let's have some Fun . . . with Food . . . and

Florrie

TOOLS OF YOUR KITCHEN WORKSHOP

If an artist were to begin to paint a picture, he would need at least one tube of oils, a paint brush, a room to work in, and an idea to put on canvas. What kind of picture can you paint with just these simple basic working tools? Nothing too dramatic or creative, needless to say . . . but it *is* a start! You begin to walk a mile when you take your first step! Given another tube or two of oil paints, a variety of sable brushes and surely, the picture produced would be more creative.

And so as the artist in your kitchen, look over your workshop, become familiar with your tools, add to your inventory, and then elaborate on their uses. The masterpiece you produce from your kitchen gallery might not make the culinary LOUVRE the first time, but then the Mona Lisa was not the *first* effort of Leonardo Da Vinci either.

At least, unlike many of the great artists, we need not starve to be inspired . . . we can survive on the "edible" canvases we create . . . we can enjoy and relish our mistakes as well as our masterpieces.

Therefore, may I introduce you to some of the tools and implements of your food sculpture gallery plus some of the terms you will become familiar with while "Creating Incredible Edibles."

Apple corer: usually a wooden or plastic handled implement with attached stainless steel coring blade with one or two serrated edges. Used to core apples and pears; used in food sculpture to remove centers of vegetables for stuffing. see ch. 7 cucumbers.

Apple or pear divider: Recommended is the *fourteen* section Wilesco (brand name): used to cut and section fourteen equal slices of apple or pear and core the fruit simultaneously. Used primarily in food sculpture to create a rose flower with fourteen perfect uniform petals from radishes. It can also be used to cut par-boiled turnips and / or beets.

Aspic cutter: See Cutters.

Assorted fruits: As in assorted medley of fruits or compote mixture; assorted melon balls and / or fruit intermixed (also see: Contrasting Fruits).

Ball scoops: Commonly referred to as a melon baller, these scoops come not only in all diameter sizes, but are also available in round, oval and scallop shaped ends. Although some are manufactured with just one melon scoop or baller at the tip, there are many that feature double

ended scoops with two different diameter sizes. The scoop ball ends vary from ¼–½" for making dainty (blueberry size) balls from fruits and vegetables (for combining and creating various flower designs) to the large well-known ice cream scoop. There are many inexpensive ball scoops on the market. It is wise to invest in a riveted handle, *stainless steel* implement *with razor sharp ball edges.* With a well-turned out ball scooper you can easily cut balls out of firm uncooked turnips and beets and cut into the heavy tough rind of a watermelon. (used in creating a watermelon frigate ship, see chapter 2). The less expensive scooper will only serve to cut the soft flesh of the watermelon or cantaloupe fruit itself.

Bamboo sticks (skewers): Thin, very pliable but strong bamboo (or wood) skewer sticks used to hold and stabilize pieces of fruit or styrofoam together in large fruit plate displays. Used for stem support of vegetable flowers for display. Can be easily cut to desired size with nail clippers or scissors. (Also see Floral Wood Picks). Note of interest: to prevent shrimp from curling, boil them with bamboo stick up back vein.

Bird's nest fryer: Sometimes called Chinese noodle basket, or potato or bread basket as bread, noodles or potatoes will look like bird's nest when fried in deep oil: makes a decorative as well as edible serving shell. Fill with creamed curries, chicken a la king, egg salad, etc. Available in various size basket cups. Place shredded potatoes, noodles or slices of bread strips in the lower of the two baskets that comprise this French kitchen implement; top with smaller basket to form nest-like mold, close clamps (provided) and deep fry until browned. Cool and fill with desired filling. To use for dessert service, line basket with left over cake pieces, fry and fill with ice cream, fruit or puddings.

Chenilles: There are many varieties of chenilles (commonly referred to as pipe cleaners) such as string chenille, stem chenille, fluffy chenille, celtigal chenille, glitter stems and bump chenilles. We will be using the stem and bump chenilles in food sculpture. The bump chenilles come in 1", 3" and 6" bumps. We will concern ourselves for the most part with 1" bumps as they are the most popular and useful. There are some magazines and booklets on chenille craft. If you wish to purchase one, it is called "Chenille Fun." The colorful booklet is published by Craft Course Publishers Inc., Temple City, Calif. The directions, diagrams and colored pictures will teach you how to have fun creating flowers, novelties and party favors. The approximate cost is $1.00. To purchase this copy or any of the other chenille booklets which feature figures and centerpieces see your local craft store or write directly to the publisher as listed above.

Chicory: Green leafy vegetable used as filler and cover up in food sculpture. It is entirely edible and very good in fresh salads or as a cooked vegetable.

Chinese noodle basket: See Bird's Nest Fryer.

Cocktail fork: 5½" long flat wood pronged fork used for cocktails or French fries: See cucumber viking ship ch. 7.

Color dye: See Food Color Dye.

Contrasting fruits: Groups of the same type of melon balls and/or other fruits placed as a whole group on a fruit plate. Lay groups next to each other in contrasting colors to add dramatic design to arrangement of fruit platter.

Cotton balls: Used in place of cotton buds, to apply food color to large areas as on the (potato) head of the pineapple peacock.

Cotton buds: Sometimes referred to as Q-tips (brand name). Used to apply food color to small hard to get at areas as for coloring the beak of the (potato) head of the pineapple peacock, the mouth of the eggplant clown, etc.

Cutters: Cutters come in all sizes and shapes and are used to cut out designs of flowers, leaves, figures and infinite different geometric shapes. These cut-outs, made from a variety of foods and pastries are then used to decorate and garnish plates, breads and pastries, hors d'oeuvres, soups, desserts, mousses, etc. *Aspic-canape cutters:* Usually measures one inch in size; used to cut out gelatin designs, meat and cheese decorations for open face sandwiches, designs from slices of vegetables, hard cooked egg white and candied fruit peel, etc. *Cookie cutters:* Bigger in size; used to cut out cookies and some large gelatin designs for decorating and garnishing, e.g. cut out large heart-shaped or star design from chilled jellied cranberry sauce for turkey garnish. Used to cut party breads for tea sandwiches for buffet or hors d'oeuvres service. *Vegetable cutters:* All sizes; can be used to cut various designs from slices of vegetables or fruit. Most popular one is the potato daisy cutter. By com-

bining different cutout pieces together you can create various new designs to lend interest to your presentation of food. *Gyalu cutter* (Hungarian version) or *Mandoline* (French version): There are many varieties of slicers or cutters; the most popular, the Gyalu and Mandoline. These slicers provide you with a stand and adjustable cutter to obtain uniform slices of vegetables and fruits for cooking as well as garnishing. These cutters are used most often to slice the cabbage heads in preparation for cole-slaw.

Dowel: As defined in the dictionary: a pin of sorts fitting into a hole in an abutting piece to prevent motion and slipping. The use of any wooden cylindrical shape (dowel) of various widths, circumferences and lengths to abut and stabilize one piece to another so as to prevent movement and shifting of design in the presentation of food sculpture. E.g. dowel stick used as mast to secure sails onto (see chapter 2 on Watermelon Frigate Ship); such as orange wood stick and bamboo sticks used as dowels to give stem support to cut vegetable flowers in Floral Bouquet (see chapter 7 on Vegetable Bouquets). See bamboo sticks; see orange wood sticks; see wood floral picks in this glossary of terms.

Egg slicer: Implement to cut hard cooked eggs into uniform slices.

Egg wedger: Implement used to cut hard cooked egg into six equal uniform wedge-shaped sections in one cutting motion.

Escarole: Green long leaf vegetable used as filler and decoration for food presentation (as in Tuna Flower Basket and as waves for whale and boat presentation). Good in fresh greens salad.

Extractor (juice): Implement used for citrus fruits to squeeze out juices quickly (see lime frog).

Floral gum tape: See Stickum Gum Tape in glossary.

Floral tape: Flexible green tape to wrap dowel sticks for topiary tree presentations.

Floral wire: Metal wire available in all gauges of weight and length. Used in food sculpture for *inedible* presentations only.

Floral wood toothpicks: There are two varieties: the more familiar one is available dyed dark green with metal floral wire attached; this is *not* used in food sculpture as we do not know what substance is used for coloring the picks. *Natural or colorless floral picks:* Used extensively in food presentation much as the dowel stick. The floral pick is available in large floral shops. (1000 to a box). It is a heavy square toothpick with both ends sharp and pointed. Being very strong and durable, it is used primarily in the vegetable bouquet. It is substituted in place of the frill pick when you do not want your pick or colors to show through or be emphasized. (See hidden toothpick method in glossary.)

Food color dye: Vegetable dye food coloring; commercially produced and available in large sizes of one particular color in liquid or paste form base. More popular and practical is the box of four small bottles of assorted liquid colors: red, yellow, green and blue. Used to change or emphasize the color of food, such as in the frosting of cakes and soft cheeses; used to color vegetables such as white radishes, turnips, potatoes etc.

Food mill: See potato ricer.

Frill picks: Toothpicks available in regular common toothpick lengths (3"), as well as four inch club size. One end is tipped and festive looking as it is decorated with frilled cellophane papers of various colors such as gold, blue, red and green.

Fruit fresh: A new commercial product from the pharmaceutical house of Merck, Sharpe & Dohme: A derivative of ascorbic acid (Vitamin C). When the white powder is diluted in water and directions are followed, it will prevent the vegetables or fruits from turning brown due to air oxidation (as in potatoes, bananas, pears, etc.). Available in small (can) size from your local *pharmacy* by its trade name of "Fruit Fresh" (see commercial product: potato white).

Grapefruit knife: A curved knife with serrated blade used to separate meat pulp from its membrane in citrus fruits. Recommended is the grapefruit knife whose blade comes to a sharp point and is serrated on *both* sides of the metal. This particular cutlery design is very important in the preparation of food sculpture for from this evolves relish cucumber boats as well as watermelon Viking Ships, etc.

Grapefruit spoon: A spoon designed to easily remove the citrus segment of your fruit from the membrane. Also used as a serving spoon for melons for easier edibility. Recommended is the grapefruit spoon I import. Its blade tang goes through the complete handle of the spoon for extra strength; the oval shaped bowl is extremely deep with serrated edges going half way down the bowl on both sides of the spoon. The tip comes to a very sharp point thus enabling you to create a beautiful cream cheese rose. It is also used as well in preparation of the cucumber Viking relish boat and to clean and prepare tomato and pepper shells for stuffing (See chapter 7).

Grater: Many varieties and shapes used to make small grated pieces of whatever food is being prepared. Graters come with round holes as well as with metal, plastic, or ceramic sharp teeth. A grater can be used to push through and grate hard cooked eggs in preparation for salads. There is also a nutmeg grater, potato grater, chocolate grater, etc. Some foods, although not pretty in their natural form, take on more beauty when grated and used as a garnish, such as red radishes, cooked egg whites, as well as drained beets, etc.

Greenery: See Chicory and Escarole.

Greening pins: See Totem Pins.

Gyalu: See Cutters.

Hidden toothpick method: Referred to in food sculpture as a technique used to present food that must be pinned or stabilized in place and yet *not* have the use of a colorful cellophane frill toothpick emphasized. Therefore, in place of a cellophane frill pick, a wooden floral pick would be used. Place wooden floral pick in proper position; push

onto its exposed point the egg, vegetable, olive or strawberry or fruit so that the point of the pick does not extend beyond the food thus positioned. See illustration; see appropriate chapters using this method.

Kitchen helper: My very favorite, all purpose kitchen implement comprised of a large-mouthed lemon stripper, a grater, a potato or vegetable peeler, and a fruit notcher. The aforementioned are self-explanatory; the latter, the fruit notcher, is a triangular-shaped cutter which when used will cut melons, citrus fruits and vegetables. With the notcher you create V shaped cuts by pushing notcher end through to the center of the fruit. By going around the melon or vegetable or fruit completely, you will then automatically divide it into saw-tooth cut sections.

Knives: All shapes, sizes, metal and plastic strengths. The oldest tool known to mankind, it is the most used and *abused* tool by mankind. Your husband would never think of using his tool—e.g.: a hacksaw instead of a coping saw in his carpentry workshop yet . . . the woman in her workshop, her kitchen, will use her tools, her knives, to open jammed drawers, bottle tops, jars; use her knife as a screwdriver, hammer, etc. Treat your culinary tools with proper use and they will last longer. *Plastic knives:* Rather new to the market, the see-through knives, (some advertised under the brandname of Dionne Lucas) have been well received for their strength and see-thru quality. *Carbon steel knives:* Preferred by the chefs and those in the know of the culinary world, they are found in most restaurants, institutions and hotel kitchens. A carbon steel blade holds a sharp edge longer and is usually hand forged. They do not often find their way into the housewives' kitchens for they pick up stains easily and therefore do not have the shiny quality of stainless steel. If, however, they were to be washed and wiped as soon as used (a custom a housewife does not practice) they would *not* stain so easily. Stains on carbon steel can very easily be removed with a soap scouring pad. May I recommend a soap-filled pad called "Rescue" I have found it not only cleans, but since it contains a polish, my blades, although made of carbon, look as shiny as any stainless steel knives you can hang in any kitchen. This same pad can be used on stainless steel pots as well. *Stainless:* Most cutlery manufacturers produce knives of stainless steel (sometimes with an additive of sorts). These are favored by the housewife for their carefree quality as many are dishwasher proof and retain their shininess for many years. I personally do not recommend washing *any* knives in a dishwasher or for that matter, throwing them carelessly into a drawer. This does not lend to the long life of a piece of fine cutlery nor to its retaining its sharp blade edge. Knives would be best cared for if placed on a magnetic bar or kept in a knife rack, handy to your cutting board and high enough away from children's curious hands.

In buying a knife you must purchase it yourself to get the "feel" of it. If hubby does the carving of the roasts, let *him* choose the knife best fitted for his handgrip. Knives are sometimes contoured, even for left or right handed  use, so it grips better and feels better to the user. *What to look for in a knife, before purchase:* After deciding if you prefer stainless steel to carbon, it is suggested you look for these other fine features of a good knife. After finding type, size and grind you want, the final test is: How does it feel to *you?* Are you comfortable holding it? Does it feel too heavy? Is the blade the right length for most of the practical purposes you would be using it for? See diagram.

Using diagram above as a guide, does the tang of your knife extend into at least ⅓ of the length of the handle? Even more superior are the knives with tangs that extend into the *entire* length of the handle and those where there is no visible crevice to catch food particles. Better quality knives have the blade riveted into position. Is the handle size good for *your* grip? A good knife will often carry the manufacturer's repair or replacement guarantee on it for a specified period of time and/or often, for the lifetime of the knife or its user. Is the grind the type you want? (Do you want it to slice meat or do you need a serrated or scalloped edge (grind) to cut bread or cake?)

Basically there are six types of knives. Often referred to as the "starter set," your workshop (kitchen) should contain: paring knife, utility knife, boning knife, roast slicer, French cook (chef's) knife and a knife with a scallop or serrated grind, to be used to slice bread or cake. The knives' names being self-explanatory, we will only concern ourselves with their use to us in our world of food sculpture. *Paring knife:* Small in size with a short blade, it's most useful in outlining, trimming and carving vegetables and fruits. *Boning knife:* Used for butchering; to carve meat e.g. to separate turkey breasts from bone. (See chapter 10 on carving a turkey). *Utility knife:* Slices and quarters melons; slices large vegetables. Used to cut cavity openings for fruit presentations such as in the pineapple peacock, pineapple flower basket, etc. *Roast slicer knife:* Possessing a long narrow blade, this knife is used to slice roasted meats and the boned turkey breast (see chapter 10 on carving of turkey) and/or to shave vegetables into very thin slices for decorating and garnishing. *Chef's or cook's knife:* Available in 8", 10" and 12" sizes, its triangular blade is used primarily for its strength. It is used to slice off the stabilizing base of large fruits. Its main purpose is to chop, mince and dice onions, nuts, parsley, celery, peppers, etc. *Serrated or scalloped knife:* Used to cut all citrus fruits and tomatoes into thin slices, used to cut breads and cakes. There are many other types of knives available for use in the kitchen only to be matched with as many types and methods for sharpening them. I still prefer keeping my knives sharpened using a carborundum stone for carbon steel blades.

Lemon leaves: Long stem with dark green shiny leaves used often to decorate or fill in a large centerpiece or to decorate the table itself. Available at nominal charge at florist.

Lemon stripper: Primarily used as a bar tool, it strips a continuous ribbon of citrus rind from a fruit for use in cocktail drinks such as a "horse's neck." Used in food sculpture as a stripper to create the groove designs on citrus fruits as well as vegetables such as carrots, radishes, cucumbers, eggplants, beets and melons. (See appropriate chapters). Often mistakenly referred to as a "zester" for it releases the zest (flavor to enhance something) from the citrus fruits. (See Zester). More commonly for sale in a bar and restaurant supply store.

Mandoline: See Cutters; subtitle, Slicers.

Melon ballers: See Ball Scoops.

Mobile decoration: The special one referred to in this book is a standing mobile (see illustration) that separates from its stand. Available at large department or chain stores, such as Rickles, Two Guys, etc., the top part consists

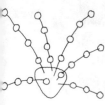

of heavy duty wire with colorful and sometimes iridescent plastic balls. It is used to simulate the blow hole and water on the Whimsical Whale creation. (See chapters on Whimsical Whale).

Molds: As in the dictionary: the cavity in which anything is shaped, also the body containing the cavity. Thus, there are many shapes, sizes and uses for molds made of many materials such as aluminum, copper, plastic, tin, ceramic, etc. Used to hold and shape gelatin or foods such as chopped liver, herring, tuna, etc. Used to bake in, they are referred to as muffin tins, ramekins, custard cups, etc. These baked forms can then be used as containers or molds to hold foods such as chicken a la king, seafood salads, etc. Even the bountiful earth provides us with many natural molds, such as the citrus family e.g. melons, oranges and lemons which hold such desserts as ice cream, sherbets and berries. Other container molds for holding relishes, appetizers and salads are made from vegetables, such as bell peppers, cucumbers, cabbage heads, tomatoes, mushrooms, squash and acorns.

Many of these copper molds are so beautiful in shape and design they have found their way into many homes as merely decorative ornaments for the kitchen and dining room walls rather than for their utilitarian purposes.

For those of you who think you do not own even one mold, you are mistaken! Our hands are molds . . . for we use our hands as "containers" to round out and shape free form designs such as tuna baskets, fishes and ducks shaped out of chopped liver, etc. (See chapter 6 on same).

Parsley: A green curly leaf vegetable (American variety) or long stemmed flat leaf (Italian variety), it is used primarily as a garnish or filler for food presentation. Actually, it is a valuable food staple, high in vitamin A and is available all year round. If slightly wilted, place stem ends in cold water and snip off tip's ends while submerged.

Pastry tubes and tips: Used primarily for garnishing and decorating, may I recommend a bag with a plastic inside or lining for its attractive feature of easier cleaning and drying. The use of various tip points determine the shape and style of that which you wish to create with the use of this unique garnishing device. Used primarily for cake and pastry decorating, it is used extensively in food sculpture to pipe out whip cream border designs on dessert molds; to highlight the trim on tuna baskets or liver creations with the piping of a "riced" egg mixture, (See potato ricer in glossary), used to garnish and fill small cooked beet cups and cherry tomatoes with cream cheese mixture, or fill mushroom caps or hard-cooked egg whites for hors d'oeuvres. Fill pastry tube with sweet potato, swirl on top of pineapple slices or fill orange baskets with potatoes to accompany turkey dinner, etc.

Pineapple knife: A long blade knife, its grind is deeply scalloped to facilitate cutting in and around with an up and down sawing motion and thus release the meat from the shell of the pineapple. As there are not too many around now-a-days a serrated grapefruit knife can be substituted if you can't find a pineapple knife.

Potato peeler: See Vegetable Peeler.

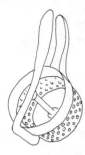

Potato ricer: As in the dictionary, a kitchen utensil designed for pressing potatoes and similar cooked vegetables through a perforated container, the resulting product emerging as strings about the size of a grain of rice, thus the name ricer. Used in food sculpture to force through the entire egg white and yolk to prepare it for mixing with mayonnaise. It can then be squeezed more easily and finely from a pastry tube for decorating and garnishing. See chapters on Tuna Basket and Liver designs.

Potato white: A brand name, a commercial product in powder form. When combined with water to form a solution, it is used to dip fruits and vegetables in. Immersion in this solution will then prevent the vegetables and fruits from browning and oxidizing. Similar to Fruit Fresh (brand name), this commercial potato white is less expensive since it is available in one pound units. Usually only available to commercial and industrial institutions, restaurants, hotels, caterers, etc. If you cannot obtain any through any of these sources write to me.

Pre-hole: Term used meaning to push a toothpick into a tough rind or surface in order to create a hole for easily inserting a larger pick or dowel later.

Pu pu platter: A large selection of assorted tidbits usually served as an appetizer with its own hibachi form of heat. Very popular in its presentation at Chinese or Polynesian restaurants. Create your own variation. See section on Pu Pu Platter in chapter 1 on pineapples.

Scoops: See Ball Scoops.

Screweye: A round eyelit atop a screw as depicted; used in households to hang pictures or to hold implements. used in food sculpture in simulating a "football." See chapter 3: Touch Down! Football Melon.

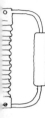

Serrator: A cutting tool with a 7" stainless steel blade and riveted handle. Its serrated or crinkled edge which never needs sharpening is used to tenderize meat and give design to the cutting of potatoes and other fresh or cooked vegetables. Cheeses and meat, sold in bulk form, can be cut into small attractive pieces or chunks with this implement. Similar to the old fashioned potato crinkler mother used to make french fried potatoes, this new and better version can cut longer pieces of melons and vegetables with one motion and is sharp enough to cut through the heavy rind of a watermelon.

Socle: As in the dictionary, a low plain block supporting a wall or beneath the base of a column pedestal or the like . . . in food sculpture, a term used to describe the base form used to hold up and support, as in the presentation of the turkey sliced and put back on frame. See appropriate chapter.

Stabilizing base: A term used very often in food sculpture, meaning to slice off a small piece from the base of something to stabilize it and prevent it from moving, rolling or shifting.

Sterno: A small can of jellied substance when ignited, is used to heat food. It is used in pineapple hor d'oeuvres piece. See appropriate chapter.

Stickum tape: A floral gum substance used in food sculpture to adhere one piece to another and therefore prevent shifting and moving. Available at florists in white or green.

Styrofoam: As in dictionary: a trademark, a polystyrene foam used for insulation; more familiar in craft decorating.

Styrofoam base: Used often as a stabilizing piece or as a base to help lift the height of a presentation as in the pineapple flower cart.

Styrofoam centerpiece: Styrofoam base used to lift up higher and therefore focus on and bring attention to some particular feature on the food presentation plate or tray.

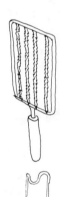

Tomato slicer: A kitchen utensil with several (10) serrated stainless steel blades approximately ¼″ apart; used to slice tomatoes or a small cucumber into uniform ¼″ slices.

Totem pins: Metal, its strong hair pin shape is used to hold philodendron plant stems onto a supporting wooded plant bark. Totem pins are sometimes called "greening pins." In food sculpture, they are used to pin chicory, flowers, etc., into styrofoam or such.

Traffic pattern: Referred to as the way you would like your guests to move along a buffet service table so as to avoid confusion and overcongestion in one particular area.

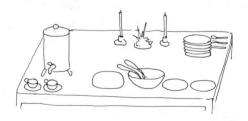

Vegetable peeler: By far the most useful household item. Used to peel or pare potatoes' skins, cucumber, carrots, celery, etc. The point of this instrument is used to clean out the "eyes" found on potatoes and pineapples. Used in food sculpture not only as a cleaning implement for paring vegetables and fruits, but when the better quality peeler is purchased, its swivel action blade will permit you to create carrot curls and attain paper thin layers of vegetables, such as beet slices to use for decorating and garnishings in trays and in aspics.

Zester: This utensil is often confused with a lemon stripper for they are both used to release the zest or flavor of a citrus fruit. With small hole like openings the zester releases its citrus skin into small gratings or shavings. It can also be used to release shavings from carrots that can be used to decorate salad plates.

JARGON OF YOUR KITCHEN WORKSHOP: Although these two terms are listed in chapter (5) on Eggs where they will be used for the first time, let's make note of both types of pastes and their uses under this heading for a quick easy reference.

Egg yolk cream paste: mix cooked sieved egg yolk with a little seasoning, mayonnaise and creamed butter to form a thick paste. Food color may be added as desired to bring more contrasting emphasis to your work as needed. Since this is a natural yellow (yolk) coloring and forms a thick paste it is used as an adherent, to bind one component food particle to another, while emphasizing and utilizing the coloring itself. As an example, egg yolk paste would be

— 35 —

used to adhere the salami cone hat to the egg while simultaneously acting as the hair on the clown (see Ch. 5, Egg-Head Clown) and is also used as the buttons on his hat; it is utilized as a paste to bind one to the other while adding color and more dimension to our theme. See footnote on egg yolk cream paste for more diversified detail on Egg-Head Clown.

Gelatin paste: Also used as an adherent to bind one to the other, this particular paste form is utilized when color needs to be de-emphasized and not brought to the attention of the eye. An analogy might be that the use of color frill picks is to egg yolk cream what floral wooden picks, used in the hidden toothpick method, is to gelatin paste. Subsequently, in many instances the gelatin paste might be substituted for the hidden toothpick method. As an example, in the chapter on creating a snowman egg, you wish to set one egg atop the other thus forming the body in two parts and then add the third egg as the head, atop that body. This can be done with hidden floral picks or with the gelatin paste; it cannot be done with the aforementioned egg yolk paste cream as it would be too obvious and not lend at all to the finished work.

To make a gelatin paste: to create a colorless gelatin paste sprinkle 1 pkg. Knox gelatin over ¼ c. cold water. Allow crystals to be absorbed and let stand until thick paste is formed.

Pastry tube method, or overlaying a design: Utilize an egg yolk cream paste. As an alternative, so as not to waste any egg whites, place the whole cooked egg or eggs through a food mill or ricer so it is sieved extremely fine. This prevents the clogging of the fine tube tip openings. Continue as in preparation for egg yolk cream paste, mix with seasoning, butter and mayonnaise to a thick consistency. Place egg yolk cream paste or egg mixture into the canvas pastry decorating bag. Utilize same to superimpose as one would a cake frosting mixture, so as to decorate a design and/or to write messages on a cake. Use the egg mixture to overlay or superimpose a particular design. Use the overlay design of egg yolk cream paste or egg mixture to outline or emphasize a feature, as in the hair and pom poms on the egg head clown and hat (ch. 5). Use as a border edge trim and to emphasize the outline of the wing area of the butterfly molds, as in ch. 6 on liver molds and in ch. 8 on fish molds. Use to write in lettering or numerals as in New Year's Eve chopped liver clock (ch. 6). As you read on we will refer often to the pastry tube method or overlaying the design. This same principle of overlaying can be utilized for dessert molds as well, simply by substituting whip cream for the egg yolk cream paste or whole egg mixture. Using whip cream all these concepts of overlaying designs can be then utilized in pudding, gelatin and cake presentations (see ch. 9 on butterfly gelatin mold as example.)

1 THE PINEAPPLE

History of the fruit: What other way to start off our book than with the pineapple, for it truly wears nature's crown of leaves proudly and is known as the "King of Fruits."

In days gone by, only on special occasions could one relish its succulent sweetness, as the pineapple was so rare and costly it was served by the King, usually only to the members of royalty. The fruit therefore became synonymously known as the symbol of hospitality. Although Marco Polo found pineapple growing in Chinese provinces, it was Christopher Columbus who brought pineapple plants home to Queen Isabella from the island of Guadalupe on his second voyage to the New World. It took many years however, before the new fruit from the West Indies found its "native home soil" in Hawaii and took on the role of the second largest industry of our 50th state, sugar being its first. Although the smooth cayennne Hawaiian pineapple is best known, many other varieties of this tropical growing plant also flourish in Australia, East Indies, Mexico and West Africa.

History records that Oliver Cromwell was presented with the pineapple plant as far back as 1657. At that time only the wealthy could "afford" the King of Fruits, for they had to be grown in hot houses . . . artificially trying to reproduce the climate this plant ordinarily thrived in.

The pineapple grows on a plant attaining a height of 2–3 feet, with a spread of 3–4 feet. At about 12–14 months it begins a two month flowering process. Actually the pineapple is a multiple fruit which is formed from approximately 150 purplish-blue individual flowers which bloom for one day only. In about 2 weeks all the flowers have opened and closed and form the "eyes" of the fruit. After a growing period of 20 months the fruit is ready for harvesting and usually weighs about 5 lbs., abundant in sugar, citric acid, protein, vitamins (especially Vitamin C) minerals, carotene (for golden color) and fiber. From field to cannery, through a Ginaca Machine which cuts off the ends, removes the core and shell, the plant passes through an entire process of canning in a total of 15 minutes. Thus, we join the King and his royalty in the modern world with canned pineapple in round slices, chunks, tidbits, crushed and in refreshing thirst quenching juice form.

Let us go to the market together and pick "the fruit of hospitality" ourselves.

How to pick: The color of fresh pineapple is a clue to its maturity, the top part may be greenish, but the lower part should be yellow. Thump the pineapple; a dull thud is an indication of sweet, juicy fruit inside, while the green fruit sounds more hollow and needs a few more days to develop to its flavorful best. In picking one pineapple choose the largest one available for it is a fact that a half of a larger sized fruit will contain more of an edible eating portion than you would find in a whole smaller fruit. Keep in mind the day you are planning to use the fruit you are purchasing at the time, for it may hold for a few days, and so can be shopped in advance at your convenience. The former blossoms or "eyes" of the shell are flat and rather lustrous on a mature pineapple fruit. At first these individual blossoms are rough and peaked, becoming flatter and smoother as the fruit matures.

How to Store: If fresh ripe pineapple *isn't* to be used right away, it should be refrigerated. To keep for a few days longer, the shell should be removed and the fruit refrigerated in air-tight containers or plastic wrap. To freeze, simply wrap airtight in heavy duty plastic bags or film.

Note on Using: Bromelain, an enzyme found in the *fresh* pineapple fruit is a proteolitic substance which breaks down protein similar to digestive processess. Thus, gelatin made with *fresh* or *frozen* pineapple will not set (gel). Used in a marinade, fresh pineapple helps to tenderize meat as well as add flavor. Dairy products such as cottage cheese and sour cream should not be mixed with fresh pineapple until ready to serve. Now let us get to the art of Food Sculpture, how to serve our "King of Fruits" creatively so *our* house may become known for its hospitality.

PINEAPPLE CANDLEHOLDERS

On a limited budget even the fronds of the pineapple fruit can be put to use with a little imagination. As per the diagram, depending upon height desired for your candleholder, slice off an appropriate section of fruit as the base, leaving frond section in tact.

Be sure your base slice is level and will stand with no difficulty. Remove from crown as many center frond leaves as necessary to accommodate the diameter base of your candle. If you wish a more decorative candleholder, spray the leaves with a glue spray or use Sobo glue and sprinkle onto the "glue" areas colored sugar or glitters to make it more colorful. Let dry a few minutes. Encompass candle bottom with sticky floral tape and push into frond opening twisting into position to make it secure and steady for lighting at the table.

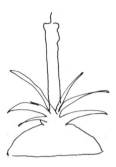

If more than a 3″ high base of fruit is used you may wish to enhance it by pinning in (with totem pins) fresh greenery or flowers, using the pineapple base as the pincushion.

SERVING A SALAD FILLED PINEAPPLE

Choose an appropriate size pineapple, depending upon the salad portion you wish to serve per person; keep in mind that ladies will of course consume less than men. Each pineapple therefore gives you two individual services.

Cut through fronds with large knife slicing fruit lengthwise in half. Empty the meat from each half leaving a ½″ thick shell intact. Refill the shell holder with fresh fruit salad and skewer with bamboo stick holding pineapple chunks, cherries and oranges aloft. If preferred, as an appetizer or for a luncheon, line shell with bed of lettuce and fill with a fresh fish or meat-type salad. Garnish with fancy skewer holding lemon wedges, so tasteful with fish, or substitute olives and pickles for meat presentation. See diagram.

To add that special touch, if it is a holiday or a special occasion

such as a bridal luncheon, a sprig of lilies of the valley or some-thing symbolic can be placed on the cut surface of each frond section.

The same principle can be applied to make a dessert-filled pineapple.

SERVING A STRAWBERRY FILLED PINEAPPLE BOAT

As you created one idea suitable for a luncheon such as a salad filled pineapple in the preceding chapter, so you create a vari-ant of it. This new one can be used as a dessert for a sweet table and/or can be encompassed into a larger centerpiece such as the gazebo or chapel. (See chapters on same). To create your pineapple boat follow the directions cited previously.

Cut and empty the meat fruit from the pineapple shell. Two complete shells can be obtained by cutting fronds in half or, if desired, merely cut off a slice from the top of the pineapple fruit leaving the *frond intact.* See illustrations.

Line entire shell of pineapple boat with fresh strawberry leaves, obtainable from your garden, or lemon leaves from the florist. Using variously cut lengths of bamboo sticks (to attain different heights) *and* wood floral picks, fill the pineapple hull with fresh strawberries. The purpose of varying the height to the strawberry filled pineapple boats is to prevent a flat look to the tray and thereby add more visual appeal to your arrangement.

Garnish with fresh peppermint leaves and if desired sprinkle with coconut for "Ambrosia." *OPTIONAL:* Fresh sprigs of flowers may be tucked in amongst the frond leaves.

If served on a sweet table surround with fresh dips such as whipped cream, sour cream, brown or white sugar or sugar color sparkles and other fruits such as bananas and other choice seasonal berries and fruits. This strawberry pineapple boat is truly most beautiful and effective in a large gazebo or chapel arrangement.

QUARTERED PINEAPPLE BOATS WITH FRONDS

Select large pineapple with full crown of fronds. Leaving fronds intact, cut pineapple in half through hull, stem and leaves; halve again creating four quartered sections from your fruit with frond pieces in tact on each quarter. Using a paring knife, cut directly under the hard core section atop each quartered piece leaving a 1″ section on each end *uncut*. See diagram.

Utilizing the curve of a grapefruit knife or a pineapple knife, undercut the flesh from the hull leaving the meat in place on the hull. With a paring knife make convenient eating size slices still leaving it intact and in position in quartered shell. Push every alternate slice to opposite sides creating a staggered affect. See diagram.

In these open spaces place large size strawberries creating a yellow (pineapple) red (strawberry) effect in zigzag fashion. Using the core top on each quarter of the pineapple as a pincushion, overlay sections of canned mandarin oranges on top and hold in place with frill toothpicks for color and easier handling of fruit for your guest's nibbling delight.

A BARREL OF PINEAPPLE

Select a pineapple with full crown of fronds, preferably with sharp pointed tips and barbed leaves. Two inches down from base of frond crown cut off top of pineapple leaving fronds intact. Cut off one inch from base of fruit also. Save crown and discard base slice. Using the curve of the pineapple knife, (or you can make do with a grapefruit knife), cut around the circumference of the fruit to release a cylindrical-shaped meat section. Push entire section out through the bottom. This cylinder of fruit may now be sliced into spears, rounds or into bite-size pieces and mixed with other selections of melon fruits, berries, etc. Line pineapple "barrel" with plastic baggie before setting rind shell holder on serving dish. This will prevent leakage of juices.

Now fill with pineapple spears or medley of fruits. Set the frond top back on so that the pineapple looks uncut and decorate the frond tip points with blueberries or cherries and small grapes. Intersperse the frond leaves with frill toothpicks so your guests may use these picks for picking up the fruits within the "barrel" once the top is removed. The picks add just another touch of color and practicality to your creation. This Barrel Pineapple may be served alone on a small plate or set on a larger one and surrounded with a section of fresh "hand fruits"

such as apples, pears, grape clusters or even more melon balls presented in the pretty paper frill muffin tin liners used to make cupcakes. Decorate these pretty filled paper cups with mint leaves and coconut sprinkled atop for an ambrosia effect.

For that extra piquant flavor to the pineapple: To add extra sweet taste to pineapple cut meats without addition of granulated sugar or other sweet additives, simply cut pineapple meats as desired into chunk shapes. Refrigerate to chill until ready to fill fruit dish. About 15 minutes before placing in presentation form (such as aforementioned Barrel) soak cut pineapple pieces in a bath of 1 qt. cold water to which 2 teaspoons of salt have been added and diluted. Drain after submersing in chilled solution for 15 minutes. Fill presentation holder and serve pineapple as is or mixed with other fruits. Your guest will never figure out how you always manage to pick the sweetest tasting of all the pineapples from the supermarket.

PINEAPPLE PU PU PLATTER

Take a "Palm Tree Leaf" from the Happy Hawaiians' book of fun and entertaining . . . combine your fresh pineapple with a Hawaiian Pu Pu Platter.

Needed for this would be your favorite selection of tropical island type hors d'oeuvre: Rumaki (chicken liver and bacon wraps), butterfly shrimp, chicken wings marinated in soy sauce, etc. Choose a tall rounded fresh pineapple, stabilize base and cut off crown section, leaving 7–8" section of the fruit. Cut out enough of meat from top opening of fruit so as to allow room to fit in a can of sterno. Cut fruit into bite size pieces and dip in rum and then sugar and chill until serving time.

To serve: place pineapple shell in center of Pu Pu platter and surround with hors d'oeuvres and pineapple chunks . . . supply long bamboo skewers and light sterno and lo and behold . . . a homemade hibachi . . . island style . . . aloha! For that added touch supply the bamboo skewers by placing them into the base of the frond leaves on the crown and top each end off with red and green cherries, or for variety add and place here and there the cute minuture Japanese-type umbrellas used as souvenirs.

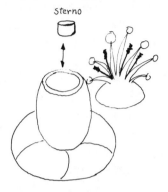

Sterno

THE PINEAPPLE OWL

As with all things creative, the first time you see something gets your own creative juices going. So a moment to thank my friend, Charlie Wong, the *garde mangere* of the Nevele Hotel in the famous Catskill area. This is where I first saw a sculpted owl which in turn started all my own creative juices working. May I now then introduce you to the Pineapple Owl to follow, the watermelon owl in chap. 2, and the meat and fish owl in chapter 8. This then in turn gave rise to the fact that all meat platters can then be created with the same simple concept: the application of layering the meats properly to create other figures or displays too (as in: Presentation of Meat, chapter 8).

To make the owl: Needed to create this pretty and unusual centerpiece would be 2 pineapples, a piece of carrot, celery stalk, olives, white of an egg, orangewood stick and a hammer.

Head section: completely pare a ⅓ section of a pineapple or use a very small-sized whole pineapple as the head of the owl.
   Body: completely pare a large-sized whole pineapple.

Beak: pare a carrot chunk and shape as a curved beak of an owl.

Eyes: use hard cooked albumin egg slices as the background white of the eye; slices of black olives as the pupils of same.

Feet: use 2 small slices of carrot cut wedges to shape like claws of an owl.

Tree branch: Use a large stalk of celery with some leaves intact as tree branch limb to set owl upon.

To prepare head section: Using small pineapple or a ⅓ section of a larger pineapple, pare off all rind and remove all visible "eyes" of the pineapple. Stabilize base of head by cutting off small slice at bottom. As per diagram, cut out (shadowed) sections to give owl-like facial appearance to head. Set aside cut out pieces to later use as body wedge for under wing areas. Cut out (shadowed) section for mouth-like area to later be replaced with (carrot) beak. Pare and cut curved beak shape from large chunk of carrot. Set aside for placement later onto owl's face.

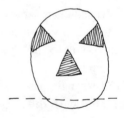

To prepare owl's body: Use the large-sized pared pineapple for the owl's body. Remove all rind as well as "eyes" of fruit. Slice small piece off base to steady and stabilize your figure; slice small piece off top of body to accommodate addition of stabilized head section later. As per diagram, *do not cut off,* but slice up both sides of pineapple to give appearance of wings (see

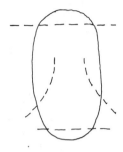

eggplant penguin, chapter 7 for similar procedure). To push away wings from the body of the owl figure slightly, wedge a small piece of pineapple chunk (removed eye sections) under the "armpits" of each wing.

To combine figure: see diagram: *Head to body section:* With the use of a hammer, force an orange wood stick into the hard core center top of the whole larger pineapple (body); leave enough of the orange wood stick exposed to then receive the smaller pineapple head section. Force head stabilized base side down onto top of owl's body.

To decorate face: Using floral wooden picks, push on slices of cooked white egg slices. Cover center of egg slices with 2 small pieces of black olives as pupils of owl's eyes. (use hidden toothpick technique accordingly).

    Beak: Using floral wood picks (hidden) attach curved carrot beak into section of owl's mouth.

    Feet: With floral picks insert carrot claw-like shaped feet into the base of the pineapple body at least two inches up from base of the pineapple fruit.

    Tree branch: directly *under* claws of owl, insert stalk of celery, leaves intact; hold in place with floral picks thus simulating owl resting upon a tree branch.

Your wise old owl would be an attractive conversation piece at a child's party and be even more of a hit as the theme for a graduation celebration. Surround with small tea sandwiches rolled and shaped like diplomas. E.G.: to create diploma like sandwiches (and graduation caps) see chapter 6: rolled-up party sandwiches. Place either and/or both cap and diploma sandwiches surrounding raised up owl. (Use owl as raised styrofoam centerpiece see: Tools of Your Kitchen Workshop, preceding chapter 1.)

This wise old owl will spread the word around you are a very creative "Hostess with the Mostess".

SOUTHERN BELLE MEAT DOLL

Tired of serving the same old type cold cut meat trays? Create a sensation by presenting your cold cuts in the form of a Southern Belle. If its a bridal, engagement or wedding party, with a little variation to your doll you can even create a bride's centerpiece breath-takingly and beautifully attired in white. See unit on "Bridal Doll" to follow.

How do you make a meat doll resplendent in a bouffant

Also see: Watermelon Owl: chapter 2
Also see: Fish Owl: chapter 8
Also see: Owl: assorted meat platter chapter 8

ruffled skirt of cascading cold cuts? Easy as going to the butcher or supermarket and buying a couple of pounds of economical cold cuts such as bologna, spice ham, salami, or any selection of cut meats that will not fall apart when folded into a "ruffle" for our old fashioned belle's skirt. If our Southern Belle is from an "old family" where money is no object her "dress" may consist of more extravagant cuts of meat such as roast beef, turkey, ham, breast of chicken, etc. The top part of her dress sets the mood for the evening or holiday spirit. If she is to grace your table for Sunday buffet any old "rags" she might have around would do, discretion as to color and style would be up to you . . . however if it's for the celebration of Christmas, why not don her in the spirit of the holiday by dressing her from the waist up in green and red finery to pick up the mood of the holiday season?

Your basic investment for this conversation sparker is a small standing 9" doll. This can be picked up in your local 5 & 10¢ store and can be used over and over again. If your young daughter happens to have an old doll with the legs broken off you've just saved yourself a half dollar, for our doll will only be visible from the waist up. Sew fabric scraps right onto your doll to create the bodice of her dress (from the waist up). From her waistline down, cover the doll with saran wrap or aluminum foil. If you wish you may deliberately cut off the legs of the doll since they will be covered anyway and of no particular use.

Take a large sized pineapple, (cabbage will do if pineapple is not obtainable) and stabilize the bottom. Remove the core and fronds by cutting out enough to be able to make room to fit the doll into the top of the pineapple so that only the head and top part of your doll is left showing. Cover the pineapple with saran wrap and insert your doll. Now begins the fun of dressing her by creating her bouffant skirt. If you possess a lazy susan tray of any sort you will find it much easier and quicker to design your meat skirt by placing your pineapple on the center of the lazy susan tray and just turning the tray to pin on your selection of cold cuts. Starting at the base of the pineapple take a slice of round bologna or salami and fold in half and then half again, forming a triangle shape out of the meat slice. These meat slices will then be pinned in place into the pineapple base with frill picks to hold them. Try to give extra fullness to each triangular piece of meat by placing the toothpick under one of the folded flaps (have the three sides of your meat triangle folded down and lift the 4th side upward so your frill toothpick can be placed between the fold of the 3rd and 4th side of the slice of meat).

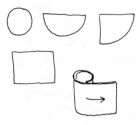

Continue following this pattern with more meat slices until a layer is formed completely around the bottom of the skirt. If you wish to have some variation to the design of your hoop skirt on your Southern Belle, you might try to roll your ham slices into cylindrical shapes instead, and then place them in a vertical

position to form the first layer of your skirt. Start your next row of triangle meat slices and place alternately in position above and in between the first layer of meats. See diagram.

You may keep the meats all the same or intermix the selection of cold cuts, as you prefer. To bring more color into play for contrast of "eye" and taste insert some pieces of canned or fresh pineapple chunks on the same pick as some of the meat slices. Stick in black and pimento filled olives or cocktail onions with frill toothpicks at random. It is also nice to see little puffs of fresh parsley peeking out of our belle's skirt here and there. As you reach the top of the skirt you might find that you have a little space left around the waist line of the doll. This can be covered with more meat or trimmed up with pretty pickle fans or a ruffle of fresh parsley.

To make a Pickle Fan: Take a small gherkin pickle and make three cuts not *quite* thru to the bottom. Spread out fan style.

Hold in this position and press uncut section slightly with thumb to keep fan in open position. Place around waistline and secure with toothpick to trim up doll's waistline.

The meat doll is attractive featured by herself for a small party or featured prominently (raised on styrofoam) on a tray surrounded by more cold cuts. See chapter on vegetables for suggestions as to relish holders for mustard and/or mayonnaise.

A BRIDAL DOLL
FOR SHOWER, ENGAGEMENT OR WEDDING PARTY

With the following slight variation to our Southern Belle doll we can create our bride for the engagement party, wedding rehearsal buffet or shower party.

Variation: Nice and Easy . . . I promise you . . .

Dress your doll as a bride using scraps of left over white material (chiffon or nylon is nice). Her head piece can be made by sewing on a small flower and veil effect with some netting material. Follow the simple directions for the Southern Belle Meat Doll but create the bouffant skirt by using only *white* chicken roll or turkey meats thus keeping with the traditional white of a bridal party. Garnish with yellow American cheese cut-outs (cut of course, with a heart-shaped aspic cutter) and place amid slices of meat on your skirt. If you do not have an aspic cutter handy use one of those handy squeeze tube type cheese rolls so popular in the supermarket dairy case.

For a light repast, surround tray with lovely tea sandwiches for the shower party or more selections of cold cuts and rolls. Our best wishes to the bride, and if it's the shower you were chosen to make for her may I share this idea with you. With every invitation sent out, include a 3" × 5" index card so that the recipient (whether she can make the party or not) can write down her favorite recipe (with her name and telephone number in case of emergency) and return it to you. Gather these up into a book or index file for the bride. Thus, less tears and frustrations for that new cook, for her friends have not only shared their good wishes but also their favorite recipes. What a wonderful cookbook for a new bride, don't you think? Please do include my own favorite one on preserving (see last chapter).

SEAFOOD PINEAPPLE . . .ALOHA!

Cut off stabilizing slice from base of fruit. Using large sharp knife, cut down thru center of the frond crown to a depth of ⅓ from the top of the fruit. Now cut crosswise to meet initial cut as pictured in diagram. Remove this piece but do *not* discard.

Remove the flesh of the fruit remaining in that ⅓ section on top. Excavate enough of the meat in the top area so as to create a cavity opening large enough to hold a small plastic dish or a disposable aluminum baking potato shell, (illustration depicts where all meat has been removed.) This area may simply be lined with silver foil paper. This silver foiled area or plastic dish placed within will eventually hold your cocktail

sauce. Using totem pole pins decorate edge of pineapple shell
open area with frond leaves pulled from the discarded section

of crown. Insert sauce holder and fill in void areas between
frond leaves with fresh parsley sprigs. Utilizing the pineapple
as a pincushion base secure in place (with frill toothpicks), fresh
cooked chilled shrimp and baby scallops. Garnish with fresh
sprigs of curled parsley amid your seafood pieces.

With the use of totem pole pins, decoratively complement
being careful not to completely cover the exposed halved frond
section crown with a pretty fresh or plastic colorful flower or
two. Fill inset aluminum or plastic dish with the cocktail sauce
of your choice for dipping. Set up as centerpiece (see use of
styrofoam) and surround with chicory or greenery of some kind.

Even the use of "Easter grass" is very effective against a back-drop of Hawaiian leis, seashells and Tiki gods. The very popular flower-shaped candles may be put adrift in a nearby "lagoon" (water filled container of some sort).

This is a very beautiful edible centerpiece for an impending trip abroad, a Bon Voyage party or even a seafood dinner. If it is for a trip to Hawaii or the Islands your local travel agency would be most happy to provide you with posters as a backdrop for your festivities.

For a Luau party the Home Economic Consumer Service, Dole Company, Virginia Street and Fifth, San Jose, California 95112 would be happy to send you their booklet of ideas and recipes entitled "How to Have a Wikiwaki Luau" as a courtesy. Aloha, my friends . . .

PINEAPPLE TREASURE CHEST

Resembling a rectangular shaped receptacle, your pineapple treasure chest will hold a juicy reward as a repast for your scavenger party or dessert table. (also see ch. 6—treasure chest.)

Obtain a large well-rounded pineapple and remove the entire frond crown section by twisting it off (use towel to protect your hands) as per instructions for pineapple flower cart. Using a large chef knife, slice off sections of the pineapple shell from all four sides of the fruit, thus squaring it off (as per diagram).

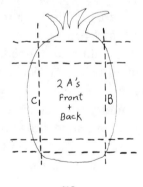

Try to keep these four sections large and intact, as they will then be used as the cover on the sides of your pineapple treasure chest. Having removed these four rind sections you are now left with a rectangular shape of the pineapple pulp. The only remaining rind shell on the fruit that will then be left over will be a little on the top and bottom of the pineapple. Slice this remaining shell off. With a sharp knife cut around and excise out (by pushing through opposite side in one chunk) the inside pulp section of your chest as per diagram. Set aside to be later cut up and used as filler.

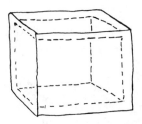

Two of these four pieces of removed rind shell will be custom cut to correct size and height to match and be used as the outside covering of the front and back sides of the chest (2 A's) as depicted in diagram. The third shell piece of rind will, after being cut to fit properly, act as the open lid cover of your pineapple chest (see B in diagram). The fourth rind section will be divided in half and custom cut to fit on the opposite ends of your treasure chest (see 2 C's).

To custom cut and fit: Holding the shell rind against the side it is to cover, trace with toothpick or pencil the outline of that side. Trim and cut to size to fit so this covering will fit properly. Before attaching to corresponding side (of rectangular shaped yellow pulp chest), cut away the fruit meat attached to the inside of this rind shell, (use same for filler or salad). By cutting away extra pulp and thus trimming down the inside of each rind

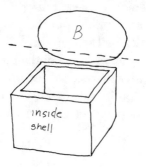

shell section, the rind will be more flexible and fit closer against its corresponding side of the chest.

To secure the coverings: Place the first shell section (A) in position and secure with frill toothpicks at each end corner. Follow the same procedure of custom fitting, cutting and removing excess inside pulp on each of the other rind shell pieces before securing with toothpicks. (Sides: 2 A's, and 2 C's).

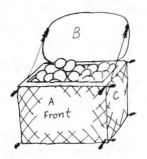

The remaining shell side (B) will be fitted as the open lid to the chest; the edge adjoining and abutting to the top edge of the treasure chest must also be custom fitted and cut accordingly so it can lie flush against the back side of the chest. See diagram. Hold lid ajar by placing two club frill picks into angled positions as per diagram.

A plastic baggie or foil may be used to hold the fruit and juice within the cavity opening of your treasure chest. Refill cavity with assorted fruits and pineapple tidbits. Garnish with mint leaves or such.

To embellish your new found treasure place a necklace of jewels draped across the top and down onto the side of your chest. *To make your necklace:* using dental floss and needle, thread, together raisins, different colored grapes, cherries, etc. to form a necklace. To add a touch of realism to your scene, place a sea diver or pirate and some pretty sea shells nearby. Stand back and watch your guests devour their newly discovered succulent treasures.

PINEAPPLE PEACOCK

Picture in your mind your finished creation. (See color picture). Select a proper large pineapple with fronds pushed to one side and curved upward, for this will be the tail of your peacock. For a bright green color on the fronds, wash your leaves with a soft brush and soap and water. If you cannot find one with a curved frond crown create it yourself by immersing the frond

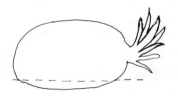

leaves in hot water for a minute or two and push up against a wall with a weight in front, to hold while it dries in this position (approximately one hour). To prevent the fruit from rolling, stabilize the pineapple by slicing off a thin flat piece with a large knife, as per dotted line in diagram.

*At this point see directions under Optional for a more colorful presentation of this bird.

You must now create the cavity opening in the bird, later to be filled with assorted fruit. For easier cutting of this rectangular cavity opening, place markers (toothpicks) positioned ⅔ of the way up from the stabilized bottom in the following manner. Place two parallel markers 1″ in from frond base. (A and B as pictured in diagram). Also place two markers parallel 1″ in from opposite end of frond (C and D).

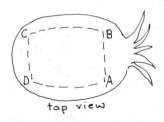

top view

Your markers will then be the corners of the rectangular cavity opening. Using a large knife, cut from A to B and also from C to D. When cutting from A to D and from B to C cut at an angle toward the cored center of the pineapple. To facilitate the release of the top section more easily, use the curve of a grapefruit or pineapple knife to help undercut the tough core of the fruit. Lift off this cut section and using pineapple knife, separate meat from shell. Do not throw out this rind . . . see optional. Cut meat into small pieces and set aside. Remove the remaining meat in like manner from the body of the bird, leaving a sufficient shell to later contain your fruit salad. To prepare bird's head, slice a ¾" thick lengthwise section of a long white Idaho potato. Place ¾" piece flat and trace or free hand draw a bird's head with pencil as per *full sized* diagram. Using illustration color and decorate as follows:

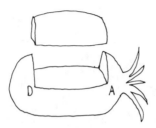

Cut out shape of head, being careful not to break potato. Be particularly cautious and work slowly around beak and the narrow neck areas. Round off cut square edges by using a potato peeler to give a more natural rounded effect to your bird's head. To prevent discoloration of the white potato wash with pineapple juice or use "Fruit Fresh" (commercial product available in drug stores) or solution of potato white. Paint entire bird's head with yellow food coloring using a cotton ball. Allow ten minutes for drying; (This is to prevent colors from running together.) Paint beak with red food dye; allow to dry. Create eyes of bird by pre-holing and pushing in whole cloves in appropriate area. If you wish to create eyelashes on your bird's head and to enhance the colorful effect, affix the hull of a strawberry first and then hold the hull in place with the whole clove "eyes." The comb on top of head is created by taking several red frilled toothpicks, (usually 4 are sufficient), break in half and push the celephane frilled half into top of bird's head. To create space to hold the peacock's potato head, cut a ¾" opening centered between C and D to a depth of 1" as shown in illustration.

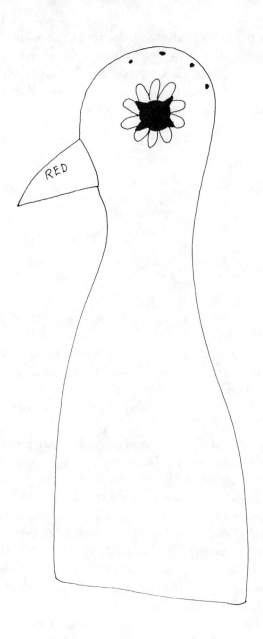

Fit head into opening and secure with turkey skewer or heavy wooden floral toothpick. Below the head piece, pull out

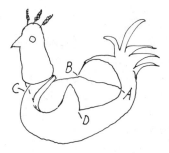

any left over dried leaves from original base of pineapple.

To provide more fruit for your guests nibbling and to beautify the breast area, pin in place small clusters of fresh grapes backed by strawberry leaves using totem pole or greening pins.

Refill body cavity of your lovely peacock with bite size pieces of pineapple and assorted melon balls, e.g., Honeydew, cantaloupe and watermelon. For more contrasting color intermix canned Mandarin orange sections; garnish with peppermint leaves and strawberries. Serve chilled with frill toothpicks for easy picking.

Your newly created pineapple peacock will be a refreshing conversation piece when served alone for 2 or 4 people. To please a larger crowd continue to refill bird as the fruit salad is eaten with additional chilled pre-cut fruit stored in a refrigerated container or you may wish to serve your bird as a styrofoam raised centerpiece and surround it with an array of fresh plums, peaches, etc. or fresh cut-up fruits served in muffin paper liners as individual servings.

OPTIONAL: After having mastered the above simple version, you may like to try a fancier looking presentation. After selection of the proper pineapple, and *before* doing anything such as stabilizing the pineapple etc., cover the pineapple with a plastic bag, leaving only the fronds exposed. Using a can of aerosol glue or hair spray, hold can 2 to 3 inches from fronds and spray all surface sections of the exposed leaves only. Better still, if you have a bottle of Sobo craft glue handy, pour some of the glue on the up-turned frond leaves—spread glue around with a cotton bud or frill pick end so leaf area is well covered. While glue is still wet sprinkle fronds with sugar color sparkles which will then adhere easily. Allow to dry, then remove plastic bag and proceed as per previous instructions up to the point of filling the cavity with fresh fruit. Before adding assorted fruit, to further beautify and give more color to the tail cut red and gold bump chenille pipe cleaners in half and cut smaller various lengths; insert push in amongst the frond leaves. Curl the exposed tip ends of the bump chenilles. If you wish to you might make it more authentic by using some actual peacock feathers placed amidst the frond leaves.

When fresh blueberries are in season they look very attractive when pushed onto the sharp tips of the frond ends. This same idea may be carried out with the use of grapes, maraschino or peppermint green jarred cherries, the addition of each little thing bringing more color to your pineapple peacock's plumage. Take the discarded rind from the cavity opening and with knife form two triangular looking pieces from it to resemble wings, trim and shape up and insert on either side of top edge of cavity opening with wood floral picks, close to points C and D. These wings will add more "color" to your bird and also help in holding a larger amount of fruit salad within the cavity opening.

OUR PINEAPPLE PEACOCK GOES TO A COCKTAIL PARTY

In case your pineapple peacock is invited to a cocktail party and you know your hostess has already provided the fruit arrangements, may I suggest the following variation of our pretty bird.

Proceed as in previous chapter on the pineapple peacock except we are about to "dress" our bird a little differently. After emptying the cavity opening (use the fruit for another time) raise your "feature creature" onto foil covered styrofoam, for it will truly be a centerpiece (although all it will hold is a simple dip recipe of your selection).

After stabilizing it onto the styrofoam (with orange wood sticks), line the cavity opening with foil. Fill with the dip. In place of the grape clusters usually pinned onto the front of the pineapple peacock, we will substitute hors d'oeuvres tidbits. Skewer your bamboo sticks with an assortment of black olives, pimento filled olives, pineapple chunks, cheese bits, ham chunks, cherry tomatoes, gerkin pickles, cocktail onions etc, etc. Garnish with parsley sprigs. Set in center of large tray. Surround with crackers and vegetables for dipping.

Also see chapter 6—Helps, Hints and How to's for a Hostess' cocktail party.

With your creative juices now working you can easily see that our pineapple peacock could also hold a large amount of mustard or relish for a larger party. Surround with salami, cornucopias or ham roll-ups, etc. Present an hors d'oeuvres "front" filled with pickled onions, olives, gherkins, cheeses, etc.

"FRUIT FOR SALE"
OLD-FASHIONED FRUIT CART

This delightful fruit piece will require the following:
1 large pineapple—for the body of flower cart
1 small pineapple—to produce two wheels for cart
4" × 8" block of styrofoam 1" thick for base . . .
to be covered with silver foil.
2 orange wood sticks

Plastic flowers of red or pink preferably (for contrast)
Long chenille pipe cleaners for handle of cart
Assorted fruits, grape clusters, garnishes and mint leaves, and
    frill toothpicks.

Large size pineapple: Remove frond crown by *twisting* it off;
DO NOT CUT! to protect hands use a towel to cover fronds and
twist back and forth to release crown of leaves. If there is any
difficulty in accomplishing this, merely insert sharp point of
knife around base of fronds every inch or so to loosen, and then
TWIST with aforementioned towel method. Since this is to be
the body and raised on top of styrofoam and skewed in place,
it is *not* necessary to cut a stabilizing base.

To create cavity opening (later to be filled with assorted fruits:)
Follow procedure as in peacock. For easier cutting on this rectangular opening, place markers (toothpicks) positioned ⅔ of
the way up from the bottom in the following manner: Place two

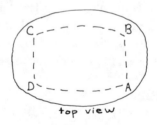

top view

parallel markers 1″ in from frond base (A and B) as pictured in
diagram. Also place two markers parallel one inch in from opposite end of fronds (C and D).
    Your markers will then be the corners of the rectangular
cavity opening. Using a large knife, cut from A to B and also
from C to D. When cutting from A to D and from B to C cut

— 66 —

at an angle toward the core center of the pineapple. To facilitate the release of the top section more easily, use the curved
blade of a pineapple or grapefruit knife to help undercut the
tough core of the fruit. Lift off this cut section and again using

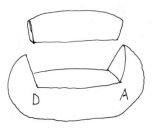

the curved blade of the pineapple or grapefruit knife separate
meat from shell rind. Cut into small pieces and set aside for your
salad. Remove the remaining meat in like manner from the
body of the flower cart leaving a sufficient shell to later contain
your fruit salad being careful you leave a very thick base of fruit
on bottom area of wagon body. Cover a block of styrofoam equal
to the size of the body of your large pineapple (or approximately
4″ × 8″—1″ thick) with aluminum foil. Place body of pineapple flower cart on top of this styrofoam piece. To secure in position, pierce an orange wood stick or two (or even a long skewer)
through the bottom of pineapple and down into styrofoam. If
top of orange wood stick extends up into the cavity, do not be
concerned so long as it does not project *above* the cavity opening.

Smaller pineapple: Turn smaller size pineapple with rind on
side and cut off two ¾″ slices to use as the wheels of your flower
cart. Use balance of pineapple meat in some other manner e.g.
fruit cup, etc. To create spoke wheel effect for your wagon
wheel, lay each ¾″ piece flat on cutting board and leaving
center hard core intact, cut out triangular shaped pieces from

wheel slice leaving ¼–½" piece in between each triangular section. See illustration. (Shadowed area has been cut out).

Proceed with second slice exactly as first wheel. Place each wheel against sides of larger pineapple body, bottom of wheel base about 1" from base of styrofoam block so that top of wheel is approximately 2" down from cavity opening. Pierce a long frill toothpick through a red cherry and then into the core of the center of the wheel, thus into and through the side of the pineapple body. Using same colored frill toothpicks insert only the toothpicks into each spoke end section of wheel and thru to the opposing body or styrofoam piece. (See illustration). Follow same procedure with second wheel.

To place flower cart handle: Use a red bump chenille or if preferred, two regular type long pipe cleaners intertwined to give twist affect. As in illustration above, at points E make a hole with toothpick (for easier insertion) and then push into holes, ends of pipe cleaner handle creating a curved handle bar to flower cart.

Decorate cart at point E only coming up a little along side of cart handle with pretty red plastic flowers. Pretty up the exposed opposite side (where frond has been twisted off) by covering exposed area with plastic flowers. To help enhance your creation place clusters of fresh grapes interlaced with cherries or strawberries along side and draped near one side of the wheel.

Fill cavity of flower cart with assorted bite size pieces of fruit and garnish with peppermint sprigs. Have on hand chilled refill of assorted fruits ready, for your company will delight in your "Flowers For Sale."

FLOWER LADY

To create our flower lady use a 1 pt. size detergent bottle refilled with water or sand (for weight). Force a 3″ styrofoam ball onto the bottle cap. Make up face of our flower vendor appropriately using buttons for eyes, flannel for eyebrows, lipstick or red flannel for mouth features. A curly type metal pot cleaner may be used for hair.

Optional: A piece of handi-wipe type cloth may be her head-kerchief if desired. Using scotch tape wrap a pink bump chenille pipe cleaner and position appropriately for hands. Using scraps of material dress up the upper portion of her body with a shawl effect; secure around waist with scotch tape. Wrap around waist a skirt made up of scrap material and top with a small apron and bow.

Enfold her hands so that she is holding a bunch of flowers (fresh or plastic artificial flowers). Place our Flower Lady next to your Fruit Cart for added realism and I'm sure she will be a "sell-out."

Alternative: If your creative mind is working you already see many uses for this flower lady with a few alterations, e.g. replace her flowers with a small rubber spatula or wooden spoon and she would make a cute kitchen gift for a new apartment.

If it's a "clean up party" for the new couple who just moved in or the church centerpiece, replace her flowers with a small oven cleaner brush or a pastry brush so it resembles our cleaning lady, "sweeping" up. A bucket filled with other cleaning equipment and sundries would make a lovely gift for that bride's surprise kitchen shower party.

HOW AND WHERE TO GET IT!

More information on pineapples:
    Pineapple Cook Book; Dole Company
    Castle and Cooke, Inc.
    50 California Street
    San Francisco, California 94111

    Patricia Collier Dept. SS
    Dole Company
    Fifth and Virginia Street
    San Jose 95108, California
Recipes for fresh Hawaiian pineapple and parties:
    Patricia Collier
    Dole Company
    P. O. Box 5130
    San Jose 95108, California
How to have a Wikiwaki Dole Luau booklet:
    Dole Company
    Fifth and Virginia Street
    San Jose 95108, California

For teachers:

Pineapple in Hawaii. A publication of the Department of Education: Dole Company, Fifth and Virginia Street, San Jose, California 95108.

For organizations:

How You Can Give Hawaiian Parties: Braniff International Public Relations Dept., 135 East 42nd Street, New York 10017. 40 page booklet. Charge 25¢

Brim fill of ideas for luaus, buffets, luncheons, beach, school, fund raisers for church and free Hawaiian posters and brochures. (Film and tapes also available).

Quick Guide to Speaking Hawaiian and *The Everything Hawaiian Catalogue.* Hawaii International Ltd., 305 Seventh Ave., New York 10001. 30¢ and 50¢.

Hawaiian Parties Indoor and Out: Hawaiian Parties, P.O. Box 293 Brooklyn, N.Y. 11208 Charge: 25¢

Hawaiian Happy Cake. Kemoo Farm Foods Ltd., P. O. Box 7973, Honolulu, Hawaii 96813. Free brochure with order blanks.

Hawaiian Posters and Islander Flight Recipes. Western Airlines, Public Relations Dept., 6060 Avion Drive, Los Angeles, California 90009. Free

Films:

Hawaiian Sound Films. Pan American World Airways, Advt. Dept., Attention: Ruth Keary; Pan American Bldg., 200 Park Ave. New York 10017. On loan.

1001 Pineapples. Pineapple Growers Association of Hawaii, Modern Talking Pictures, 2323 New Hyde Park Road, New Hyde Park, New York 11040. On loan.

Also see your local travel agents for posters, check your local commercial display firms (see the yellow pages classified directory) check your local Polynesian restaurant for ideas and help and all you need to say is "MAHALO" . . . Thank you.

2 WATERMELONS

If we were to play the game of word association, what most popular fruit dessert would come to your mind?

It was of much interest to Dr. David Livingstone of Stanley and Livingstone, in Africa. A member of the gourd family, it was born of Egyptian heritage over 4,000 years ago and introduced to this country by the Negro. Cultivated by the Indians, it is enjoyed by all Americans going back as far as 1629. Proof of its delectibility is the fact that approximately 1,057,000 tons of this luscious fruit are grown and shipped out of five of our states, Florida, Texas, California, Georgia, and South Carolina, principal growers of this product. From these geographical locations we surmise our product is a warm season crop although it has also been known to thrive as far north as Canada.

The answer of course is the popular vine growing *watermelon*. This fruit, actually 93% water, is now available in many varieties, sizes, and shapes, from the bantam type of 5–10 lbs, to a watermelon variety that can weigh as much as 100 lbs. The average watermelon weighs between 20–35 lbs., and may be round, oblong or even oval; may be green, striped or even almost all white. Although some fruit specialty shops may carry them all year round, they are most plentiful during their peak season, June through August.

Grown from seed in hills 8–10 feet apart, the one most often seen and recognized is the Charleston Gray, the all green variety. The Garrison or Jubilee variety, with a rind of light green and dark green stripes is often referred to as the rattlesnake, striped or tiger skin watermelon.

It is a known fact that the word "watermelon" was included in the Sanskrit language, and was depicted by early Egyptian artists, indicating that this fruit has been under cultivation for more than 4,000 years.

This plant, with its vines branching out 12–15 feet in all directions, first grew in Africa where it drew the interest of Dr. Livingstone. Native to Africa, it was introduced to America by the Negro and was plentiful in the Massachusetts colony as early as 1629. The melon was even grown and raised by Indian tribes along the Colorado River in 1799. To date, scientists have been experimenting with this member of the gourd family, and have been able to produce a seedless watermelon, and even a midget watermelon which turns gold when ripe.

How To Buy: Since this melon has no aroma at all to help you choose for sweetness, the surest method of choosing a delicious vine-ripened watermelon is to see and taste it after it has been cut open or at least have a "plug" removed. Look for crisp pink meat, free from white streaks. Look for seeds which resist cutting and are dark brown or black; (whitish seeds indicate immaturity) dry mealy meat or stringy pulp indicate overmaturity and aging *after* harvesting. If cutting the melon is frowned upon by your local supermarket produce manager may I suggest you look for a firm symmetrical shape; the rind should have a slight dullness (neither shiny nor too dull). The underside of a ripe watermelon should be yellowish in color. This is natural in *all* the varieties due to the fact that this is where the melon laid on the ground. The ends of the melon should be filled out and rounded.

How to store: Once cut open, the watermelon should be carefully wrapped to protect and lock in its own flavors. Refrigerated properly, the average time it will last is approximately two weeks. It has however, been frozen commercially, or can be frozen even by you, the housewife, if packaged correctly and stored frozen in its own juices. It has been known to keep in its frozen state up to one year.

The variety of its species is only matched by the many ways of "presenting" this fruit. There are so many infinite ways of using its meat and juices as treats for snack times, desserts, preserves, in champagne cocktails, punches, sherbet, and in dips and salads.

Tips on selecting watermelons and a booklet filled with recipes is available to anyone interested by writing to: The National Watermelon Growers and Distributors Association, P. O. Box 38, Morven, Georgia 31638; and now for some of my tips on novel ways of presenting this delectible and versatile fruit . . . the watermelon.

WATERMELON BASKETS
(To be used as Fruit Holders or as Punch Bowls)

Supplies needed:

One Watermelon	Lemon Stripper
Other Melon Fruits	Food Coloring
Melon Baller	Cotton Buds
Sharp Knife	Kitchen Helper

Before you embark on cutting your basket, decide just how much space is allocated for it on your sometimes crowded buffet table. If you're long on your love for watermelon and short on space, choose a short squat shape so that it may stand vertically. Conversely, if you prefer to stand it horizontally, choose a long oval shaped "tiger" melon. Whichever your choice, cut off your slice from side or end of the watermelon to stabilize base of your basket for its appropriate position.

The first step after stabilization of the fruit is to draw (with pencil) the outline of your basket (with or without handle). See diagram for suggested variations of watermelon basket.

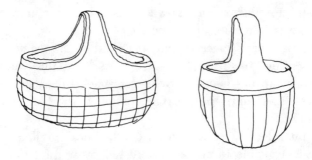

To create a more authentic look to your basket draw or outline the markings for a basket weave effect. Score the rind of the watermelon with a lemon stripper. OPTIONAL: To enhance the color scheme of your table setting, color the scored out stripped areas with appropriate food color using cotton buds. The handle may even be scored in the same manner. See diagram.

Cut out as per drawing. Start with outlined shape of handle, then meet by cutting crosswise to base of handle. Be sure you do not cut *thru* base of handle in your zealousness. Remove these large cut sections and ball meat from them. Set meat aside. With melon baller remove meat from basket. Carefully remove meat beneath handle of basket. Undercut handle and all edges of basket to make design distinct. Combine with other watermelon meat set aside earlier and with other fruit melon selections. If desired, this fruit compote may be marinated with Kirsch, rum or other liquer or wines for that extra tang. OPTIONAL: Decorate entire circumference edge of basket with border of canned mandarin orange sections. Hold in place with frill toothpicks. Refill basket cavity and garnish with fresh berries, peppermint or strawberry leaves.

There are as many variations to the creation of a watermelon basket as there are facets to a diamond. For example: See ice formed handle for fruit basket in chapter 8 (Seafood Basket Holder.) (1) Instead of scoring handle, the handle can be overlaid with scallop designed orange slices (use lemon stripper to scallop oranges). Hold in place with frill picks and garnish with maraschino cherries. (2) The handle can be overlaid with fresh strawberry leaves, small kumquats and spiced apple rings. (3) Fresh or plastic flowers may be pretty atop the handle. (4) If desired, using melon baller remove only half of the ball scoop of watermelon rind every 2–3", being careful not to pierce *through* the handle. Replace this cavity with an equal size cantalope ball and/or alternate with contrasting honeydew balls. (5) You might like to use the smaller melon ball end, removing the rind in similar fashion and replacing with fresh blueberries.

If desired you can create a scallop edge on your basket by making a paper pattern which then could be used over again. To do so use a cup edge or glass rim and trace your pattern onto heavy manila type paper. Transfer and trace that pattern with pencil as the outline of your watermelon basket. See diagram. ⌒⌒⌒⌒⌒ The opposite effect of the scallop can be created by holding your scallop pattern upside down and tracing same. See diagram. ⌣⌣⌣⌣ Your handle can be cut in like manner.

If pointed top edges are more pleasing to you, use your

Kitchen Helper gadget or cut with knife in zigzag staggered pattern. For another variation of the scallop effect, cut straight across as for plain basket. With melon baller scoop out a ball of the watermelon rind edge every two inches as per diagram. This melon hole may then be filled with a melon ball of contrasting color. A scallop effect is particularly beautiful when the border effect is left and has at least 3″ width. Now score your basket weave effect. See diagrams.

If desired, watermelon meat may be entirely removed to be presented in another fruit dish. Therefore you can refill basket with beverage and use as a punch bowl. Float ice mold and garnish, or line basket cavity to use as a serving dish and fill with frozen ice cream and sherbert balls and garnish with fresh fruit melon, cocoanut and nuts. To do so in advance, ball various flavors of cream and sherbert. Coat some with cocoanut or chopped nuts and freeze until ready to serve in awaiting watermelon basket.

Also see chapter 8: A Basket filled Seafood holder.

ROUND THE WORLD:
UP, UP AND AWAY IN A HELIUM FILLED
WATERMELON BALLOON

Keeping up with Mike Todd's Around The World theme you too can fly your own creative edible balloon filled basket. Doing a take off on the watermelon basket, it's just a new added touch that transforms your basket into an airborne vehicle.

Prepare a watermelon basket without a handle as per previous instructions. Carve out strips for basket weave effect with the lemon stripper. Refill basket with fresh fruit and garnish.

To simulate effect of being airborne is a simple matter of purchasing a large colored *HELIUM* filled balloon from a local vendor or store and placing it high above your basket, containing it within a cape of thin netting or ribbon effect. The ends

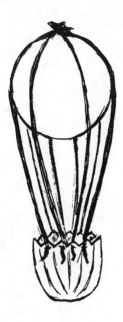

of these netting or ribbons can be secured and attached onto the border edge of the watermelon and further festooned with decorating bows and ribbons as if for a gala event. Be sure to keep your balloon anchored high above the basket leaving enough room in between basket and balloon for easier reach of those hungry hands.

WATERMELON WISHING WELL

To serve as a mood setter for a shower and to provide the proper setting as an edible centerpiece for your table, serve a refreshing punch or cut up medley of fresh fruits in this watermelon wishing well container.

To cut melon: Cut melon as in diagram for vertical standing position. Stabilize base cut and remove melon meat from both

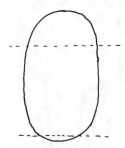

sections of watermelon. Set melon balls aside for mixing with other fruits and refilling later. Undercut all around melon shell as close to white section of rind as possible, leaving a good border of white and green rind intact. Be sure to leave a sufficient floor base to watermelon shell, especially if melon is to be used as a punch bowl, and not merely as a holder for cut up fresh fruits.

Use the wide lemon stripper end of the Kitchen Helper implement to take out strips of the white part of the rind across the flat cut surface top of the melon. The distance between these lemon strip cuts should not be measured nor uniform in size as by cutting the strips out you are trying to emulate the actual brick or stone formation of a spring water well. The stone wall housing a water well would naturally be comprised of various sized stones and bound with mortar. Therefore in this particular instance, contrary to usual procedure, we do *not* want to emphasize any uniformity to the strip cuts in any way.

Continue as above, creating the stone and mortar formation of the water well by stripping out the rind of the entire melon shell. (see diagram). I then prefer to leave the melon in this natural cut state, however, if you wish the color scheme of the evening to be accentuated, color in the stripped out rind pieces with vegetable dye and a cotton bud tip.

To construct overhead roof top of well: Estimate height necessary to station and uphold the protective roof top over the well base. Using ¾" styrofoam cut out 2 long supportive arms to do same, making them 2" in width and proportionate in length to the overall size of the melon (well). Allow enough room between roof top and top of shell base to afford a guest to dip and refresh herself from the wishing well. (contents)

Roof: Although an oak tag base can be used to form a roof, I prefer one made of stratofoam or the more sturdy styrofoam ½" board. Put together a simulated gable roof top to station overhead as the protective rooftop usually found over a water well as per illustration. Using a felt marker pen, stencil in stone type effect on supportive arms of well (styrofoam sides.); use same to stencil in shingle type roof on overhead styrofoam.

For a more colorful effect, I prefer covering all such styrofoam pieces with a red brick designed crepe paper usually used to simulate brick fireplaces for Christmas decorations. Glue or tape with transparent tape the red brick paper onto the styrofoam. If you intend to use your wishing well over and over again, contrary to making a wishing well to be given as a gift (of food), then for your own home entertaining and for more authenticity by all means prevail on that handsome guy of yours to make a roof and sides from a light weight type of wood such as balsam. Be sure the base ends on the two supportive sides are cut properly so they can be later staked into the flat surface of the wishing well, as per diagram.

Measure circumference of dowel and cut holes on both supportive styrofoam structures of well. Thread this small dowel stick through these two facing holes as per diagram. This will act as the pulley for the well's water bucket lending more authenticity to the centerpiece. Use a piece of pipe cleaner stem chenille on end of dowel as handle of pulley. Wind rope or colored twine onto dowel stick center and attach remaining end of rope to a small drinking paper cup or tortoni paper cup to act as water bucket.

To attach and assemble roof to well: Using long bamboo skewers push 2 sticks into each side of each supportive styrofoam arm to depth of 3–4 inches. Carefully prehole (use bamboo stick point) and then push remaining exposed tip point of bamboo stick into surface top of shell base.

Optional: With roof in place perch a little feathery novelty bird atop roof corner over well.

Fill watermelon well with fresh fruit and garnish or fill with liquid refreshment and float lemon slices and small ice ring. If giving this wishing watermelon well to a hospital or convalescent patient (be sure to check dietary rules for that patient with his doctor and hospital first) fill empty plastic capsules (obtained from a local pharmacy) with little slips of get well messages. Instruct patient to take one pill or capsule daily from well's water bucket and the fruit from within the well "whenever needed for comfort".

Your well of good wishes will be a big hit for a convalescent patient as well as a birthday celebrant or use as the fruit-filled centerpiece at a bridal shower.

For any other party occasion, use this "stone" watermelon well for what it was more naturally meant . . . to quench one's thirst with a refreshing drink. (fill and use as punch bowl)

Wishing well paper cups: Carry out your party theme by making similar wishing wells to hold mints or nuts for the party table. Cut a hot styrofoam coffee cup as per diagram. Stencil in "stone wall" as per larger melon well. Fill cups with cubes of colored peppermints or nuts. Top off with different colored paper muffin liners as overhead rooftop. Adhere one to the other with little dabs of floral gum tape. To simultaneously serve as a place setting marker write each guest's name on top of (well) roof as per diagram.

WATERMELON SAILBOAT

For your sailboat you will need:
One elongated shaped watermelon
Assorted melon fruit balls
Red pipe cleaners
Bamboo sticks
Wood floral picks and/or orange wood sticks
Maraschino cherries
Appropriate garnishes

Sails: Outline and cut from the removed ⅓ top section of watermelon rind.

Anchor: String or rope (or light chain for realistic effect). Attach to "anchor" piece (shaped watermelon rind or piece of oak tag will do to simulate anchor).

Select oval shaped watermelon and stabilize base. Slice off top ⅓ section of watermelon. Cut into sections as illustrated in diagram (A).

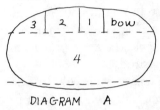

DIAGRAM A

Reserve fruit balls removed from this section for refill later. With melon baller, scoop out all meat from the boat base (sec. 4) of your watermelon. Set fruit aside for refill later. Using the distance measured between the side walls of the back of your sailboat as a guide, cut the length needed (for retaining the walls) from a piece of styrofoam. This piece (#5) will then be 1″ × 1″ × length. Cover with foil and place into retaining position as in illustration "B." This will give you the extra sup-

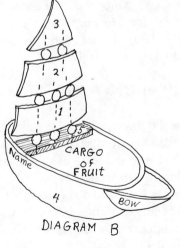

DIAGRAM B

port needed to place and stabilize the sails of your boat.

Cut out from the discarded ⅓ section as depicted in diagram "A", the bow of your sailboat. Position it onto the bow of the boat with bamboo sticks as shown in diagram "B." On top of the styrofoam retaining wall in the stern of your boat, place 3–4 or 5 maraschino cherries in position (the length of your retaining wall will decide the number of cherries needed). Hold cherries in position with wood floral picks or orange wood sticks and use the picks as a base to mount your first sail. The sails are to be cut as depicted in diagram "A" from the discarded ⅓ watermelon section. Repeat the same process to mount your second and third sail if desired.

The number of sails on your vessel is entirely up to the "skipper." At least three sails *can* be cut out from the ⅓ discarded watermelon section top although sail #2 can be omitted. Secure your rope or chain and anchor onto the base and set your anchor over the side.

Optional: With felt marking pen christen your boat with a name. If you would like portholes to your sailing vessel, cut them out with a melon baller. Try not to pierce the meat portion of the watermelon fruit as this will cause leakage of the fruit's juice. Place your sailboat onto a serving tray atop a chicory sea and set sail for a fun time with a cargo of melon ball fruits and berries. (base of boat (#4) was refilled with melon balls and garnished appropriately.)

SIMPLE SHIP FROM A WATERMELON

This ship is a real quicky and nice for a child's party. Stabilize the base of a large elongated shaped watermelon. Cut as per diagram. Note that bow and stern of ship is slightly higher and angled toward lower mid-section of ship.

With melon baller scoop out all of the meat. Set aside to mix with other melon fruits later for refilling ship. Undercut rind all around edge so that outline of ship is distinct. Create portholes

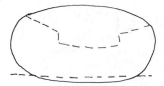

by cutting them out of rind on side with melon baller. Line inside of watermelon cavity with foil to hold in fruit and juices and also to emphasize port hole effect of the ship. Foil can be easily held in place with toothpicks. Once the fruit has been filled into the cavity opening, the foil will remain in position. See diagram.

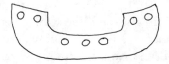

Mount one or two "sails" depending on size of ship. Cut the sails from oak tag or fashion them out of heavy foil. Place your sails into appropriate position in the hull of your ship with the use of a dowel or bamboo sticks.

With felt marking pen write the name of the birthday child on the rind of the bow end of the ship (e.g. U.S.S. Bernard or H.M.S. Cyril). An appropriate anchor or child's small toy rowboat might be hung off the side of your ship with the use of rope and totem pole pins to provide more authenticity to your sailing vessel. Push horizontally into position between stern and bow sections of your ship, long bamboo sticks to simulate walking rails of the vessel. This will also help to retain the fruit in place. See diagram. Place on tray of "chicory waves". Fill with fruit and garnish prettily.

This ship or any boat type need not necessarily be refilled with fruit. If you wish you may remove the fruit and reserve it, to be used in another fruit plate for your party or use the fresh fruit for dinner. You might then line with silver foil the entire inside of the watermelon. Fill it instead with an assortment of candies for the children or even little prizes or party favors. I would then "title" my ship with felt marking pen on bow, appropriately "Ship of Goodies" or "U.S.S. Prizes".

A WHIMSICAL WATERMELON WHALE

Your whimsical whale, adrift on a turbulent sea of chicory waves, couldn't help but catch the eye of every guest, be it filled with a compote of assorted fruit melons, or filled with a fruit or liquor punch. To create your own whimsical whale you will need:

1 suitable oval-shaped watermelon
1 Kitchen Helper gadget or small sharp knife

melon ball cutter
Large chef knife

Cut off thin slice from bottom of watermelon with large knife to stabilize melon, being careful not to penetrate into rind too deeply. Using a pencil, sketch the design of your watermelon as per diagram.

top view

To cut: For easier carving of the rounded areas of the whale cut out along the dotted outline utilizing the curve of the blade of a pointed grapefruit knife. For variety of design use the

zigzag cutter of the Kitchen Helper gadget to cut along the straight side areas of the whale figure. See diagram.

Do *not* attempt to remove the top cut section in one piece.

Remove that part of the watermelon which is to be taken out, in *small* sections carefully exposing the meat of the melon. Now remove the meat with the melon baller. Set aside for use later. Be particularly careful in working around and under the tail section as this is most fragile. Undercut the tail and all edges of the melon, removing all the meat so that the outline of the whale's shape is very discernible. Create the face of your whimsical whale by decorating the front with cherries or strawberries for eyes. With the use of a waterproof marking pen you can create the effect of eyelashes. Create the mouth by excising out a curled piece of rind (use lemon stripper). Accentuate the mouth by coloring with red food dye and a cotton bud.

If whale is to be utilized as a punch bowl, merely fill with beverage, float a pretty ice mold and garnish with strawberries and sprigs of fresh peppermint. OPTIONAL: A bunch of grapes may be hung over the tail (use totem pins) for that extra touch and for your guests' nibbling delight. A blow hole and water spout may be simulated (above the eyes of the whale) by filling a small hole with a cluster of pipe cleaners or a floral wire staggered with a few fresh grapes on it. Recently a standing mobile type of decoration made of wire and colored balls has been prevelant and if you wish, the top part of this mobile is very effective as the water spout when placed in the appropriate place. Your whimsical whale then becomes a musical one when the backyard breezes cause the balls to elicit the sound of soft chimes.

To serve, place your whimsical musical whale adrift on a sea of chicory leaves.

FRIGATE BATTLESHIP

Select long oval shaped watermelon and stabilize base. Carefully outline with pencil, the three tier decks following diagram.

Cut out the bow (section #1) using the curved back of the pointed grapefruit knife thus creating the pointed top of heart shaped effect in bow of ship. (As per instruction for whimsical

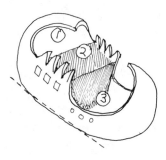

whale). Create a zigzag effect to the second deck section by cutting with the use of the Kitchen Helper gadget (or use a sharp knife to create points.) Drop down 2″ and create the stern or third deck effect of your frigate ship by cutting with a grapefruit knife. The stern line must of course be parallel and in line with the front bow of your ship and have the same heart-shape effect. As previously described in directions for watermelon whale, cut and remove outlined sections of watermelon in small pieces. *DO NOT* discard removed top rind sections of the watermelon as some of it will be used as the mast sails of your frigate battleship.

Leave a three inch mid-center section of fruit meat intact (shaded area in diagram). This will give a stronger base to mount and support your sails and mast stick in later. Remove the remaining watermelon meat from inside the body cavity of the ship with a melon baller. Two inches below zigzag effect of the mid-section of the ship, (second deck) pencil in and then cut out three square windows following illustrated diagram. As illustrated, cut out three port hole windows with a melon baller in the stern section. Try not to cut through into pulp part of melon. Fill these port holes with cantaloupe melon balls of equal size (cut with same size baller).

Place wood floral picks into the porthole openings; (push them from the inside of the watermelon ship outward). Have the wood pick extrude just enough to catch and hold the cantaloupe balls so that the ends of the wood picks *do not* show through.

(Optional: Place a few dates in the square cut out windows (with floral wood picks) thus creating an effect of cannons jutting out, ready for battle.) Line all open windows with foil to retain the melon fruit and their juices.

Decorate all curved area border edges of watermelon ship with mandarin orange sections. Hold in place with colored frill picks. *From previously removed and discarded top sections of watermelon rind, cut out two sails as per diagram.

Insert dowel mast stick into three inch meat mid-section of second deck section (#2). (Shadowed area in previous illustration). Mount sails on top of dowel stick (mast) and support with bamboo sticks and floral picks.

Run thin rope or cording (with appropriate flags if desired) from top of apex of mast sail (A) and then down to connect to top of bow and stern ends of ship (B & C). (If mast stick has small cut across top surface (A) it will hold rope more securely in

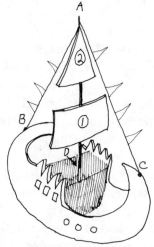

place.) See diagram. Tautness of these cording lines can be accomplished by tying the rope ends to the head of the totem pole pins. Push pins into the watermelon rind at points B and C so they cannot slip out.

Refill entire cavity opening of ship with a "cargo" of assorted fruits, pile fruits high to cover the entry point (D) of your mast dowel stick. Cover the totem pins (holding your rope lines taut at points B & C) by placing clusters of assorted colored grapes into position with totem pins. Garnish with cherries and mint leaves and a sprinkling of blueberries and coconut if desired.

Optional: Drop your anchor (made from oak tag paper or watermelon rind) over the side.

Your ship is now "ready for attack" by your hungry guests. Set frigate battleship on tray with green chicory leaves lapping at its bottom and give your guests a "fighting" chance by supplying them with frill toothpicks for quick pickings of juicy "treasures."

VIKING GALLEY SHIP

To set the mood for a Mediterranean type of dinner or for that trip abroad to the Isle of Greece you will need the following to create your edible centerpiece:
Large oval shaped watermelon
Kitchen Helper gadget
Melon ball cutter
Sharp cooks or chef knife
Grapefruit knife
For serpent head: black oak tag, base wrapped in saran wrap
For oars: Long straws
Frill toothpicks
Assorted fruits
Chicory and garnishes
Slice off stabilizing piece from bottom of watermelon to create flat base. You will need a large chef or cooks knife to do this. Outline in pencil the design of a heart shape on both sides of the melon as per diagram.

Cut, utilizing the curved blade of a grapefruit knife to get around the curved outlined section of the viking ship. Use the

Kitchen Helper gadget to create the zigzag effect of the sides of the vessel.

Remove in *small* sections that top cut portion of the watermelon rind. Remove meat from that section of the rind, and also from the body of the vessel with a melon baller. Set aside. These watermelon balls can then be intermixed with assorted fruits for replacement later. Undercut all outline edges of the viking ship. Leave a 1–2″ thickness of green and white rind to ensure that the design of your vessel ship is discernible.

For serpent's head: (See illustration). Trace and cut vessel's masthead from black oak tag. Wrap base of serpent head with saran wrap. This will prevent the mast head from getting wet, thereby bleeding and becoming limp when placed into position. At head of ship cut a vertical slash down center of vertex to allow for insertion of saran-wrapped serpent head. Place into position. Cover base of serpent's head with decorative flowers pinned in place or cover with strawberry leaves.

To make oars: Push 4–5 frill toothpicks through red cherries or apple spice rings and then into sides of vessel positioning them two inches below zigzag cut effect. Be sure to angle the frill

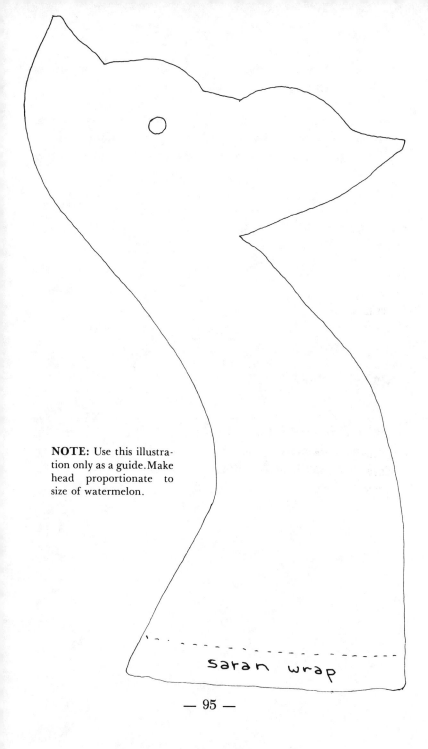

NOTE: Use this illustration only as a guide. Make head proportionate to size of watermelon.

saran wrap

picks so that the cellophane ends point downward. Slip colored straws onto the ends of the cellophane frills.

Optional: Mast sails may be incorporated by putting sails (oak tag) on long dowels of wood and setting into center of ship.
　　Refill with fruit, garnish and set sail on bed of chicory waves.

SIMPLE SWAN OR DUCK

　　Going off on a slight tangent of the Viking ship created, you can easily transform the principle of creating the Viking ship into a duck or swan by merely changing the shape of the body cavity and substituting a different head piece. Cut off the stabil-

izing base from the full well-rounded (not too elongated) watermelon, outline in pencil, the body cavity as depicted in diagram. The notched pointed outline in diagram will distinguish where the notched effect of the Kitchen Helper is suggested. Note also that the widow's peak in the front and back are carved slightly differently than in the aforementioned Viking ship.

After outlining, cut in the depicted zigzag areas with the use of the kitchen helper or use a paring knife to obtain similar effect. After cutting out the wing and tail areas, proceed to cut out all other curved areas as outlined using the rounded back of the grapefruit knife. As in the whale, cut the remaining rind top into small sections for easier removal thereby preventing possible breakage. Remove carefully. With melon baller remove meat from cavity area and set aside for refilling later. Undercut around all border edges to emphasize the distinct design of your creation.

To further highlight the feather effect of your bird, be it swan or duck, use the lemon stripper to cut out strips along the top width flat surface of all the curved border edges. If desired use the stripper to cut out rind pieces from the flat surface sides of the watermelon body to give your bird more of a feathered look.

Trace onto very thick white oaktag or heavy cardboard (for extra needed strength, covered with white oaktag for better appearance) the paper pattern outline of the duck or swan. Cut out and wrap base of figure head with saran wrap or plastic to prevent the figure head from becoming limp from the juice of the watermelon.

Draw eyes on both sides of the outlined heads or paste pretty buttons into appropriate positions to simulate eyes of your creature. At front peak of watermelon body cut a vertical slash down center of vertex and position in swan or duck head.

Refill body of watermelon cavity with fresh assorted fruits; garnish. Place on tray filled with blue or green gelatin and float your swan or duck on his private lake. If preferred, green chi-

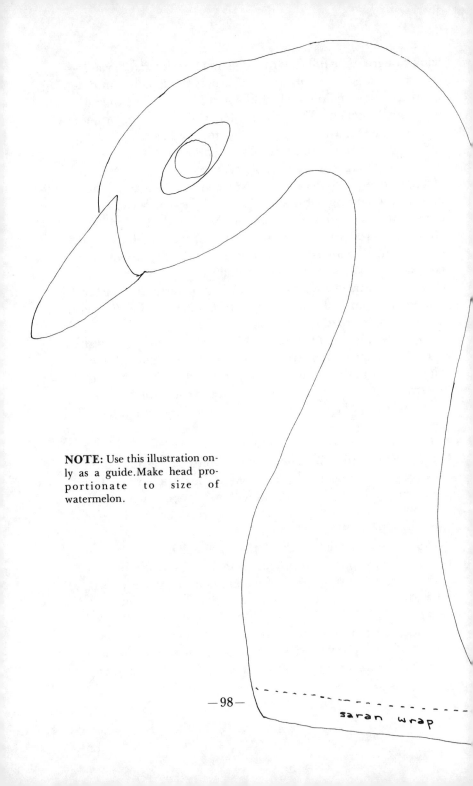

NOTE: Use this illustration only as a guide. Make head proportionate to size of watermelon.

saran wrap

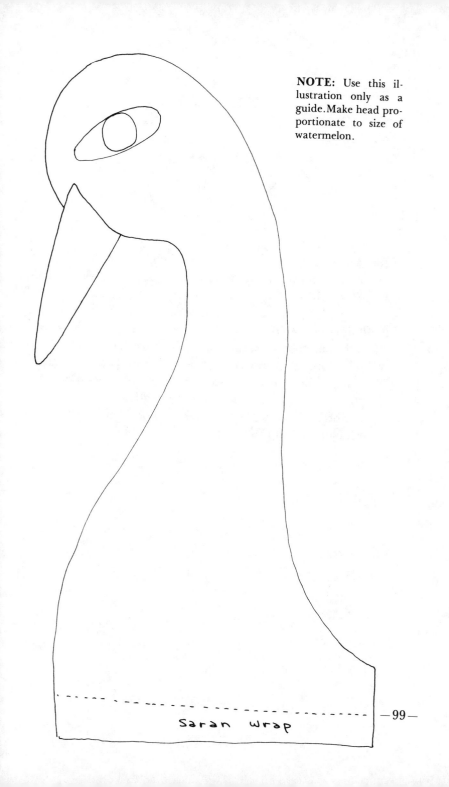

NOTE: Use this illustration only as a guide. Make head proportionate to size of watermelon.

Saran Wrap

cory leaves can be used to simulate the lake. NOTE: To obtain green or blue color to your lake water, use lime gelatin or use Knox gelatin and water solution or lemon gelatin to which green or blue food coloring has been added. Pour into a tray (with lip) to depth of ⅛ to ¼″ and let set. If you prefer a wavy effect to your body of water, after gelatin has set in a deep bowl, put jello through a grater to give it a crumbled wavy effect. Place on surface of tray and place your bird creation atop. Watch your guests "go duck hunting" with zeal.

For more advanced creative presentation of swan or duck see watermelon swan to follow.

A MORE ADVANCED SCULPTED
WATERMELON SWAN OR DUCK

To create this more advanced presentation of this edible centerpiece and fully appreciate its beauty, it is best if you work
with a very large melon of at least 50 to 60 lbs. or upward.
Although the same procedure can be applied to a smaller melon
(cutting down the figure size to proper proportions) the grace-
fulness of the bird would not be brought out as dramatically.
Obtain a very large and very well-rounded melon and stabilize
as depicted.

Using the outline, place the head of the duck or the upper
curve of the neckline of the swan at the very top of the melon.
Trace with pencil the entire outline of the paper pattern from
the neck down toward the bottom of the melon. Be sure to
leave a very wide, high base on the bottom. This base cavity will
later hold the fruit balls of your creation. Taking into account

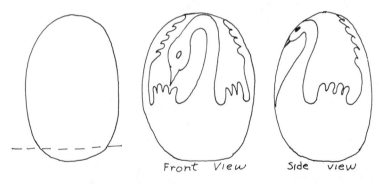

Front View   Side View

the size of the melon you are working with, continue to outline
free hand with pencil the wings, body and back tail end of your
bird as shown in illustrations.

When you are satisfied with your penciled outline, then proceed to cut the melon using the curved back of the grapefruit
blade. Use the Kitchen Helper for the zigzag affect where depicted in tail top and wing area of diagram. As in the whale, cut

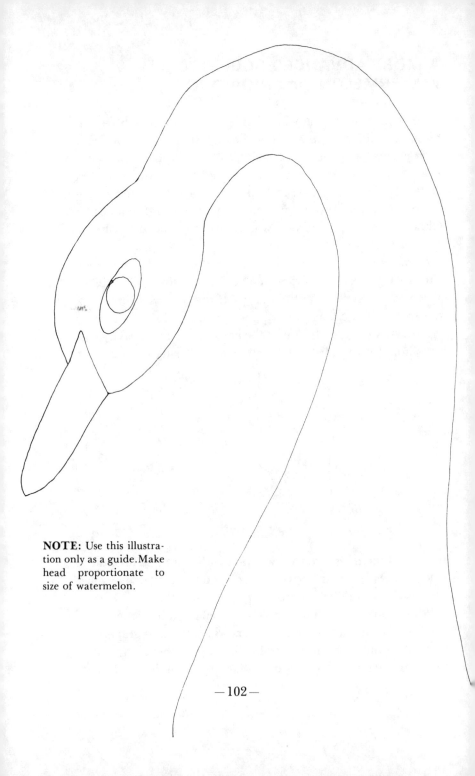

NOTE: Use this illustration only as a guide. Make head proportionate to size of watermelon.

out rind sections to be removed in small sections so as to easily remove and avoid breakage.

Remove meat pulp of the melon with a melon baller. Leave intact a wide section of the pulp as the "floor" of the base of the bird. Undercut along the border edge close to the white skin of the rind so as to emphasize the outline border of your swan or duck figure more distinctly.

Using a lemon stripper remove strips along the remaining white skin rind on the top flat wide surfaces of the bird's tail and wing to give a ruffled feather look to your bird. Do *not* strip any part along the head or neck, for this section is most fragile as is. With lemon stripper, strip out almond-shaped eyelids and color in groove strips with red food coloring, (use a cotton bud). Cut a green cherry in half and place one half into center of eye on one side, piercing pick completely through to underside. Utilize this back end tip of the pick to secure remaining half of cherry on underside of head so there are eyes on both sides of bird's head. If desired using lemon stripper, small rind pieces can be stripped out to simulate feathers of the bird, on the flat side surfaces of the creature. It is optional to fill in these strips with food coloring (use cotton bud) if desired. With a sharp paring knife remove triangular shaped section of the green rind of the watermelon (as depicted in diagram) on the bill or beak section of the head thus baring the white underlying skin beneath the rind. With cotton bud, color this beak section with yellow food coloring. Be sure to color top and *underside* of the beak section.

Refill cavity body of watermelon swan or duck with assorted medley of fruit balls and garnish. Set upon a tray of blue or green gelatin (see simple swan—lake water) or use chicory leaves to represent swan's lake.

OPTIONAL: If desired to bring more realism to your lake scene, place a few large strawberry leaves (Lily Ponds) on your lake. Set upon the leaves a large mushroom cap or two with an (egg) frog sitting on top or nearby. (See chapter on eggs: How To Make A Frog.

A more modern design to your swan can be accomplished simply by cutting the outline a little differently as depicted in following diagram. Following the cutting of the outline, proceed with instructions accordingly.

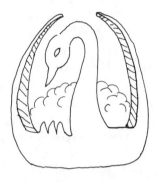

WISE OLD WATERMELON OWL

A lovely edible fruit-filled centerpiece so apropos, as summer birthdays & graduation time roll around, is the Wise Old Watermelon Owl. I prefer using the round ball type watermelon, commonly referred to as a sugar babe melon. Sugar babes are particularly available during this time of season.

To prepare: Cut off a very thin slice from base of melon to stabilize, being sure not to penetrate into the pink meat. Try on for size and fit only at this time, a mortarboard graduation cap which you can easily purchase from a novelty store at this time of year; if you like, make one yourself from black oaktag and ribbon (tassle). If necessary, change the colored ribbon tassle found on the novelty bought cap to that of the graduate's school colors, a nice personal touch. After measuring hat for proper fit on top of melon, set it aside. With pencil, outline cap crown found on an owl's head using illustration as a guide. Pencil in position of eyes of owl. Use a curved blade of a grapefruit knife to cut along the penciled outline. Carefully remove top section of melon. Scoop out melon balls from fruit within top and bottom sections of sugar babe. Set fruit balls aside.

Bottom section: Using sharp edged melon baller, scoop out from rind the penciled outline for the bird's eyes. Replace same with large black grapes or olives (use hidden toothpick method). For feathered effect, strip *UP BUT NOT OFF* little strips of rind, giving an uplifted feathery look to our owl's skin. With floral pick, push in a carved curved carrot beak in appropriate area. Raise bottom section onto piece of high styrofoam or set base atop a deep bowl. Adhere melon to bowl with gummy floral tape or adhere to styrofoam with orange wood stick pushed down through melon into styrofoam base. With bottom section of face in raised position, drape a cloth remnant of the graduate's school colors about base of melon, flowing gracefully onto the table thus simultaneously covering and hiding the tray and/or the bowl and styrofoam uplifted base.

Top of melon: With lemon stripper, peel out all along edge of (cap) top section of melon, a border of the rind skin. Color in with food dye so as to define the outline of the owl's cap. Position graduation mortarboard cap in place on top section of

melon. See diagram. Hold mortarboard cap in position with totem pins or dabs of gummy floral tape. Fill bottom of melon with fruit; garnish. Place graduation capped melon top in place.

Place as centerpiece on birthday or graduation table. If for graduation, accompany with (edible) diploma.

To make diploma: Bake or purchase a large jelly rolled cake. Tie up with a shoe string licorice "ribbon". Decorate: class of June 1975.

To serve: Remove top of melon with graduation cap in position thereon. Set to one side while your guests pick (the fruit of) this owl's "brains". For coordinated graduation theme also see Pineapple Owl: chapter 1; Meat or Fish Owl: chapter 8.

WATERMELON CARRIAGE OR BASSINET

This is always a fun one to make for a baby shower or for the Christening party of the newly arrived babe.

Required for either version:
a 15–25 lb. watermelon
cantaloupe
garnishes

Optional: bow and rattle; assorted cut up fruit mixture

For name: lemon stripper, cotton bud, food color

To make baby: canned pear halves

For features of face: cherry, raisins or cake writing tubes

For hair: coconut

For carriage handle: metal coat hanger wrapped with ribbon

For carriage wheels: pineapple ... oaktag or cardboard or styrofoam wrapped with silver foil.

For bassinette: 5 yds. of 5″ width of netting material shirred across top with gathering stitches; floral gum tape; totem pole pins; and ribbon.

Choose large oval shaped watermelon (ends fully rounded). If she is expecting twins, get an extra, extra large watermelon to fit in two babies (better her than you!). Stabilize melon. Design outline in pencil, using pointed effect or scallop effect as per diagrams. Cut along outline carefully.

For both carriage and bassinette version: Using melon baller, remove meat leaving enough fruit in back of hood so as to resemble raised pillow for baby. Cover this pillow area with cantaloupe balls.

To make baby: Place canned pear half, rounded side up on pillow. To create hair for new born babe, toast cocoanut in oven to desired brown coloring. (To color hair red or "blonde" place some white cocoanut in jar with a few drops of desired food coloring, add a drop or two of water, cover jar and shake well. Spread out on tray and allow to dry . . . DO NOT BAKE!) Eyes and mouth may be made with raisins and a cherry, or drawn on with appropriate colored cake writing tubes. Cover (pear) baby with a "blanket" of watermelon balls. Create the blanket border effect with the use of the contrasting color of cantaloupe meat. Garnish *sparingly* with peppermint leaves.

If the outline design of the body of your carriage or bassinette was cut simply then trim that surface edge with mandarin oranges. Hold oranges in place with frill toothpicks. The word "baby" or the baby's name, if known, can then be carved into the top of the carriage or bassinette hood with a lemon stripper. To accentuate, fill in with a food color dipped cotton bud.

For carriage: Raise watermelon up onto large foil covered styrofoam piece. Secure by piercing orange wood sticks through base of carriage and into styrofoam. To create handle, bend and shape a coat hanger. Wrap with ribbon and place into appropriate position on carriage hood. Slice four ¾" slices of pineapple to create the wheels of your carriage. (See wheels for Old Fashioned Fruit Cart). If preferred, cut oak tag or cardboard as wheels. Pin into place on watermelon carriage.

For bassinette: Place bassinette on tray as it is not necessary to raise onto styrofoam. Pin the shirred net skirt along the bottom edge of the watermelon. Use totem pole pins every 2–3" apart to hold netting in place. Press a dab of sticky floral gum tape onto the head of each totem pin. Now run a ½–¾" finishing ribbon along top of netting using the gum tape as the adhering point of contact.

Optional: Finish off by placing matching bow and/or pretty rattle on your edible centerpiece.

For both carriage and bassinette: When your centerpiece is positioned on tray refill with selected fruit. *OPTIONAL:* If you wish to have a *medley* of assorted fruit then place your mixed assorted fruits under the covering "blanket" of watermelon balls.

TAKE OFF!! . . . IN YOUR OWN WATERMELON PLANE

For your airborne farewell party you will need:

Airplane body: large oval shaped watermelon with flat base.

Motor head: end piece of small acorn squash or facsimile.

Propeller: bump chenille pipe cleaner.

Wheels: (optional) can be simulated with 2″ styrofoam balls or oranges held by heavy orange wood sticks or facsimile for landing gear apparatus.

Wings: purchase another quartered lengthwise cut section of watermelon to allow for two appropriately sized plane wings and rudder tail wing end flaps.

Optional: Airport runway: large tray or foil covered wood board with runway markings (colored mystic tape or ribbon to represent lane guides).

To create body of plane: **DO NOT** cut off stabilizing base (especially if you are outfitting your plane with landing gear, which is optional). Outline in pencil pilot's and passengers' windows. Leave a large space (3–4″) between pilot and passenger apertures to allow later for insertion of wings.

Cut small oval shaped opening (as per diagram) on top of plane. Remove this section using the curved grapefruit knife and ball out meat. Set rind aside to be replaced later when completed. With top of cavity opening removed, ball out meat from body of plane. Cut out all window outlines. Undercut all edges and window openings so that they are well defined. Line inside body cavity especially around the open window areas with heavy duty silver foil to prevent leakage of fruits and juices and to accentuate windows.

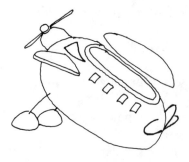

Optional: With cavity now empty it will be easier to place landing gear in position. Slice off small piece to stabilize the base on the two oranges or styrofoam balls. Place flat side down on tray in appropriate position to body of plane. Pierce with orange wood sticks or dowels through the base of the plane and down into the oranges thus lifting the front section of the plane into an inclined position. See diagram.

To create motor: Cut off end piece from a small acorn squash or reasonable facsimile E.G. base of a Delicious apple, etc. Place this "motor" on front end of plane. Secure into position with use of an orange stick, leaving a one inch end of wooden tip exposed. Wrap a chenille "propeller" around exposed tip end and secure in place with a maraschino cherry. With waterproof felt marking pen inscribe plane's destination on rind; e.g. Miami Beach, Fla., England, France, Hawaii, etc.

To create wings for plane: Sketch on paper a pattern for wings that would be appropriate to the size of your watermelon (plane). From the extra purchased watermelon quarter section, remove the meat and undercut down to the white section of the rind. Using paper illustration as an outline guide, cut 2 side wings and the rudder and flap wing ends for the tail of the plane. *For Side Wings:* Cut out appropriately sized wings. On the rounded ends ONLY, cut away as much of the white part of the rind as possible, thus making the wing ends lighter in weight. Leave more white rind toward the flat end of the wings for extra strength for this will be the point of adjoining the wing to the body of the plane. To attach wing to plane, push 3 floral picks into the flat thicker end of the wing. Pre-hole and then push into proper position on sides of plane body. *For Tail End Wings:* From left over quartered melon rind section cut out 2 flap end rudder sections. Place white rind against white rind, face to face since the outer green rind surface must be seen from all sides. Hold rudder together with totem pole pins. Position rudder end in appropriate position on rear of plane with floral pick. Now cut 2 more rounded wing tips ends from extra rind to be placed on either side of rudder; hold with floral picks. *OPTIONAL:* Place appropriate country or state flag of destination at tail end of plane. Refill cavity opening with assorted fruits and garnish. Place on (optional) "runway" tray. Replace rind cover on top of cavity opening of plane until guest of honor and company have arrived and "climbed aboard" for an enjoyable airborne bon voyage party.

HAWAIIAN OUTRIGGER
AS PICTURED ON FRONT COVER OF BOOK

Set your sails for a delicious and refreshing trip to the islands aboard your own watermelon outrigger or make YOUR OWN fruit filled outrigger for your next backyard barbecue or Luau.

Necessary for the fruit filled outrigger:

1 oval shaped Ipuhaole (watermelon in Hawaiian)

2 pieces (green) styrofoam to stabilize and raise height of peacock

2 pineapple peacocks (see chapter one on how to make pineapple peacock as raised centerpiece)

4" orange wood sticks and/or bamboo sticks for stabilizing purposes

4 asparagus spears or squash with curved tip ends

assorted fruits (hand fruit or melon ball variety and appropriate garnishes)

clusters of grapes and large can mandarin oranges (drain juices)

chicory or other greens

fresh or plastic flowers for decorating

1 oversized heavy duty tray to hold outrigger boat (obtainable in restaurant supply house or use piece of plywood of good thickness to hold weight)

Cover serving tray with foil. Cut watermelon lengthwise in half; then cut just *one* of those halves into lengthwise quarters thereby giving you 3 pieces. You now have the body of the fruit outrigger for the halved watermelon will be the center (A), and the remaining 2 quartered sections, the outrigger pontoons (B & C). Remove the meat from all sections with a melon baller. Undercut all sections for a smoother laying surface and distinctive outline. Place the half section of watermelon (A) in the center of your large tray. Decorate the border edge of body (A) with mandarin orange sections. Hold them in place with contrasting colored frill toothpicks. Cut 2 pieces of wide enough

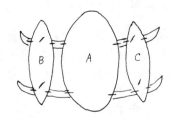

green styrofoam to use as the under base to raise height of peacock so that the outrigger sides the peacocks will later be placed upon, are level to and equal in height to section A. Stabilize rind sections B & C of watermelon to the styrofoam bases by piercing through bottom of watermelon rind of B & C and down into styrofoam cut pieces for the outriggers. See diagram side view of quarters B & C.

Leaving a space of approximately 3–4" in between the body of the watermelon and the outriggers adjoin each side of the outrigger to the main body by placing asparagus spears stalk section only or use piece of green squash in between. Use bamboo sticks (for narrower asparagus stalks) or orange wood sticks (for thicker squash sections) to join one to the other. See diagram.

Cut off the 3" curved tip ends from asparagus or squash. Place into position (using same method as suggested above) into the

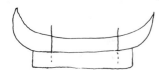

outside rind sections of the outriggers keeping them in line with pieces between A and B and A and C. Pin in chicory on top and to hang over and cover sides of sections B & C. Place prepared pineapple peacock (sans fruit in cavity opening) in center of each section B & C. Stabilize peacock to B & C sections and to the styrofoam beneath same with orange wood sticks going down through base bottom of peacock cavity, into watermelon rind and down into styrofoam sections beneath. Now fill in peacock cavities with fresh fruit and fill in main body (A) with same. Garnish and decorate. Decorate chicory filled areas of B & C bases with fresh flowers or plastic flowers to break up and bring color to the greeness of your "cover."

ALTERNATIVE: If melon is out of season in your particular locale, or even as a change of pace, you might prefer to fill the peacock's cavities with canned fruit cocktail (well drained). I would then fill the main body (A) of the centerpiece (after lining it with foil and garnishing it with greens) with assorted hand fruits (apples, pickle pears, dates, etc.) and an assortment of various *foil wrapped* cheeses. This not only makes a most beautiful edible centerpiece but also serves as an all-in-one light dessert smorgasbord.

Throw a colorful fishnet cloth over a solid colored tablecloth, place some sea shells, Hawiian Leis and a Tiki God nearby and you have "set the mood" for your island party or Luau. Mood setters such as the aforementioned Tiki Gods, or figurines of sea nymphs or skin divers can be easily purchased at your local 5 & 10¢ store or local aquarium shop and/or tropical fish store.

With a slight change of table accessories this fruit filled outrigger can be the highlight of your next barbecue party for the gang or even set the mood for a nice seafood dinner party.

WATERMELON HEART

Select a well shaped watermelon and stabilize base. (See diagram.) Carefully outline heart shaped section (A) and entire cavity opening in pencil *prior* to cutting, being sure to leave a 2″ "floor". Utilizing the curve of the grapefruit knife, carefully cut around heart (A) and penciled cavity opening. Cut and remove watermelon rind and meat sections in small pieces.

Scoop out all melon meat with the use of the melon baller. Set aside for refill later. If the occasion for celebration is an engagement or wedding party, the likeness of a ring or wedding bells can be positioned and secured (with totem pins) onto the heart of the watermelon as in diagram. If you are celebrating an anniversary or birthday, use (A) as the base and carve out with

a lemon stripper (or paste on paper numbers) the years significant to the birthday or anniversary celebration.

If the party is merely to celebrate a holiday, such as Valentine's Day, you might simply pierce the heart base (A) with a red
bump chenille to represent cupid's arrow (or use red oak tag).
Trim the entire border edge of the cavity opening with an
appropriate type of material trim such as red lace or red pipe

cleaners. If the centerpiece is for a wedding, may I suggest
substituting lilies of the valley or white lace to trim the border
edge of the cavity opening, see suggested diagrams.

To suggest "a message of love," refill the cavity opening with
only the *red* sweet meat melon balls of the watermelon fruit
and a sprinkling of the "Ambrosia" of coconut. The fruit can be
best held in place and built up high within the cavity area with
the use of hidden floral wooden picks.

OPEN WATERMELON HEART

For a St. Valentine's Day party, or wedding or anniversary
celebration, create this more open variation of a watermelon
heart fruit display to serve as a most beautiful as well as edible
centerpiece.

To add extra strength and stability to our display, we will back
it up with a styrofoam raised base so as to display it better.

Also utilized will be a cut 2″ × 2″ strip of styrofoam, the

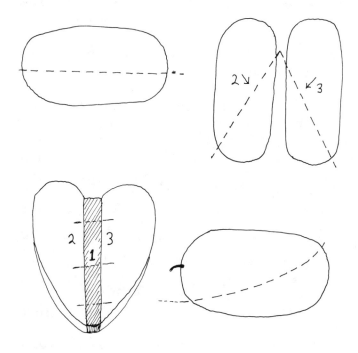

length of which will be determined by the overall length of the *cut* watermelon itself. This foil covered styrofoam strip (1) will act as the catalyst, or the abutting piece to join both halved sections of the melon together thus forming the heart design. Choose an oval shaped watermelon. No stabilizing slice will be necessary as it will be raised and secured into styrofoam backing.

As per diagram, the easier method of cutting this melon would be to merely slice it in half lengthwise. It would then be sliced so as to form two halves that would abut each other, forming a heart shape from the two sections of cut watermelon.

To achieve a more rounded and uplifted effect to the heart shaped design of your melon display, I prefer to cut mine in the following manner. Using the melon's stem end as the center of the melon, draw an imaginary line in your mind to ascertain the exact opposite point center on the other side. From these two points measure the same distance as outlined in diagram. Outline with pencil and cut *diagonally* as per diagram. Slice off proximal edges so they can meet to butt up against the prepared foil covered styrofoam centerblock (1) as depicted in diagram.

Remove melon balls from inside each melon half leaving 2" of melon meat as the walls (2 & 3) on the butting sides to the styrofoam strip (1) of the heart design. Set melon cut balls aside for refilling later. Using strong wooden orange wood sticks, abut each wall (2 & 3) of the melon halves against and into the styrofoam block center strip (1) as in diagram. This now formed whole heart shaped melon shell must be backed up and stabilized into a raised styrofoam backdrop. (Use orange wood sticks to do so). By so doing you have stabilized the entire displayed piece while simultaneously raising it up for better viewing and edibility. Fill in heart shaped watermelon shell with *just* the red watermelon fruit to accentuate the heart effect. The alternative of course, is to fill it with a medley of mixed fruits, the choice, of course, being yours.

To emphasize and cover the outlined edge or framework of the open heart design, decorate the border of the watermelon heart with fresh lemon leaves. (use totem pins to hold stems of same in place). A nice effect, especially for a wedding, is to intersperse the lemon leaves with little sprigs of lilies of the valley or fresh orange blossoms.

Optional: If using all red melon meat within heart shell, try to complement your red heart displayed effect with a Cupid's Bow. As per directions on "Cupid's Arrow" in chapter 6 on the makings of a "Red Heart Berry for Special Occasions", use the described red oak tag to create the Cupid's Arrow; place the two divided sections of the red oak tag arrow into the rind sides of the watermelon heart. To accentuate this theme more fully, fill in the melon (heart) holder itself with an equally wide band of red maraschino cherries, laying the cherries on the same plane as that of the arrow sections.

THE WATERMELON CHAPEL

Following are the simple step by step instructions, to create the watermelon chapel. This is a most beautiful and entirely edible fruit piece, and is most appropriate as the table center-piece for a wedding or an anniversary party. By merely sub-stituting the figures or symbolic artifact within the domes, this same watermelon creation can serve equally well for a bar mitzvah or a christening party.

Place some small champagne or wine glasses within the dome, or even a simple vase of fresh flowers, and it can serve

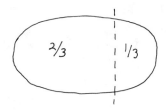

steps

as the attractive centerpiece for a large cocktail party. (Substitute the emblem for the Elks Club or Masonic order or whatever is most appropriate for the special occasion). These aforementioned emblems or centerpieces can be purchased at the local bakery or party goods stores or at a large 5 & 10¢.

To display your chapel centerpiece, you will need: A very sturdy large tray (at least 12″ × 24″); hubby can quickly improvise one for you by nailing a lip frame around the edges of a 12″ × 24″ piece of heavy plywood. Line serving tray with heavy duty foil.

To create the chapel dome: Keep in mind the actual size of the appropriate figure or emblem centerpiece you will be placing within the dome of your chapel. Cut chapel dome from a large elongated type watermelon; (see diagram). Usually the dome piece would be about ⅔ of the entire watermelon. Reserve the ⅓ remaining watermelon section left over as it will be cut and used as the steps leading up to the dome chapel piece later.

Being sure to leave at least 1½–2″ base to act as your "floor," carefully outline in pencil the cavity opening of your chapel dome such as shown in diagram.

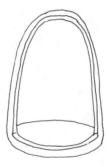

Using a melon baller, remove the meat from within the cavity opening of the dome shaped altar section. Set aside to be used as filler in your fruit platter. Line cavity opening of dome with foil. Hold foil in position with totem pins.

To create styrofoam platform with steps: Cut a two inch thick piece of styrofoam large enough to receive the bottom base of the chapel dome. Cut a second piece of styrofoam of the same width, but two inches longer than the styrofoam base for the

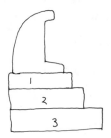

chapel dome. Cut a third piece of styrofoam same width so piece #3 is two inches longer than piece #2.

Wrap each styrofoam section in foil. Place styrofoam sections #1, 2, and 3 into position alligning back edge sides together, as in diagram. Secure by pushing long bamboo sticks into each corner of section #1 and down through the second and remaining styrofoam sections.

Place watermelon dome into position on top of styrofoam section #1. Secure chapel dome into position by forcing 1 or 2 bamboo sticks through the floor of the watermelon chapel and down through the styrofoam platform. Place figures of bride and groom or a heart shaped decorated styrofoam inside of chapel dome. Line outside border edge of dome chapel with flowers, such as lilies of the valley, and decorate with wedding bells. Totem pins can be used to hold decoration in place.

Optional: Place white love birds (available in 5 & 10¢ store) above dome top.

For fruit tray you will need: Remaining ⅓ section of watermelon;

(Depending on the size of the watermelon used for chapel dome) another watermelon may be needed to use as filler for the fruit tray;

Assorted melon fruits to be used for melon balls to fill fruit tray, (honeydew, persian, cantaloupe);

Two whole cantaloupes: cut into Lotus flower designs, (see melon chapter);

Two fresh pineapples with fronds intact;

A large can of pineapple spears;

A jar of green spearmint pears;

A jar of kumquats;

A jar of spiced apple rings;

A jar of spiced whole crab apples (aforementioned are available in specialty shops or the gourmet section of your supermarket);

Canned mandarin orange sections;

Canned pineapple rings or chunks;

Red and green cherries;

Fresh berries; if in season;

Clusters of grapes;

Artificial or fresh flowers;

Totem pins, frill toothpicks and floral wood picks;

Bamboo sticks (used frequently to hold and support accompanying pineapple boats and cantaloupe Lotus flowers at unusual angles in decorative fruit display of plate);

Strawberry, peppermint leaves and chicory.

To create fruit platter for chapel setting: Slice remaining ⅓ section of watermelon into two inch pieces. Cut each slice so it can be set flush against the styrofoam steps. Start building your steps by placing the first watermelon slice on the bottom of the tray itself. Proceed with the remaining steps and build up. Force floral picks or (appropriately cut to size) bamboo sticks into each side of the watermelon "steps" thus stabilizing it into the styrofoam. Cover the mid-section of each watermelon step with 1 or 2 slices of the canned pineapple spears. Using floral picks place spiced apple rings standing on edge (so pick does not show through top of apple ring) as a border on each side of step. If desired, a cantaloupe Lotus flower (see chapter on melons for instructions) can be placed against base of the chapel dome and secured (into styrofoam piece #1) with use of bamboo sticks. Fill center of "Lotus" flowers with whole crab apples or grape clusters. In like fashion, pineapple boats with fronds intact can be utilized. Secure and fill with assorted fruits or line the pineapple boats with strawberry leaves and fill with fresh succulent large strawberries.

If it is a bridal or anniversary celebration tuck in among the fresh pineapple fronds, fresh or artificial lilies of the valley. Now build up your fruit centerpiece by filling in the plate with fresh melon fruits, such as the watermelon, honeydew and/or cantaloupe and persian balls. A large variety of canned fruits can be used as filler. Use the gourmet items such as mint pears, kumquats, etc., sparingly only as contrast for color.

After the build up of assorted fruit balls and gourmet and canned fruits, fill in the area against the spiced apple ring border of each step with the contrasting colored canned mandarin orange sections. Cover and fill in the exposed back of the styrofoam base and chapel with chicory and strawberry or lemon leaves. Fill in with flowers to break up the "greenery." Place small grape clusters about as fill in on your fruit centerpiece. Excluding the step build-up (as you want this to stand out) garnish remainder of chapel creation with peppermint leaves and a very sparse sprinkling of coconut.

If you wish this fruit centerpiece to be placed in the center of the party room rather than on a table against a wall, may I suggest a variation of the fruit piece. Please see following section on how to create a watermelon gazebo.

THE WATERMELON GAZEBO

If your edible fruit centerpiece is to be used as the main focal point of the table located in the center of the party room, and will therefore be seen from all sides, or if centerpiece is needed to provide more fruit for a larger number of guests, may I suggest this variation of a watermelon and fruit plate. The creation of the gazebo is based on and therefore follows the makings of the aforementioned watermelon chapel.

What you will need: A large sturdy heavy duty serving tray with a lip frame around it.

A large elongated type watermelon.

Another smaller watermelon or piece of watermelon to be used as filler balls for the fruit tray.

Two cantaloupes to be cut into Lotus flowers designs, (see melon chapter).

Two cantaloupes and 2 or 3 other melons to be used as melon ball fillers for fruit tray.

Two fresh pineapples with fronds intact.

Large cans of peach halves (drained) for fruit tray.

Jar of spiced apple rings.

Spiced whole crab apples.

Two cans of mandarin orange sections.

Two cans of pineapple spears.

Can of pineapple rings or chunks.

Two boxes of fresh strawberries; cherries and blueberries for color contrast.

Jar of minted pear halves.

Kumquats; grapes (assorted variety—total of 2–3 lbs.), green and red cherries; dates; and coconut.

Bamboo sticks, floral sticks, frill toothpicks and totem pins.

Styrofoam for platform of steps.

Chicory, strawberry leaves, and fresh mint leaves.

Artificial or fresh flowers, paper or plastic doilies and saran wrap.

To create gazebo: Follow directions in previous unit on watermelon chapel. Cut off ⅔ section of melon to give you a dome shaped effect, which will then be the gazebo top. Being sure to leave at least a 1½–2″ "floor". Outline (with paper pattern) in pencil, four to five openings appropriate to the size of watermelon dome. Be sure to leave enough width of watermelon rind in between gazebo openings to assure strength for each "post". See paper diagram suggested for aperture openings on a 30–40 lb. watermelon.

Cut along penciled outline using pointed grapefruit knife to

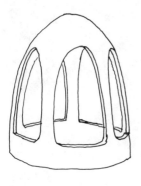

easily cut out rounded areas. Remove sections carefully. Set aside for balling meat to be used as filler for fruit plate later. Ball out meat from cavity openings of gazebo shaped dome and set aside for later use. See diagram.

To create styrofoam platform with steps: Follow directions to create styrofoam platform for steps leading up to gazebo as previously described in preparing styrofoam base for watermelon chapel. However, in placing styrofoam piece #1 onto #2 and then onto #3, substitute and use diagram drawing below as sample.

By so doing you now have steps ascending on *both* sides of tray leading up to dome shaped watermelon gazebo. Continue to follow directions in positioning and stabilizing watermelon dome onto platform base of styrofoam piece #1. Drive bamboo sticks through all pieces. Now cover gazebo "floor" with a piece of saran wrap so juice of melon will not soak through the white paper doily you will place on floor center of the gazebo.

Place within gazebo dome the appropriately chosen bridal couple or flowers or symbolic emblem. On top of gazebo dome may then be placed either a pair of love birds or fresh small bunches of hanging grapes. Continue creating gazebo watermelon centerpiece exactly as in directions for "How To Create Fruit Platter for Chapel Setting" in previous unit. Since all sides *plus* front and back must be filled with fruit start again by placing the watermelon steps. Place into position both cantaloupe Lotus flowers as well as full sections of pineapple boats as described previously. Continue as in previous unit on "chapel" until all of large tray is brimming with fruit.

Use clusters of grapes as filler and garnish with mints and strawberry leaves.

3 MELONS

To be better able to choose the proper type of melon for our "Incredible Edibles Creations" we would do well to learn something about the variety and choosing of same for proper ripeness and edibility. I think the following glossary of fruit terms or jargon would therefore be helpful.

Blossom end: The more rounded end, opposite to the stem end is called the blossom end. The opposing stem end, the part broken away from the vine, will have a scar or remains of the stem from which it was cut or broken off.

Decay: Due to the growth of bacteria or fungus infection, the fruit or melon will start to decay. This will be noted by a greenish moldy appearance especially prevalent at the blossom end.

Full slip: A muskmelon will have a fully rounded depressed scar at the stem end and is therefore termed "full slip." This is so called because the fruit's stem end came off its vine fully and smoothly with no portions of the stem adhering, thereby leaving "scars." Melons have developed the full sugar content when they are "full slipped" but must be picked while still very firm for shipment. They then need only soften at room temperature for 3 to 4 days for full flavor peak and enjoyment. When fully ripe they must then be placed in plastic bags and refrigerated. A muskmelon need not necessarily be served chilled. Some, like the honeydew or honeyballs are more flavorful when served at room temperature.

Mature or maturity: Maturity is often confused with the state of ripeness. A melon must reach a stage of both maturity and ripeness to be fully appreciated and to savor its peak of flavor. A melon picked at its maturity is ready for harvesting although not necessarily ripe. It is at the stage where its sugar content and its growth are at the fullest. If this same fruit was picked immaturely it could never ripen properly during shipment to markets or even at the stands of the marketplace itself, a factor which must always be kept in mind. Maturity is therefore best defined as the state at which it is judged right for harvesting in order to bring it to you, the consumer, in its best possible condition. There are laws in most of the states decreeing when a fruit is mature enough for harvesting and subsequent shipping.

Muskmelon: A round or oval melon with sweet juicy light green or orange flesh, and a rind with a ribbed or netlike pattern, e.g. a cantaloupe "muskmelon" is also referred to as the plant it grows on.

Netting: Vine like network of lines running randomly across the rind or skin of only some melons. See individual descriptions of melon fruits.

Ripe: A fruit ready to be eaten.

Generally speaking, melon-wise: There is a melon for every household depending on the need and size of each family. The cantaloupes and honeyballs are fine gourmet fare for 2 to 4 people. The honeydews belong to the larger sized muskmelon variety such as the casabas, cranshaws, persians, etc., and are good for large households.

For the peak of flavor the cantaloupes and watermelons are best ripened on the vine, (look for full slips), whereas the other melon varieties do better ripening at room temperature at the market or in your home. After reaching ripening stage at room temperature, store in plastic wrap to prevent other refrigerator odors from permeating. Once cut however, it is of utmost importance to carefully wrap well to contain its flavor as well as its aroma. Since flavor loss is at its greatest then use as soon as possible after cutting. It may be served plain or with the piquant garnishing touches of lemon or lime sprigs or with just a dash of salt to peak its flavor. It is as good at breakfast time as right through after dinner and for our diet conscious folks what a nice pick me up for those hunger hours in between. Half a medium sized cantaloupe = 25 calories; a ¼ of a honeydew = 50 calories; a ¾″ × 6″ slice of watermelon = 100 calories. Melons cannot only be purchased nowadays in commercial frozen form at the supermarket but you can even freeze them homestyle yourself. All you need do is make up your own 30 percent syrup for freezing by mixing 2 cups sugar with 4 cups of water. This will give you 5 cups of syrup. Leaving container head room (for expansion during freezing) pare, slice or ball melons (free from all seeds); submerse in this freezing solution and store in well sealed containers. The melon balls can also easily be prepared for freezing *or* refrigerating by packing in ginger ale or 7–Up soda instead of the 30% solution syrup. You might taste a little of the flavor of the soda while eating but that should be good too!

The art of food sculpture needn't even come into focus as this wonderful selection of muskmelons do just as well served as is, or combined with gelatins to make shimmering salads. For that nose tingling sensation try pretty cut melon balls in sherbet glasses with champagne or even carbonated soda poured over; for a more intoxicating effect try kirsch or an appropriate liqueur to marinate your melon balls as a starter. Served in a punch, or combined with meat or cheese, sherbet or ice cream, it is still delicious and so easy to prepare. For those with more of a creative flair try your hand at any of the edibles creations to follow.

Recommended reading: California Summer Fruits: Calif. Tree Fruit Agreement P. O. Box 4640 Sacramento, Calif 95825

How to buy fresh fruits . . . U.S. Department of Agriculture-Home and Garden Bulletin #141. Cost 15¢.Washington, D.C. 20005

Selection and Care of Fresh Fruits and Vegetables . . . October, 1971 issue prepared by the United Fresh Fruit and Vegetable Association, 1019–19 St. N.W. Washington, D.C. 20036 Cost $1.00. Single copy. Lower prices on larger orders for groups and teachers. Listing of Publications and Materials as of April 1974 available on request to United Fresh Fruit and Veg. Assoc.-address above.

A GLOSSARY OF MELONS:
HOW TO PICK AND HOW TO STORE SAME

Due to the fact that they must be first shipped from farm to market place and then eventually sold to you, the consumer, melons must be harvested at a very firm stage and arrive at their destination still firm. Although some are more ripe than others at the time of final sale to the consumer, they may not have reached the peak of their best eating stage. Therefore purchase them with thought in mind as to when you would actually be serving them. Once purchased, it is best to let the cantaloupe stand at room temperature for 2 to 4 days to complete the ripening to that delectable "best eating stage" we spoke of. Once ripened it may be chilled before serving.

Cantaloupe: Of all the melons known, the cantaloupe is the most popular. This muskmelon is available May to September, shipped in from such states as California, Arizona and Texas. To choose a good melon look for a yellowish cast to the rind and actually sniff it with your nose to try to detect a sweet aroma. A ripe melon would be a little soft when touched at the blossom end of the melon. The "net" appearance to this cantaloupe should stand out coarsely above a yellowish skin color underneath. If however, the rind is too yellowish, and the entire rind feels too soft to touch, or you find the beginnings of mold growth (look especially at the blossom end) then your melon is overripe. Choosing a good melon is a real challenge even to the most experienced shopper.

Casaba: The casaba melon is pumpkin shaped, slightly pointed at the stem end. Its ripeness can be denoted by its golden yellow rind color and slight softening to the touch at the blossom end. Contrary to the "netted" cantaloupe, the casaba melon has shallow furrows running from blossom end to stem end and its meat is a soft creamy white color and has a very sweet delicate flavor. Produced mostly in California and Arizona this melon can be found in supermarkets from July to November. Although of the muskmelon family, the casaba, unlike the cantaloupe, will never possess a "full slip" as this is a melon that must be actually cut from its vine growth at harvest time. It would be useless also to look for the sweet aroma of ripeness, for only the casaba and the watermelon have no odor at all to them. Avoid *any* melon with dark, sunken in water soaked areas.

Citron melon: See footnote following Wintermelons.

Cranshaw or crenshaw: Here's an easier one for you to pick. This newer variety of the muskmelon family is pointed at the stem end, more fully rounded at the blossom end and has only shallow lengthwise furrows. Its ripeness can be quickly denoted by the change of color from its golden green skin to a deeper more golden yellow color. Its sweet aroma is matched only by the beautiful bright salmon color of its meat, which is plentiful, as this muskmelon usually weighs approximately 7 to 9 lbs. Grown in California, it is available July to October, reaching its peak shipments to market during the months of August and September.

Honeydew and honeyball: The main difference between these two varieties of melons is that the honeyball is smaller and very round, and has a slightly irregular "net" surface over the rind. The honeydew is larger, 4 to 8 lbs., somewhat oval and generally very smooth with a little trace of netting. The stem of these melons, like the casaba, must also be cut from the vine at harvest time. It is more available as a year round fruit for dessert, due to importing during winter and spring. During the peak months of June to October and also in March, the produce comes mainly from the farmlands of California, Arizona and Texas.

Maturity is recognized by its soft velvety rind; its ripeness by the sweet aroma and yellowish-white to creamy rind coloring. Purchase of honeydew and honeyballs should be avoided if the melons possess a dead white or greenish white color and/or water soaked bruised spots. This variety of muskmelon is at its best flavor when served at room temperature. Delicious as an appetizer or as a dessert; for that change of pace, combine it with meat such as prosciutto ham and serve as a main entree or salad combination.

Persian melon: The persian melon might be described as a first cousin to the cantaloupe, as one must look for the same quality and ripeness signs in both these varieties. This globe shaped muskmelon measures approximately eight inches in diameter and weighs about 4 to 8 lbs. The average weight is 7 lbs. The rind's dark green coloring with its fine netting turns to a much lighter green as it ripens. Although they do not gain sugar or therefore become sweeter after harvesting, they do become much juicier upon standing. Similar to its first cousin, its meat also has a deep orange pink color. It is shipped from the fields of California and is available from July to October at your local markets. It is best served cold and should be refrigerated as soon as it has been given time to soften properly at room temperature for that extra added juiciness.

Santa Claus melon: The Santa Claus melon is grown on the farms by its largest producers, the Turlock Fruit Company of California. It has only been known of in the last 40 years and is not as popular as its neighboring crops of persians, cantaloupes, honeydews, etc.

It is not a hybrid or a cross however, but a true strain of its own, grown in rows similar to the melons in the fields of the San Joaquin Valley of California. Much like a football in size and shape, its ripeness is determined by its deep yellow coloring under the green striping. Its meat, like that of the cantaloupe, is also pink-orange and very sweet to taste and particularly juicy. Abundant during mid-July to late-October, ironically in time for football season, it is delicious served as is or in combination with ham or other meat selections.

If you're at home watching the game why not whip up our special "football melon" for in between game quarters. See section entitled "Touchdown" in this chapter to follow. Since this melon is not as well known and not even listed in the afore mentioned sources, the only information available would be thru the Turlock Fruit Company, P.O.Box 7, Turlock, California 95380.

Watermelon: See chapter 2 on subject of watermelon.

Wintermelon: The only purpose in my writing of this melon, very much in the vegetable family of the squash, is so that it will serve as a point of information. Called the wintermelon because it is grown through the winter months, this melon is the size of a basketball. With a heavy rind of green, its pulp is of white flesh with its heavy spongy portion inside filled with white seeds. It is very much like a summer squash and can be found in Chinese groceries as it is used primarily for Chinese cuisine. Combined with ham and chicken broth and other ingredients it makes for a most unusual and delicious soup. Since the average winter-melon is so large, it is usually sold in a 1″ or 2″ piece and is purchased by the pound by the consumer.

Citron melon: As in the aforementioned the only purpose of making note of this melon is to avoid confusion and give infor-mation in re same. The Citron melon is a kind of watermelon, bearing a small fruit with firm, white flesh which is used, like the citron, in candied form.

The reason the last two aforementioned "melons" are listed in this descriptive section of melons is to help you avoid confu-sion in thinking it is of the same family of melons heretofore previously mentioned and worked with in food sculpture.

HOW TO MAKE USE OF COLORED FRUITS AND GLAZES

To bring dramatic contrast of color to your fruit centerpieces one need go no further than the supermarket. There, one can purchase many varieties of different colors and tastes of fruits to suit any and all appetites. There are maroon colored spice apples in ring form as well as small crab apples, green pepper-mint pear halves as well as red cinnamon pear halves, gold colored kumquats, purple plums, the deep browned cooked (jarred) prunes, all shades of pitted canned sweet and sour cher-ries as well as the more familiar jars of red and not so familiar jars of green maraschino cherries. This is not to go into such delicacies as pickled watermelon rind, and the more mundane pears, peaches and chunks, slices and even spears of pineapple available, canned in heavy syrup or in their own natural fruit juices for the diet conscious. If some of these aforementioned colored delicacies prove to be a little too expensive for your entertaining budget, marinate and prepare your own variation of the same fruits.

To marinate and spice up a can of halved pears, for instance, drain off ¾ cup of the fruit's syrup. To this liquid simply add enough desired food coloring to acquire the desired shade. To spike the flavor, add to this mixture a drop of appropriate extract such as peppermint extract or creme de menthe to the green syrup liquid combination; try adding red hot cinnamon candies (called "hots") to the red dyed fruit syrup coloring. Be daring: try flavoring fruit with almond extract, rum or cocoanut extract added to the fruit. *HELPFUL HINT:* The only rule to follow is to be sure you do not add any additional food coloring (to deepen shade) *WHILE* the fruit is submersed in liquid mixture. This would cause the immersed canned fruit to be streaked and unevenly colored. Immerse your drained canned fruit in each separate bowl of desired spiked color mixture for 45–60 minutes. Remove fruit and wash off under cold water. Set on paper towels to drain off any excess colored juice run-offs.

To make fruit glaze: To create a fruit glaze, in a cooking vessel, heat ¾ cup of apple juice (set aside balance of one cup (¼ c.) to be used later. Any other type of clear fruit juice can be substituted such as apricot, canned pineapple juice, the more exotic papaya juice or passion fruit juices or nectars, etc. To add thickening agent and thus form glaze, add 2 teaspoons of corn starch (pre-mix first with ¼ c. left over cold juice until smooth paste) and add to heated juice. Stir over low heat with rubber spatula until thick and clear. Cool and use to glaze fresh or canned fruits in display centerpiece.

To make a fruit tasting glaze: For a light colored jelly fruit glaze to cover peaches, pineapple, etc., use a similar clear jelly such as apple for a clear aspic. To create textured jelly glaze for your fruit use a marmalade jelly for peaches. In either case, combine ¼ cup of the fruit jelly with one tablespoon of water and merely let stand over boiling water in top section of a double boiler until melted. For dark fruits such as plums, crab apples, blueberry or strawberry use a currant type similar jelly. Mix with water accordingly over double boiler. Let cool slightly and brush on fruits with a pastry brush.

To create clear plain fruit glaze: Cook together one cup of sugar and ½ cup of water until granules are dissolved. Add lemon or lime juice to taste. To add color to this glaze, simply add a few drops of desired food dye a little at a time to achieve shade of color desired. Cool and then dribble over fruits to coat and bind together. (see chapter to follow on Christmas using Honeydew Melons).

See also glazes for white colored aspic and brown colored aspic for liver molds in chapter 6 and other molds in chapter 8.

MELON RINGS

As a refreshing dessert: Cut cantaloupe crosswise into one inch slices. Remove seeds, pare skin if desired or merely cut and release the meat pulp from the rind leaving rind in tact as a border trim. Use the curved blade of your grapefruit knife to do this. Top each melon slice with a scoop of lemon flavored sherbet: (1 pt. of sherbet will be enough to provide you with about 4 to 6 servings). Garnish with fresh blueberries or, if out of season, substitute 1 to 2 tablespoons of canned blueberry pie filling.

Alternate suggestions for dessert combinations: Using the same principle of presentation you might like to try the combination of cantaloupe with vanilla ice cream or sherbet topped with a dash of creme de menthe or creme de cocoa; for an exciting color presentation try blackberry ice cream topped with crushed pineapple preserves; try vanilla ice cream topped with grated or whole semi-sweet chocolate tidbits or butterscotch tidbits grated usually used for baking, etc.

As a salad: As a change of pace try using a honeydew melon and follow the same procedure as cutting ring slices to serve approximately 5 to 6 guests. From the left over end sections of the melon (or another whole melon) cut out cubes of melon meat. Around each of these melon cubes wrap a small one inch strip of appropriate meat (e.g. Italian prosciutto goes well with the honeydew melon). Present on a plate of Bibb lettuce or other salad green of your choice and serve with a pretty cut lemon slice or lime wedge. Depending on the size of melon section and the other accompanying tablefare this presentation may be served as either an appetizer or as a main entree especially welcome on a hot summer night.

Alternate suggestions for salad combinations: Casaba, crenshaw or cantaloupe melon may be substituted with a helping of lobster salad or tuna salad on top, or whatever your taste buds and imagination can decree. Try chicken salad atop cantaloupe and garnish with bacon strips; add cranberry aspic cutouts for that extra touch of elegance. Highlight it with skewered chunks of pineapple and cherry tomatoes on a bamboo stick. (See section on: Serving A Salad Filled Pineapple).

MELON BASKETS, WHALES AND CARRIAGES

Baskets: For any and all of the many varieties of a basket shaped melon see watermelon chapter 2 on creating (watermelon) baskets. Carry out directions and procedure, applying same to substituted choice of smaller size melon.

Whale melon: Same principle can be applied for a watermelon whale to any smaller melon.

Carriages: For creating carriage (or bassinet) centerpiece follow procedure as to making a carriage from a watermelon (see chapter 2) Since your melon carriage will be smaller in size keep your wheels of an appropriate size to the body of your carriage. May I suggest therefore making your wheels for the smaller melon carriage from orange or grapefruit slices instead of the previously suggested larger pineapple slices as was used on the *watermelon* carriage.

SALAD FILLED MELON

It's time to invite the gang to brunch . . . and as usual some of our ladies are watching their figures; (that's so the boys will keep watching them!) If melons are abundant, and therefore less expensive, you might want to serve each guest an individual service of a salad filled melon. You might choose to serve 1 or 2 large melons as the main centerpiece and use for actual serving dishes. The number of large melons and salad needed depends on how many guests "brunching" and what else is being served that day.

Whatever your choice, cut off stabilizing slice from bottom. Mark off with pencil or point of Kitchen Helper the outline you will be following to cut off and remove a ⅓ section off the top of the melon. Cut with zig-zag end of Kitchen Helper to create the desired saw tooth effect, or use paring knife or grapefruit knife and/or scallop paper pattern as previously described in other chapters. Remove top ⅓ section; cut and use meat for melon balls. Clean out all seeds and stringy portion; drain well. *Greens optional:* if you prefer, you might like to line the melon cavity with lettuce leaves or some sort of mixed cut up salad greens before filling the melon with your chosen salad mixture. E.G.: chicken or turkey salad goes well with cantaloupe melon; bacon curls are good as a garnish or can be mixed directly into prepared salad. E.G.: Crabmeat, or any seafood combination, goes well in a honeydew, persian or cranshaw melon. To make a "Veronique" of your salad presentation simply add chopped seedLESS grapes; to make a "Florentine" combination add chopped spinach leaves. If you have gone ahead and lined your melon (holder) with salad greens, try egg salad in a cantaloupe, top with bacon strips or Julienne strips of smoked ham or garnish your egg salad with fresh thin cut green pepper rings; for change of pace: try lining the melon cavity with boiled ham slices (use cut 1–2″ narrow strips instead of 1 large slice for better edibility) and then fill with egg salad mixture. Whether presented to your table as individual service in small melons or as a large serving dish centerpiece—for that added touch, decorate with trails of ivy coming up and around sides of melon as

pictured in diagram. Place on serving tray on bed of "greens"; surround with cranberry slices (if serving chicken or turkey salad); for service with fish salads accompany and garnish with lemon wedges and/or lemon baskets filled with tartar sauce or seafood cocktail sauce.

For a variation use cottage cheese to fill melon.

FROSTED FILLED CANTALOUPE: AS AN APPETIZER OR DESSERT

1 3 oz. pkg. lime flavored gelatin
¼ teas. peppermint extract (optional, or a drop according to taste)
1 med.-large sized cantaloupe
⅓ c. fresh seedLESS grapes; (⅓ c. of fresh cut-up fruit or drained canned fruit salad may be substituted)

1 8 oz. block form type cream cheese
optional: 2 tbsp. milk or juice
optional: chopped nuts or minced parsley

Gelatin: Prepare lime gelatin as per package directions reducing amount of cold water to ¾ cup. If using canned fruit cocktail, drained syrup from canned fruit may be substituted for ¾ cup water. After dissolving gelatin powder and adding cold water (or syrup), if desired, add mint extract. Refrigerate as this must be chilled and thickened to the consistency of egg whites before adding grapes or fruit.

Cantaloupe: From top of a ripe and sweet smelling cantaloupe, cut out a small hole just large enough to allow a serrated grapefruit spoon through the opening or use an iced tea spoon (recommended for its length). Either one will do to clean out the seeds and stringy portion of the melon's cavity. Rinse out by flushing with cold water. Set melon, hole side down to drain for a few minutes. Slice off stabilizing slice from opposite side (of hole cavity). Pare off melon rind. Score entire surface with a lemon stripper or fork. Pat dry. This will enable your cream cheese "frosting" to adhere better to the melon. Place on plate with small hole opening facing up.

To fill: cut grapes in half (or use fresh or drained fruits) and mix with thickened lime gelatin. Pour gelatin mixture into cantaloupe cavity through the opening; fill to top. If any gelatin is left remaining it may then be served at another time as a dessert treat. Refrigerate gelatin filled melon once again to firmly set.

Cream cheese frosting: While gelatin filled melon is setting, remove block form of cream cheese from refrigerator and allow to soften at room temperature.

Optional: To add flavor or hasten softening stage, beat orange juice or milk into softened cream cheese until mixture is easy to spread. This softened cheese combination will then serve as the frosting for our melon. As you would frost a cake using a

spatula so frost the entire surface of your cantaloupe. Refrigerate to firm up cheese frosting for at least one hour. Melon may be served as is or. . . .

For that extra touch as a dessert: To serve our frosted filled cantaloupe as a dessert, spread chopped walnuts (pecans or for that unusual taste flair try Macadamia nuts) on a piece of wax paper (for easier handling). Roll and press frosted melon surface into chopped nuts. Refrigerate until serving time.

For that extra touch as an entree or first course: To serve as a first course, roll into chopped parsley in place of the nut covering. Refrigerate until serving time.

To serve: Cut into 1" slices crosswise with sharp knife (that has been dipped into hot water first for easier handling and cutting) see diagram. As a dessert serve accompanied with garnish of mint leaves or watercress. As a luncheon entree or light repast at midnight this melon can be served on a bed of greens and accompanied simply with tea sandwiches. So colorful to look at and even more refreshing to eat! For that dramatic flair to entertaining, may I suggest you bring your frosted filled melon to the dining table on a pretty cutting board and slice amidst the oohs and ahhs of your guests as its colorful surprise cavity of gelatin is revealed.

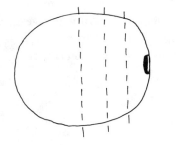 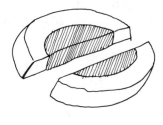

Serves 4–6 depending on size of melon chosen and appetite of guests. For variation of gelatin filled melon sans frosting or fruit filling please see chapter 4 on citrus fruits; Baskets or Shell Cup affect; gelatin filled basket shell with Kitchen Helper.

HAWAIIAN MELON

Select a cranshaw, persian or even a cantaloupe melon for your Hawaiian style melon dish. Use diagram to follow as guide.

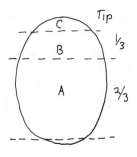

Cut off small, stabilizing base so it can stand on its own easily. Slice off ⅓ section of the melon (B). From that, cut off a small section (C) from the top; set aside. This same cut will be used later as a stabilizing slice. Clean out seeds and stringy portion from ⅔ section of melon (A). Use this part to cut out your melon balls. Using ⅓ section (B) as a base (do *not* deball it as it will have to be firm to hold weight of top section), place section A on top of section B. Secure and stabilize section A onto section B with

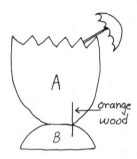

orange wood stick. If desired cut scallop or saw tooth design on rim of section A for variety. Refill scooped out melon (A) with assorted fresh fruits and other melon balls. Top off at jaunty angle section C. Attach to section A with large club frill pick. See diagram. If you prefer you might substitute a pretty Japanese party umbrella parasol obtainable in a party goods store for section tip C.

This presentation lends itself beautifully to individual servings, and can also be used as a centerpiece if entertaining 2–4 people. If more fruit is desired use as styrofoam centerpiece, (raise up) surround with other fruit selections. Decorate with use of Hawaiian leis and Tiki Gods to set the mood.

This same presentation can be modified and used to present fruit and/or beverage as individual services substituting a whole fresh pineapple for the melon.

CORNUCOPIA OF FRESH FRUITS—HORN OF PLENTY

To serve a variety of fruits, hand fruits as well as cut-up tidbit sizes may I suggest an arrangement that can combine both. The principle of same can be used as a base for many other presentations (see salad cornucopias to follow.)

Use a large honeydew or cranshaw melon. With paper pattern (such as one used for watermelon basket) outline with pencil the zigzag or scallop effect border edge you wish to create. Keep in mind that you wish to add interest to this basket type variation to give it a horn of plenty effect, so place the paper pattern on an angle as per diagram.

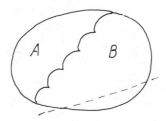

Cut along outline of melon with knife; remove all seeds and stringy portion from both melon halves A & B. Place section B of melon in one corner of a large tray. Cut stabilizing slice at angle thus emphasizing the effect of the horn of plenty by lifting it higher. Leave meat intact in melon section B. Cut melon balls from meat of section A. Mix melon balls with other bite size fruit pieces and fill melon B. Place fruits as if overflowing and tumbling out of your horn of plenty down onto the *center* section of the serving tray. Garnish and supplement the fruit display with small clusters of fresh different colored grapes, strawberries and peppermint leaves.

Border edge center section of medley of assorted fruits with decorative foil or paper muffin liner cups. Fill these holders with arrangements of fresh and/or canned fruits. Surround these fruit filled cups (if desired) with an assortment of small hand fruits such as sickle pears, small apples, dried fruits, etc. Border edge of tray with bananas if desired as that will provide more to eat and will help to retain the fruit display. Garnish with pretty lemon leaves amidst the hand fruits; peppermint and strawberry leaves in amongst cut fruits. Strategically place *fresh* juicy strawberries on tray and emphasize color contrast with a sprinkling of *fresh* blueberries. (Do not use frozen or canned berries as they will tend to bleed and discolor the other fruits. See diagram.

CORNUCOPIA OF MIXED SALADS

Even if we are watching our weight to keep our waists, keep your meals eye-appealing! For that buffet lunch for the girls, keep it light and refreshing and garnish yourself an "A" for appetite appeal as well! Follow the preceding directions for creating the cornucopia horn of plenty. Cut the melon and place in center at one end of a large serving tray. Fill melon cavity with assorted fresh and canned fruits. This time, however, we will cascade the medley of fruits down from the center of the melon cavity of the cornucopia onto both sides of the tray as the border effect. Now fill mid-center section of tray with decorative foil cups (for extra strength it is suggested to use only foil holders; they may be potato bake holders or such). Line these aluminum holders with lettuce or "greens." Fill with desired mixed salad or furnish an assortment of different varieties of salads to choose from such as tuna, shrimp, salmon or chicken salad. For variety of choice as well as color, fill some foil cups with the dramatic colorful contrast of yellow egg salad, brown chopped liver, red deviled ham salad and the white purity of cottage cheese. Fill some other cups with accompanying tid-bits of pickles, green and black olives and fresh cut vegetables as well as the colorful cherry tomatoes and parsley clusters. With this simple presentation, your guest may select her own choice of salad and greens, fresh vegetables as well as fresh fruit accompaniment.

LOTUS CUT MELON FLOWER

To create this flower design choose any melon with a rind that is soft and pliable such as a honeydew or cantaloupe. Cut off a small stabilizing base so it will stand well. Outline in pencil 6–8 equal (petal) sections leaving a one inch base at bottom. Cut along outlined design. Carefully separate sections slightly to clean out seeds and stringy portion. Utilizing the curve of the grapefruit knife blade carefully, cut away and separate the fruit meat from the rind to within one inch of the base. Leave base intact. Pull rind away from meat gently. Working carefully fold each rind petal down (toward meat side) and tuck top section of each petal down in between its own petal base and the meat section so the petals appear to be folded in half.

Fill cantaloupe melon cavity with cottage cheese or honeydew melon with fruits or with other type salads. Serve individually as an entree. (see salad filled melon and cheese filled melons in this chapter for variations) To serve as a dessert, fill with ice cream and garnish. To serve as a refreshing aftermath to a lovely dinner, fill with sherbert and top with a liquor such as creme de menthe or top with crushed pineapple.

See variation on lotus cut melon to follow.

LOTUS MELON FLOWER VARIATION FOR TWO

To make your dollar go further and still provide a pretty flower effect we can utilize the idea of the lotus cut melon flower by cutting it in such a manner as to provide us with two serving pieces from the same melon. Select a nice shaped melon with a soft pliable skin such as honeydew or cantaloupe. Using a pencil, leave a one inch base on top and bottom of melon and outline 5–6 wedge type v-shaped petals as per diagram.

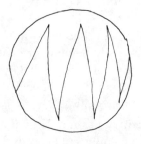

Following outline, cut melon and you will find the two halves of the fruit will separate very easily thus giving you 2 separate flower designs. Proceed now as in simple lotus cut melon flower description preceeding this. Cut small stabilizing base. Still leaving base section in tact, use grapefruit knife and carefully cut and separate the rind from the meat of each petal to within one inch of base. At the one inch base of the melon flower, in between the meat and the rind of each flower petal place (thus wedging) a stemmed maraschino cherry with stem pointing upward. Hold cherry in position with a frill toothpick of contrasting (cellophane) color. Fill the center cavity with your choice of entree or dessert. For individual service it looks especially elegant placed atop a paper lace doily.

To provide that extra frill or extra petal effect to your flower melon: if you have an abundance of fruit skins left over (if you're making a large fruit tray and need meat for balling, use the left over melon shells to provide you with the extra cut petal shells as previously described). Cut the extra flower shell in half. This will provide you with an extra frill to your flower by placing one half on each underside of your main flower arrangement. Hold in place with wooden floral picks. See diagram.

This particular melon-cherry variation is especially beautiful when combined and used in the dramatic presentation of the watermelon chapel or gazebo. (see chapter 2) on same.

FOOTBALL MELON: TOUCHDOWN!

On their appetites on the goal line with a football melon!

It's football season and if you are a football widow, keep yourself busy and please those fans of yours by making them a football melon for snack time in between quarters or for use as a centerpiece for the buffet table for the gang returning from the high school game. In either case you'll be voted outstanding honorary athlete of the year . . . and not even a scratch!

During the months of Mid-July through Fall you will find an oval shaped yellow and green streak colored melon referred to

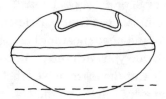

as a Santa Claus melon. (See glossary of melons: Santa Claus). Hold on side and make stabilizing slice as diagramed. With use of lemon stripper, mark off and strip out what would actually be the seam lines on a football as per picture.

Along top, mark out and then cut (using the curved blade of a grapefruit knife) the top (shoelaced) section of a football pigskin as depicted in top view of our Santa Claus melon illustration.

Using 6–8 small screweyes (overall length 11/16" recom-

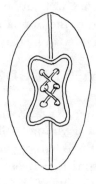

mended and obtainable from your local hardware store), place them at intervals for lacing the shoelace of the pigskin for true realism. Proceed to actually lace and tie the shoelace.

Color in all lemon stripped grooved out areas with red food coloring for color emphasis. Ball out meat with melon baller, mix with assorted other fruits if desired and replace in shell. For authenticity it may be placed on a football tee (but be on guard for the juice run-offs). As centerpiece, surround on plate with pompoms, batons and pennants of your favorite football team. If it's been a cold day in the cheering stands for your football fans, you might try spiking the melon balls by marinating them in some kirschwater or gin before refilling your melon pigskin. *Note: Not* recommended for the high school team! In either case you would have scored big in the hearts of your own football fans!

CHRISTMAS USING HONEYDEW MELONS

To celebrate the Christmas holidays in the warmth of the southern sunshine states is indeed fortunate for you would then have an abundance of melon fruits available all year round. Use the honeydew melon to create a Christmas wreath or tree. Serve as a refreshing edible centerpiece for your holiday buffet table.

Stores in snow bound or sunshine areas will be well supplied with styrofoam cut shaped Christmas trees and wreaths as well as other mold pre-cut shapes to welcome in Santa's season.

To create tree: cover styrofoam tree shape (flat styrofoam *not* cone shape) with green foil covering available this time of year (or use regular foil). Using a large ball scoop cut honeydew meat from several melons. Using the hidden wooden toothpick method place first layer of large balls onto styrofoam. With two other different smaller sized melon cutters cut and place more honeydew balls on top of first layer, thus building up and filling out your tree.

To create trunk of tree: cut cantaloupe slices with serrater and lay in position as tree trunk.

To create holder for tree: Slice a large red Delicious apple in half, remove stem and place rounded side up to simulate pot holding tree.

Decorating your tree: to simulate Christmas bulbs, use colorful cut round slices of canned peaches halves, pears, etc. Garnish tree with red and green cherries. The star on top of the tree can be cut from canned peach slice or made from a kumquat.

Optional: If you like, a glaze can be used to bind and hold your melon creation together, and simultaneously highlight its effect. If desired, a drop of green food dye may be added to the glaze mixture (before or after cooking) to further emphasize and darken the leaf coloring of your tree.

By using a glaze you will find you will not need to use as many floral toothpicks to hold together and build up your edible centerpiece. *To make glaze:* cook together one cup of sugar to every ½ cup of water, add some lemon juice or drop of extract for taste. If darker green coloring is wanted (be sure not to put it on cantaloupe tree trunk) merely add drop or two of green food dye to mixture. Allow to cool before dribbling it over to cover main body of the Christmas tree. If you wish to add tinsel effect and design to your Christmas balls refrigerate for one hour before applying. . . .

Tinsel and Ball Decoration: to add an edible tinsel effect to your centerpiece "hang" your tinsel by using a white or yellow Cake Mate* decorating gel (available in all colors in squeezable tube form in bakery aisle of supermarket). Use various different colors of Cake Mate to decorate and design the pattern effect on your Christmas bulbs (peach halves, etc.) Garnish your edible Christmas melon tree with sprigs of fresh strawberry leaves tucked in place here and there.

To serve: place on serving tray and angle at 45 degrees for

*Trade name for decorating writing gel used by bakers.

better view and overall appearance to table.

To create Wreath: Using same procedure, substitute wreath or ring cut shaped styrofoam as for tree form: cut and place similar layers of honeydew balls onto ring mold. Use glaze (with deeper shade of green coloring if desired) to bind and cover honeydew balls. To represent holly garland effect, decorate with lemon leaves and red cherries on 3–4 strategic places of wreath. Create large bow for wreath by cutting bow shape from canned pear halves which had been dyed with red food coloring (see beginning of chapter on how to make change of color).

To create other holiday designs: with your creative juices flowing you can easily see how with a little thought and same principle applied one can design almost anything as a holiday centerpiece. Using a pre-cut store bought bell shaped styrofoam mold substitute red watermelon balls. Add red food coloring to the glaze. Use miniature marshmallows to outline and add contrast to the piece. If using a pre-cut mold sled form use watermelon balls for body, marshmallow for contrasting outline and cantaloupe slices as sled runners.

For All Year Round: With styrofoam as a base for your chosen motif design, you can see a whole new world of edible table decor available to you. Using the same principle, a styrofoam (foil covered pattern) pre-cut and sold in stores or cut and designed by you for a special occasion, can be used as the base to layer and display meats, cheese spreads, etc. See chapters on same.

Even if it's not any special time, try serving a pretty melon ring of fresh honeydew or cantaloupe meats, Glaze ring (sans food coloring) and fill center with contrasting colored and differently shaped melon fruits; E.G.: use ball scoop to cut melon for ring's mold and then cut melon with serrater into small tidbit sizes to fill center area of ring. Do *not* glaze center filled section of melon meats. This absence of glaze will provide even more contrast of color as well as texture. Garnish as you wish with fresh strawberries and border with lemon leaves or whatever. If serving a honeydew ring try bordering melon ring with pretty lemon slices. Fill center of ring mold with rolled prosciutto ham on a bed of lettuce or other greens.

MELON GRAPE CLUSTERS

As stated so many times before, one creative thought leads to another. Try your hand at this one when melons are not in season.

To add a touch of class to that first course: Use a base of "greens" and place on top a pear half, preferably fresh and pared. If necessary, use a canned, pear half rounded side up. If using canned pear, drain well and pat dry. Cover rounded surface with the whipped type cream cheese, or use block form of cream cheese. If using the block type cheese, soften with milk or juice to a spreading consistency. Cut seedLESS grapes in half and press into the spread cheese, so as to resemble a grape cluster. To add realism, garnish by placing a piece of the grape stem at the large end of the pear half. Serve as is, glazed or with a fruit dressing as an entree, or as a light midnight snack with wine (how apropros) and choice of cheese and crackers.

If honeydew melons are available: Follow same procedure as above; however, first place folded pieces of prosciutto ham on bed of greens. Top with pear half rounded side up as center of plate. It is optional at this point to omit the cream cheese frosting all together. Spread pear half with glaze, substituting melon balls cut in half, in place of grapes. This same presentation may be easily served buffet style for a larger party group by presenting as a centerpiece on large tray. Bed tray down with lettuce or greens and border with slices of prosciutto ham. Place pear halves with different colored assorted grapes or melons as center section of serving dish. Your guest then has the option of choosing what he prefers: pears with green, red or ribier grapes or assorted melon "grapes," with or without choice of accompanying ham.

For variation, and to add contrast of color to this large center plate, intersperse design of platter with spots of drained canned peach halves cavity (hole) side up. Fill cavity with cottage cheese or with chopped ham salad or even fill with a simple jelly or other fruit filling. As you can see, again we have gone the gamut from melons to grapes, to ham, to peaches with ham salad; from individual service to a buffet table presentation; all with just a little "associative" creative thinking.

See chapter 7 on vegetables, tomato and cheese rose for another variation of using cream cheese.

4 CITRUS FRUITS

By definition, a citrus fruit is any of the genus of small, often thorny trees and shrubs of the rue family. (Rue family: a group of chiefly tropical or subtropical shrubs or trees, which yield an aromatic oil.) Said plants bear a pulpy fruit with a usually thick spongy rind. They are a great source of vitamins C and a quick energy picker-upper especially for athletes. *E.G.* citron, grapefruit, lime or orange.

Citron: (not to be confused with citron melon; see chapter 3, glossary of melons) The citron is the fruit of a shrub or small tree somewhat like a lemon but larger, with a thicker rind and less acid. The candied version of this member of the rue family is primarily used in preparation of fruit cake, plum pudding and candies so popular around holiday time.

Grapefruit: This pale-yellow roundish fruit, likened to an orange but larger and more sour, grows in clusters (like grapes, thus the name) and is cultivated chiefly in the warm climate states of this country. The grapefruit serves as a delicious sustenance for most dieters as it is a most filling, refreshing snack or first course permitted on most diets. It is recommended by the medical profession for its great source of Vitamin C while still low in caloric count for those watching their weight.

Lemon: This sour light-yellow citrus rue member serves many purposes and fields of endeavor. The juice of this fruit is used for flavoring and making beverages as it yields its citric acids. The rind yields its oil or essence for use in cookery and is used greatly in the perfume industry. Needless to mention, the sight of just a bunch of these bright colored pretty fruits with its attractive pale green lemon leaves have easily graced and brought elegance and pleasurable eye appeal as a centerpiece to many a table setting.

Lime: Smaller and more sour than its kin cousin, the lemon, this green tropical tree grown citrus fruit is raised extensively in Asia. It is used primarily as a flavoring for cookery and beverages and also in the field of medicine.

Orange: This round-reddish-yellow skinned juicy fruit with its fragrant white blossoms is the floral emblem of the state of Florida where it is chiefly grown. The blossoms of this edible fruit are almost as popular as the fruit itself, as it has been traditionally carried by many brides in their bouquets and is known as the symbol of love; hopefully, their future life may be as sweet and fruitful as the aromatic fragrance of this beautiful flower. As the story is told in Roman mythology, Jupiter, the Roman ruler of Gods and men, gave an orange to Juno, the Roman Goddess of marriage and childbirth as a symbol of his love for her on their wedding day.

Citrus in general: There are other members of the citrus clan which belong to the rue family. These will be discussed in more detail later on in this chapter. As a point of information, and to give us some general knowledge about this tree and shrub bearing fruit, there is also the kumquat, tangerine, bitter orange, and mandarin, all of the orange tree family. Then, there is also the shaddock, (like a coarse dried grapefruit) and the bergamot, (an orange-lemon related fruit) grown especially in Italy.

The citrus trees, familiar to us as we drive through the warm climate states of Florida, Arizona, California and Texas are seen in acres of unending groves. The fruit in these groves literally have got to be *picked* off for unlike other fruits they do not fall from their tree when ripe. Skillful citrus workers are hired to pick the fruit, for it is only they who would know which fruit must be clipped off with special fruit cutters and which fruits must remain untouched to grow sweeter and juicier or larger, as in the case of the lemon. This particular citrus fruit is picked and clipped off by *size* alone. It is a fact that each lemon picker is supplied with a ring like implement that the lemon must *not* be able to pass through before being allowed to be picked for marketing.

It is interesting to note that although citrus fruit was around and given as a gift to emperors as a symbol of future happiness as far back as the 12th century, it wasn't until 1750 that the vitamin value of it was used successfully as an experimental cure of the death-dealing illness to sailors of the high seas, scurvy. Citrus fruits first grown in China and India over 4000 years ago, were brought by Columbus from Spain to the New World in 1493; from there to Mexico and then, in 1796 the first citrus was planted in California. A lot of travel and a far cry for us who walk to the local supermarket a block or two away and bring these citrus flavored vitamin filled fruits to our own home table in fresh, frozen, powdered, canned, bottled and or container forms; our pick of edible hand fruit, frozen concentrates, jars of powder forms, mandarin orange and grapefruit canned forms of fruits and fresh bottled fresh juice.

It is said that by the 12th century in the land of the Kubla Khan, there were 27 different varieties of citrus fruits to choose from. Today, with hybrid crossing, proper irrigation and development through scientific study, we have almost as much to choose from, and more than enough to be confused with. Perhaps with an assist from the Florida Citrus Commission, the U.S.

Dept. of Agriculture and the United Fresh Fruit and Vegetable Association the following notes on how to pick and store and the glossary to follow might prove very helpful.

Citrus Fruits: must be picked well matured before being harvested and shipped out to the waiting consumer market. Look for firm and heavy fruit with a bright reasonably smooth close fitting skin (for its variety).see glossary—tangerine for exception. Avoid fruits that are light, puffy or spongy to the touch as they would prove lacking in juice and dry in pulp. *#1 Rind color:* It is not indicative of inner color or even ripeness. There are those orange or grapefruit skins that will bear green splotchy areas. This is called *"regreening,"* and occurs when extra chlorophyll is produced by the fruit bearing tree for the new blossom as it grows. Ironically, ripe citrus is the only fruit that regreens in this manner. *Russeting:* a tan or blackish mottling or specking on the skin most often found on the Florida and Texas shipped oranges. There is no effect on the eating quality and in fact, mostly occurs on the thin skinned more superior quality eating oranges. In marketing, you might come across oranges marked "color added" so be aware that there are some oranges to which color is actually added to give them the more commercialized "orange" appearance that some consumers might look for. Although here again, there is actually no effect on the eating quality of this orange by law, it must be labeled "color added" on the very rind of the fruit.

Grapefruit's principal difference is that although there are many varieties, they all basically fall into two categories: seedless or with seeds, self explanatory terms in themselves; white or the pink fleshed fruit developed in 1913 in Florida. (see glossary of citrus fruits to follow.)

Fruits with thin rind covering would have more juice than coarse skinned ones. If a grapefruit is pointed at the stem end it is likely to be thick skinned and therefore less meaty and juicy inside. The same holds true for the lemon fruit. Also to be avoided would be a lemon with pale or greenish-yellow color.

This is indicative of high acidity to the fruit.

Lime: Although limes are generally purchased green (yellowed fruit denotes lack of acidity), there is an exception to this rule of buying green limes, for also available at the produce market is a Mexican grown key lime which *is* actually supposed to be light yellow in color when ripe, a contradiction to its cousin, the domestic Persian lime. *To store:* Both lemons and limes may be kept at room temperature for a period of time extending from a few days to two weeks. They may also be kept fresh under refrigeration for up to six weeks. These and other citrus fruits such as the oranges, grapefruits, etc., may be refrigerated to keep longer and simultaneously be chilled for serving. To obtain more juice from a citrus fruit try this trick: after leaving the fruit at room temperature and before cutting, roll the citrus between your hands or on the table. If you are not in need of the juice of the entire lemon try rolling it first, poke a hole through the citrus rind and into the flesh using a floral pick. Squeeze out the needed drops of juice; replace the toothpick and refrigerate. Did you know that if your recipe calls for a small amount of buttermilk you can make your own by adding one tablespoon of lemon juice to one cup of sweet milk; (skim will not do). Let stand for five minutes and voila! buttermilk. If a recipe, especially one for a marinade or salad dressing calls for vinegar, try lemon juice instead for a really fresh taste. For those of us (for health reasons) who must abstain from a heavy salt intake, try a dash of a juicy lemon instead. Stuck with slightly wilted vegetables? Try perking them up again by adding the juice of a whole lemon to a basin full of cold water and soak the wilted greens for a while. Although every supermarket spice rack sports grated or peeled forms of orange, citron and lemon, try making your own. The next time you are in need of the juice of a lemon or citrus fruit, don't be tempted to throw away the left-over skin shell. Use the juice needed for your purpose and then grate, chop or make slivers of the leftover rind skin to be used for candy making, cake decorating or whatever. Not in the mood for all that cooking at the moment.

. . . fine, then prepare the grated or slivered rinds and freeze them for another time. Incidentally, an average lemon or lime will yield 2–3 tablespoons of juice and about 3 teaspoons of grated peel. Five to eight medium-sized lemons will give you one cup of juice while its citrus cousin, the orange will yield one cup when you squeeze the juice from 3–4 oranges; one medium orange will afford you 2–3 tablespoons of juice, and the rind of that orange will give you 2 tbsp. grated peel.

The grapefruit, not used as much for its grated or slivered peel value none the less does afford you 10–12 sections of edible meat from a medium-sized grapefruit or, if sections are chopped, one cup. When squeezed it will make ⅔ cup of juice. Speaking of grapefruit juice, try substituting some canned or fresh juice in place of the water called for in the preparation of cooking up a swiss steak for dinner next time. Makes for a real yummy gravy.

For a continuence of these helpful ideas see Hints, Helps and Garnish Cuts under the subtitle of HOW TO USE:

A GLOSSARY OF CITRUS FRUITS
TO HELP AND FURTHER CONFUSE YOU!

Bergamot: orange or tree, named after the town of Bergamo in Italy, where it is primarily grown. Grown also in states bordering on the Gulf of Mexico and in California, its oil derived from the rind, is used to give the pleasant odor to perfumes.

Citron: a sour fruit that actually grows wild in India, it is grown commercially in Italy. The citron's flavorful rind is used for cakes, candies, etc, while the oil derived from the rind is used in the perfume industry.

Grapefruit: closely related to the shaddock citrus fruit, the grapefruit was first grown in 1820 when it was brought over from the West Indies and planted in Florida. However, it did not attain popularity for home use until almost 60 years later when northern people, having vacationed in Florida, created enough demand for it to be shipped from its warm climate to the northern dining tables; broken down into two catergories, seed or seedless, and white versus pink meat (although there is no discernible difference in taste as to the color of the fruit inside.)

Duncan Grapefruit: pale yellow meat filled with clusters of seeds, it is large yellow and thin skinned, tinged with green or russet. (Oct.–June)

Marsh seedless: white meat *nearly* devoid of seeds, usually has 8 seeds total it comes in small to medium sizes and is usually flat on both ends (no stabilizing slices needed here). Since its sections separates easily from its rind sack it is good for salads. (Oct.–June)

Pink seedless grapefruit: small to large size, its characteristic is that its meat varies in color from light pink to a reddish tinge (Oct.–May)

Ruby seedless grapefruit: similar to above. The meat is of a deeper red blush and the skin casing has a red blush to it. (Oct.–May)

Burgundy: more flavorful and larger in size, this citrus also has a red blush to its skin with juice and flesh of deeper pink and sweeter meat within. (Oct.–May)

Kumquat: fruit related to the orange, although only slightly larger than a brazil nut, it is grown on a dwarfed evergreen. It is used primarily for candies, preserves, marmalade and jelly. It is very decorative, and goes well served with duck or ham meals. It can be eaten fresh, but would prove rather bitter in taste and very pulpy to chew.

Lemon: a tart fruit available all year round, with few or no seeds at all, it is high in content of Vitamins A, B, C as well as mineral salts. Of all the citrus rue family members, this one has the most usefulness. By the homemaker, it is used primarily for garnishing, adding spice and refreshing flavor to a salad etc. (see Helpful Hints, etc.) By the commercial industry, its juice and flavor is used for cookery, beverages, and toilet preparations. Its oil is used for flavorings as well as in perfumes. In medicine its pectin, a grainy powder made from its skins and membranes, was used by the battlefield wounded World War II soldiers who sprinkled it in wounds to help blood clots form. Never picked before reaching a diameter of 2½", it is picked green and ripens under special conditions in curing houses to the gold color we are familiar with.

Lime: A green rounded fruit pointed at both ends, it was carried aboard vessels in the 1700's by the crateful as the sailors drank its juice to prevent scurvy. Imported primarily from India and the Mediterranean basin, its chief source, stateside, is the southern area of Florida. It is used as flavoring for drinks and salads. Squeezed on top of some varieties of melons, the juices make the melons taste more savory.

Mandarin: see orange classification, tangerine, as this is a common term used for a fruit that is actually a small sweet orange with a very loose peel.

Orange: Blood Orange: a term not heard too often in the U.S., but so that you are aware of same, there is an orange especially popular with Europeans that actually exudes a blood colored juice. The outside rind will also possess a blood coloring blush to its skin.

Hamlin: excellent for juice; medium size with no seeds. (Oct.–Dec.)

Honey Orange: Likened to a large tangerine with easy peeling skin, it is very juicy and unusually sweet to taste. (Feb.–April)

Navel: best for hand eating variety, since it peels and sections easily; extra bonus is that it is usually seedless too. Its name was simply derived, since it is actually a double orange, a small fruit that does not develop and is caught in the spiral end. (Nov.–Jan.)

Parson Brown: a deep golden juicy citrus of sweet flavor, possessed of few seeds with a light brown outer coloring usually tinted green in spots. (Nov.–Jan.)

Pineapple: As news to many, there is the pineapple fruit you have already learned much about, and now the pineapple orange. Like its namesake, it is very sweet and juicy with a few seeds and a smooth skin. (Dec.–Feb.)

Tangelo: easy to peel, since this is a hybrid deep orange colored fruit developed by crossing the tangy sweet tasting and easy peeling tangerine with the tart tasting and easily sectioned grapefruit. (Dec.–Mar.)

Tangerine: Very easily peeled due to the loose skin encompassing this deep orange colored fruit, it has gotten the nickname "zipper skinned fruit". This citrus will appear to feel spongy and *not* firm to the touch, its flat ends feeling equally soft . . . all signs of a poor orange for consumer choosing . . . however, this is typical of *this* fruit although the *exception* to the rule of the entire citrus family. It sections easily, possesses few seeds and is therefore popular as an excellent salad service or for good hand eating. (Nov.–Jan.)

Temple: small oval shaped orange with few seeds. Peels and sections easily and is therefore good hand eating fruit (Jan.– Mar.) Under the overall heading of Temple oranges let us note:

King Orange: like a tangerine except darker in color it is easily peeled and sectioned for hand eating and salads. (Mar.– April)

Murcott: a comparatively new variety of orange its later developement shows its best work by being a superior hand eating fruit with rich exterior and interior color. Very juicy and very sweet. (Feb.–Apr.)

Valencia: Having done more than any other orange to help spread the word "that there is nothing like a Florida orange for juice" this Floridian grown orange accounts for nearly half the transported crop from that state. Oval shaped and large since it contains so much rich flavored juice and aroma it is shipped north in great quantities to quench many thirsts while providing its abundance of vitamins. (Mar.–July)

Shaddock: the shaddock must have been the ancestor of our present day grapefruit having grown prior to the 1700's in southeastern Asia. A larger fruit than its present day grapefruit it has a thicker rind; its flesh is merely meaty rather than juicy, it is more pear contoured than round in shape. It is likened to a coarse like inferior grapefruit. It is not grown commercially.

Ugli: Since we're not sure whether this new found Caribbean-grown oddity would be classified under grapefruit or orange but surely under citrus, let us list it by itself. A new and recent but odd looking citrus it has been appearing of late in some of the specialty fruit produce shops rather than the local supermarket. Its name and its appearance usually throws the average housewife off and therefore it is left for the epicurean gourmet who would be shopping in a specialty shop and appreciate an expensive odd ball fruit such as this. Its rough pebbled shell appearance, often yellowish-black or even green in color encompasses orange flesh segments that are mellow in flavor although its outer appearance is that of a badly colored and misshapen grapefruit.

HINTS AND HELPS

How to peel: there are two commonly used methods for shedding the skin rind of citrus fruit such as grapefruit or orange; called the basketball method and the spiral or round and round method.

Basketball: with one of the many citrus tools on the market or an ordinary knife, section the rind all around the fruit as per diagram or like the lines that would be found on a basketball. Remove small piece top and bottom and the rest will easily peel off in sections.

Round and round method: as it sounds, merely using a sawing motion, cut around the entire skin of the fruit, spiraling, thus releasing the rind casing. as per diagram.

To section fruit: once the citrus rind is peeled, cut with sharp knife along each side of the membrane of the fruit, thus releasing each section from its core membrane center.

To chop sections: divide the fruit in half and lay cut side flat on chopping board, cross cut and then cut lengthwise. Proceed to chop into small bite-size pieces or finer if desired.

To sliver peel: strip off peel rind and clean out all fruit meat from shell. Scrape as much of the white membrane from shell rind as possible. With sharp knife slice into thin strips as for slivers. Good for candying or making marmalade.

To grate rind: after cleaning outside skin of fruit, grate rind against a medium-size hole grater or put through a Mouli-type grater. Whichever, be sure not to exceed beyond the white inside membrane as this will give your gratings a bitter taste, whereas you only wish to obtain the essence of the flavor-giving oils that are in the rind.

To frost fruit sections: after sectioning fruit segments from the citrus fruit, pat dry (like the frosted grape method) and dip entire section or just the cut angle of the segment into beaten egg white. Roll or dip into fine granulated sugar or the different fine color sugar granules available nowadays. Allow to dry until crystallized.

To make candied peel from rind cuttings: as per slivered peel strips, cut strips into wider ¼″ widths (use grapefruit or orange or lemon). Boil in solution of one quart water to which ¼ teaspoon salt had been added for a period of one and a half hours. Drain off at that time and add peel slivers to a saucepan containing one cup sugar dissolved in ⅔ c. water. Boil together rapidly for 20 minutes; then reduce heat so as to cook slowly until a few tablespoons of this thick syrup remain on the bottom of the saucepan. Be careful not to burn the peels. To cool properly, lift out citrus strips and place onto wax paper to cool before rolling and coating with white or color sugar granules or color (square) sparkles sometimes called party sparkles.

If your forte is not making preserves or candied grapefruit peel, try your hand at tantalizing your guests' appetites with a simple or a fancy cut grapefruit half and a unique grapefruit topping.

There are so many more ideas than those already covered in this chapter in preceding pages it would be difficult to list all of them . . . on the other hand, it would be unfair not to mention and list them at all so I'll just start and you can add your own. . . . Needless to say some of these ideas can be applied to *all* citrus fruits. The most useful of all: *the Lemon* . . .

Beverages uses: Although you've tried a lemon slice in iced tea try dipping that cut quarter lemon wedge into chopped fresh mint leaves first before hanging it over the side of that tall glass. Try a twist of lemon or even better, lime served with a cola beverage; it cuts the sweetness down and makes the drink really thirst quenching.

In place of that lemon, lime or orange wedge try using just the wide or a spiral section cut of parings of the citrus rind and rub the inside of the glass with same. Leave it there as it is actually the rind peel that gives off a more sharper, keen flavor than the juice itself.

To pretty up that beverage glass try slipping in a twist of lemon in the water of the ice tray cubes so when they freeze they will look especially pretty and decorative in your drinking glass. Take that one step further, and when you have leftover tea pour that tea with its lemon strip into the ice cube trays; then, when it's time to serve iced tea, you can be sure yours will not only look good but the ice will not dilute the strength of the beverage as it melts.

For the guest who favors the stronger stuff, try rubbing his cocktail glass rim with a twist of lemon or lime. Dip into a fine granulated sugar and chill for that frosted look. If guests prefer Marguerita drinks, rub the glass rim with lime or lemon and dip in coarse salt and chill.

CITRUS GARNISHES . . . HOW TO CUT THEM AND SERVE THEM!

All the effects of garnishing with citrus fruits evolve from three basic cuts.

The round slice, the wedge cut, and the basket or shell cup effect, the latter used primarily as a holder of sorts as well as a pretty garnish (e.g., lemon shell filled with drawn butter or tartar sauce to accompany fish or an orange shell filled with cranberry sauce to accompany turkey). These will be discussed more fully presently.

Although garnish cuts can be applied to any member of the citrus family such as the lime, orange, grapefruit, etc., we will concern ourselves for the moment and use as an illustrative point the lemon, since it is the citrus most commonly used and at the same time is small and economical enough to handle for purposes of practicing garnish cuts. Keep in mind that whatever is done to create a lemon garnish can also be applied to any other citrus fruit.

The Round Slice: meaning the round slice of a citrus obtained by cutting crosswise between the two pointed ends of the fruit. The rind of same may be left intact and just cut crosswise, or it may first be stripped with a lemon stripper (strip out pieces of citrus rind vertically from the lemon all the way around ¼–½" apart and then cut thickness desired crosswise. This will give a scalloped effect to the slice of lemon cut. See diagram to do this.

The round slice of lemon, scalloped or cut as is sans stripper effect, is used very often and seen most frequently hanging over the side of many iced tea glasses or liquor drinks; it is seen set floating on top of a beverage filled punch bowl, pitcher of tea or frozen in a pretty ice mold centerpiece for display.

A simple round crosswise slice of lemon is a colorful contrast and most attractive garnish; however, if I may suggest some of the following means of using that same basic round slice and to that add some innovative changes, we can have some really

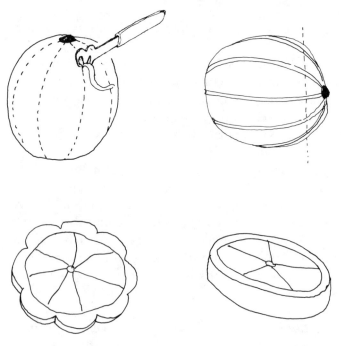

different and various garnishes. To use in its simplest form as a swizzle stick: impale the lemon slice (scalloped or left as is) onto the forked end of a cocktail fork or a cinnamon stick to use as a stirrer in a tall drink.

Using either the rind left intact or the stripped scalloped version, decorate the outside rind edge slice with studs of whole spiced cloves. This garnish adds a bit of spice to your eye as well as to your taste buds. It is especially nice in a cranberry or sweet beverage punch; back up or float that lemon slice on a straw-berry leaf cluster. To hold it bound to that leaf cluster, place a cherry on top of the lemon slice and hold in place with a frill pick. Float in a punch bowl or pitcher of tea or lemonade. For individual service, do a take-off on the same idea by making a small hole in the center of the lemon slice, enough space to pass through a drinking straw or a long sprig of fresh peppermint stalk. Serve individually in a tall glass of liquid refreshment. Don't forget the lesson we learned earlier, so try to sugar frost the rim edge of the glass for that extra pretty "cool" touch.

A very simple and most commonly used lemon or lime garnish is to make a diagonal slice to the center of a citrus round and then place this cut over the rim edge of the glass. To this common garnish add an original touch by first frosting the rind border as per the frosted grape method using beaten egg white and sugar sparkles or the new colored sugar granules. Coat the lemon rind edge before draping the cut over the glass rim edge.

Now let's do a take-off on even that simple garnish slice by cutting the lemon thicker. Cut off a ½″ wide lemon circle slice

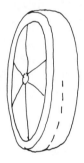

and follow the same procedure as you would to "butterfly" a shrimp; create a wing effect to your lemon slice. Follow diagram and proceed as if attempting to slice that ½″ width into two ¼″ thicknesses but do *not* complete the cut, leaving ⅓ of the lemon rind intact.

Position this cut area over the glass rim, thus leaving one wing inside the glass and the other on the outside of the glass.

Optional: Frost the uncut rind edge with sugar granules or

place a cherry or olive (whichever is more appropriate for that particular drink) on the uncut lemon rind edge.

Folded over citrus round: By the simple method of folding your round citrus slice in half you can create a somewhat different garnish. Fold lemon slice over so edges meet. Secure and hold position by fastening edges together with a cherry-pierced frill pick; nice as a plate decoration or served in a whiskey sour drink. Substituting the larger orange slice, arrange the following version as per diagram, using a bamboo stick. Start your skewer off with a green maraschino cherry, then place one slashed end of the orange in position. Place a pineapple chunk in position next and now skewer the other slashed end of the

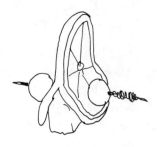

orange onto bamboo stick. Finish off with a red cherry or straw-berry (see diagram).

Try this one if your preference runs to pineapple.: Use an orange slice and wrap it around a pineapple spear. Hold all together by skewering center with a frill picked cherry and mint sprig. Lay across top of the drinking glass horizon-tally.

Starting with a simple slash cut to the center of a lemon circle slice, this version can serve as a basic cut for many new garnish-ments. Make basic cut to center, as pictured. Pull ends slightly

toward each other thus overlapping and forming a cone-shaped cup. This can be held secure with a frill picked cherry center as is or caught up in the center of a canned pineapple ring slice. Float in a punch. To serve with a fish accompaniment merely substitute a rolled anchovy or olive (for cherry) within your lemon cone and use to decorate your serving plate.

To create cartwheel slice: Use same basic slash cut to center of lemon slice. Holding each cut end, pull and twist away in opposite directions sort of forming a figure 8, laying ends flat on serving tray. *Optional:* slashed edge cuts can be dipped or dusted with parsley or paprika for a salad plate or for melon or dessert service, dust with chopped fresh mint leaves or colored sugar granules. You needn't limit yourself to just the slashed cut inner edges of the lemon slice . . . try dusting one whole side cut with your choice condiment.

Many other cuts can be created from the ordinary crosswise cut slice of lemon by cutting out portions of the lemon

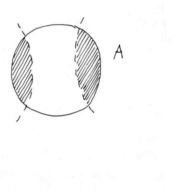

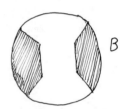

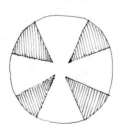

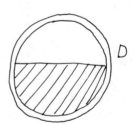

pulp itself. For variety, these cuts or parts of these cuts can be dusted with condiments. Follow diagrams for suggested cut-outs.

Within cut (D) there can be many various designs created from that same basic cut: e.g., if working with lemons and limes of equal size leaving the rind intact, the meat half of one citrus can be removed and replaced with the meat section (only) of

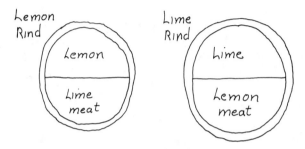

the other citrus. This two-tone effect is especially pretty when in a frozen state of an ice ring.

Halved lemon curl slice: once half of the citrus meat is removed as in previous cut, make a cut through the rind near one side of the lemon meat. Roll the remaining rind peel in a curl to the

opposite side. As in (A) See diagrams to follow.

Before thus curling the peel, the *inside* of the rind skin might be dusted with mint leaves or paprika or the outside rind can be studded with whole cloves or the curled edge can be caught up with an olive or cherry placed within the peel curl or topping it.

Decorative lemon slices without rinds: These lemon slices were cut from a whole lemon with rind skin left as is or first stripped and then cut thus creating a scalloped edge to it. With all the many variations on the lemon slice cut in mind, a new look can be given them very simply. Basically start off with all of the rind *removed*. Duplicate the various decorative touches sans rind on each slice. E.g., with all of the rind removed and just the meat left intact, cut into each horizontally sliced lemon ring to remove tiny wedge pieces from the entire border edge creating an entirely different look although it will still have a zigzag effect. The center can be decorated with cherry slices or olives or for fish presentations use capers or anchovy centers on top of the lemon circles. Thus, following suit, all the cuts with the rind thus removed *first* can be simulated to appear as bowtie cuts, cartwheel twists, frosted with sugar, dipped or dusted with paprika, mint, etc.

Lemon rose: This is the best time if any to go into the creation of a lemon rose for if we are about to shear all the rind coverings off our citrus fruits why not put them to good use and create something new and especially pretty as a garnish using the rind that would ordinarily have been thrown away. In removing the rind peelings from a citrus we can do so by making any kind of cut to get the skin off and then make strips or gratings from same for immediate use or for the freezer. However, by removing the rind more carefully and in one long spiral piece or at the most two we can then use it as a decorative touch to a tall drink or even as an integral part of the drink. E.G.: Ask any bartender for a Horse's Neck Drink and you would get a spiral cut lemon rind placed in a tall drinking glass with its lemon end cut hanging over the glass rim, to which is added some ice and ginger ale to make a most refreshing thirst quencher. Nice for those non-drinkers who want to look like they are (drinking); For those who are not teetotalers ask for a "kick" to your Horse's Neck by having the bartender add 2 oz. of your favorite whiskey.

To use the rind of the lemon (or lime or even a tomato skin) the rind of the citrus *must be cut in one continuous* spiraling piece of lemon strip *without* removing the knife. Using a serrated sharp knife begin at the top (opposite pit end); cut in one continuous ½–¾" strip (depending on width of flower petal desired) from top to bottom without breaking spiral peel that is forming. To form rose recurl spiral rind to resemble a rose flower. For a nonedible decorative vegetable rose apply the same method to the (scrubbed clean) outer skin of a white turnip. Stand back to admire the pretty fusing of the natural white to light lavender shade coloring on your turnip rose.

Wedge cuts: As previously stated over and over again, start with an idea and apply it to many things thus creating even more beautiful garnishes. As we have worked with lemon slices so we will apply these same principles to a lemon wedge.

How to cut: To determine the size of each wedge, depends upon how many times we cut each section into the number of pieces desired. . . . therefore a wedge of lemon can vary from a quarter cut of a whole lemon to a 1/16 cut of that same lemon. All wedge cuts, however, must start out the same way by simply cutting the lemon in half vertically (pit side base on cutting board). Cut in half, then cut each half into half or thirds, etc. For pretty effect pass lemon wedge for squeezing on fish, etc. in colorful nylon net material. No fall out of pits while squeezing for juice.

These wedge cuts can then be treated as any other lemon slice; the (meat) center edge can be dipped in chopped parsley, paprika, mint, etc. The rind of the larger wedge pieces can be stripped with a lemon stripper for a more decorative look or it can be frosted with sugar or studded with cloves; it can be butterflied to hang over a glass rim edge, or try this pretty take-off on the basic lemon curl slice: cut lemon into ⅓ wedges (cut lemon in half and then cut each half into thirds). Peel away, starting at top point ⅔ of the rind leaving base of rind attached. Now curl and catch under the lemon meat wedge, the partially peeled-off lemon rind. Place as is or first dust cut edge of meat and also the white membrane inside of rind skin with parsley. To glamorize, place olive or cherry inside or on top of curl of lemon slice as depicted in diagram. Hold with frill pick. Use as garnish for large serving tray.

How to make: basket or shell cup effect: Since we have gone the gamut of creating basket shapes from watermelons (see chapter 2 on watermelon baskets) and have already done some other shell type effects with melons (see chapter 3 on melons) merely refresh your memory with the following diagrams and apply same method to create orange and/or grapefruit baskets.

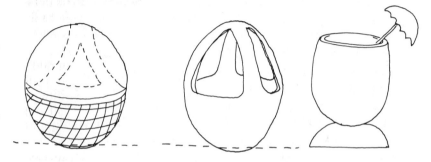

With these larger citrus fruits merely cut out the meat sections and clean out the remaining pulp or membrane left on shell. Use the meat for a fresh fruit salad and the basket shell as a holder for cranberries, sweet potatoes, sherbet, or utilize as a basket to display edible fresh cut carved vegetable flowers (see chapter on vegetable flowers and how to carve). Since lemons and limes are smaller, first squeeze out the juice of same. Reserve refrigerated for future use in covered container. Clean out remainder of membrane netting and pulp. These smaller shells can be filled and utilized for attractive individual service. Try slipping a lime basket shell into a larger lemon basket for a dual contrasting color effect. Be sure, however, that each basket has a flat base or is stabilized so as not to tip over and for a better custom fit. Serve these smaller citrus baskets as holders for drawn butter, cocktail sauce or tartar sauce as a fish accompaniment; use to hold mustard or relish for cold cuts or mint jelly when serving lamb, etc. Follow suit as per melon; basket edge can be cut sawtooth effect with Kitchen Helper notcher or scalloped; these pretty designed edges can then be dipped in parsley or mint flakes or paprika; the lemon shells are very pretty when studded with cloves or strips of rind can be removed with the lemon stripper in crosswise fashion thus forming a basket weave effect (see basket in illustration above).

To add new refreshment to our variety of basket shells let's learn how to do what follows, as these can more easily be done with a citrus fruit rather than a melon. It will be simple to do by just following the illustrations to create baskets such as those depicted in diagrams.

A: Cut grapefruit (or orange) in half between blossom ends. Use grapefruit knife to sever meat all around skin shell and cut sections into bite-size pieces, separating same from membrane.

Cut horizontally ¼" down from top surface of citrus half and along entire edge leaving a 1" area uncut on opposite sides of fruit. These ¼" grapefruit strips will then be the handles of your basket. Join them and hold together *above* the basket surface with a frill picked cherry; use a pipe cleaner with a name tag attached to also serve simultaneously as a name place setting for dinner.

As per instructions for A, cut a ¼" wide strip along entire border edge of citrus leaving a one inch area uncut on opposite sides. This time however, we will also cut these 2 strips in half

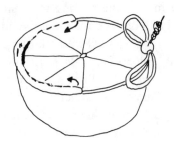

midway. Now, fold over and tuck each strip piece in place at uncut areas (see diagram). By doing so you have created 2 bows on opposite sides of grapefruit. Hold in position with frill pick and cherry.

The halved lemon curl decorative slice can be applied to the basket shell vertically (provided cherry is not included, as this would put too much weight on the delicate handle effect) as well as horizontally. Follow illustrations to accomplish the effect desired, using the lemon curl.

VERTICAL   Horizontal

Sunburst effect; if you can imagine a bright yellow sun with extending rays you can easily see how pretty this design of fruit presentation can be. Cut citrus in half between blossom point ends. Cut out all flesh from citrus fruit. Set aside to mix with other selected fruits for fresh fruit salad mixture. Using the French lemon stripper (its opening is narrower and extremely sharp) begin to strip the rind vertically at ¼ inch intervals. *DO NOT COMPLETE* cutting the strip (as is usually done) to the base of the fruit. Merely strip the rind down vertically to a depth of 1″. Retrace your cut by bringing the stripper tool up again thus releasing the cut 1″ grapefruit peel strip. The result will be that the top surface of the grapefruit half will be scalloped and the 1″ partially stripped vertical rind pieces will droop gracefully out as a sunburst. If desired and you wish to bring more color to your table, you can color these drooping rind 1″ pieces with a food-colored cotton bud. Refill with mixed

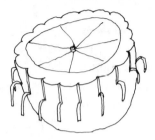

fresh fruit salad. Optional: If you wish to carry out the theme of the sunburst cover the fruit salad with a canned peach half, rounded side up. Use the Cake Master* writing tubes or a decorating gel to "paint" in Old Sol's smiling face.

SPOKEWHEEL DESIGN: to create this spoke wheel 3-dimensional design on a mere grapefruit half (or melon) you must use a sharp knife to cut a large zigzag sawtooth edge to your citrus leaving enough space in between each sawtooth edge point to fit in a pineapple slice or shrimp. *E.g., for fruit service* place in between each notch cut a canned half slice of

*Trade name

pineapple or orange section so that tips of same meet in center of citrus and curve still overhangs the grapefruit side. *For Shrimp:* place the curve of the shrimp overhanging the grapefruit side and in between each sawtooth cut; one end will then meet in the center like the spokes of a wagon wheel. For a

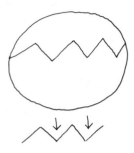

take-off on this theme but with a slight variation, cut grapefruit in half, (between blossom ends) release the meat and place a thin slice of red apple skin side up (skin is left on for contrast of color) or a jarred spiced apple ring in between the citrus sections, thus forming a flower design. The juice of the citrus will automatically prevent the white of the apple from turning brown. Actually the white of the apple will not even be showing, as only the skin of the apple is visible in this particular display. Whatever presentation you choose, do decorate and garnish the center of the citrus grapefruit appropriately.

For gelatin filled citrus wedges: As you would cut a lemon in half for wedge cuts thus cut an orange or grapefruit in half vertically through the blossom end. Release segments of meat. To hold steady for filling with gelatin later, set in a deep bowl so it will not tip over. Prepare package of gelatin according to package directions, cutting down liquid portion by ½ cup (for thicker and faster setting.) This rule holds true in *all* molds for gelatines. Choose a contrasting color of gelatin for the shell to be filled; e.g., prepare raspberry gelatin to fill a grapefruit shell,

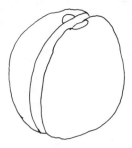

lime to fill an orange shell, etc. Fill citrus shell or shells with slightly thickened prepared gelatin. Return to refrigerate until firmly set (minimum of six hours, also a general rule in preparing molds). Cut into wedge cuts with a sharp knife that has been dipped in hot water (to cut through gelatin more easily). For a dramatic touch frost side or edge cut with sugar granules or dip into chopped mint leaves. Use to set off a pretty poultry tray or fill with minted lime gelatin to accompany a leg of lamb dinner. (*when preparing gelatin add a drop or two of mint extract to mixture before refrigeration)

Gelatin filled basket shell to create special effect using the kitchen helper: Want to puzzle your guests completely? If they were dazzled by your segment cut color-filled wedges of oranges and/or grapefruits, hear the conversation get off to a flying start with this one. It's one thing to cut an orange or melon into a sawtooth design, but when you can also cut that shimmering colored substance within it called gelatin into a sawtooth effect you'll really earn your chef's hat . . . at least in their envious and admiring disbelieving eyes. Your guests will stand there trying to figure out how *you* stood there to cut each shimmering gelatin section so perfectly into a sawtooth affect . . . especially when some of them have difficulty in just getting a gelatin dessert to release from its mold container without breaking up (see chapter on gelatins later in book).

To earn your chef's hat, try it on a grapefruit or even a melon. The same procedure will work for both. Follow illustrations. Use a flat bottomed grapefruit or cut off a *very* small stablizing base from the blossom end of the citrus or melon fruit so it can stand. Now slice off from the opposite stem end enough of a piece to allow you to get a grapefruit spoon in to remove the meat and pulp from the grapefruit. If using a melon,

just remove seeds and stringy portion, wash out and let drain. Prepare contrasting colored gelatin as already described. After slightly thickening, fill holder to the *very top* with the gelatin.

Refrigerate to set until very firm. As per diagram, draw a guide-line 1″ from top of surface. Just as you would cut a cantaloupe for sawtooth border effect, use this guideline to cut into with the zigzag notcher end of the Kitchen Helper. For easier cutting into the gelatin midsection, I find it better to first dip the notcher end of the implement into hot *tap* water before insert-ing into citrus or melon. Gently lift off this now separated one inch cut section. You will find a very unique and pretty saw tooth gelatin cut surface as well as a complementary border edge to your container.

Garnish center of citrus appropriately. Put a small dab of whip cream in center of filled melon but in either case be sure not to hide the sawtooth cut effect of the gelatin. Now stand

back and listen to the buzz in the room as they try to figure out how you did *that* one! After all, they may not have read this book or even own a culinary implement like the Kitchen Helper. They will really know what a true friend you are if you *do* share this with them; better still, give them one for a birth-day present or house gift next time!

CITRUS NOSEGAY—OLD FASHIONED BOUQUETS

Although I will go into more detail in presenting food in floral bouquet form (see chapter 7 on Vegetable Bouquets), we can start practicing on something smaller, such as using a citrus fruit as a pincushion base to form a small nosegay version of an old fashioned bouquet. Choose an orange or grapefruit as a base, depending upon what size you wish to use as individual service for each guest's table setting. Stablize the base with a small thin cut Saran wrap to prevent juices from running out. Using the grapefruit or orange as a pincushion base, position into it small vegetable cut flowers or hors d'oeuvres using wooden tooth-picks and frill picks. E.g., pin in cheese balls, peperoni, salami, and ham chunks, etc. Try placing your citrus pincushion atop your liquor bar to hold such goodies as would go with a cocktail drink: e.g., strategically place several pincushion holders along the length of the bar top, filling them with "pinned in" black and pimento-filled green olives, cheese bits (foil wrapped Laughing Cow tidbits are colorful, small and yummy) midget gherkin pickles, cocktail onions, etc. Utilize this same idea or principle and create a pincushion base as a holder for colorful gumdrops, candies and chocolate kisses for individual favors at a child's birthday party. Place a little card into the candy pompom as a place setter—a "sweets" bouquet for Susie Smith.

Use your nosegay bouquet to express your love for that special occasion or on Valentine's Day by filling your citrus cushion-holder with lush fresh strawberries (use hidden toothpick method).

Encircle your citrus nosegay bouquet with a pretty white paper lace doily held in place with greening pins or Scotch tape.

The beauty of these individual nosegays is that they can be prepared in advance, Saran-wrapped and refrigerated if necessary, as with hors d'oeuvres and the fresh fruit and vegetable nosegays.

JUICY FEATURE CREATURES

Looking for something a little unique? Try the following innovations for having lime or lemon juice available for a buffet service. Nice-looking and so handy for your guests at a dinner table, tea table, or even handy for bar service.

THE LEMON PIG

Buy a nice large lemon—choose one with extra-thick rind and extreme heaviness at the blossom end. Follow illustration and directions to transform the lemon into a pig. Simply leave the heavy stem end as is, to form its snout.

Use the lemon stripper to pull up but *NOT strip off* enough of the rind to form an eyelash on both sides just above the thick snout end of the citrus pig. Push in 2 whole cloves to simulate

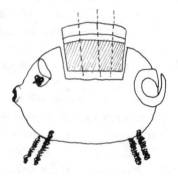

the eyes under these pulled-up lemon-strip eyelashes. On the opposite end of the lemon, release a curled-up long strip of the rind to act as the tail, or with a sharp knife you can attain the same effect by cutting the lemon rind in a spiral cut fashion and allow it to hang loose to simulate the pig's tail.

With the tail and eyes thus prepared, now outline and then cut out a cavity opening from the large area within the lemon ends. Remove the cavity opening piece in one large wedge section. OPTIONAL: at this point, if desired you can strip off the surface rind area lengthwise so the cavity area is emphasized.

In either case now proceed to slice the removed lemon wedge section crosswise into individual serving pieces being sure to keep slices in the same cutting order. Replace the sliced lemon pieces back into the cavity opening. Insert wood ends of 4 yellow cellophane frill toothpicks at angles into the base of the lemon (cellophane ends remain exposed) so that the pig can stand properly on his newly formed legs. Be sure to place a cocktail fork or hors d'oeuvre fork nearby for "easy pickings" by your guests. Our citrus pig is a unique way of serving lemon slices and providing a table conversation piece at the same time.

PORCUPINE TOOTHPICK DISPENSER

Going off on a tangent apply some of the principles of our lemon pig to create a porcupine toothpick dispenser. Follow directions for creating facial features on the front end of the lemon. Using the remaining area of the lemon as a (pincushion) body. Push in toothpicks at a 45-degree angle thus simulating the quills of a porcupine. Before positioning the legs of the porcupine cut down on the length of the frill picks as porcupines are by nature closer to the ground.

In place of the lemon strip to simulate the tail, it would look more effective if you placed the longer club size frill picks in position at the far end of our little figure as a porcupine's usual 3-foot length of tail does not hang but sort of drags along behind him.

JUICE DISPENSING LIME FROG

Keeping in mind the home-remedy trick previously recommended, prewarm the citrus lime in the oven or roll it on a hard surface such as a table top to provide a juicier citrus fruit, try your hand at creating this versatile juice dispensing lime frog. For this feature creature you will need:

1 large green lime 2 gherkin pickles or 6 green frill picks
1 acorn squash   1 juice extractor
2 cocktail onions

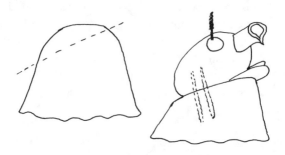

Try to obtain a cylindrical shaped green lime. If not flat enough, stabilize the base of an acorn squash to serve as the "toadstool pad." Following the diagram, slice off a slightly angled stabilizing cut from the top of (same) acorn squash upon which to set your lime frog. To stablize the frog and secure him into position, use the hidden toothpick method (see glossary) and set the lime frog onto 2 floral toothpicks which have been pushed into top of acorn squash; two cocktail onions for eyes (use frill picks to secure); use gherkin pickles for feet or position 3 green frill picks in proper position as each frog leg at base of lime leaving just the green cellophane frill of the pick exposed. Push a juice extractor tool (see glossary) in place as frog's mouth. Thus by squeezing the lime, your guests can extract the natural citric juice through the frog's mouth.

A most versatile conversation piece, and so useful, too.

MEET THE LOCAL SALOON CHARACTER. . . . AN ORANGE BIRD THATS ALWAYS HANGING AROUND YOUR BAR!

For a unique bar decoration that goes well with drinks, here's one that can be eaten as well as visually enjoyed. Try your hand at creating an orange-bird and make several in advance as they will disappear fast. You will find even your teetotaler guests enjoy this one.

Follow diagram, cut a large orange wedge to use as the body of the bird. Stabilize the orange section (use the hidden tooth-pick method (see glossary) or raise the orange wedge on 2 frill picks by positioning the body of the bird into a bulk piece of cheese or meat such as a salami chunk or thick peperoni slice; if preferred, use a piece of cucumber or carrot as a base. Use a large pimento filled olive or pitted black olive as the bird's head.

Position the olive in a crosswise position atop the orange wedge section. By so doing, the holes or the pimento of either selected olive will act as the eyes of the bird. Push a small carrot or pretzel into the front of the olive as the bird's beak.

Enjoy!—as everything is entirely edible and goes well with a good cocktail or for just plain nibbling.

HOW AND WHERE TO GET IT. . . . RECOMMENDED READING

For mothers, organizations, teachers and students and of course, domestic engineers who are just plain interested in these versatile and healthy citrus fruits there is an abundance of information and recipes waiting out there for you. Drop a postcard to obtain more literature, background history and best of all recipes in which to utilize these vitamin giving fruits. You will find these booklets or pamphlets not only informative but many of them also provide recipes. I will mark the recipe containing literature with an *R" for "really refreshing" ideas.

Dept. of Citrus, State of Florida, Florida Citrus Commision Lakeland, Florida 33802: Citrus Is . . . A Fabulous Fruit *R; Citrus Fruit & Nutrition *R

Sunkist Growers, Inc. Consumer Service P.O. Box 7888, Valley Annex, Van Nuys, California 91409: Merry Citrus from Around the World. *R also contains Christmas craft ideas; Build a Better You with Fresh Citrus; Happiness Is a Cool Drink *R contains beverage drinks only.

Sunkist Growers, Consumer Service, Box 2706, Terminal Annex, Los Angeles, California 90054: The Glorius Age of Grapefruit *R utilizing grapefruit only; Sunkist Growers California-Arizona Citrus Fruit Growing Areas (well-written pictorial history, Teacher's Unit).

Scholastic Book Service, 50 W. 44 St., N.Y.C., N.Y. 10036: Nutrition Science and You by Olaf Mickelsen (price 50¢).

PINEAPPLE PEACOCK

"FRUIT FOR SALE"

CLEANING LADY

BRIDAL MEAT DOLL

WHIMSICAL WHALE

FRIGATE BATTLESHIP

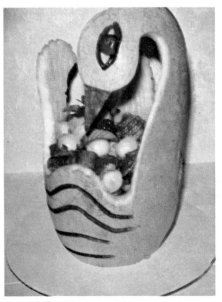

WATERMELON SWAN

WATERMELON PLANE

WISHING WELL

WEDDING CHAPEL

WATERMELON GAZEBO

FRUIT CORNUCOPIA

FOOTBALL MELON

EGG MENAGERIE

EGG CORNUCOPIA

NORTH POLE

EASTER CHEESE DUCK

LIVER BEEHIVE

FROSTY WONDERLAND

CHRISTMAS HOLIDAY

VIKING SHIP

EGGPLANT CLOWN

SPRING SCENE

TUNA BASKET

NOSEGAY BOUQUET

ARTIST'S PALETTE

VEGETABLE BASKET

POTTED VEGETABLE PLANT

CHEF'S WINE PARTY

DESSERT MOLD

BUTTERFLY ENTREE

CARVED TURKEY

5 EGGS

Although eggs are used for many purposes such as to prepare vaccines, in shampoo products, paints and varnishes, fertilizers, etc., we will confine the subject matter for this book to the purposeful use of eggs in the more popularly accepted version of omelets, cookies and cakes, soufflés, casseroles and in the presentation of creative ideas in our newly found food sculpture craft.

Although duck's eggs are widely used in other countries, turtle eggs for soup, and we ourselves consider caviar to be a delicacy, we will confine ourselves to the vitamin-giving chicken eggs more readily available to the consumer at her corner store or supermarket.

One hen's egg contains 73.7% water content, 14.8% protein, 10.5% fat and 1.0% ash. Therefore chicken eggs are an excellent source of protein, iron and phosphorus. Although the egg does not contain vitamin C as found in all citrus fruits, it is still nonetheless most important to our diet. The egg yolk, though high in cholesterol, is still very rich in vitamins A, B and D. The white or albumen (which is allowed even for the cholesterol patient) is high in vitamin B. To enhance the egg even more, let it be noted it that although high in protein it is very low in calories and therefore usually recommended on all diets. One large egg contains 80–85 calories, a medium egg 75–80. If you were to substitute instead the protein quality of one lean 3 oz. serving of hamburger meat you would have to account for 245 calories. Do you weight watchers see the immediate beauty that little old egg has suddenly taken on?

Facts & fallacies: There is no difference between white or brown eggs, since both contain the same vitamins and food value. Shell color is merely the result of pigment, the depth of yellowness of the yolk is the result of feed given to the hen. There is, however, a difference between the grade standards as noted on the carton box set up by the federal government's Dept. of Agriculture in classifying eggs into Grades AA, A and B & C. Grade C primarily used for dried & frozen processing, never reaches supermarket stores. This grading is based on the condition of the shell, yolk, albumen and air cell size. The candling of eggs is important also to determine a stale or infertile one. Choose Grades AA and A—they are best for serving as the more popular breakfast fare: poached eggs, frying them or serving cooked as is in its natural shell. Grade AA & A are also best used to make a superior milk shake or eggnog drink. The federal government has also stepped in to determine for the producer and consumer just what constitutes the size classification listed on the grade seal (or elsewhere on the cardboard egg container) you bring home from the market. Keeping in mind not to confuse size, which is a determining factor in establishing price, with the quality of the egg (AA, A, etc.) the carton of eggs are classified and labeled by their collective minimum weight *per dozen.* Thus, although one egg within that container might appear smaller than its neighbor, the container of a dozen eggs must equal out to minimally weigh at least 30 oz. to be jumbo, 27 oz. to be classified extra large, 24 oz. large, 21 oz. medium, 18 oz. small and sometimes found in the dairy case, those designated peewee weighing 15 oz. per dozen. Depending on the weekly supply of various sizes, egg prices will vary by size for the same grade. If there is less than a 7¢ spread between one size of a dozen eggs and the next smaller size (of the same grade) you would do better purchasing the larger eggs. When a recipe calls for an egg it means a large one unless otherwise noted.

Storing eggs properly: Purchase eggs from your market that are always kept under good refrigeration. Eggs tend to deteriorate faster when exposed to heat. With modern refrigeration in large stores nowadays this worry is entirely unnecessary. Speaking of modern refrigeration, many new produced refrigerators off the assembly lines feature an open area on the door in which to store your freshly purchased eggs. *Do not!* Eggs are best stored in the cardboard container in which they were purchased as the shell covering of the eggs, being very porous, take on other refrigerator odors and will lose flavor as well as moisture if left uncovered. This type of opened egg storage compartment on a constantly swinging open refrigerator door will not tend to help contain the moisture and flavor so needed. Be sure, however, to look over the eggs in your container before refrigerating the carton to be certain they are all standing with *large ends up.* Storing eggs with the large ends up serves two purposes: the yolks are kept centered (important in the making of hard-cooked eggs for deviled halved eggs presentation; storing eggs in this manner will also allow for the natural air space within the egg to expand. Freshly purchased eggs have a smaller air space and therefore peeling the eggs after cooking will be more difficult. With proper purchasing and storing as just recommended, eggs can be kept 3–4 weeks.

To store egg portions separately, once opened: egg whites: To store egg whites when the yolks were used elsewhere such as in the makings of mayonnaise, Hollandaise sauce or such, store whites in a tightly covered jar in refrigerator as they will stay 1 week to 10 days. An easy trick to freezing the egg whites if opened in large number, is to slip one egg white into each cube unit of an ice cube tray. Plastic wrap entire tray to freeze.

To store egg yolks when the whites were used elsewhere: when egg whites were used to make meringue tart shells or meringue pie toppings, or angel cake, etc., place egg yolks in tightly covered container, fill above yolks with water. Refrigerate to keep 2–3 days. *To cook egg yolks alone* once separated from whites and *to store:* to hard cook egg yolks only, separate yolk from white and immediately slip into a pan of rapidly boiling water (no salt necessary) as this prevents sticking. Cover pan and cook until yolks are cooked thoroughly. Remove yolks with slotted spoon, cool and refrigerate. Use as a "mimosa" garnish. To create mimosa effect, push hard cooked egg yolk through a sieve or fine strainer for decorating atop dishes. See "Hints and Helps" to separate whites from yolks easily later on in this section.

To store whole eggs after cooking: It is a fallacy to refer to an egg as "hard-boiled" as this is the worst manner in which an egg can be prepared, for it will result in just that—a hard-boiled egg: tough, rubbery and poor eating! Boiling eggs or allowing them even to stand in boiled water too long is the cause of the distasteful appearance of the greenish-gray color to the yolks therein. See "To prepare perfect eggs" to follow later on in this section. After the preparation of these perfectly cooked eggs, store them in their shells or peeled, in an enamel container or plastic ware covered with cold water under refrigeration. They will stay for days. If not submerged in water, they will tend to become hard and tough.

HINTS AND HELPS

1 egg = 4 tbsp. liquid
4–6 whole eggs, 8–10 egg whites, 12–14 egg yolks = one cup

Handy cooking substitutes: 1 whole egg, for thickening or baking purposes USE: 2 egg yolks or use 2 tbls. dried whole egg + 2½ tbls. water (dried eggs are more economical and are available in some supermarkets or at your local bakery); do not confuse dried eggs with frozen eggs.

1 whole egg use: 2 egg yolks + 1 tbls. water
1 whole egg use: 2 egg yolks without water for custard desserts or such
1 whole egg use: 3 tbls. thawed frozen whole egg
1 egg white use: 2 tbls. thawed frozen egg white
1 egg yolk use: 1 tsp. thawed frozen egg yolk

To use leftover egg yolks: make some home made mayonnaise or sauces such as Hollandaise; find some recipes calling for more than one egg yolk or use as substitute as listed above; cook egg yolk in boiling water and use as a mimosa garnish as previously suggested.

To use leftover egg whites: whip up some meringue tart shells for filling, toppings for pies, for angel food cake, for baked alaska pineapple, and citrus fruits Having Trouble *Whipping up Cream?* . . . any cream will whip if the white of one egg is slipped into it and it is then chilled before whipping (or add an unbeaten egg yolk or a few drops lemon juice or pinch of unflavored gelatin powder or pinch of salt and keep whipping cream). For a lighter hamburger patty fold in one egg white which had been beaten until stiff. Cook as usual for a jucier and lighter hamburger.

Egg whites and yolks will separate much easier if well chilled before separating one from the other. . . . however . . . *egg whites*, once separated from yolks must come to *room temperature* (let stand at least one hour) if they are to beat up properly to a high volume.

To separate albumen from yolks there are several culinary egg-separator implements on the culinary market. There are also old home remedy tricks: use an old narrow funnel. Break the egg gently into the funnel mouth, be sure egg is well chilled. Watch how easily the albumen passes through leaving the yolk intact. The more familiar method is to crack the egg sharply in half on the rim of a dish pass the yolk back and forth from one shell half to the other permitting the albumen to slip away into the waiting bowl or gently slide cracked egg into loosely closed fingers allowing the albumen (which should be heavy in a fresh egg) slip through your fingers and into the bowl.

Separate eggs while very cold and once separated, *TO GET GREATER VOLUME FROM YOUR EGG WHITES:* allow to stand at room temperature for a few hours or at least a minimum of 1–2 hours. Properly prepared egg whites should triple their volume if: left at room temperature several hours, beaters and bowl for beating should be moisture free as well as grease free, the slightest speck of dropped egg yolk in the albumen will hinder the volume affect so be careful in separating eggs. If using a hand electric beater hold at 45 degree angle for even greater volume. Add cream of tartar to egg whites for greater volume and it makes for a more tender meringue. *TO FOLD EGG WHITES* to incorporate into your recipe: after putting forth all that effort to incorporate air (beating of egg white is in effect doing just that) maintain that aerated feather-like substance by gently folding the beaten egg whites in gently to create that melting light angel cake, sponge cake, mousse or soufflé concoction. *EXCEPTION TO THE RULE:* here's a hint not too well known. To lighten the batter base to which you wish to incorporate your beaten egg whites, first gently *stir* in ¼ of the beaten egg whites thus giving the batter itself a lighter texture to work with. Now *fold* in the remaining beaten egg whites to the lighter textured batter. You will find folding in the egg whites much easier to handle now that the batter has already been lightened in effect too. When preparing even commercial box mix cakes, add the egg yolks where it calls for the whole egg. Beat the egg whites separately. Add the beaten egg whites to your cakes mix last and they will come out higher and lighter in texture. Don't take my word for it, give it a try.

To cut through that lemon meringue topping easily (notice how the meringue always rips away from the pie itself when cutting portions?) slightly butter your knife before cutting. *TO ADD EGG YOLKS WHEN A HOT MIXTURE IS CALLED FOR IN YOUR RECIPE:* To prevent curdling, always add a small amount of the cooked hot mixture to the beaten egg yolks stirring constantly. Then reverse the method, and stir the egg yolk mixture just concocted into the remaining hot mixture. Stir until smooth.

How to hard cook & peel eggs: To create the many "feature creatures" we will learn how to do as this chapter progresses, we must first begin with nicely shaped and perfectly peeled unblemished eggs—therein lies the problem. Tell me if I've been peeking over your shoulder in your kitchen when I say how many of you like myself, for quite a while found that to get one or two hard cooked perfectly shelled unblemished eggs to create penguins or other figures (see later on in this chapter) or to use perfectly peeled eggs for deviled halved eggs, we had to cook 6–7 eggs. How many of you had to cook up another batch because the ones we just shelled had half of the hard cooked albumen missing—stuck to the shell we just peeled off? No more, ladies . . . take heed . . . take hints!!!

This is the best way I have found to prepare the perfectly shelled egg for figure creatures or pretty deviled eggs for food sculpture buffs like myself!

Rule 1: Since we now are so much more knowledgeable, having read what preceeded this page, we are aware that shells will stick tenaciously to fresh eggs (I didn't say freshly *purchased* eggs. Since there is no way of determining whether those eggs you picked up at market were shipped in that day or a week ago you have got to "age" your own eggs). Since shells will not stick as easily to older eggs, purchase your eggs several days or a week in advance and store large end up. This is usually no problem at all, for one usually keeps at least a dozen eggs in the house at a time anyway. Remove eggs from refrigerator to stand at room temperature the night before or at least a couple of hours before cooking. Pierce (make a hole) only at the large end of the egg deep enough to pass through the membrane of the egg. Use an egg pricker, an implement available in gourmet shops or use a hatpin or straight pin as I do. As a little vinegar in water when poaching eggs* will prevent the albumen from spreading so a teaspoon of salt in the water while cooking should prevent the albumen from escaping if the eggs should crack. Fill an enamel pan with a handle with enough water to cover one layer of eggs. Avoid using an aluminum pan as it will be terribly stained by cooking eggs in it. Avoid using cracked eggs for cooking, as the whites have a tendency to run rampant in cooking water and much of the albumen and vitamin source would be wasted. Save these accidentally cracked eggs for your omelets or cake baking. Bring salted water to a full boil. With a slotted spoon gently lower hole pierced eggs into the water. Place a tight fitting cover on pan remove from heat and let stand covered for 20 minutes. *IMMEDIATELY* run cold water on eggs for five minutes to stop their cooking action. Tip pan cover once again to run off water. The trick now is to gently shake the pan; hold handle firmly so that each egg knocks gently against the others until all the eggs shells are well cracked. Cracking the egg shell is most important as it is a means of letting the cold water in to shrink the membrane away from the egg and firm up the albumen. The immersion in cold water will prevent the aforementioned dark greenish area from forming around the yolks. Once all the eggs are "mapped" with cracks, run cold water over the eggs at full force. You will find that many of the shells will start peeling away on their own. Always start peeling off the shell coverings of eggs from the large pierced hole end as this will be where the greatest formed air sac will be. If preferred, the shells may be removed while the eggs are still warm if held under fast heavy pressured running cold water. The alternative to this is to allow the eggs to

*Try poaching your eggs the next time in chicken broth for poached eggs with a yummy extra flavor.

sit in their bath of cold water for an hour before shelling; (add a few ice cubes so the heat of the eggs won't change the temperature of the water). If other matters are more pressing, by all means tend to them. Once the eggs are submersed in cold water, merely refrigerate them for several hours or even for several days.

It is advisable at this point to note that if the eggs were being prepared in large quantities for deviled egg service, they should be turned several times while being cooked to the hard stage. This is to help center the yolks so that when halved for serving they will be well formed and symmetrical for filling. Cut and separate the cooked egg yolks from the hardened albumen. Store the cooked egg white halves in a container and cover with lightly salted water solution. The yolks can be mashed in advance and even seasoned to be stored and held for a few days. Be sure to cover the containers to avoid the strong permeating egg odor from circulating in the refrigerator for the 2–3 days they will thus be kept.

To carry deviled eggs on a picnic and to serve: Since there are so many various ways to prepare deviled eggs and you probably have a favorite (if not look at any dozen number of cookbooks for recipes) we won't go into that phase of it. To handsomely garnish the egg halves use your imagination or for that matter anything that is handy as eggs go so well with everything like A,B,C. Try topping them with anchovies, bacon, caviar, dill, etc.; add a dash of paprika or fresh parsley for color. For many ways to present them in some manner more unique than a dish see ideas to follow later on in this chapter. If you must travel with deviled eggs, that might be something you will not find in every cookbook so may I make some suggestions along *those* lines. Place two filled halves together and saran wrap, be sure you twist and then securely tuck the ends under so it is airtight. *To carry,* place back into the egg carton in which they were purchased to carry them to the picnic grounds without mishap. If you need to bring more than a dozen gently layer the wrapped eggs into an old shoe box. Use newspaper in between layers of eggs to prevent shifting and banging. Make sure the eggs are well wrapped in Saran or foil before so doing.

Implements to use with preparation of eggs: Although there are some professional culinary tools used in conjunction with eggs, such as an egg beater, egg poacher, egg slicer and egg timer, I will list just as many more commercially produced devices that are less known and used by the consumer. Still, above and beyond even these there are many other tools in your kitchen workshop which you can utilize without going out to purchase one of the aforementioned commercial egg gadgets. Although some devices are used much more than others in the art of food sculpture, and are therefore listed under "Tools of Your Kitchen Workshop" in the beginning of this book, I will now list all that are known to me. Try some of their conveniences if you care to indulge yourself and would like to expand on the culinary inventory of your own workshop.

Aspic canape cutter: small cutters used to cut put designs from a hard cooked egg white. Used for decorative purposes in garnishing food.

Bird nest fryer: two section frying basket used to shape and fry bread, noodles or potatoes into basket shape within which to serve chopped egg salad or such (see this chapter on same, see also glossary, "Tools of your Kitchen.")

Egg boiling basket: a wire liner basket used to hold a large number of eggs for steeping into a larger pot of water. Convenient with handle for cooking and removing eggs from cooking water in one motion.

Egg beater: implement with 2 rotary blades with metal or wood handle. Used to beat eggs manually as versus other electric operated beaters such as mixers with bowls and other attachments as well as electric portable beaters. Some manual egg beaters are manufactured with a reversible feature so one can convert the rotary turner for lefthanded use.

Egg coddler: usually a decorated porcelain cup used to coddle eggs.

Egg cup: glass, porcelain or plastic cup used specifically to serve a cooked egg within its shell.

Egg cutter, scissors or shearer: do not confuse this with an egg slicer, as this implement is used to cut off the top of the egg shell to give access to its contents. Scissorslike in design, it is often referred to as an egg cutter, egg scissors or egg shearer.

Egg (electric) cooker: an electrical unit, usually a decorative ceramic, in which several eggs can be simultaneously cooked at the breakfast table in unison. Incorporated in its manufacture is usually a timing device which is the most attractive feature. It is this built-in timer which can guarantee perfectly cooked eggs to the absolute minute.

Egg frying rings: Used to keep eggs uniform while being fried, they are sold individually or in sets. They are usually round with stand-up handles for easy lifting. One company has manufactured an egg fryer with a square shape for eggs that are specifically being prepared for making sandwiches. This implement can also be used to shape and hold hamburgers while frying. Some frying rings are sold with fitting individual covers thus helping to avoid the inevitable spattering of grease and juices.

Egg omelet pan: A two-section hinged pan that folds and is used specifically for the making of omelets.

Egg piercer: used to punch small hole in eggs to prevent bursting while being cooked.

Egg poacher: device with handle used for holding egg in water while being poached. Sold individually, multiple or in sets of a combined holders with pan.

Egg separator: cup-like holder device used to catch and allow the white of an egg to pass through the openings to a waiting bowl to catch same while the egg yolk is simultaneously caught in its cup center. A useful implement to have around when having to separate the albumen from the yolk of many eggs as sometimes called for in sponge cake or angel food recipes.

Egg slicer: usually a two-part hinged type holder with fine wire slicing blades used to cut an individual egg into ⅛″ uniform slices. Although a butter slicer or tomato slicer can be substituted for same to slice the egg, the holder section of this slicer is specifically designed in shape and contour to hold the egg. Some manufactured egg slicers will cut an egg crosswise as well as diagonally and lengthwise. By cutting your egg through crosswise and then lengthwise or vice versa, you can in essence therefore chop or dice an egg. Such an egg slicer would be referred to as a 4–way slicer.

Egg (wood)spoon: a (Swedish imported) manufactured hardwood spoon specifically designed with egg-shaped concave bowl with hole in bowl center. Used to lift and cradle eggs while being placed into or removed from cooking water.

Egg timer: an hourglass timer filled with sand used to time a 3-minute egg (or telephone calls); available also is a combined set of holder and three hourglass timers with various colors to depict 3, 4 and 5 minute eggs.

Egg tree: a standing sometimes rotary mobile type holder featuring 12 dispensers for holding one dozen eggs (on end) at room temperature for utilitarian purposes and/or for featuring Easter eggs as a centerpiece display for the table.

Egg tulip flower cutter: a cutting implement used to cut hard cooked eggs into tulip shape designs for garnishing and decorative serving.

Egg wedger: usually a scissorslike implement consisting of an egg shaped holder and an opposing wire cutting slicer. Used to cut an individual egg into 6 equal wedge cuts for garnishing and easier handling of egg sections.

Egg whisk: many metal fine wires curved and fixed to a handle; available in all sizes and lengths with which to beat up eggs or whip cream. Used for whipping eggs to a froth or to blend sauces, gravies or creams until smooth in texture.

Fine sieve or strainer: use back of spoon bowl to push hard cooked egg yolk through sieve or strainer to obtain a crumbled "mimosa" effect for garnishing.

Grater: My favorite grater is a fine mesh rectangular shaped grater with handle. I use same to push the eggs through to mix in with tuna fish salads or such.

Knife: any small cutting knife that can be used to cut hard cooked eggs in half for serving.

Muffin tin: you are probably wondering what a muffin tin has to do with eggs, but this is what I use when I have to prepare a lot of eggs at one time in "bread nests." After removing crust borders from white bread, butter *both* sides of bread and fit snugly into cups of muffin tin pan. Break egg into each buttered bread nest; season eggs to taste. Cover pan with foil and bake in 350° oven. Walla! eight (cup) or 12 (cup) eggs for serving simultaneously. You can even sit down and join your guests for breakfast or brunch.

Pastry decorating tube set: usually used for decorating and frosting cakes. To use for food sculpture, first finely sieve or use food mill or ricer to strain through only the egg yolks or even the whole egg. If you do not wish to be left with many egg whites since utilizing only the egg yolk, I put the whole egg including the whites, through the sieve or ricer until finely strained so there is no chance of a large piece of egg white clogging the tube tip of my pastry bag. It is thus more economical to use the egg in its entirety; in either case strain yolks or eggs finely, season and mix with mayonnaise. Fill canvas pastry bag and press through the pastry tube tip to design and garnish your tuna or chopped liver molds (see chapter on same).

Pie tin: another "homey tip" for making lots of bull's-eye eggs simultaneously. Grease a pie tin or large pan. Break in many eggs depending on size of pan utilized. Add a bit of water and eggs will spread a bit. Bake in 350° oven until degree of doneness desired. Cut eggs apart with edge of wide spatula. Serve guests as many eggs as they wish and sit down and join them.

Serrator: implement with stainless steel 7″ crinkle blade cutter (see Tools of your Kitchen Workshop). The same pretty crinkle design you get by cutting carrots, radishes, and potatoes with this implement will lend itself beautifully to egg slices and pieces for garnishing and serving. Before cutting eggs into crinkle-faced slices or sections, due to the dryness of the hardcooked egg yolk which has a tendency to stick to cutting blade (knife or serrator), spray blade with aerated can of oil spray now available on the market for Teflon pans.

FEATURE CREATURES

To create a snowman for an ice skating party or as theme for a Winter lunch party for the kids, follow directions to make some snowmen.

Body of snowman: stabilize end slices of 2 jumbo eggs so that one will set upon the other.

Head: to be made from a small or peewee egg or from a large pared red or white radish. Stabilize base of head to set atop body of snowman. Affix to body with gelatin paste* or hidden toothpick. Use cloves for eyes, carrot stub for nose etc. SCARF: use narrow strip of pimento to wrap around and hang down over the shoulders and neck of snowman.HAT:use lengthwise thick cut of pitted black olive for brim of hat; place a second whole black olive on top of brim for stovepipe section of hat. Use gelatin paste to hold hat sections together or use hidden toothpick.

Studs: Use whole cloves or bits of black olives to simulate coal chunks usually placed on snowman's front.

Snow: to set realistically upon a snow covered base create the whiteness of snow in the following manner. Using a tray with a lip, pour in and refrigerate this recipe for gelatin to use to simulate snow: bring to boiling point only—½ c. sugar with 1 c. heavy sweet cream; in the meantime, sprinkle 1 pkg. Knox gelatin over ½ c. water; allow gelatin to dissolve and thicken and add to sugar-cream mix. Let cool ½ hour before beating in 1 pt. sour cream (or sour dressing) and 1 teas. vanilla. Mix to blend well and pour into tray to set in refrigerator. To serve place several snowmen on tray of snow gelatin, etc.

---

*Gelatin paste: to create a *colorless* gelatin paste in contrast to yellow color of egg yolk paste, cover ¼ c. water in shallow dish with 1 pkg. Knox gelatin (sprinkled over) until crystals are absorbed and dissolved. Allow to stand until *thick* paste is formed. Use this *colorless paste* in place of yolk cream paste for adherence qualities.

APPLE EGGS

To transform an egg into an apple is a feat for any magician except if that magician happens to be you at work in your own kitchen. The magic of this trick is to work with the egg while it is still very warm, right after being cooked. Hard cook egg and shell carefully. Allow to cool just until point that you can comfortably hold it. *While still warm* apply pressure at opposite ends of the egg simultaneously, being careful not to puncture it with your fingernails. Press and hold until rounded in shape to resemble an apple. After apple shape is formed, hold and run under cold water or submerge in a bowl of ice water to help retain apple shape permanently. Submerge egg in light green colored food dye and water solution for an hour. Rinse with cold water, let dry. Color only one side of egg with a dab of diluted red food coloring to create that "Mackintosh" look. Push in a small frill pick with attached (peppermint) "leaf" on top to simulate that "just picked" look.

Use as garnish for salad plates. Egg apples would look particularly nice and go well as an accompaniment to the cornucopia salad setting. See chapter 3 on Melons: cornucopia of salads, cheeses, etc.

BASKET NESTS

There are many ways to simulate the straw-built nest of a bird in which to present our fish and meat salads, egg salad or to emphasize our creature features like the Baby Bird, Chickadee and Duckling described in this chapter.

There is available on the culinary market a professional implement called a Bird's Nest Fryer with which these basket nests are most easily made. (see: Glossary, Tool of your Workshop; see: This chapter, Implements to use in preparation of eggs.) To make a basket nest using a Bird's Nest Fryer implement: line the larger bottom basket of the two section Bird's

Nest Fryer with thin cuts of peeled potato slices or line with peeled and finely shredded potatoes (do not wash after shredding, 2 medium potatoes shredded will yield one basket) or line with strips of bread or line with fine or medium size widths of pasta or egg noodles. Basket can be lined with pre-cooked pasta, drain well but do not rinse with water or with uncooked noodles which, when fried in Birds Nest, will then actually be the familiar Chinese chow mein noodles. With larger basket lined with your selection, insert smaller basket on top thus forming a nest-like mold. Slide clamps, provided with Bird's Nest Fryer, over handles locking the two baskets together. Deep fry in hot oil to golden brown. Loosen edges with fork or knife to release the fried edible basket mold. Drain on paper toweling to absorb excess oil.

If this implement is not available, try these other suggested methods of creating a variety of other edible nests to set your birds, chicks or salad fixings into.

Fine noodle basket: after cooking according to directions, drain ½ pound of fine egg noodles and mix with enough butter to bind the two together. Place buttered noodles in a well-greased muffin cups. Press noodles against bottom and sides of muffin cups using the back of a spoon. To hold the shape while baking in 375° oven for 30 minutes, I place the bottom of a second muffin cup on top of the noodles (be sure to grease entire *outside* sides and bottom of the second cup to avoid sticking and assuring easy release). The alternative is to use heavy duty foil to hold shape of basket accordingly. Remove inset cup or foil; continue to bake nests for 5 more minutes at 500° for extra dryness as well as crispness. Release noodle nest with knife and cool on wire rack. Half pound of fine cooked noodles will yield 10–12 nests for filling.

Quickie chow mein noodle nest: to one small can chow mein noodles mix in 3 oz. shredded cheddar cheese (¾ c.). Bind together with one egg white. Proceed as above placing into greased muffin cups. However, since Chinese noodles are actually already in cooked form, you need only bake them for 15 minutes in slow 325° oven to yield 4 nests for filling.

Unique quickie pasta nest: Cook fine noodles or fettucini pasta or the like according to package directions. Drain well but do not rinse. Season and bind together with beaten eggs. For change of pace, depending on what your choice of filling is to be, try different spices or add poppy seeds or such. For example, use your own creative ingenuity; cook up some spinach, noodle or pasta form, mix with eggs and add fresh chopped parsley. Place mounds of the seasoned mixture on well greased baking tin. Using back of spoon, form a well in center (leaving ½" base of noodles to cover and form bottom of nest). This last one tastes best when a raw egg is dropped into the spinach nest before being popped in the oven and baked together for a nice high protein brunch bite.

Mashed potato nest: another quickie: cook enough potatoes to make as many potato nests as needed or use the new easy box prepared mixes of potato flakes; prepare according to directions. Either way, keep mashed potatoes to thick consistency. For that added touch and change of taste, mix in shredded cheddar cheese while potatoes are still hot. This will not only add an au grautin taste to your dish, but will also help thicken the consistency, firm up and bind the potatoes for better forming a deep yellow colored basket nests. Place on greased baking tin, dust well with paprika and/or light coat mix of bread crumbs and chopped fresh parsley for color and extra crispness. Bake until lightly browned in 375° oven. Any of the above basket nests can be filled with a fresh raw egg. Season and bake as previously mentioned to serve as a light midnight repast or brunch in place of bread nests described in this chapter under the heading of Implements to use with eggs: muffin tin.

After removing desired created bird's nest, fill accordingly with salad after optionally lining nest with chopped salad greens.

If filling nest with hot chicken or crabmeat salad use a hot type of basket nest such as potato mounds or hot noodles. *Omit greens.* To serve cold chopped egg salad or tuna fish or to feature creatures (bird, duckling, etc.) use a cold noodle basket variety such as the Quickie Chow Mein Noodle Nest lined with greens.

For other nest type ideas, refer to Jack & Jill in the Box, this chapter. Substitute tomato and pepper cups for cooked basket nests to feature creatures or present salads, lined with chopped greens.

EGG HEAD CLOWN

A nice way of serving lunch for a child's party is to provide them with clown eggs for their uniqeness of presentation as well as for their protein value and source of vitamins A,B and D. Egg head clowns also provide certain fringe benefits such as entertainment and exciting table conversation for the youngsters. Try it as the whimsical touch for an adult's party and see how a circus clown can still bring out the child in your guests too.

To create your egg head clown:

Collar: for collar and stabilizing base for your egg head clown, use cookie or vegetable cutter to scallop or daisy cut the collar design from a thick slice of bread. Remove the crust. Use a dark (pumpernickel) bread for color emphasis and contrast. If preferred, substitute and use a collar cut from a bulk form of thick cheese or meat or fresh vegetable (e.g., beet or large carrot slice).

Head: to stand egg in vertical position, slice a very thin stabilizing cut off the bottom of the large end of the egg. Use thick egg yolk cream paste* or use hidden toothpick method to vertically place and secure egg onto collar, placing it large end down.

To create facial features: EYES: push in whole cloves for eyes or use large round olive slices. *NOSE:* optional: use carrot "Pinocchio" nose or tip of a red cherry for a clown's bulbous nose effect. *MOUTH:* Use cherry or pimento for mouth. Alternative, which I prefer, is to strip out smiling mouth from albumen in appropriate area (use sharp French narrow lemon stripper implement). Carefully with a cotton bud and red food dye, color the border edge surrounding the stripped out area thus creating the red lips of the mouth. The uncolored remaining stripped out albumen within the lips will then be emphasized as the teeth of the clown.

Hat: to create the dunce hat for your clown, appropriately slash cut a thin slice of salami to roll cone shaped. Secure slash cut sides together with club frill pick exposing pick end to secure into top of egg to stabilize hat.

*To make egg yolk cream paste: mix cooked sieved egg yolk with a little seasoning, mayonnaise and creamed butter to form thick paste. It is the butter addition that helps hold it together better for storing under refrigeration; the mayonnaise for spreading and fluffiness when pushed through a pastry tube for decorative work. In the egg head clown the egg yolk cream paste is being used as an adherent as well as for its decorative quality. See Filled Egg Halves later in chapter for highly seasoned deviled egg filling as additives for egg yolk paste form.

Optional: if you are already utilizing an egg yolk cream paste, follow through and use some of the yolk paste to create the pompom balls usually found on a clown's hat. If desired to add that extra-nice touch, use yolk cream paste to give your clown some blonde hair or mix the paste with a drop of red food dye to create a red-haired clown. I have always loved redheaded clowns as they seem more authentic to me!

JACK OR JILL IN THE BOX

Planning a children's luncheon party or if you wish to bring a charming note to your own luncheon party for adults, try this entirely edible centerpiece to present your eggs in vegetable nests. I call them Jack (or Jill) in the Box, for that's what they remind me of.

For red colored jack in the box: choose a firm medium-large tomato. With Kitchen Helper implement, cut off in zigzag design an ⅛ section from the top part of the tomato or use knife to create a straight cut on your tomatoe thus creating the box (holder) and its cover. If fortunate enough to grow your own tomatoes, by all means leave the natural blossom stem end attached as is for handle effect to your box cover. Set aside ⅛ cut off section for replacement later. If remaining bottom section of tomato is not flat enough to stand, stabilize base with thin slice cut. Use grapefruit spoon to clean out some pulp and seeds from the tomato box (holder). Fill this bottom with cooked spinach or cut up salad greens. Set the egg in vertically, placing small end down. From large end of egg, slice off a small stabilizing cut. Onto the new stabilized top surface, replace the ⅛ removed tomato section as the cover to your Jack in the Box.

To decorate egg head:

Eyes: push in 2 whole cloves or small ends of pimento olive slices.

Mouth: for a really cute touch, cut out a small wedge section for mouth area. Fill in with a triangular long piece of pimento tongue.

For green colored Jack in the Box: for variety of presentation of your egg plate centerpiece, apply this same principle, substituting a suitably sized green pepper for the red (tomatoe) box. Proceed as per previous directions to create box. After scooping out seeds, refill pepper nest or cup with macaroni salad or potatoe salad for variety. Dust with paprika to bring out contrast of color before nesting in egg. Set hard cooked egg atop macaroni salad. Replace pepper top (leave natural stem in place to act as handle) as cover for Jack in Box.

To create Jill in a Box: for further change of pace and to add distaff side to your centerpiece presentation of eggs, create Jill by adding on celery leaf hair or hair made of egg yolk cream paste (see hair for clown egg head previously described).

Decorate hair with pretty pimento ribbon or large bow. Omit pimento tongue. Substitute smiling cherub mouth detailed in directions for clown egg head's mouth. If serving Jill-eggs, omit cover for box so hair and ribbon are emphasized and highlighted instead.

CREATURE FEATURES FROM A MENAGERIE:

The Penguin: Pare a large sized carrot and cut off crosswise a 2 inch piece to serve as feet, the base for your penguin to be set on.

(A) Cut off stabilizing slice lengthwise, as per diagram so it has a flat surface and will not fall. (B) In center cut out a small v-shaped piece. (C) Cut off small slices at diagonal angles from both ends on sides of carrot as diagram depicts.

(D) Push into carrot base just above V-shaped cutout section in center, a floral heavy wooden toothpick. (E) Push onto toothpick a hard cooked egg, large end down using hidden toothpick method (see glossary) as pictured in diagram above. (F) Place large size black olive (pit in) atop a halved (shorter) floral toothpick. Make two little holes where eyes would appropriately be positioned. Place into each hole a silver candy dragee (the type used for wedding cakes), piece of almond nut, piece of carrot or any suitable edible "eyes" for your penguin. Mount olive head onto top of hard cooked egg. Cut a small wedge shape piece of carrot, push into position to form beak for penguin.

Slice one pitted olive in half, each half will then be an arm for our feathered friend. Hold olive arms in place by piercing into each side of egg with a *dark* colored frill toothpick. See

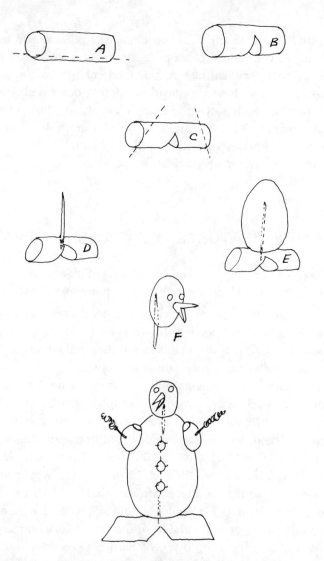

diagram. Optional: Place in 3 whole cloves down center of egg
(body) to simulate tuxedo studs.

Chickadee: To attain yellow (body) coloring for egg chickadee,
place shelled hard cooked egg in food dye colored water mix-

ture (in cup of water, drop enough yellow food dye to obtain shade desired.) for at least one hour. Remove, rinse egg with cold water. Using 3″ crosswise cut piece of carrot as feet and base, set a floral wood pick into front end of carrot chunk after stabilizing carrot base so it stands and receives egg body properly. Follow diagram to make 2 stabilizing cuts.

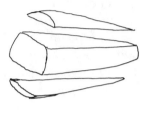 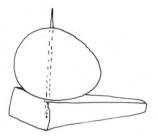

Position larger end of egg as front of chickadee. Position and push down over floral pick so that the floral wooden pick will penetrate through the top of the egg. This exposed floral wooden tip point will then be utilized to hold and stabilize head of chickadee.

For head: shape and cut from pared white icicle radish or pared red radish an appropriate carved shaped head and beak

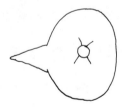

for chickadee as per diagram. Color head yellow with food coloring and cotton ball; color beak area red with cotton bud. Prehole both sides of head and position whole cloves to act as eyes of the figure. Force onto the exposed pick point of the body thus creating the head of the chickadee.

Wings: To place wings into position push floral wood pick through body of egg so two pointed tip ends are exposed on either side of egg. Wings are simply made up of two carrot slices (shaped accordingly) and then secured onto pointed ends of picks on both sides of chick's body hidden toothpick method. See diagram. Also See chapter 7—How to Present *Vegetables,* as chickadee.

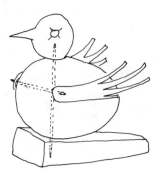

DUCKLING EGG

Body: Using hard cooked egg proceed as per directions to make chickadee, omit coloring procedure.

Head: Using pared red radish or pared white radish cut and shape head as per proceeding directions. Place whole cloves as eyes in position on either side of radish head; color beak orange.

Wings: proceed as per wings on chickadee, however, substitute white icicle radish slices shaped like wings in place of carrot wing slices as in chickadee. (See Vegetable Duckling in chapter 7.)

SWAN

For those of us who prefer a more edible swan than the turnip vegetable swan suggested in chapter 7 on vegetables may I suggest the swan made from an egg. Keep in mind once again that this (egg) swan would be more perishable than the (turnip) vegetable swan used and incorporated in our springtime setting featured later on in this same chapter.

Swan's body: stabilize and place horizontally, a hard cooked egg to represent the body of the swan.

Head and neck: to create the graceful neck and head of our swan, choose, a suitably long shaped white icicle radish. Pare skin. Using a knife, shape thickest part of radish to resemble head and beak. Using a potato peeler, proceed to shave to slim down and curve remaining portion of radish into neck of swan. Cut off stabilizing slice at base of radish neck for slightly angled placement against (large end) front of the swan's body.

Carefully push floral pick into front of body, leaving enough of pick extruded to receive radish neck and head of swan. Push angled base of radish neck carefully onto toothpick point and up against egg body. (It's best to pre-hole this point of entry for the toothpick in advance so it can be slipped on easily to prevent breaking (egg) body. Color in beak with yellow food coloring. Pre-hole eyes to receive whole cloves on either side of head. OPTIONAL: if desired place white radish wings (as per duckling or chickadee wings) on both sides of swan using same pick method as for duckling and/or chickadee previously outlined in this chapter.

FROG

Body: submerge a hard cooked and shelled egg in green food dye and water solution for 1 hour. Rinse with cold water. BASE: slice a 2-inch cross section of a cucumber, one side of which is to be cut at a slightly elevated diagonal slant upon which to perch your frog.

Frog's legs: slice an appropriate sized gherkin pickle in half lengthwise. Place them atop diagonal slant cut of cucumber positioning pickles toward outer edge of base so that feet are overhanging base.

Hold in place with 2 regular toothpicks placed in pickle feet at 45° angle. Place egg body in position, large end facing front of legs. Use hidden pick method. In appropriate area for mouth, carve out a wedge shape section. Fill this mouth opening with a long triangular cut piece of red sweet pepper or pimento to simulate frog's hanging tongue.

Eyes: Place 2 pickled onions in position as eyes. To secure hold with red frill picks.

For authenticity place a large mushroom cap or two nearby and surround with "chicory" grass.

A BABY BIRD HATCHES

Using an egg tulip flower cutter (see implements to use with eggs), or Kitchen Helper, carefully cut off an ⅛–¼ *albumen* section from small end of a hard cooked egg. Set aside. Remove yolk from within egg, mash and combine with small amount finely chopped or cooked ground turkey or chicken (for thickening) and enough liquid bottled margarine or melted butter to bind mixture together. Season properly to taste, and with fingers, shape to resemble a baby bird's head and top of body. Stabilize (very thin slice) remaining ¾ albumen section of egg shell and fill with bird's (yolk) body poking out above shell edge. Replace removed ¼ section of egg white top, perching it lightly on bird's head. Secure to adhere to head top with dab of mayonnaise thus simulating bird just emerging from broken egg shell.

Decorate head of bird with eyes (olive slices) and large carrot beak. Set "hatched" shell on lettuce bed or move appropriately into a basket nest. (To make basket nests, see previously detailed directions in this chapter.)

CORNUCOPIA BASKET PRESENTATION OF EGGS

Speaking of edible centerpieces for your table, why not combine deviled egg halves and whole shelled eggs together, giving your guests a variety of choice. Using a long half sheet cake tray, left over from your last birthday party (or see your local baker or restaurant-supply house to purchase one as they make marvelous narrow but extra long serving trays), position a wicker cornucopia basket on one end of the tray. To stabilize the basket adhere it to the tray with a blob of floral sticky gum tape. Fill the cornucopia inside and line the tray with salad greens. Place, as if tumbling out of the mouth of the cornucopia and onto the tray itself, a load of whole shelled eggs, as well as halved deviled eggs. OPTIONAL: intersperse with a few Baby Birds just hatching as they always draw rave notices no matter where they (literally) pop up. For an added touch, sprinkle tray with colorful orange and yellow candy corn kernels. On the top edge of the cornucopia mouth opening and along the rim of the tray itself, position (use floral gum) some of the furry artificial chickadees or ducks left over from the children's Easter Candy Basket.

FIREPLACE HANDLED BASKET

Smaller crowd to feed? Apply the same principle to a lovely handled open fireplace basket available in floral stores or 5 & 10¢ shops in assorted (plastic) colors or natural wicker shades. Follow suit; line the basket with salad greens and fill with deviled eggs this time. Place one or two of your feathered artificial friends left over from Easter along the handle of the basket. This time fill in here and there with some whole shelled eggs for balance and variety.

Whether using a Cornucopia tray or fireplace basket, have some extra eggs on hand for you'll never see them disappear so fast as when they're presented so nicely!

SUN BONNET BASKET

No fireplace basket or cornucopia handy? Don't despair. Get out your old big summer gardening bonnet or your old wide-brimmed sun hat or try Dad's old straw hat for a novel effect; push in crown slightly to create flat base to stabilize. Be sure to first line it with plastic wrap before placing in those salad greens. Follow through with the eggs and decorate surface of brim with your old leftover artificial feathered friends.

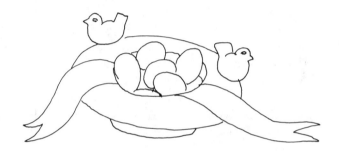

FILLED EGG HALVES FOR HORS D'OEUVRES SERVICE

Throughout this part of the chapter I've referred continually to halved or deviled eggs and have used an egg yolk cream paste as a binder for joining food staples together so that everything is completely edible. Let's take a moment now to go into it in more detail.

Now you are aware of the fundamentals in cooking the perfect egg and also how to obtain one by proper shelling. If using these prepared eggs to be cut in half for refilling with yolk mixture, it is best to refrigerate the peeled egg for at least 2 hours to firm up the albumen before handling. Egg yolk filling basically is to remove the hard cooked yolk from the albumen of the egg; set the albumen shell aside for refilling later. To make a yolk paste mixture is to basically mash or sieve the yolk, season with salt and pepper and mix with butter *and* mayonnaise . . . the butter for storing it better, the mayonnaise for its spreading and fluffy quality (especially when being put through a pastry tube.)

What we do to this basic mixture before returning it to the albumen shell half is up to our taste and imagination. Here are some basic recommendations to get you started.

Deviled egg mixture: to the basic egg yolk mixture above, add any of the following spices to give the egg filling a hot flavor. Add to taste: prepared or dry mustard, lemon juice, Tabasco sauce, cayenne pepper, etc., and so the name derived: deviled eggs. Refill halved egg white shell with the deviled yolk mix. To carry out the devil in you, decorate the yolk filling with a facsimile of the devil's features . . ., carrot horns or pepper horns (green or red), etc.; black olive eyes, pimento nose, dill beard, celery leaf eyebrows, etc.

As a surprise *filling* to your egg halves try any of these: Before replacing the yolk mixture, fill the well area (area from which the yolk was removed) of the white albumen shell with a spoonful of caviar, a smoked oyster, anchovies, chopped sardines, etc. Decorate with the egg yolk paste mix.

For a surprise *topping* to your egg halves try some of these. Dust with paprika for extra color enhancement: capers, standing baby shrimp, rolled anchovy, bacon bits, olive or radish slices, etc. Not enough caviar to make it as a surprise filling in the well? Economize and merely use it in combination with smoked salmon . . . (better known as lox) . . . spread mix of minced onions and black caviar on a wide strip of lox, roll up jelly roll fashion. Refrigerate to firm up and chill; slice crosswise and place pinwheel slice of lox atop egg yolk filling. This surely meets the D for dramatics of our A B C rules . . . all the D's, for that matter. It's Decorative, Different, and Definitely gourmet!

For an unusual combination of design and gourmet service do a small take off on the Baby Bird. Fill well in albumen half of egg with caviar (try red for a change of variety) or any other well filling that suits your fancy or your pocketbook. Following suit for preparing and shaping Baby Bird head and neck, set on top of filled egg half. Omit shell top cover used in Baby Bird to decorate head. Use carrot beak and olive eyes for facial expressions on bird. Place a few of these smaller version birds among your Filled Egg Halves for hors d'oeuvre service. For a unique color variation add some tomato paste (and oregano) or colored food dye to the yolk cream paste; blend well. Fill shells or use to top fillings already in the well as per many of the aforementioned suggestions. Extremely decorative and colorful when put through a fancy tipped pastry tube and garnished appropriately.

FROG'S EGGS IN A MUSHROOM PATCH

Now that we have learned how easy it is to whip up frog's eggs (see this chapter; feature creatures: menagerie) let's delight the small-fry by incorporating them in a main centerpiece for a child's party. For a more diversified version for an adult party see chapter 7, Spring Scene.

Using a large piece of 1" thick styrofoam as a base, cover with foil, pin in "chicory grass" to cover top as well as sides of styrofoam base. Use hidden toothpick method to place small groupings of full mushrooms (caps with stems) in position. Place a few frog's eggs to set upon some of the mushroom caps and place some frog's eggs into the chicory grass. If desired, place in just a few cut vegetable flowers on green cellophane frill pick "stems." Too many flowers will detract the attention away from your frog menagerie.

SPINACH GRASS GELATIN MOLD

If you happen to have some "Popeye" spinach lovers around, try this recipe I found and adapted to serve as an edible green grass lawn for our frog's setting. Originally prepared with 4 diced cooked eggs (added at the last stage before setting) for a 3 c. spinach-egg loaf mold try this doubled version to serve to enhance our edible centerpiece.

Sprinkle 2 pkgs. Knox gelatin over 1½ c. cold water in saucepan. Heat over low heat until gelatin is completely dissolved. Remove from heat and stir in 2 teas. salt, ½ teas. dry mustard and ½ teas. tabasco pepper sauce. Chill, stirring occasionally until consistency of unbeaten egg whites. In the interim, mix together 3 c. chopped fresh spinach with ¼ c. lemon juice. Put 1½ c. of cottage cheese and ⅓ c. of cold water into blender; cover and process at high speed until smooth. To the now thickened gelatin add the spinach and cottage cheese. Mix well. With a can of aerated vegetable oil (Pam, etc. now available in supermarkets for Teflon pans and such) spray a rectangular 9 X 13" deep pan. Pour in gelatin mixture. Refrigerate for 6 hours or overnight. Loosen edges and turn out onto tray. Use this edible spinach gelatin base in place of the chicory covered styrofoam block. Proceed to set mushroom, frog's eggs and vegetable flowers as previously directed for frog centerpiece.

PENGUIN EGGS WITH IGLOO SCENE

Too hot to cook? Your turn to entertain for lunch? Are the ladies dieting? For the answer to any or all these questions, there is always the old standby of eggs, cottage cheese, a light gelatin dessert and some fruit to help you keep the calorie count low and still healthily provide you with the necessary vitamins and protein. Sounds familiar, the usual eggs, cheese and fruit? What will be different about it is the manner in which we will present this same old standby menu. Let's be imaginative by incorporating all of the aforementioned courses into a beautiful main serving piece, thus making it light on the work involved, light on the dishes to clean, as well as light on calories.

Use a large serving tray with a lip edge border. Prepare a refreshing lime gelatin dessert (optional: mint extract added) a day or so ahead. If you wish to include a fresh vegetable in place of a dessert type gelatin, substitute the spinach loaf (with or without the chopped eggs) as outlined in this chapter: The Frog and Mushroom Patch scene for the children's luncheon party. I'm sure the youngsters won't mind at all if you partake of some of their spinach and transform their grass lawn into a green ocean to set your igloo upon. When the green gelatin of your choice is set and you're ready to serve, chop up or mash the gelatin. The chopped gelatin will simulate the effect of a wavy ocean base. Accordingly then, cover your serving tray with your ocean floor. Use canned (drained) peach slices, pineapple spears or rings to frame out and border the North Pole picture you are presenting. Border the edge of the tray with plenty of this drained fruit to serve as dessert.

To create the igloo: The Eskimo hut or igloo can simply be contrived by filling a deep round bowl with cottage cheese and then turning this mounded cottage cheese "igloo" out onto the tray. Use your hands to shape up the entrance area in front of the hut. (See diagram.)

If you prefer something a little more dashing, prepare your own favorite recipe for a gelatin combination so long as it will pick up some cottage cheese or sour cream or dressing in the preparation of the mold to give an overall white igloo appearance to your eskimo abode; e.g., following is a quickie recipe that is simple. Poured to set in a deep bowl, then turned out and released it will yield a glazed gelatinized white dome hut, an igloo. Bring 1⅔ c. of unsweetened canned pineapple juice to a boil. Turn off heat and sprinkle a 3 oz. pkg. lemon gelatin over the boiled juice. Dissolve completely. Refrigerate to chill just until thickened. Beat 1 c. small curd cottage cheese until fluffy. *Fold* cheese into thickened gelatin. Pour into deep bowl mold to set. Depending on the number of guests expected to partake of this plate and the size of the tray used, this recipe can be doubled, tripled, etc. It can be put to set to mold in a small bowl or a large mixer type beating bowl, etc. Pour some into a *cone-*shaped paper drinking or coffee cup to jell. Turn out and set up as mountain scenery in background setting. To form the tunnel entrance to your igloo, pour some of the gelatin mixture into a *rounded* paper cup (these also come in assorted sizes). Chill gelatin mix to set (at least 6 hours or overnight). Farmer cheese, ricotta or whatever your choice of cheese may be substituted for the cottage cheese specified in this recipe. Invert bowl and unmold. Remove gelatin from paper cups. Place on tray atop lime gelatin and/or spinach ocean.

Use cake writer gel tubes or * egg yolk cream paste (see footnote to Egg-Head Clown this chapter; putting yolk paste through the fine tip of a pastry bag) to outline the ice block forms that comprise the makings of an igloo. (note illustration above)

To create ice float: if desired, the surrounding area immediately bordering the cheese igloo can be simulated to look like a large ice float. Sprinkle said area with finely chopped hard cooked egg whites (or put cooked albumen through potato ricer or mill) (use the leftover egg yolks to make your egg yolk paste to outline your ice block forms of your Eskimo hut). If you prefer to incorporate more fruit into your picture, substitute well-drained crushed pineapple for the ice floating area.

North Pole inhabitants: Place several penguins (see how to make penguins in this chapter under Feature Creatures: menagerie) about the ice float, stationing some of them about the igloo entrance. To add a touch of humor to your center-piece, have one or two penguins stationed at the edge of the ice float ostensibly fishing for a dinner from the wavy (lime) ocean deep.

To create a penguin fisherman: Proceed to prepare a penguin. This time, however, substitute a spiral cut long piece from a colossal or giant black olive (or use spiral strip of eggplant skin). Place in usual wing position on sides of penguin figure. (See illustration)

Fishing rod: Place appropriate size of bamboo skewer eminating from under olive wing. To stabilize and hold at the proper angle and in position, push point end of orange wood stick or bamboo skewer into carrot (feet) base of penguin. (see illustration above)

Fishing line: In keeping it completely edible, use candy shoe string licorice rope (red or black shoe string licorice rope is available in confectionary stores.) Tie candy rope onto fish pole so it dangles over ocean base.

Fish: If one of your penguin fisherman was lucky enough to hook one, his little fish (cut free form outline of fish from flat 1″ X ¼″ piece of carrot (see diagram) would evidently be hanging from his (licorice) fish line just above the ocean waters ready to reel in.

It might be eggs, cheese and fruit you served for lunch but thats not what the girls will be raving about, believe me! It's not what you have but what you do with it that counts!

A WINTER WONDERLAND OF PENGUINS: OR HOW THEY SERVE RELISH AT THE NORTH POLE:

A big hit at a buffet dinner dance, whose theme for the evening was "A Winter Wonderland," was the centerpiece I dreamed up to serve the necessary mustard and applesauce needed for the accompanying hot dogs and potato pancakes. The mustard and applesauce was set up on a main buffet table to accommodate the 300 attending guests. Needless to say, it can be modified and used to serve just about anything you'd like to complement the particular main entree being served as your dinner fare. The preparation of the centerpiece itself was done in advance and refrigerated until time to bring it to the reception hall. Leave enough time to fill the holders and place the penguins which were made earlier in the day into position.

To create the ice float area: Since I am a "saver" I happened to have at hand the styrofoam packings that came from a recently purchased TV set (or radio or whatever leftover packings are handy around your house). These packings usually have wells in them to cushion your purchase for handling and shipping. If need be, you can even create your own quite simply. Purchase two 2″ thick styrofoam blocks. In one cut out, free form, two well openings. Place this block form with its wells, on top of the second purchased styrofoam block. Adhere one to the other with floral gum or stabilize with floral wooden toothpicks or orangewood sticks. Line the well openings with heavy duty foil, covering the remaining styrofoam float area with heavy foil too. When the dance or occasion is over, cleaning up is easier and the entire unit is reusable.

To create icebergs: To add background and realism to our winter North Pole scene, cover some different sizes of (A) styrofoam cones and/or cut up large (B) cliff like pieces of styrofoam with foil to simulate (A) icebergs. or (B) mountainous background. Stabilize the positioning of same, by placing into the styrofoam base (the simulated ice float) with bamboo sticks or orangewood sticks. Place these icebergs and cliffs strategically in the background leaving easy access to the relishes being served in the well openings.

Optional: igloo: If you wish to add an igloo to your Winterland setting do so by following these easy instructions for designing an artificial one, that can then be stored for another time, along with the rest of our Winter Wonderland scene. An igloo can be formed by cutting a large styrofoam ball to appropriate dome size or use a wiglet styrofoam hair stand; attach a halved paper styrofoam hot coffee cup horizontally as the igloo entrance. Stencil in with felt marking pen to simulate ice block forms of the Eskimo hut.

For snow or ice coverings: to simulate the white icy snow covering of the North Pole, prepare a Seven Minute cake frosting or use a commercial frosting box mix. Frost your ice float, mountain cliffs and icebergs. If preparing frosting is not your cup of tea, you can simply use ordinary canned vegetable shortening to ice your North Pole scene. Use chopped coconut or finely chopped or riced hard cooked egg whites to simulate the snow itself to cover the icebergs, mountains and float. Refrigerate to store and firm up.

To set scene: to serve: fill well openings with desired accompanying relish, mustard, applesauce, tartar sauce, ketchup, etc. Place your penguins (see this chapter, Feature Creatures: menagerie) in position about the ice float area. If you like, have one or two penguins fishing into the mustard or relish well. (See this chapter: Penguins with Igloo scene; Penguin Fisherman). Strategically place the accompanying dinner fare best suited for the well holders next to them convenient for all to go "dipping."

For a similar scene to set the mood for this same dance see chapter 6 and see what you can come up with when you're given (brown) chopped liver to incorporate into the same Winter Wonderland Scene for this dinner dance.

HOW AND WHERE TO GET IT . . . RECOMMENDED READING

Needless to say, there are loads of books on the market containing chapters on eggs and their preparation in many ways too numerous to list. There are also specialized cookbooks available on the subject of just eggs alone. I know of an entire book on how to use the leftover egg yolks and/or the whites of eggs in recipes and in other ways. As always, I urge you to run to your nearest library to scan their homemaking shelves not only for cookbooks but for "How To's." Keep your eye open for hints and ideas written in as many newspapers and magazines as there are cookbooks giving you the how-to on what to do with leftover eggs yolks or whatever. I always suggest the library first, unless you have an unlimited bookshelf to house the many cookbooks you are apt to collect over the years. The rule of thumb I exercise and recommend to my students is, if you've heard of a good cookbook, *don't* run out to buy it immediately. Go to your nearest library where, if it is that good, they would have already purchased it to share among your own townsfolk. Take it out and live with it for a while. Try the recipes. Write down the few you like; if you find there are too many to copy for they are that inviting *then* go out and buy the copy for your own collection.

Look to the free market for help and advice . . . you can never argue about price if it's free.

Write to New York State Dept. of Agriculture & Markets, Division of Markets, Albany, N.Y. 12226. They will be most happy to send you a set of egg recipes designed to be cut out for your own recipe files.

Write to Supt. of Documents, U.S. Government Printing Office Washington, D.C. 20402 for Consumer & marketing Service Home & Garden Bulletin #144 & #442 on eggs.

Write to: Ralston Purina Foods Box—Box 9162 Dept. FW, St. Paul, Minn. 55177 for "How the Shrewdest Shoppers Buy and Use Meat, Dairy Products and Eggs," pgs. 27–31; 25¢ for postage & handling.

6 THE COCKTAIL PARTY

Come on over . . . we're having a few friends drop in. It'll be fun; we're all just getting together for a few drinks. Your husband, that frustrated bartender, went and did it again, didn't he? Can't you just kill him? What to him means picking up a quart of scotch and a fifth of rye, a bottle or two of club and ginger ale soda, brings nightmares of things to come for you! Don't let it! Now is the time for you to learn to enjoy the party too! Get into the swing of things and use hubby's invitation for a little social get-to-gether as an opportunity to practice. A little get-to-gether now can lead to bigger and better parties later. Its not a sit-down, no silver or plate service, no expensive extra help . . . now is the time to practice a little bit, at a little time for a little intimate group of friends.

It's called a cocktail party! —where refreshing beverages and mixed cocktails make for a few hours of relaxation for everyone while partaking of little *nosherei* (many of which can be prepared and frozen in advance for use at anytime). Set it out self-service style as "less work for Mama" is our motto.

Under the all-encompassing heading of cocktail party can be found: candy, pretzels, potato chips and dips, alcoholic beverages as well as teetotaler punches, fish and meat spreads as well as cheese spreads, hors d'oeuvres, tiny tea sandwiches, large party sandwich loaves (served hot or cold) looking like cakes or spoke wheel rounds) etc. Since this book is on the presentation of food, I am not about to give you the actual breakdown of recipes on how to make sandwich fillers, canape toppers, cheese balls, liver patés, etc., for everyone must own at least one cookbook where recipes for such things are found. The bookstores and libraries are filled with books devoted to cocktail parties, freezer type hors d'oeuvres and otherwise, party canapes etc. Since the actual recipes can be found in such cookbooks we will restrict ourselves primarily to how one can present this party food with a bit of a creative flair. Remember our basic guidelines: It's not what you have, its what you do with it that makes it creative!

If you don't own a pretty crystal punchbowl, be different and serve your refreshing punch in a watermelon whale shell (see chapter 2); present that dip via the peacock pineapple (see chapter 1: our Pineapple Peacock Goes to a Cocktail Party). In this chapter we will learn that cocktail party *nosherei* need not be presented on expensive silver trays or priceless china plates. Present your hors d'oeuvres, vegetable and fruit bites, as if they were growing in their natural habitat, on trees and bushes (see topiary and vegetable trees, this chapter). For a festive holiday touch, present your hors d'oeuvres and nibbling sweets as Christmas trees and wreaths. We know liver spreads, fish, and cheeses can be presented in a bowl, but following the directions and illustrations in this chapter, these spreads can be displayed in the form of a shirt for a Father's Day celebration or as a cake for a birthday.

Try a liver or fish bonnet for Mother's Day, liver roosters and/or hens with baby chicks can be presented for a unique buffet service. These spreads can be presented looking like a pineapple but in actuality the aforementioned are really liver patés and cheeses. Cheeses can also be displayed in forms of balls, logs, hearts, ducks, etc. Cabbage heads as well as pineapples (see chapter 1) can be utilized to hold sterno cans to heat hors d'oeuvres hibachi style right at the table. The usual party loaf be it bread or meat loaf can be frosted and served hot or cold. The sandwich bread party loaf can look like anything from a floral box of long-stemmed roses to the flowerpot itself for buffet service or individual entrees. But whatever, it is *completely edible!*

All this under the guise of "Hints Helps and How-to's for a Hostess' Cocktail Party:" You may serve self-service style via a buffet table where everyone helps themselves or you may wish to serve it more personally by passing around the tray of canapes or hors d'oeuvres yourself. Whatever, do it creatively!

Personal Tray Service: If you are passing around a tray of simple canapes, present the service tray covered with a pretty white paper lace doily. In one corner, or, if preferred, center it on the tray, place a small foil-covered styrofoam piece. Attach the styrofoam to the tray with floral gum tape so it doesn't shift while being carried about. Fill styrofoam with a chicory-filled background. Pin in (use frill picks) just a few iced and opened vegetable carved flowers (see chapter 7). Mix in some black olives for contrast. ALTERNATIVE: if preferred, simply fill in corner or center of tray with a half of a green or red pepper shell basket and use as a pot to hold gathered vegetable flowers and celery stalks. If you like, use styrofoam base as setting to stabilize a feature creature from your menagerie (see chapter 5 on eggs). Set in center or corner of your serving tray, a chick, frog or penguin. This small addition to your serving tray as you pass it around adds such glamour and wins many compliments. Some guests might even like to partake of some of your vegetable flowers, so have some being chilled for refills. Leaving each styrofoam setting as is in place on each serving tray, merely slip into the kitchen for refilling of hors d'oeuvres and goodies, using the same tray to make the rounds just once more. After the second round (exception: if they are hot hors d'oeuvres you would want them to be passed while always hot) set down the tray and your guests will get the message the rest of the evening is self service. Just keep a watchful eye out for need to refill the tray at intervals during the party.

To serve a punch: Utilize the watermelon whale or the viking ship (shell) as a punch bowl (see chapter 2). More appropriate would be to use the watermelon wishing well as a holder for your shimmering cooling beverage; where better to draw liquid refreshment to quench one's thirst than from a wishing well. Your refreshing punch and the manner in which it is served will have it evaporating in no time at all, so have some on hand ready for refilling from time to time.

Party sandwiches As in all bread forms of sandwich presentation: one usually uses thin slices; use an electric knife for cutting and removing crusts on all sides of baked bread (use electric knife or serrated knife to cut finished loaves at table for more ease and efficiency); pinwheel breads must be rolled flatter with rolling pin before applying spreads; after slicing bread sections be sure to cover with a spread of a basic butter paste (herbs may be added for better taste if desired (see cookbook recipes); the butter spread paste is to seal up the bread's pores, so that the applied filling will not soak into the bread base thereby making it soggy.

While working on bread sections, remaining bread should be covered with a damp towel to keep moisture in and the bread fresher to prevent drying out. After fillings are added, wrap entire loaf in Saran wrap or damp towel and refrigerate overnight or at least several hours to firm up and bind together which will make for easier frosting and slicing. If preferred, sandwich loaves can be made in advance and frozen sans frosting and garnishing. Wrap securely and airtight in foil or freezer paper and store in plastic container. This precaution will prevent accidental crushing in an overloaded freezer compartment. If freezing loaves, be careful in choosing fillings, as egg yolks freeze well but whites do not; (there goes the egg salad mixture!). Mixtures containing loads of mayonnaise do not freeze well, so stick to your sliced or ground meats, fish or poultry mixtures, peanut butter, American and cream cheese, as they do well and hold up to two weeks in freezer. Allow for thawing (approximately 3–5 hours depending on size of loaves).

Now that we have laid some of the ground rules for successful and easy sandwich preparation, let's learn some of the variations for making these party winners.

Open faced sandwich: sometimes called a canapé, it is a bite-sized open sandwich wherein just one slice of bread is used as a base to hold the spread filling without the benefit of a cover. The variety of cut shapes and filling spreads used is not as important to the canapé itself as the attractive colors brought to the tray by their individual garnishings such as red radish roses, black caviar trims, colored cream cheese designs, green pickled fans, etc. The different bread cut bases add to the concept and color of the platter design by the intricate cookie cutter forms used to hold the spreads. Even this need not limit you for using this open faced method produces a square or rectangular small (white cheese spread) bread cut base and can produce mahjongg tiles (decorate with cake tube writers in corresponding colors) or use black olives and pimentos to reproduce the hearts and clubs of playing cards the next time the ladies join you for bridge.

Fold-up sandwich canape: a square of thin sandwich bread sans crusts and flattened with rolling pin which is then covered with desired butter paste and filling spread. Fold over 2 opposite corners to meet at center. Press to hold and secure if desired with frill pick or olive slice or pickle garnish.

Cornucopia: same as above except bring two opposite corners together to form cone shape or cornucopia form. Press to seal to hold cornucopia design and fill in open area with sprig of parsley or watercress, etc., peeking through cornucopia mouth.

Roll up: same procedure for bread as above. Flatten out completely with stockinged rolling pin. Spread butter base and filling. Roll up jelly roll fashion like a log. If roll is to be served hot, place roll seam side down on baking tin to heat through.

Graduation party service: using roll-ups: (A) prepare a cold rolled hors d'oeuvres, place seam side down on tray and decorate with pimento strip or use cake writing gel tube thus creating the graduate's *diploma.* To create *graduation hat:* (B) cut out 2″ dark bread (pumpernickel) rounds with cookie cutter. Top with filling. Cut dark 3″ squares of bread for mortarboard top of graduation hat. Place atop 2″ rounds and decorate with carrot or pimento tassel. Roll-ups remind us of two associated party sandwich services: the pinwheel and the rollatinis which in turn remind me of my favorite fish type roll-up, all of which will follow.

Pinwheel: With electric knife trim off all crusts from an unsliced sandwich bread. Cut loaf into ¼″ slices horizontally or have baker do this. Flatten with rolling pin. Butter side facing up on each slice and place filling spread on top. (Have you covered the remaining slices of bread while you're working on this one to keep them from drying out as outlined in overall directions?) Roll, wrap, refrigerate slice into ½″ slices for serving. Will look like a pinwheel or snail design.

Filled variation of pinwheel: optional but nice: I consider this a must, not an option but you're the boss in your own kitchen so do as you like. Here's the how-to for it: Along the narrow end of the bread slice I line up 4–5 pitted black olives, or green pimento filled olives, or cocktail onions or whatever complements my filling for taste to bring color contrast, and added interest to my pinwheel. Roll up, starting at this filled narrow end, jelly roll style. Wrap in damp towels and chill for several hours before slicing into ½″ crosswise cuts for finger lifting service.

Polka dot variation of pinwheel: In place of filling used at narrow end, this time lay at equidistant lengths, narrow strips of green or red pepper or scallion green strips all along the length of the filled bread slice. Roll up, wrap, chill and then cut as before for a polka dot pinwheel sandwich affect.

Customize your creations: Blend to customize your family's tastes with that of your imagination. Make up some of your own variations for spreads using different substitutes for the rolled centers and spreads; e.g., try chicken spread filling with 6–7 whole water chestnuts on narrow side for rolling; try deviled ham spread with a pineapple spear at narrow end for roll-up; work red caviar into the butter base as the filling spread and place a 1″ molded cut block strip of cream cheese on narrow end for rolling. Try the polka dot method with a cream cheese spread and vertical ¼″ line spreads of black caviar to roll for pinwheel affect.

Children's customized creations: Make some goodies the next time your little girl is having a birthday party. The little ones love to be treated like grownup ladies with a sampling of pinwheel sandwiches served just like at Mommy's tea parties. Make the little ones, who like to play grownup, pinwheel sandwiches topped with peanut butter and jelly. Place within at narrow end before rolling, similar blocks of 1" strip of cream cheese. Try some of these other variations for them: Egg salad rolled with sausage link. Try chicken spread with a good juicy pickle-centered pinwheel. Chill and slice and watch how fast the young ones will devour them. Don't wait for an occasion. If she or he is a poor eater try it for lunch sometime for just a party for two, you and yours.

Rollatinis: is a pinwheel sandwich made without using bread at all as a base. E.g.: use a slice of meat such as ham or turkey as the base *in place* of bread; spread meat with filling as you would have the bread base. No need for butter paste except to add for flavor. For decorative affect proceed as before, using olives on narrow end or pickle or try where apropos, a pineapple spear or a thin block chunk of cheddar cheese or Swiss or whatever. Try if you like the combo of spreading a slice of turkey or chicken roll with Russian or French dressing; place a cooked asparagus stalk within meat at narrow end and roll; chill well before cutting. Slice and serve as is, a rollatinis, or place on party round bread (pumpernickel goes well with this one) thus combining a bit from both new concepts you've just learned. A fish that lends itself well to becoming the seafaring version of a rollatinis would be to use slices of smoked salmon (lox) cut thin but preferably cut wide, spread with softened cream cheese or chives and cream cheese combo. Place pickled cocktail onions or pitted black or green pimento-filled olives along narrow end. Roll in wax or foil paper. Refrigerate several hours, preferably overnight to thoroughly chill before slicing. This one is particularly good when served on black bread party rounds for contrast of color as well as taste. If preferred try it on a saltine.

A take-off on this concept, getting away from bread for the moment but still sticking to suggestions for cocktail service, would be to roll firm cream cheese around a pitted olive, macadamia nut or pineapple chunk for *cold service.* For *hot service,* try hiding a pickle chunk or pineapple chunk or waterchestnut inside an hors d'oeuvre bite-size meatball. To make it into the so called Porcupine, merely push pignola nuts (pine nuts) into the meatball at angles to resemble porcupine. A cousin to this form would be referred to as the *Wrap-Up or Wrap-Around* so called because you literally wrap one edible food around another. The well known Beef Wellington is in essence a wrap-up since the beef rump is wrapped in a breadlike crust and served as one. The commonly known and most often eaten hors d'oeuvre, a hot dog covered with a bread dough, called a pig in a blanket, would be to the pinwheel breads as Rumaki, a chicken liver wrapped about in a bacon slice would be to a rollatini. Rumaki is a delicacy served often in Chinese restaurants. The kosher version of same for Jewish delicatessen might well be a pineapple spear wrapped in pastrami, heated and served. Either one goes well with a hibachi type serving at a cocktail party, using the cabbage sterno method (to follow) or the pineapple hibachi as described in chapter 1: The Pineapple Pu Pu Platter. To prepare *Cabbage Hibachi:* simply follow concept of the Pineapple Pu Pu Platter stabilizing the (core) base of a large head of savoy curly leaf cabbage, cutting away (top) center well to allow for the fittings of a sterno fuel can. Pull outside leaves away from firm head as graceful border surrounding cabbage. Use the firm cabbage comprising head as a pincushion to stick in bamboo skewered hors d'oeuvre for heating over the sterno. A nice one to serve as a prelude for an intimate dinner for two. Using iceberg lettuce same manner, cavity can be filled with dip and serve similar purpose as pin cushion. Back to the breads now. . . .

Bread wells: cut whole bread into thick 1" lengthwise slices. With 2" cookie cutter, cut and remove rounds from bread slice. From out of each round snip out (use scissors) center well leaving ¼–½" floor base. Seal inside walls and base of bread well by "painting" with butter base. Fill with desired filling, mounding high in top. Garnish and serve as raised open-faced hors d'oeuvres in place of, or in conjunction with, some of the usual flat open faced type canapés. The addition of these bread wells will lend a unique overall presentation to your tray when combined with other assorted tea sandwiches, adding further color, variety, height and dimension to your selection of cocktail nosherei.

Finger breads: Basically a finger sandwich is 2 slices of bread held together with a filling, cut and served in 1″ × 3″ strip lengths. They are most easy to prepare by the hostess and easy to pick up and handle by the guest. Finger breads are a small scaled down version of the more elaborate ribbon sandwich.

Ribbon sandwich bread: is simply a take-off on the finger bread. The former, consisting of longer horizontally sliced lengths that are stacked higher, thereby accommodating more assorted fillings. A ribbon party loaf is made from a whole bread, usually a Pullman size loaf. A Pullman loaf is a 2-lb. white bread, measuring 16″ × 4″ × 4″. By placing a special order with your local bakery (giving him a few days' notice in advance) not only can a Pullman be baked for you, but for a few pennies more can be baked in whatever colors you choose. Pink, yellow and pastel green are favorites. Alternate and layer the colored cut ribbon bread slices with that of the white bread slices. When cut into sandwich portions for guests, it is most attractive, bringing lots of eye appeal and color to your platter. A regular sized white (or colored) sandwich bread loaf can be prepared for you by your local bakery in similar manner. This regular sandwich bread usually weighs 1 lb. measuring 11″ × 5″ × 5″. A store bought commercially produced one, called a stuffing bread, an unsliced whole white bread can be similarly used. The size of thickness and the number of slices cut, plus the variety and amount of fillings used between the slices will determine the size of the finished ribbon loaf evolved for the occasion. If left with an unused ribbon of bread, since for easier handling it is best not to stack the loaf too high, the white or colored bread can be used to make pinwheels rounds or open faced canapes or croutons for soups and salads.

Cut the bread horizontally lengthwise into 4–6 slices, depending on how thin you wish each of the ribbons to be in order to accommodate the amount and choice of fillings. Use the butter paste to seal both sides, the top and bottom of each ribbon bread slice. This will prevent the fillings from saturating the breads. Fill; refrigerate overnight wrapped in damp towel or saran wrap to prevent the permeating of other odors, and to keep the bread moist while simultaneously binding one slice to the other to form a compact loaf shape. Cut the ribbon loaf vertically into portions giving you a technicolored filled ribbon affect to each slice. You might at this point prefer to

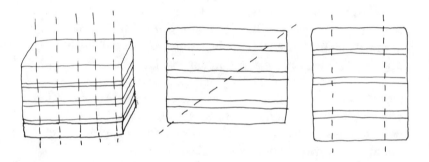

cut each sandwich into smaller (triangular) halves or into finger strips to serve with other assorted canapes on a tray. To provide a sweet repast as a dessert for a tea, prepare a variation of a ribbon bread using a commercially sold presliced thin date-nut bread. Fill with colored cream cheeses (use food dye) or assorted spreadable cheeses. Stack only 3–4 slices together. Wrap each stack separately to refrigerate. Do *not* frost! Cut vertically as for ribbon loaf. Cut different shapes from each ribbon slice. The colorful cheese spreads contrast against the dark bread is a tempting delight for both the eyes as well as the appetite.

Party sandwich loaves: is a take-off on the ribbon breads. The former is presented as a whole loaf, frosted and decorated to be cut into its ribbon sliced portions at the table. Purchase an unsliced white and/or whole wheat (for change of pace and color) combination at your local bakery. The baker will usually cut them for you free of charge into lengthwise strips. If you prefer to do it yourself, first mark out the width sections with toothpicks. Use the picks as a guide when slicing with an electric knife. Remove all crusts from bread also. By ordering some colored loaves at the same time and stacking and filling the ribbon slices alternately, one pink, one white and/or brown (whole wheat) and one yellow, the yield can thereby be tripled. You can prepare three party loaves for immediate use or freeze the leftover ribbons for another time. If you choose, prepare and fill one party loaf and use the remaining colored ribbon slices to make trays of pinwheel filled rounds or open canapes for tray passing service, thereby making a little of the same look like a lot of many (varieties). The party loaf can be prepared in advance if you like and be frozen for a period of up to two weeks. A party sandwich loaf will yield about 14–16 ¾"–1" slices.

Serve all three loaves if a crowd is expected as they can all be frosted, decorated and garnished to look different. E.g., see: Floral Box of Roses, Sailboats, Treasure Chest, etc., in this chapter. Slice breads, butter both sides of bread slices, top and bottom thus locking out the moisture from the fillings. To fill, here's a *helpful hint:* If you're going to cover or decorate with a cream cheese frosting later, keep aside some cheese. Place in pastry canvas decorating bag and *after* buttering but *before* adding the filling mixtures, pipe a border of cream cheese all along the top edges of those sliced bread ribbons. With this piping now in place, fill in with your salad mixtures. I promise there will be none of the usual oozing or running of the salad mix down the sides of the loaf. Place one bread ribbon slice upon the other as you fill with the salad. Wrap in dampened towel or Saran wrap and refrigerate overnight. Frost the next day; decorate and garnish as you wish. Basically this is a cold sandwich type loaf. To frost a 16″ loaf you will need three 8-oz. packages of cream cheese as a base for mix. We will review hot sandwich loaves as we go further into this chapter. If you wish, you may write a message on a cold party loaf for it surely looks as pretty as a birthday cake.

Floral box of roses . . . sandwich loaf style . . . completely edible!
If you really want to impress your kinfolk, the next time it is a "bring something get-to-gether" for the cousin's club, bring your hostess a dozen of her favorite roses, flowers that are completely edible and won't deplete your weekly budget money of $15–$20. March down to your nearest floral shop to purchase a long white floral box. Flower shops use these to deliver fresh long stemmed roses to their customers. Share this idea with his wife and perhaps she'll give you the box gratis. White floral boxes come in 25″ × 5″, 30″ × 5″ or 34″ × 5″, depending on the roses chosen and the length of stems. Since Pullman loaves are 16″ × 4″ or regular loaves are 11″ × 5″, allowing for crust removals, etc., with a little mathematics (you don't even need the "new math" for this one or I'd never have figured it out!), we know we can put the loaves together to fit nicely into whichever size box you choose. When having to combine 2 loaves to look like one merely bind together with some cream cheese frosting mix. Saran-wrap and under refrigeration it will set and bind together; treat as one loaf when frosting. Prepare your pretty sandwich ribbon loaf, double checking the allowed height you can build up to with fillings included. Be sure the finished loaf will stand 1½″ lower than the top of the floral box for you must allow room for piping on the roses. You are sure to be left with extra slices when making this one so leave some filling to make a few canapes or ribbon sandwiches to pass around on a tray. Wrap and refrigerate overnight. Frost with cream cheese the next day. Keep the cheese coating simple, smooth and as flat as possible. With a heavy consistency of red (yellow or pink) food dyed cream cheese, pipe out 12 colored

roses onto the smooth top surface of the party loaf through a "rose" tipped tube on a canvas pastry bag. With plain round pastry tube tip, pipe out the roses' green stems. Use a "leaf" tube tip to add in the green leaves and gel writing tube for fern-like effect if desired. Your hostess will really be surprised and pleased to learn that this is one dozen roses she and her guests can really enjoy—eating!

Alternatives: If your forte is not pastry bag decorating and you cannot wield that bag like a pro, try these other alternatives: use flat Italian parsley leaves and stems for the greens of your rose flowers or use fresh dill leaves; use scallion greens or, if you prefer, the American curly parsley leaves and stems. Use fresh vegetable cut radish roses (see chapter 7) as the blossom head of your roses. For a change of motif, fill in the sandwich loaf with assorted cut vegetable flowers to form a lovely bouquet of wild grown flowers tied up with a nice big red pimento ribbon.

For a child's party: If our birthday celebrant is a young child, this same concept can be worked out with a ribbon loaf of jelly and cream cheese or peanut butter. Frost in cream cheese with flowers made from marshmallows or gumdrops; use spearmint candy gum leaves for greenery; green gel writing tubes for green stems.

Optional: red bow: for latter trim up in red licorice shoe string bow; for the former party loaf, use a pimento cut bow at base of flowers.

To deliver flowers: Just prior to traveling time, cut and foil wrap heavy cardboard to fit bottom of floral box. This is most impor-tant for extra carrying strength and to act as cutting board later. Place sandwich loaf on top of foil wrapped cardboard and gently place onto center of flattened out floral box container base. Now fold up sides of box. This method is easier than trying to lower a long sandwich loaf into a high standing pre-folded box container. With box cover in flattened open position, glue on pretty ribbon across top. Attach suitable card to bow.

Fold; cover bottom box container. Transport with care so as not to jostle frosted loaf against sides of container.

Which brings to mind *FLOWER POT CONTAINERS:* These adorable flower pot sandwich loaves can be made in large sizes as edible centerpieces for a buffet party table or can be scaled down as miniatures to serve individually and act as dinner appointments for a seating plan. The concept for preparing either one is to cut 3–4 round slices of bread in graduating ½" sizes. E.g., 2½", 3", 3½" cut rounds. Butter the bread slices on both sides. Stack the bread slices using the *smallest* in size as the base. As you build up, fill with spread or salad. The largest slice

will then be the top of the flower pot. Frost the pot in red "clay" cream cheese coating, using green frosting as base for the grass on the top bread round. Cover with chopped parsley.

Flowers: use cut vegetable flowers on bamboo skewers and frill picks as blossoming flowers. *LEAVES:* Fill in with celery stalks with leaves attached for fullness; use green pepper cuts as leaves at stem base. If done in smaller scale version, frost as per directions and then pipe onto the frosted clay pot "A PLANT FOR TONI." Each guest need only look for her edible flower plant to know where she is to be seated. The larger flower pots look most attractive when placed at both ends of a buffet table. Its even nicer to watch your guests' reaction when they realize not only do your flowers smell good but they taste delicious too. Share your bountiful harvest with them by cutting them a piece right there at your garden table.

For a sweet flower planting for a child's birthday: To make really dainty flower pot sandwiches, use date-nut-loaf bread rounds. Fill with whipped cream which has been firmed up with very well drained crushed pineapple. Cover top layer with green cocoanut grass. *CANDY FLOWERS:* Pre-hole and push into top bread round short licorice stems with marshmallow or gum drop candy blossom tops. Use spearmint leaves at base of stem. An even bigger hit with the small fry is to find their garden plant actually grows a large Sugar Daddy Lollypop amidst licorice leaves or candy canes which they may pick "to harvest" and bring home for "preserving" for another time.

TREASURE CHEST SANDWICH LOAF: Try this party loaf variation as an exciting entree following an exhausting scavenger hunt party. Use a store purchased regular sized uncut loaf of stuffing bread. Following drawing carefully, cut as illustrated.

Section 1. Cut and remove top crust in tact. This will be the cover of your pirate's chest. Wrap in damp towel and set aside under refrigeration. Remove all remaining crusts.

Section 2. Second slice is cut very thick. As in illustration, remove shallow well cavity (shadowed area) in this slice to later hold the precious stones (onions, tomatoes, olives, etc.) of the pirate's bounty.

Sections 3. & 4. The remainder of the loaf can then be cut in 1 or 2 slices as per thickness and number of fillings desired. Butter all filling sides. Fill in between slices leaving the top section (#2 well cavity) unfilled. Wrap and refrigerate as usual. *Frost* cavity depth of first bread layer (#2) as well as the entire outsides of the chest loaf.

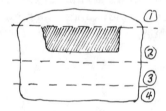

Precious stones: Fill inside well cavity with well drained and patted dry "precious stones." E.g., EMERALDS: green olives; BLOODSTONES: pimento-filled olives; ONYXES: black olives; PEARLS: cocktail onions; TOPAZ STONES: pickled (tiny) yellow onions, etc.

Optional: with colored frosting simulate wood and carvings on treasure chest to more closely resemble a pirate's trunk. *COVER:* frost *only* the underside of the removed crust top (#1) Place at angle onto frosted border edge on long side of treasure chest. To stabilize cover in this raised angled position hold up with club frill picks, celery stalks (rounded side up) or crinkled ½" cut carrot sticks on short side as per illustration.

(Use hidden pick method) Use as edible table conversation centerpiece. *To serve:* Remove top crust cover and slice ribbon sandwich loaf vertically through jeweled top (use electric knife whose blade has been wet or buttered for easier slicing at the table). Each guest may "stake out" his fair share of the "loot" so divide up the chest and the precious stones within and give each "matey" that portion of his claim!

Simplified quickie version of treasure chest: To prepare: use uncut whole store-purchased loaf of stuffing bread. As in preceding directions for treasure chest, remove top crust; set aside, etc. Remove all crust trims from bread. Cut out rectangular area from inside the bread being sure to leave a 1" base on

bottom (See diagram.) Fill this area with desired filling up to ½"
from top of well cavity. Frost treasure chest on all exposed
bread areas. Cover filling with "precious stones" mounding
over well cavity area as in previous directions. Frost underside
of chest cover and continue as per previous instructions. Use
buttered electric knife to cut more easily at table.

THE RAILROAD SPECIAL

Whether it be a retirement party for a union official or railroad buff or a luncheon celebration for your little boy's birthday, this variation of a sandwich party loaf draws pleasure-
seeking passengers every time it rolls 'round the bend!

To prepare train caravan: From your local bakery, order a Pullman loaf or pick up 2 unsliced regular loaves of stuffing bread.
From the grocery shelf, pick up a *can* of *round* Date-nut loaf
bread or have baker prepare bread in round loaf form. They
have such molds.

Car trains: Cut the Pullman loaf in half vertically giving you 2
whole breads or use the purchased individual loaves of stuffing
bread. *RAILROAD TRACKS:* Use electric knife to trim off all
bread crusts. Crust should be cut in at least ¼–½" thickness. Set
aside to be cut again later into wide strips. These long strips will
be the railroad tracks upon which the train will be set. Prepare
a long serving tray by covering with foil. Set down (use cream
cheese frost) your wide cut bread crust tracks, browned side up.
You will be setting each of your train cars atop these bread crust
tracks. Allow for some of the track to be exposed on both sides
of train cars. see illustration.

Locomotive: To prepare rounded locomotive section of train,
slice round date-nut bread horizontally as for sandwich loaf.
However, date-nut bread has no crust to remove. Prepare and
frost as per directions for loaf bread. Place locomotive's base on

bread crust track in front (#1 position of cavalcade of cars) *WHEELS:* place into frosting on both sides of car appropriately positioned. Use round crackers as wheels or cut out spoke design to make wheel from a slice of a beet or turnip as outlined in chapter 1 on Flower Basket wheels.

Coupling: Use the narrow celery branch stalk end pieces, rounded side up as the couplings found between connecting railroad cars, one to the other. *HEADLIGHT:* On front of locomotive push on a 1″ round thick slice of white radish as headlight of train.

Cow catcher: The grating on the front end of a locomotive is called a cow catcher. To simulate same on our edible locomotive, prepare a rounded cut section of a green pepper. Cut out vertical gratings like the teeth of a comb. Push into cream cheese frosting in the front of the lower part of the locomotive. With egg yolk cream paste or cake writing tube gel, pipe on the conducting engineer's window.

Coal car: The second and middle car of our train procession is to be prepared following the directions for the aforementioned Treasure Chest sandwich loaf but omit the chest cover. Place a celery coupling in back of coal car. Place onto track behind locomotive. Push front of coal car into celery coupling already in position on the back of the engine car. Place wheels on coal car as previously done on locomotive. *COAL:* Fill entire recessed top (1″ well cavity area) of sandwich loaf with small pitted black olives or fill in with large black olives that have been coarsely chopped to represent coal chunks.

Caboose: Prepare as for regular sandwich loaf with filling. Following previous directions, soften cream cheese to prepare for frosting the party bread. Add red food dye to the softened cream cheese mix. Blend well and frost caboose. The caboose of a train, usually red, is the last car where the railroad workers are bedded down and take their meals. Pipe on windows as per usual method.

Caboose smoke stack: Place a one inch round by two inch high chunk of carrot on top of caboose as its smoke stack chimney. Before placement of same, whittle out part of the carrot core within (use the bud eye removing end on a potato peeler.) Stuff carrot cavity with small sprig of celery leaf top to simulate the smoke belching from the chimney atop the caboose.

To set the scene: for a birthday: with colorful cake writing tube gel (or use egg yolk paste cream through fine hole tip of a pastry bag) pipe out on the side of the locomotive car: "DOUG'S BIRTHDAY SPECIAL" or simply "BIRTHDAY SPECIAL." Place green coconut grass along route of tracks. If script writing on locomotive side is kept in simple form: e.g., "Birthday Special," use a road marked signpost to signify name and age of child. "DOUGLASTOWN—12" (mi.) *SIGNPOST:* to make signpost for train route, simply stand a dowel stick with shortened cocktail fork ends depicting town name on it. Secure with a drop of floral gum tape. Place some purchased toy cows or horses about as if grazing in the nearby field. *Alternative:* if preferred, place about some of the Easter purchased friendly feathered chicks we met in chapter 5 on eggs: see Cornucopia Basket Presentation of Eggs.

To set the scene: for retirement party theme: For a retirement party prepare edible centerpiece as above. Change written message on side of locomotive to read "STEVE'S EASY LIFE SPECIAL." If the couple plan to retire to Florida or wherever, place a railroad marked signpost nearby that reads: "FLORIDA —42" (number of years with the railroad company). It would be nice if couple were leaving for Florida to welcome them along the route by planting one or two authentic Florida palm trees.

To make palm trees: Use long thin cucumber or zucchini as the tree trunk. With paring knife, cut skin of the vegetable to give usual ring layer look found on the trunk of a palm tree. See

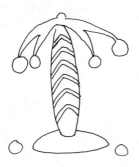

illustration. Cut a green pepper into umbrella leaf affect as per diagram. Place on top of the stabilized sliced palm tree trunk using hidden pick method. Using same method, attach small cluster of black or red grapes or use brown chocolate covered peanut M & M's (for shape) to represent coconuts. Place some on grass adjacent to tree as if the coconuts had just dropped off. To stand palm tree in vertical position, attach to tray with heavy frosting mix or push into small end stabilized cut slice of cantaloupe, rind side up. (Note: since vegetable is edible we do not use same method of stabilizing as previously done for signpost using the floral gum tape.) *To serve:* slice as previously recommended for sandwich loaves. A big treat for anyone who works for, travels on or just loves the rails.

CIRCUS TRAIN SPECIAL

As we have created the train for a child's birthday party, we can easily customize it to delight another child's whim by changing it to a circus theme.

Following concept as outlined previously, prepare a loaf bread made of peanut butter and jelly. For the wheels of train use some large cookies or 1″ thick cut pinwheel sandwiches. Place an animal cracker of a lion, tiger or elephant inside each window compartment of your train car's traveling circus express. Use egg yolk pastry cream tube method to outline the windows of each car or if preferred licorice swizzle sticks can also do the job. Push in end tips of black shoe string licorice to simulate the slightly concave stand out bars of the caged windows. Onto the outside of the train loaves, use cake writing gel to spell out "DONNELLY'S ANIMAL CIRCUS EXPRESS."

ANIMAL ZOO

With a slight change from up our kitchen magician's sleeve, what was a circus train can easily become a small zoo. If preferred, make just one large loaf bread and customize it to look

like an animal zoo cage following premise above sans wheels. Fill in accordingly with licorice shoe string bars, etc. On top of cage front, write in "LARRY THE LION . . . 10 YEARS OLD"; on bottom fill in "NATURAL HABITAT: ALLEN AVE" or whatever is suitable. A big hit with animal lovers of all ages.

A FIRE TRUCK PARTY LOAF

With some of the concepts used for creating our trains and baby blocks (to follow) we can just as easily please some of the bigger boys with this one. Follow diagram to create a fire truck sandwich loaf as above. Keep it simple and inexpensive by using peanut butter and jelly spreads. As depicted in diagram stack the number of ribbon layers accordingly and cut proportionately to different sizes. Frost sections together with cream cheese frosting. Refrigerate to solidify binding. Frost entire outside of loaf with a red tinted cream cheese frosting. Use one small pinwheel sandwich roll (uncut) as holder for the fire fighting hose reel. Roll black shoe string licorice around same to simulate truck's water hose. Place on top of sandwich loaf. Use the wider more stable swizzle stick type of black licorice to create sides the fire ladder, shoestring to create steps of same. Press into side of truck in appropriate position. Use marshmallow for headlights and square or oblong (plain) cookies as fire truck windows. Label door side of truck . . . "F.D. ENGINE CO. 9" (or whatever age of birthday child). Write in birthday celebrant's name under same. . . . "STEVEN'S CITY, N.J." or "DOUGLASTOWN, N.Y." The kids really love to play firefighter with this yummy equipment to work with.

As you can easily see with these concepts in mind, you can decorate many other sandwich loaves tailored to create a whole trucking fleet most little boys love to play with. For the California set on the West Coast, customize it to create your own familiar trolley car using the shoe string black licorice for outline details and the more stable swizzle stick of black licorice as the connecting electrical conductor atop the car.

BABY BLOCK PARTY LOAVES

As pretty as it is edible is this unique theme setter for a baby's birthday party, a shower for an expectant mother or a christening. These cubed baby blocks are made from several Pullman sized breads, prepared, filled and presented as smaller cubed individual party sandwich loaves.

Using a Pullman loaf (get colored breads to intermix to make several loaves) prepare as for sandwich ribbon loaves. Cut each Pullman loaf horizontally in half thus giving you a 2″ high bread loaf to work with. Slice each one of these in half again lengthwise for filling. The ¾–1″ of salad filling will then bring up the finished height of the party loaf. Cut loaf vertically into 3″ cube sections thus giving you five approximate 3″ × 3″ finished baby blocks. Wrap individually to refrigerate and firm up. *TO FROST:* Apply a smooth simple coat of white frosting or a lightly tinted yellow (wood coloring) frosting or use light colored yellow cheese spread to coat each toy block. Pipe on a large colored letter on only one side of each cube if table is to be set against the wall. If table is to be set in center of room for traffic pattern, apply letter to both opposite sides of each block cube. Try to use different colors for lettering blocks. Each toy block will then spell out a colorful letter of the birthday child's name or for a shower, "Welcome Baby". If name or message is particularly long capsulize, as depicted in diagram, by

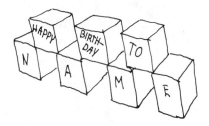

writing Happy on one cube and Birthday on another, etc. Some extra coated but *un*lettered blocks will be needed to act as supports to hold up the colorful lettered block cubes thus lifting it up to a higher plane.

Use wax paper or foil, custom fitted to the bases of the lettered blocks on the second level of the centerpiece. This is done so each cube block sandwich section can be easily separated when it is time to serve your gathered guests.

For baby shower party, add some rattles or umbrellas from 5 & 10¢ store to the centerpiece to enhance the mood setting. (The new rattles can be given to the newborn babe or to mother as party favor.) Set up as edible centerpiece for buffet table. If necessary, decorate a pretty carton (use yellow or white, pink or blue paper) to place the long rectangular sized serving tray upon, thus lifting and displaying the set of (edible) sandwich blocks higher than the other party fare goodies on the buffet table.

Pretty and exciting enough to give the girls ideas about making more babies instead of sandwich loaves! (Tongue in cheek on that one for me girls!)

SANDWICH SAILBOAT SETTING

For a nautical approach as a centerpiece theme, be it for a boating enthusiast or a little boy's birthday luncheon, prepare a sandwich loaf sailboat (or two) for a buffet table. If preferred, prepare a smaller scaled down version of same to serve as individual edible entrees that will act as the same time, as place setters at the birthday table.

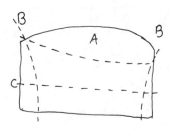

For a buffet table: Purchase two 1 lb. individual regular loaves of unsliced breads for sandwich making. If you wish to have a longer sloop boat use a Pullman bread and cut proportionately. Remove top crust of bread, cutting at angle as shown (A) in illustration. As per illustration, cut off at angles depicted, the front and back of each loaf to more closely resemble the bow and stern angle of a boat (B). Remove all other remaining crusts of bread and set aside. Depending on height of boat desired and number of fillings used, cut bread into horizontal ribbons (C) for filling.

Proceed to prepare; fill and refrigerate to wrap as per usual instructions for making a party loaf. *TO FROST:* Frost top of deck with softened white cream cheese (or whatever frosting used). Use jarred Cheez Whiz spread or tint remaining frosting cream cheese spread with yellow food dye. Frost sandwich loaf-boat with the yellow cheese coating. Use a frosting comb (available in gourmet or culinary departments, a frosting comb is a metal triangular shaped sawtoothed comb-like implement) to create the wooden plank effect of boat.

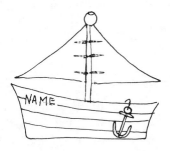

Sails: Cut previously removed and set aside bread crusts into sails for boat. OPTIONAL: use American cheese slices for smaller version of sail if preferred. Use edible celery stalk as mast. Attach bread sails to celery mast with floral toothpicks (hidden toothpick method as per diagram.) Use olive to top mast head. *ANCHOR:* Use remaining small piece of bread crust to cut out simulated anchor for boat. Attach as shown leaving anchor's browned crust side facing up. Pipe on (use writing tube gel or egg yolk paste through hole tip on canvas bag) the boat's destination or the guest of honor's name. Place this edible centerpiece on chicory base ocean on tray. If necessary, place tray on blue or green (ocean color) carton box in order to raise the entire centerpiece higher than the rest of the table thereby making it a focal point of interest (using same concept as styrofoam raised centerpiece in this case raising up an *entire tray* of goodies).

To prepare individual smaller scaled boats: Purchase as many regular loaves of bread as necessary to individually feed the

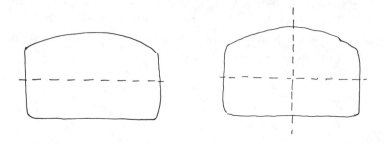

number of children invited to the birthday luncheon party. To scale down to size, keep in mind each loaf will yield 2 large sized sailboats (diagram) or 4 smaller boats (diagram) depending upon age group of youngsters and their respective appetites. Cut each loaf horizontally in half giving you 2 hull boat sections to work with. (Cut vertically in half again to yield 4 boat hulls from the one loaf) Following illustration proceed exactly as described previously to cut properly, using cuts A, B and C.

Use bread crust A or use American cheese slices as sails. Use olive to top mast head. Cut and attach anchor over side of boat. Pipe on side of each boat, the (guest) child's name for his or her sailboat. E.g., "Steve's Sloop" or "Diane's Dinghy" or "Doug's Dreamboat," etc. Set on individual plates with lettuce greens as ocean. (I find children prefer lettuce to the sharper and bitter tasting chicory leaf).

The small-fry love finding their seats at the birthday table in this fashion and your party celebration is headed for some smooth sailing!

HOT & COLD FROSTS FOR LOAVES

Loaves, as you know, can be served hot *or* cold. The hot loaf most of us are familiar with is the ordinary ground beef version, commonly called a meatloaf. Sometimes in the past, you may have gone so far as to partially edge it with a "frosting," not realizing it is so called. You may have "planked" your loaf with some whipped potatoes. To plank, in the culinary vernacular means to serve food hot on a board or sizzling hot dish platter planked or edged with a fancy encompassing border of pastry tubed whipped potatoes (or vegetables). Serving a hot loaf is merely taking a loaf form of food, such as chopped or ground meat (beef and pork) loaf or ground ham loaf or even a sandwich filled loaf and "frosting" it with a mixture of such ingredients to complement its taste, to be baked completely covered in its frosting until heated through and then to be served immediately for cutting at the table. E.g., to complement a ground ham loaf frost with a whipped *sweet* potato or yam mixture such as the blending of the potatoes, mashed or pureed, with melted butter, orange peel, nutmeg, salt, pepper and hot milk to make it more spreadable. The meat loaf may be similarly frosted with a whipped together mix of white potatoes, milk and/or cream etc. Perhaps you'd like to try this very nice light meringue frost (direct from the Hellman Kitchen as found in a magazine advertisement): for a 1½ lb. chopped meatloaf which will serve 6, beat 3 egg whites with a ½ teas. cream of tartar until soft peaks form; gently fold in ½ c. of mayonnaise. Remove meatloaf from oven after baking 30 minutes. Place loaf onto heat resistant platter. Frost and return to oven and bake until brown, approximately 20 minutes. Use this very same hot frosting spread on a sandwich filled ribbon loaf but bake it in a hot 450° oven for only ten minutes or until browned.

A variation of a slightly different hot meringue frosting follows: beat 5 egg whites until frothy; add ½ teas. salt. Beat until stiff but not dry; gently *fold* in ½ c. sour cream until well blended. Frost top and sides of loaf and bake in a 350° oven for approximately ten minutes or until browned.

A much simpler and quicker hot frosting for a sandwich or a meat loaf is to mix together to blend: 3 cups grated American cheese with a little more than ¼ c. milk. For a sharper flavor, add ½ teas. prepared mustard. Coat loaf with this frosting and return to oven for only enough time as to soften the cheese which should be approximately 1–2 minutes. *HELPFUL HINT:* If using on sandwich party loaf, it is suggested that the outside top and sides of the loaf be first brushed with melted butter. Place on heat resistant serving tray and pop into oven to heat through and be toasted lightly. You will find it much easier to spread a cheese frosting onto a preheated buttered sandwich loaf. After removing from oven, garnish with olives, cherry tomatoes, etc., for decorative designed presentation to table. This is just a sampling of hot frostings one can use on a sandwich loaf or any other type loaf for that matter. There are many more one can find to experiment with through cookbooks, magazines, newspapers and of course through friends who have tried and tested some good ones that they might like to share with you. Give them a start on some of these *COLD FROSTINGS* YOU MIGHT LIKE TO SHARE WITH THEM: as you can readily see from my frequent references, I prefer working with a cream cheese frosting. (1.) I happen to like cream cheese (with lox, date-nut bread, in gelatin desserts, in pies and to frost cakes). (2.) Because it comes commercially prepared in block and whipped form it is as easy as going shopping to prepare it. Incidentally, there is even a substitute cream cheese type spread now on the market for those watching their diets. (3.) There is not too much you can do to ruin cream cheese and much you can do to improve it. By adding coloring (food vegetable dye), spices, seasonings or other additives such as chives, pimento, etc. or whatever, you are given much lattitude in color variations, taste and texture to experiment with to create your own frosting patterns, designs and motifs.

Some general *HELPFUL HINTS:* In handling cream cheese frosting, whether it be for sandwich loafs or cake, always coat yours with a very thin spread of the frosting as the first coat. (this is the same rule that holds true when waxing the floors in your house; you're far better off with two thinner coats than one heavy one). The first thin frosting coat will bind in and seal off the crumbs so they cannot surface later as you apply your second frosting application. Allow the coat to set before applying the second thick decorative frosting to the loaf. Cream cheese, for easier handling, must be allowed to soften by standing to room temperature. If you are in a hurry, the cream cheese can be beaten until of creamy spreading consistency or you can add 3 tbsp. milk or cream for each 8 oz. cream cheese used or you may add mayonnaise to bring the cheese to spreading consistency. If the cheese is to be used to form a flower or create a swirl or as a border design, it must be of heavier consistency to hold its shape. Therefore *omit* the milk and/or cream and any other additives. For decorating and garnishing in the aforementioned style, set aside approximately ¾ c. of the frosting mix. Commercially available nowadays are many other spreadable cream type cheeses which can be used to frost sandwich or meat loaves. If you find the consistency of same too thick, allow to stand to room temperature or beat slightly or add milk or cream to soften enough for workability. Refrigerate afterwards to firm up. As there are many bulk cheeses available in the supermarket to use as bases for many cocktail "put-to-gethers," so are there now "store bought" basics for hors d'oeuvres one can easily throw together with no one the wiser. Look into the freezer compartment and find a light strudel paper thin pastry leaf (sheet) called a Filo dough. Use it in casseroles or for pastry sweet filled goodies or cut into strips to form filled triangular bite sized hors d'oeuvres. Purchase store bought packaged little miniature tartlets to fill for individual quiches. Try making your own pinwheels or wrap-ups, using commercially sold canned biscuit doughs (crescents or buttermilk rounds, etc.) These can be found in the refrigerator compartment in your grocery store. Like to include a little touch of Italy in your cocktail party fare? No need to start fussing with the commercially frozen pizza doughs, let alone making your own from scratch. Substitute a ready baked split English muffin; on each half spread some tomato paste or sauce, crumbled meat or sausage, a drop of olive oil and oregano and top with shredded mozzarella cheese. Broil and bring forth your individual pizzas; no cutting, no fussing . . . just good eating!

Try this open faced sandwich for the bigger men in your life . . . the growing teenagers love this one! Use ordinary bread and cut out 2½" rounds (toast one side and butter the other which will give it more substinance when handling this hot one). Prepare tiny meatballs and place on each toasted round. Make indentation on top of meat with your finger or spoon. Broil until meat is done. Fill meat centers with chili sauce or relish or top with a cocktail onion, olive, water chestnut or canned crushed pineapple, or chunk or tidbit size cut pineapple. Shake some Kikkoman or soy sauce on or baste with a sweet and sour sparerib sauce to add that dash of Polynesian flair to the latter.

For more of these quicky eating tidbits look further into any cookbook for many more ideas for concoctions and recipes. These and the many other "How-to" suggestions found in this chapter will keep your house humming with beautiful and delicious table fare for many evenings to come when he says, "Come on over—we're having some friends in for a few drinks" —bless him! It is nice getting together now with all these goodies hidden up your magical kitchen sleeve!

SMORGASBORD BREAD WEDGE

This is one form of canape or open sandwich I particularly favor, for it is done so quickly, as if on an assembly line. There is no need to stand and prepare individual canape sandwiches for these wedges give you an assorted smorgasbord all your own. "Follow these simple directions and you will see, life of another complexion, where you'll be queen" . . . sounds like an old song? Well, it is and the words will ring true for you for you'll just breeze through this one that easily crowns you with the title, "the hostess with the mostest."

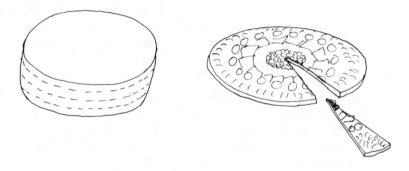

Although I favor pumpernickel for taste, color and texture contrast, any other thick round center slice cut from a round bread loaf will do as the smorgasbord "table" (canape base). Spread the cut round bread slice with a thickened butter base. Starting at the center, fill with assorted circles or bands of fillings or spreads, E.g., for a *FISH ROUND:* To fill the bull's-eye center, lay in some black caviar which adds that necessary tang of the brine that's so good. The caviar is used in the innermost and smallest circle for we need use as little as possible (the good stuff can be a little expensive) so let it be used most dramatically. Surround with a circle of piped cream cheese which will complement and hold the caviar in its place; encompass cheese with its kissing cousin, chopped smoked salmon (lox). Next, band chopped herring encircled by black olives and yellow pickled cocktail onions. Border in piped on rosettes of pimento cheese. Garnish with fresh sprigs of parsley curls. Since one loaf of bread will yield several sliced rounds, with your imagination and talent you can make each one of them look different by simply varying your fillings and colorful spreads (chicken salad, eggs chopped, baby shrimp standing on end, etc.). Cut into wedges. Present each guest their own private smorgasbord "table."

HOW TO CUT HORS D'OEUVRES

By merely using the professional serrator in place of a knife, you can cut various shapes from *bulk* type cheese such as Munster, cheddar, Swiss, etc., to make them appear more appetizing. The same principle can be applied to bulk meats such as salami, bologna, pepperoni, etc., to create some variety to your presentation of simple cold cuts for hors d'oeuvre service. Using the professional serrator you can also lend more interest to vegetables by cutting them with this kitchen utensil. You will find a bonus to this when cutting cucumbers, carrots sticks, white icicle radishes, etc., for with the pinked edges created by using the serrator your dip will adhere better to your meat or vegetable.

Combine the cheese and meat varied shapes, add a canned pineapple chunk or add an olive and now you have created an hors d'oeuvre tidbit for your cocktail party. *To create a two tone cheese wedge using grocery packaged sliced cheese cuts:* purchase a package of deep yellow and lighter yellow American cheese. For better working ability, let stand at room temperature.

Alternate 3 slices of dark with 3 slices of light yellow American cheese and stack up one atop the other alternating the colors. Press together to adhere to each other by pressing with the palms of your hands. (This is the reason you wanted the cheese at room temperature). Now trim off all outside edges with the serrator thus "pinking" them.

For triangular shaped cheese wedges proceed to cut squarely stacked cheese slices in half diagonally and then cut each piece in half again and/or again depending upon how small or large you would like to serve your wedges. If preferred, you might try creating square or more rectangular shapes by cutting accordingly. If you are more adventurous, try using an aspic or vegetable cutter or a small cookie cutter to acquire some more interesting cheese shapes. Refrigerate to serve chilled and to firm up cheese stacks.

These cheese stacked wedge cuts are pretty served as is for hors d'oeuvres or used as an accompaniment surrounding a hot apple pie or may be used as aforementioned, as the base of combined meat and fruit tidbit. For a more contrasting and colorful wedge cut hors d'oeuvre, alternate the light yellow American cheese square with a similarly cut cold cut meat (spiced ham). Proceed to cut as previously recommended and be pleasantly surprised with the pink and yellow layered effect gotten by stacking the meat with the cheese as described.

TOMATO FILLER-UPPERS

If you prefer, the *cherry tomatoes can be filled* on the inside rather than decorated with cheese on the outside as for tomato cheese rose. Here's a suggestion for you: cut off the stem top of

a cherry tomato and set aside. Hollow out (use a demitasse spoon or tip of grapefruit spoon to make this job a cinch). Fill cavity center of fruit with chopped egg salad, cheese, liver or fish mix or mousse. Mound it high over top. Place removed tomato cap cover on top. Hold decoratively with frill pick if necessary. For a more colorful filling contrast, fill cherry fruit bottom with a large pitted black olive. Fill olive hole with piped on egg yolk cream paste.

Cherry tomato accordion fan filler: cut cherry tomato in 3 vertical cuts, fan style. Fill in with egg yolk cream paste or try rounded black olive wedge slices for dramatic contrast.

TOMATO FILLED BUTTERFLY FOR HE-MAN EATERS!

For a larger man eating version of a filled tomato see and follow the diagram. Laying an egg tomato, sometimes called a

plum tomato, on its side, slice off a ⅓ section from the top. Clean out and set top aside for use later. Fill lower basket-like section of the plum tomato fruit with a filling, mounding the filling to overflowing the top. Divide the scooped out removed ⅓ top section in half lengthwise. One inch from the front mound of filling, push in the halved horizontal sections at angles as if to resemble the uplifted wings of a butterfly. Fill in 1″ front area with pimento filled slices of olives using the stabilizing frill picks to act as eyes and antennas of the winged creature.

MORE STUFFED VEGETABLES FOR THE HE-MAN EATERS

Speaking of stuffing, one need not be limited in that area either, for almost anything can be stuffed and served as part of a delicious luncheon or hors d'oeuvre offering; e.g., cut off one end from a large round cucumber and for the decorative touch, lemon strip its rind all around. Hollow out the inside seedy portion (use small demitasse spoon or grapefruit spoon if cuke is large enough to warrant same). Refill with a contrasting meat or fish paté and refrigerate to firm up. Slice in rounds. The same principle is applicable to green peppers or very firm tomatoes. Fill with cheese or mixture and slice in rounds.

For mouth stuffing pop-in quickies: stuff mammoth black pitless olives with shoe string carrot sticks or celery fans.

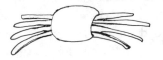

Speaking of celery: lay open a bunch of celery stalks. Fill with varied colored cheeses. Push one stalk into the cheese fill of another. Reshape the celery bunch together and wrap tightly in foil or tie with string. Refrigerate preferably overnight or at least several hours. Slice into ½" rounds revealing the multicolored cheese filled celery rib cuts. A lovely sight to see . . . all those little colorful tidbits bring interest and variety as they are passed around and offered on a tray.

PINEAPPLE CHEESE AND OTHER FORMS

Mold cheese mixture into a pineapple shape on a horizontal plane or use a more stiffened cheese mixture to form a vertical standing pineapple shaped presentation. Proceed as for chopped liver pineapple presentation in this chapter. Score and press in sliced pimento filled olives as pineapple eyes. Use celery or (pineapple) frond leaves for crown of pineapple. Serve with crackers or bread rounds. However, one needn't be limited to pineapple shaped forms, for you can free form any shapes of cheese spread or liver patés you wish. With the use of self-designed and cut styrofoam shapes as a stable under-base, a whole new exciting avenue once again is wide open to you. Let us use Easter as an example, for that's when I came up with this one for some visiting children at this gay holiday time.

Use any of your favorite but firm cheese spread mixtures. Draw on scrap paper (use large paper shopping bag if oversized figure or shape) the outline of your design. In this case it was (just) the body of a duck. Cut out the paper outline and trace onto ½" styrofoam block. Cut out body and cover completely with foil (thus making it reusable once again). With foil wrapped in place, cover styrofoam shape with the spread of thick cheese mixture. Garnish and decorate. E.g., for the duck, I used bugle shaped corn chips (or Frito corn chips will do nicely) for the uplifted feathered effect for tail and wing areas. Use a pimento filled olive for the eye and for the comedy touch (which my guests got a particular kick out of) I placed on curved cut long slices of black olive as his eyelash. Use food dye to color some of the cheese spread to fill in the beak area or merely fill in with a carrot beak. Place in carrot feet, rounded side up. Push wood floral picks into carrot base end and connect the opposite exposed pick tip into the base of the styrofoam. Make and connect claws similarly. On remaining tray space left, use the cake writing gel to spread your message—in this case, "Happy Easter to Gracie and Joey." Serve with crackers and party rounds.

As this shape was outlined on paper, traced and cut from the styrofoam so can any other motif, design or figure. So we can, with a little imagination and some cheese, liver or whatever, create any and all themes for our party or snack purposes. Picture, if you will, the tracing of a mouse's face, carried out with a white cheese spread, mounded high in appropriate (nose) areas, celery whiskers and black olives pressed in for that unmistakable Walt Disney's Mickey or Minnie look.

To create the bumpy fur effect of a Peter Cottontail, mix up a concoction of softened cream cheese and chopped Macadamia nuts. For the eyes and pink inside of Peter's ears mix the cheese with a mere speck of red food dye to create the pinkish tone needed. Accentuate the floppy ears and tail of the bunny by covering with flaked cocoanut. Use black shoe string licorice for whiskers—cherry for a pert nose. Your children will be so delighted with you Mrs. Disney, they might even keep you on for another few years.

THE ART AUCTION COCKTAIL PARTY

I had fun coming up with this mood setter for a cocktail party when I volunteered to serve on a fund raising committee for an art show.

You'll find the more you volunteer your services, the larger your scope becomes to meet interesting people (for they are out doing things too), the more opportunity you will have to practice and create new ideas experimenting with somebody else's food. Sometimes it's quite a challenge just trying to stay within a budget and still come up with refreshing ideas. So here's one for you. . . .

For the art gallery, I created a painter's palette which not only set the mood but made good pickings complementing the champagne and cocktails being served our art patrons at the fund raising auction. Outline free hand on paper, a painter's palette. Cut out and trace onto a 1" thick stratofoam panel sheet board. Used for insulation with aluminum sidings and in ceilings and for packaging, the panels are available in lumber yards or home improvement centers. Cut out palette outline and cut a hole for the artist's thumb, lending more authenticity to it. To avoid having to place the food directly in contact with the stratofoam, pin in various colored (flattened out) muffin paper liners. As a play on words, as an artist would use colors to paint a picture, you will use colors to paint the palate. On each of the paper liners, push in wooden floral picks leaving the tip ends exposed. Place onto pick ends (hidden toothpick method), in a contrasting color sequence, bold groupings of cherry red tomatoes, black olives, pink shrimp, green broccoli florets, cubes of yellow cheese, red radishes, cocktail onions, salami chunks, and on and on. . . .

Taking your choice and "paint" your palette with your favorites!

Paintbrush: Use the hidden toothpick method to place a large rhubarb across the artist's palate spreading out the leafy end part as the bristles of a painter's brush.

Attach this food bedecked palette, as one would a canvas, to an artist's easel. Off the top of the easel hang a painter's smock with the large pockets holding some cocktail napkins handy for use.

Place the easel near the cocktail bar or table. If easel is not available, simply set palate on table and raise at 45° angle for better viewing.

No artist's ball to go to or prepare for? Apply the same principal using a large round flat circle styrofoam or a cone shaped flat styrofoam as a base. Cover with foil. Inbed it with chicory and using hidden toothpick method in combination with some frill picks for added color, place onto the displayed chicory covered shapes, large groups of contrasting foods for holiday tree or wreath pickings. Your tree or ringed circle can grow edible clusters of shrimp, black olives, cherry tomatoes, scallops, red radishes, etc. Fill center opening within ring with a bowl containing a dip that would add to your tidbit variety.

For a variation to this principle, attach little foil cups to the styrofoam ring shape. Use a dab of floral gum tape on the bottom of each foil cup to stick it to the styrofoam. Fill each cup with a different dip or mixture spread. Fill center of styrofoam ring display with a deep fitting bowl to hold assorted crackers and party bread rounds for spreading and dipping. (Also see vertical displayed topiary trees this chapter and also Santa's Salmon holiday displays in chapter 8.)

TOPIARY TREE

A topiary tree can be used as a means to present most any type of food from an hors d'ouevre snack to a dessert treat. This attractive manner of presenting these edibles is partially for the uniqueness of its appearance; primarily because the tree, presented in a vertical position, takes up very little table space.

Utilize a flower pot as a simple base, which when prepared properly will hold an inserted and stabilized wooden dowel. This dowel stick acting as the trunk of your topiary can in turn hold any size and shape of styrofoam (e.g., cone or ball). Your styrofoam shape would then be used as the basic pincushion to display your choice of edible goodies. Pre-hole the insertion area for the placement of this wood dowel. To pre-hole it be sure to use the same identical dowel for it must be re-inserted later as the trunk of the tree. This is to assure you of a proper and custom tight fit. Pre-hole the trunk area for insertion to at least a ⅔ length of the dowel stick for proper balance. Follow diagram for simplified guidance.

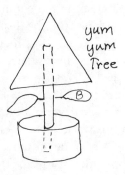

After pre-holing the dowel stick, remove it and set it aside. By pre-holing and removing the dowel you are now at liberty to pin into the styrofoam shape (pincushion) your edibles; the chief advantage to this procedure is that when the food is perishable you can refrigerate it separately until time to set it up on the tree trunk in readiness for your guests. Therefore it must be noted that the circumference of the wood dowel chosen must be in ratio to the weight of the food intended to be pinned into it, e.g., strawberry filled styrofoam top need not have as strong a dowel trunk as one that would be heavily laden with a vegetable filled pincushion of broccoli and cherry tomatoes; a nice feature for the holiday Christmas season. To prevent an imbalance of and to avoid tipping over during snack "picking time" be sure to use a wide mouthed or heavily weighted flower pot as a base.

To stabilize pot base: to give extra weight to the flower pot bottom, you may have to fill it with a rock base and plaster of paris (available at hardware or paint stores) or use clay as a filler. I have tried rock and sand alone as pot base weights but find that the dowel shifts as your guests pick off the topiary goodies thus creating an imbalance. Pre-wrap with green floral winding tape that part of your dowel that will remain in view. OP-TIONAL: At this point if you wish, attach 1 or 2 artificial green leaves (obtainable from a 5 & 10¢ or craft store) on the dowel trunk of your tree. With felt marker pen, inscribe those leaves (B) to read "Yum Yum tree, Nibbling Tree or Shrimp Tree" or whatever.

To prepare plaster of paris filler: If you wish to feature a green grass appearance to your pot "soil" simply dye your water green (use food dye) before adding the powder of the plaster for mixing. The alternative is to cover the white plaster or clay "soil" with left over Easter grass or tinted green cocoanut grass. If it is to be a candy tree, simply cover the "soil" with foil and then lay in a bed of candy sweets such as M & M's or dark raisins. Prepare your soil bed and plant your (dowel) tree (trunk). If using plaster, be sure to hold dowel in upright position until plaster hardens and trunk is firmly implanted. Thus you have the basics for any type of topiary tree ready to receive whatever shape styrofoam pincushion you have chosen; the former, which can be prepared in advance and refrigerated until serving time. Following are a few suggestions to present foods for their particular effect to place on your buffet table.

FOR HORS D'OEUVRES: after pre-holing process, cover styrofoam ball or cone with foil or plastic wrap. Using totem pole pins, place on chicory leaves as background cover. Using wooden toothpick (hidden method) and frill picks for the light touch of contrasting color, use your topiary top as a pincushion to hold: foil colored covered wrapped cheeses, salami chunks, pineapple, cherry tomatoes, etc.

FOR FISH ENTREE: try an assortment of pinned shrimp and scallops.

FOR COLD CUT TREE: pin on cone shaped rolls of salami and bologna; supplement with chunks of chicken, ham, peperoni and pickle fans, gherkins and olives.

PREPARE A SWEETS TREE: pin in cookies and candy; use the pop sticks themselves to push on lollipops or sugar daddies for a youngster's delightful pickings at a birthday party.

VEGETABLE TREE: pin on cherry tomatoes, cauliflower and broccoli florets and cut vegetable chunks for dipping.

CITRUS TREE: pin in citrus cuts as a tea and/or bar service.

That was so easy, let's double the height and the food by topping one with another.

TO CREATE A TWIN TOPIARY TREE: Using 2 smaller foam balls prepare the top ball as previously detailed. Set aside. To prepare the lower ball for insertion, you will have to pre-hole it, this time completely penetrating the dowel through both sides of the ball. (see illustration).

To prevent the ball from sliding down after placement on the lower section of the dowel, line the hole with floral gum tape. Keep the goodies pinned onto the lower ball of a lighter weight; e.g., for Easter: set the holiday mood by including some Easter marshmallow bunnies on the bottom ball, some cookies and lollies can be placed on the top (which can be varied by using a cone shaped styrofoam on top if so desired). Place some chocolate Easter candies as the "soil" covering of the flower pot.

TO PRESENT A TOPIARY CHRISTMAS CANDY TREE: set your *cone* shaped styrofoam up as a gum drop candy Christmas tree to the delight of visiting children (and adults) for the holiday season. Use the spearmint gum candies sold in shapes of little (green) leaves and pin into the cone styrofoam (use hidden toothpick method). A 9" cone will hold about 2 lbs. of these candy leaves. Fill in with colored gum drop balls or Christmas wrapped gold and red foil covered chocolates. For that festive touch add a few strands of tinsel and top with a poinsettia or star! Your colorful array of edible Christmas balls amid the green leaf boughs of this Yule tree makes it beautiful to look at and absolutely good enough to eat . . . Try it, it is! Apply the same principle using a round styrofoam form to make a Christmas wreath.

TOPIARY CHRISTMAS TREE OF VEGETABLES: pin in (hidden toothpick method) the full cluster heads of broccoli florets. Intermingle them with the bright red coloring of plump cherry tomatoes. Fill in with large bunches of fresh curled parsley sprigs. Add an artificial poinsettia in place of the green leaves on the tree trunk base.

STRAWBERRY DESSERT TREE: set your topiary on a large

revolving lazy susan. Pin in (hidden toothpick method) large succulent fresh strawberries pointed tips up, hulls down. Always leave the hulls intact for easier and less messy handling for your guests. Hulling a berry will bleed it of its natural juices so it is best to always wash and hull berries in that order just prior to eating. Surround the berry topiary with dips of sour cream, whipped cream, brown sugar, sugar sparkles, etc. Try melted chocolate a la fondue style for a change of pace. See also strawberry heart, this chapter.

Need to pick up a bright note to your entertainment table? Set the mood for spring by presenting a topiary of blooming fresh garden flowers: pin in lemon leaves as background (or use chicory) and pin in lovely cut flower forms of fresh vegetables. (See chapter 7 on how to cut vegetable flowers.) Speaking of lemon leaves . . . review chapter 4 on citrus fruits to present a citrus tree as a centerpiece for an afternoon tea party for the ladies. As you see, the same topiary tree, base and styrofoam top, made once, can be used over again and again.

With a little imagination it can open a whole new world—presenting many types of different foods, suiting a lot of individual tastes and varied moods and taking up an absolute minimum of table space.

And you thought you didn't have a green thumb and couldn't grow anything! Happy pickings from your new found tree arbor!

A RED BERRY HEART

Strawberries need not be limited for presentation as a vertical space saving topiary tree. If there is more room available on your buffet table at that wedding, birthday or anniversary party, try your hand at this easy but most impressive display. Thinking of strawberry topiary trees brings to mind the strawberry heart I made for my husband's birthday, a quiet affair with just the children and myself, for he had reached the golden age of forty. A red berry heart is such a nice way of saying LOVE to that special someone on his or her birthday. Better still, make it even more significant by presenting it on a day that has no special meaning and then see the meaning that day will especially take on. Your berry heart now says . . . for no special reason or occasion . . . just that I love you!

Your presentation of red berries can be a big one to feed a large party crowd or a small 4″ personal berry heart just enough for an intimate dinner for two if you've invited that special someone.

TO MAKE HEART: Pre-cut styrofoam heart forms are sold in 3″, 4″, 5″, 9″ and 12″ mold shapes at your local craft or 5 & 10¢ store or at floral houses. If you need a bigger one or prefer to save money by cutting your own its quite simple. Outline and cut out a heart shaped paper pattern. Trace the outline of same onto a large enough size of 1″ or 2″ styrofoam block. Cut out the styrofoam heart and cover with foil (thereby making the whole thing reusable again). Use totem pins to cover the one or two inch wide border edges of the styrofoam form with strawberry leaves (if you grow your own) or substitute chicory or lemon leaves or fresh curley parsley. Leave two small areas open on sides to place on cupid's arrow.

HOW TO MAKE CUPID'S ARROW: Cut cupid's arrow in two sections from red oak tag. Following diagram proceed to

tape the oak tag onto long bamboo sticks leaving a one inch tip of the bamboo exposed, push these one inch exposed bamboo points into the open side areas of the heart form. *OPTIONAL:* on cupid's arrow can be spelled out the occasion for the party. E.g., Happy Birthday, Fred, etc. *TO FILL STYROFOAM HEART FORM WITH BERRIES:* To create a double heart and create an even prettier effect (this is optional) outline another 3″ area in the center of the large heart shape form. Have the smaller heart shape follow the contour of the larger form. Slice large strawberries lengthwise. Starting at the outside border edge of the 3″ heart in the center, place in the larger strawberry slices, cut surface and points facing upward and outward (using hidden toothpick method). Continue to overlay berry slices in similar fashion. Use the smaller berry slices and work them in toward the center. Fill in apex of center with one large whole berry point tip up. If you wish to bring emphasis to frame out the smaller heart, outline same with fresh parsley or small strawberry or mint leaves. Alternative is to place in slices as detailed sans parsley border. Continue either way, with or without inner second heart, and place whole strawberries on larger styrofoam heart form. (Use hidden toothpick method, fruit point tips up.)

TO RAISE FOR BETTER EYE APPEAL: Something that looks good lying flat on the table will look far better if just raised up at a slight angle for better viewing. To set your berry heart at a 45° angle, follow diagram and set heart up on two vertical

column stands supported by one horizontal base. Attach all pieces one to the other with totem pins, wood picks or floral gum tape. If you do not wish to have attention brought to these stands simply "drape" them by vertically hanging down graduated chicory leaves. Pin the chicory into the border edge originally designated for decorating with strawberry or parsley leaves.

ACCOMPANIMENTS: Using the now readily available foil potato shells for baking (5 to a plastic bag package) reshape the potato foil into a heart form. Fill individually with sour cream, brown or white sugar or colored sugar sparkles or whipped cream. Station your dips near the strawberry centerpiece you have just lovingly created.

Also see "Open Watermelon Heart" in chapter 2 for heart designed all fruit presentation.

CHOPPED LIVER

To present chopped liver and expect it to hold its shape or mold form, the consistency must be very thick and binding (hold together well). The alternative to insure the mold's firmness to hold its shape is to encompass it by using an overlaid glaze or aspic (to be discussed later.) If the chopped liver is purchased from the supermarket's appetizing department or from the store's freezer case, it might be necessary to defrost and add a few cooked, chopped chicken livers. This will give the mixture a thicker binding consistency thus making it better to handle and prepare the shape into its desired form. If the liver is to be molded by packing into a commercially sold form (as opposed to free hand molding, as will be discussed later), the liver filled mold should always be refrigerated a few hours before turning out.

Once shaped into its formed design, it can be preserved to hold up better for a longer period of time by encompassing it in an aspic. Simultaneously, this aspic will also lend a beautiful glazed overall appearance to your displayed food creation. Also see the use for such a purposeful glaze to follow in this chapter on chopped liver called "A Winter Wonderland." In this instance, a glaze is used to actually change the outward appearance of the brown liver mold to that of the whiteness of snow covered ski slopes. With the addition of food coloring to this white glaze, any color can be achieved as in chapter 8: See Santa's Salmon. Since an aspic, when applied, is actually in liquid form, it tends to run off the mold and onto the (serving) tray. To avoid when necessary (leaving remainder of tray with a clean look), treat your mold as you would a cake being prepared for frosting. Cover the edge of the tray with triangular pieces of wax or light foil paper. Place the mold form on top of the ends of these "clean up" papers so they can be slipped out easily later. Lay aspic coating over liver mold using several thin coats. See directions for recipe to follow. When the last coat is set and garnish is then applied, carefully lift edges all around mold, using a flexible spatula, and gently withdraw the "clean up" papers. Clean balance of tray if necessary with a clean cloth or paper toweling. The following glaze applied *before* garnishing would lend added beauty to many of the liver displays to follow: liver birthday cake, heartshaped liver, bonnet (can be done in white aspic also), bowling ball, horse's head, etc. Use your discretion in choosing which aspic to use and which mold to use it on! E.g., for the face of the liver clock, I would use a white aspic as I would use the white aspic to create the ski slopes in Winter Wonderland. Although I would choose the beef aspic (to follow) for a horse's head (smooth shiny skin natural to the animal) I would not use *any* aspic at all on the liver owl. I would prefer the owl to have a feathery look and would achieve that effect by "picking up" the liver into points, using the tines of a fork to do so.

The recommended glazes in this book are to be used as a light covering aspic. They mainly consist of nothing more than broth (of choice) and unflavored gelatin and therefore do not influence the taste of any food it would be used upon.

TO MAKE A DARK COLORED COVERING GLAZE

To every 3 c. of broth or consomme, use 2 envelopes of unflavored gelatin. Place broth in saucepan and sprinkle with gelatin. Allow to soften at room temperature for 15 minutes. Place on heat; stir to slowly dissolve completely. Chill *only* until syrupy. Spoon over mold using ½ c. at a time covering mold with a light coat in each application. It is not unusual to have 3–4 *thin* coats applied before the mold is evenly coated. This same aspic can be poured into a shallow tray to set like a gelatin. Cut up into small pieces or mash. Use aspic in this form as "dirt" background coloring for a display such as land surrounding train (Railroad Special) in chapter 6 on Party Loaves.

Chopped liver can then be served as an hors d'oeuvre form, as a cocktail spread with crackers or as a main entree. Use as appetizer as in a salad platter or use as a filler to present tomato baskets or as filler in noodle nests. Want to try something a little different, very simple but very yummy? Try chopped liver (or chicken salad) topped with a few pieces of crisp bacon slices as a garnish or use in salad or sandwich form. Chop up those crisp bacon slices to mix directly into the chopped liver when preparing it yourself. Another nice one to compliment chopped liver are green pimento stuffed olives . . . let's start with that combination now presenting it differently to make it even more interesting.

Pineapple (liver) mold: Use an extremely thick binding chopped liver mixture for a vertical free standing form of pineapple. You may utilize a less binding mix of chopped liver if presenting your pineapple shape on a horizontal plane (lying flat on a platter). Whichever one you do choose to reproduce the color, design and shape, mold the liver into the contour and shape of a pineapple using your hands to do so if you do not own a pineapple mold form. Smooth out by patting with wet hands.

To achieve the scored affect usually found on the rind of a fresh pineapple, use a knife edge to cross cut in the diagonal indentations (also see optional). Fill in scored design of rind with small slices of pimento filled green olives thus creating the eyes of your fruit. Top off with actual pineapple frond leaves from a fresh pineapple or substitute lengthwise slices of green pepper or celery leaf tops. Surround with party breads or cracker rounds for spreading and enjoying.

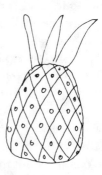

OPTIONAL: if you prefer to overlay the design (see Jargon of Your Kitchen Workshop); use the pastry tube method of overlaying the diagonal criss cross scored effect, using the egg yolk cream paste to emphasize the rind of a pineapple. Proceed to place sliced olives in rind effect as previously described.

OTHER LIVER DESIGNS: As you can now readily see by using the principle of overlaying designs of egg yolk cream paste (or alternative suggested in Jargon of Kitchen Workshop) and pressing this mixture through a pastry decorating canvas bag, a whole new avenue of designs and display pieces are opened to us. Using our hands as molds or utilizing commercially sold molds or even using ordinary baking pans many other motif designs and presentations can be created.

CHOPPED LIVER BIRTHDAY CAKE: Any round cake pan or tube baking pan can turn your liver out and onto a tray to look like a cake. Using the overlay design method, it can be decorated with the use of the pastry canvas decorating bag to resemble a real birthday cake, one that can be used as the party theme centerpiece and yet be eaten as the main entree. Use the decorating bag to outline and trim up the liver cake as a birthday cake would be; so as not to cover the whole area accidentally, it is suggested that the egg yolk decorative roses (forms) be made on wax paper, dusted heavily with paprika and then transferred to the top of the birthday cake. If you prefer, use the method of mixing the egg yolk cream paste with some red food dye to create a pink coloring to your egg paste before pressing through the pastry tube; you need not dust at all to highlight the pink rose thus formed. Use (Italian) flat parsley leaves and stems for rose's greenery. Use a fine hole tube tip to write the message to the birthday celebrant across the top of the cake. This liver cake is always a hit for its uniqueness and the fact it serves as a spread for an hors d'oeuvre at a cocktail party or if you wish, (provide salad greens and) cut everyone a slice of birthday cake to serve as the main entree. By using a heart shaped mold pan the theme can be used for Valentine's Day also.

PARTY THEME FOR A MAN: For a Father's Day gathering or for his birthday celebration give him a replica of his favorite *shirt*—one he can eat!

Using a rectangular shaped baking pan, fill with chopped liver and refrigerate to firm up. Turn out onto party tray to serve. Use that extra reserved chopped liver to build up and create the *collar* of the shirt or if he likes two toned colored shirts build up a contrasting collar of chopped egg salad instead. Using pastry tube method, overlay the design of a collar and shirt pocket. *Buttons:* use sliced or whole pimento filled olives *BOW TIE:* use black olive halves pressed below collar area as tie. If you prefer he be more dashing substitute a red pimento tie instead.

This is one time he can literally eat his shirt . . . and like it! Does this give you ideas? How about a chopped liver (or egg salad) *bonnet* for Mother's Day—use deep round bowl for her —cake pan for *straw hat* for him. As you can see your imagination and your hands can be the basis for many creative endeavours. Working with chopped liver, chopped egg salad, chopped herring, tuna fish, salmon, etc., of proper thicknesses, many of these ideas can be adapted. E.g., *FOR A BAR MITZVAH CELEBRATION:* the *Star of David* can be shaped and overlaid with egg yolk paste using the pastry tube method to write in the occasion and emphasize the star's outline; form a *menorah* for the holidays or for such an auspicious occasion by free forming the chopped liver into a menorah, use celery stalks (rounded side up) as the candles, with graceful cut carrot shapes for burning flames with a touch of pimento red tips. Are you and your friends more sports-minded? Here are just a few suggestions to get you started. Top off that trophy winning bowling season with a little party. Use an edible bowling ball and bowling pin as a delicious centerpiece to set the mood! Cover the *chopped liver bowling ball* (which has been formed, refrigerated and turned out of a mixing bowl of the right size) with minced black olives; use round carrot slices to differentiate the finger hole grips. Accompanying the ball of course is a lighter colored (egg salad) *bowling pin* with pimento cut out number for same. Football season? Do a take-off on the *football* itself as the coloring of chopped liver couldn't be more suitable; fill in the pigskin seam lines with the overlay design of egg yolk paste, use capers or olives for the shoelace holes found on the ball. The horsy set coming for lunch after the morning canter? Again the color of chopped liver is most suitable to free form design a *horse's head* using slices of cooked egg white as the background white of the horse's black olive eye, utilizing fresh dill or Italian parsley for his mane. and so you can go on and on and on. . . . and on!

Now for the *nature lovers:* make a *beehive* by shaping up a tall mound of chopped liver. Using the back of a demitasse spoon or whatever, indent the curved lines graduating upward as you would find on a beehive; outline to emphasize with pastry tube method using egg yolk paste. Leave an opening at the base center for entry of the bees. Decorate and garnish with artificial bees (from novelty store) or make your own *butterfly*. (also see chapter 7 on edible Daikon butterflies). Speaking of butterflies make a butterfly mold (there is such a commercially produced mold on the market) or shape one up free form with your hands). Fill mold with chopped liver, turn out onto serving tray and use pastry tube method to outline and highlight the design and spread of the butterfly's wings. Use olives and frill picks for eyes and antennae. See ch. 8 & 9 for other suggested butterfly themes.

Nature reminds us of chickens doesn't it? Let's make one, then, in the natural background setting of her own nest, surrounded with her baby chicks.

CHICKEN IN NEST: using a minimum of 3–5 lbs. of liver, shape up a large mound of liver for the body. To add extra strength and stability to keep her head raised higher than the body, peel a thick carrot of 3–4″ length. Push into liver body to act as the neck. Mold liver over the carrot base smoothing out the contour of the breast front. Shape a smaller mound of liver into an oval shape for its head. Press onto (carrot hidden) neck. Place on a large carrot beak and large olive eyes on either side of head. With extra liver shape up wings and add onto sides of chicken. Do the same to add on tail of chicken. OPTIONAL: overlay design of feather effect on wings and tail, using egg yolk pastry tube method and a very light hand.

NEST: surround base of chicken with bed of canned onion rings or Chinese noodles.

BABY CHICKS: Create a few little baby nests (see recipes and directions for same in chapter 5 on how to make various noodle nests). Fill in noodle nests with sliced greens. Nestle in a small chickadee, or, if you prefer, set in a bird hatching . . . either one can be found in chapter 5 on eggs: feature creatures for a menagerie. Place 2 peewee eggs, hard cooked and left in shell, nearby, for realism as if ready to hatch. You've set the scene so don't be surprised if there is an egg or chicken snatching thief in your party . . . everyone goes big for these little ones and their Mama Hen.

CHOPPED LIVER & EGG SALAD ROOSTER

And why should the male counterpart be neglected? He too would like to be sculpted in edible delicious chopped liver! Just as we had created a vertical standing chicken (hen) surrounded by her babies, a chopped liver mixture, lacking the extra heavy consistency needed for a standing vertical hen, can nonetheless be presented as a rooster in a horizontal position. What's even nicer is that we can combine two different salad entrees into one centerpiece; for those who are not liver lovers, there is the alternative of eating a chopped egg salad tail.

BODY: Turn out onto the proper sized serving piece, the mounded liver; shape accordingly with your hands into a (flat) rooster body and head. In this instance I prefer *not* to have a smooth wet down liver pate (such as the one for the chopped liver pineapple fruit earlier in this chapter). To simulate the feathery look of the rooster, pick up the liver mixture with the tines of a fork (like one would swirl a cake frosting).

FEET: Use celery stalks or (halved lengthwise cut) carrots for feet in vertical placement at bottom of rooster's body. Place feet rounded side up.

EYES: use cooked egg white slices for background of eyes. Place in whole mammoth black or pimento filled olives as eyes.

BEAK: Place in position a large carrot beak, rounded side up.

COMB: Push in a red pepper as comb atop head and use pimento for beneath chin. You want his comb top rigid so each comb section stands up properly; you want soft pliable pimento below the rooster's chin to hang loose, which in turn would make the wattles appear more realistic.)

TAIL & WING EFFECT: To provide your guests with a choice of two different salads or entrees, prepare egg salad, deviled if you prefer it spicy. Prepare it by putting it through a food mill or ricer so it is applicable to pipe through the pastry tube canvas bag and tip. For realism be sure to follow the diagram provided. Note the sickle feathers on the tail of a rooster go upward gracefully before they descend downward into a cascading feathery effect.

Using the pastry bag to hold the fine deviled seasoned egg salad paste, pipe out and add on the tail of the rooster in graceful curved lines as per diagram above. If desired use short strokes of the same egg mixture to add on the wing spread on the side of the rooster. Alternative: use Frito corn chips and push in at angle to represent wing of bird.

Although this was done in chopped liver you can readily see it can easily be made with a thick and binding fish mixture such as tuna or salmon. Use the egg salad as the tail, as eggs complement these fish salads well while at the same time giving your guests a choice of entree.

AND FROM THE AFRICAN JUNGLE . . . . . .
. . . THE LION!

If poultry isn't your bag and you prefer to bag the bigger game found on an African safari, try your hand at making this chopped liver lion. Using a suitable sized serving tray, turn out the chopped liver mound and mold with the use of your hands

a close facsimile of a lion's head. The prettiest part of a real lion and the edible one you are about to make is the fluffy mane around the lion's head. Be sure to put that extra big mound of liver in front to act as this big cat's mouth and heavy jawbones. Leaving room to add the facial features, push in all about the head corn Frito chips simulating the mane and also acting as cracker picker-uppers for the liver. *OPTIONAL:* to bring emphasis to the mane fill in egg yolk paste using pastry tube method on top of the Fritos, giving more dimension to the mane. Outline the mouth and border eyes with the overlay design of the egg yolk paste, pastry tube method. *Eyes:* pimento filled olives; *nose:* made from cut-up slices of black olives; the cat's *whiskers:* very narrow thin long pieces of carrots.

Listen to the roar of the crowd when they find this lion good enough to eat!

AND FROM THE TREES . . . THE OWL

If you really want to give your guests a hoot and they are not as adventurous as to tangle with the lion from Africa, why not make them a gentle old owl?

To prepare, hand mold the shape of an owl onto a rectangular shaped tray. Following same concept of garnishing as in other chapters on owls, overlay owl's cap with some egg yolk paste; for feather effect, pipe some of the paste on wing areas and tail too. For eyes, place white of egg and cover with black olives using flat parsley to accentuate eyelashes and socket. Use pepper triangles for ears. (optional) Follow suit as for rest of our feathered friend with carrot nose and celery branch stalk to set upon, etc.

If you like the family of gray owls better, merely substitute chopped herring for liver.

CHOPPED LIVER CLOCK

This is a nice one to make for a get-to-gether for a New Year's Eve party or for that farewell when it's time to retire.

Form shape of clock's face in whatever pan you like (as nowadays clocks do come in every conceivable size and shape). Personally, I'm old-fashioned and still prefer the round ones, so I merely pack my liver into a round cake baking pan. Always remember to refrigerate mold for several hours to firm up liver. Turn chopped liver mold out onto serving tray.* Use the pastry tube method to overlay the numerals on the face of your clock. Position hands at 12, as if ready to strike, for New Year's Eve party. Use 2 green pepper strips or serrated carrot strips for hands of the clock. If tray is large and room on it remains, with a fine tube tip on your pastry bag write across the tray itself,

Happy New Year, and the year.

If the party is for your favorite foreman whose time it is to retire, you might need a little more food stuff than the face of a clock would supply for a crowd. Do a take-off on the theme; prepare enough liver to make the encasement outside of his time clock puncher or a grandfather's clock. For this you will need a long rectangular tray to turn out or free form your chopped liver wood encasement upon. You can also use the brown of the liver similarly to reproduce the case of a grandfather's clock. For variety, use chopped egg salad or chicken salad* or whatever as the face of the clock within, thus giving you 2 different salads to choose from. If you like the combo of egg salad and caviar (if you want to show him you threw cost to the wind) invest in a small jar of black caviar with which to carefully write in the Roman numerals on the clock face. Use carrot stick Roman numerals for us plebians. Position in green pepper hands; use celery stalks, rounded side up, as the pendulums of the grandfather's clock. Overlay the more intricate design of a grandfather's clock or factory punch-in timer with egg yolk paste cream.

Your new enlarged replica of a clock can now feed a bunch of old business pals or a whole family.

A FROSTY WINTER WONDERLAND

Just the title sounds intriguing enough to make you read further. Let's see just what magic transformation can take place in your own kitchen using ordinary every day food staples. Personally, I didn't find the whole thing amusing or intriguing at all! I was merely presented with 15 lbs. of brown chopped liver for the dinner dance and then was told the theme for the

---

*Optional: If desired, cover face of clock *only* with white aspic coating. (See Winter Wonderland) on separate tray before transferring clock face to larger tray & surrounding with liver "wood encasement".)

evening was "A Frosty Winter Wonderland." With some thought (as previously touched on in chapter 5, see penguins, igloo, and icebergs), following is the manner in which I decided to present the buffet table to help set the mood for the attending 300 guests.

Give it a try the next time its your turn to play "Committee" for the next big winter binge! Try a smaller scaled version of it for the hungry ski crowd coming over for a hot toddy party get-together.

The height of your ski slope winter scene will be determined by how much *very firm* chopped liver you have prepared or purchased. With many other accompanying main entrees for this community buffet table, I used 15 lbs. of firm chopped liver for this particular edible and most well received food centerpiece display. Working with a minimum of at least 5 lbs. of liver you can create a smaller scaled down mountain or ski run. Using a large foil covered tray, set your liver mountain at one end leading down and onto the side of the tray. Prepare your mountain or ski slope by mounding it, packing and shaping it free-form with your hands. Now for the magic: somehow using only the facility of your own kitchen we must transform this dark massive hill shaped "blob" into a magnificent white ski slope run. Following the recipe and directions given, cook up a white glaze which can then be used as an aspic, giving a thin coating effect to the chopped liver (or for that matter to anything such as egg salad, chicken salad or whatever, see chapter 8: chicken salad basket with aspic coat.

This recipe for a glaze coating aspic will cover 5 lbs. of ham, liver and chicken salad or use to put a shimmering coat on a molded form of potato salad.

HOW TO MAKE A LIGHT COLORED COVERING GLAZE*

2 envelopes Knox gelatin
1 c. cold chicken broth (or substitute cold beef broth or make
    your own vegetable broth and allow to cool)
2 c. mayonnaise

Soften gelatin in cold broth in small saucepan. Dissolve over low heat. Remove pan from heat and stir in mayonnaise until smooth. (I find a whisk does this job well.) Let stand to set 30 minutes (time it; it's important) or until slightly thickened. Spoon ½ c. glaze over food (liver, ham, potatoe salad or whatever is being coated) so that top and sides are lightly but evenly coated. (Similar to putting a light covering of frosting over a cake to cover the initial loose crumbs and then following with thicker coat of frosting to actually decorate the cake—you did know that trick, didn't you?) Let first coat of aspic set. Continue until completely coated using one or two more thin coatings rather than one heavy one. If any decoration (cut out flower designs) or garnishing (finely chopped egg whites) are to be placed do so *before* last coating has time to dry or it won't adhere properly.

Allow this white aspic to run down and completely cover the brown liver mountainous ski slope. Be sure the bottom surface of the tray itself is also covered with the white aspic glaze as this will be the snow or frosty image we are looking to attain.

Ski run path: Using a narrow strip of foil lightly cover the middle "run" of your ski slope so it remains glistening and looks used. With your (ski run) cover in position, place only cooked egg whites through a food mill or chop very finely. Drizzle your newly created "snow" (egg whites) over the mountainous terrain and ground. Be sure snow is drizzled and lightly pressed

*Also see How to Make a Dark Colored Covering Glaze earlier in this chapter.

in to glaze after last coating and *before* it dries! Remove foil strip.

TO CREATE LAKE OR SKATING POND: Although chopped blue or green gelatin would do nicely for a lake you might prefer the quick method of merely laying down an old large hand or shaving mirror (no longer being used) on top of the flat surface of your snow covered tray. Since you have just created a skating pond put upon it a few skating figures (look in your old Christmas collection or raid the novelty stores or children's toy shops for same). I was even fortunate enough to find a couple of skiing figures to set upon my ski run to add that true touch of realism. If you can't find any skiing figures, don't fret—merely close the ski run down for lunch. Put up a notice "Ski Run Lift Is Closed Today!" and so there would be no one up there skiing. Go one further if you'd like. Name your mountain slope . . . put up a little sign "Ski Mt. Fujiami at Your Own Risk! Enjoy the excitement as your first guest comes along and cuts into the frost covered ice mountain and realizes its all not make-believe—it's truly a Winter Wonderland, only one that you can really eat!

CHOPPED LIVER BONNET

As one thought quickly gives birth to another you can easily see that with this new aspic coating new dimensions are open to us once more.

For that finished look and to cover whatever we wish to actually change in color or sublimate to suit our needs, more can now be done with this concept of simply aspic coating it; e.g., the chopped liver hat touched upon previously: if we wish to coat it to make it into a pale yellow bonnet, would merely necessitate the drop or two of yellow food dye into the cold beef or chicken broth liquid prior to mixing with the mayonnaise to prepare the aspic covering. Proceed to cover the bonnet hat in deep canary yellow aspic. Place a pimento ribbon around its

base and fill in with a few cut vegetable flowers around the brim
(see Chapter 7).

CHOPPED LIVER IGLOO

Take a chopped liver mold(turned out from a deep round
mixing bowl), cover it with a white aspic coating as the one
previously described. Overlay with the egg yolk cream paste to
outline the ice bricks (use the pastry tube method) to transform
it into an igloo. Set about it a few penquins eggs (Chapter 5).
Cover the tray bottom with some aspic and egg whites chopped
fine. You have just created another winter scene!

And so on to bigger and greater things, using the same
learned principles of food sculpture over again and again.

7 TABLE DECORATIONS AND FRESH VEGETABLES

BARBECUE CHEF

To make a barbecue chef use contents of bleach from plastic gallon size bottle and clean out thoroughly; fill with sand or water to give weight to it so it won't tip over. Recover with screw top cover. Using handle in front as chest, draw on with felt marking pen, arms holding fork. Slip over top of bottle a piece of material cut out to look like apron and tie around waist with bow in back. Glue into position. Add cut out black felt feet, and glue onto base of bottle. Position into place around bottle neck a 1″ band of cardboard so that it will act as neck to raise up head of figure. Secure into position (use floral gum tape) an appropriate sized styrofoam ball for head of figure. For the eyes, use buttons. The top cover of a "Bic" pen for a nose (if he's a gourmet chef, give him a blue nose), use imitation fur material to create the brows, hair and mustache for our chef, use red felt for a mouth if desired instead of mustache; glue or pin onto styrofoam head. Design a chef's hat from tissue paper and pin in place on top of head. Create a neckerchief from a remnant of red checkered cloth material and wrap about (cardboard) neck. Place chef on runner of material from checkerboard design and place in center of table as centerpiece. For barbecue surround with barbecue tools.

TO CREATE ITALIAN FIESTA CENTERPIECE

Using same runner place chef on top and off to the side slightly. Next to him place empty wicker wine basket and proceed to fill back section of basket with fresh chicory or greens of choice, base of leaves wrapped in foil. Fill narrow front end of wine basket with assorted bread sticks (garlic, plain or sesame seed), top with Italian hot peppers or any selection of green and red peppers for color. On top of the peppers place some wrapped cheeses and top with red, black and/or green grapes. You don't need fancy napkin ring holders as you can make your own to fit in with this theme. Take uncooked manicotta shell and pull through a large red paper napkin. Write "welcome" or name of each guest on each manicotta. (Use felt marker or tube of *Glow Writer obtainable in craft store)

TO CREATE WINE CENTERPIECE USING CHEF BLEACH BOTTLE

Place chef bleach bottle off to one side of table centerpiece. Set on large size tray atop checker print material runner. Place a wicker cornucopia along side. Fill cornucopia so it overflows onto tray with crackers, bread sticks, sesame sticks, foil covered assorted cheeses, nuts in their natural shells, some apples, etc. Decorate top of wicker basket with grape clusters. Gather nearby an assortment of wines and glasses and if desired you can add the pretty colored drip type candles in background for

*TRADE NAME—can also be used to write name on watermelon ship's rind: chapter 2.

effect. Also see Flower Lady in Chapter 1 on Pineapples: Flower Cart.

EGGPLANT CLOWN

Choose for your eggplant clown a suitable eggplant, one with a rotund shape. Cut off small slice from base so it is stabilized and will not roll and fall over. Cut off small slice from top section of vegetable so it is flat also. Take an appropriate size lemon to

be used for its head and cut off stabilizing base from bottom. Cut off ⅓ section from top of lemon and set aside. Using a toothpick, make two holes to accommodate two whole cloves for eyes in the larger ⅔ lemon section. Use the melon stripper, strip out

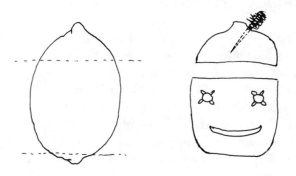

a piece of lemon rind for a smiling mouth and color it in with red food coloring and a cotton bud. See diagram.

Place some chicory or other "greens" atop of body of clown for his collar and partially push in toothpick to hold collar. Leave toothpick exposed to receive lemon head. Push on ⅔ section of lemon for head. Place on top of cut lemon some more greens for hair of clown and replace removed ⅓ top section of lemon for hat. Hold hat in place with a long frill colored toothpick. Pare and clean fresh carrot and cut off a one inch section from thick end stub of carrot. Halve and shape to resemble feet.

Use floral or heavy type of toothpick to secure carrot feet into place at base of eggplant. Cut off appropriate size (approximately 2"), section from remainder of carrot to be the arms of your clown. However, cut carrot in half lengthwise with the serrator thereby giving crinkle-effect arms. Secure in appropriate position with heavy toothpicks. With large frill toothpicks pierce red cherry tomatoes into center front of clown as the buttons of his costume.

TO CREATE BABY EGGPLANT CLOWN

Use small eggplant and proceed as above using appropriate sized cut carrot sections for arms and feet. Use kumquat for head if lemons are too big and scalloped carrot slices for buttons.

EGGPLANT PENGUIN

To make eggplant penguin cut off small slice from base of eggplant to stabilize figure. Set aside. Leaving green "collar" top intact, merely cut off stalk stem (if any) so it is flattened to later receive head of penguin. Cut off thin slice from front of body of penguin. Brush with lemon juice or cover with light coat of white vegetable shortening. With sharp knife cut out two flippers on your figure, slicing from base of flipper toward top. Be sure *not* to cut deeply or cut the flippers off completely. See diagram.

To wedge flippers away from body of penguin use small unobtrusive pieces of eggplant from discarded base and wedge just under "armpit" of figure so it does not show.

Paint on (use felt marker or glue felt scrap pieces into position) the face of a penguin onto a hard cooked *unshelled and uncracked* egg. Pierce *carefully* base of egg and secure to top of eggplant with use of floral wood pick or skewer. If desired, the egg *can* be shelled and secured into position with wood pick. NOTE: I find in using a peeled egg it very often breaks up in transporting as it is fragile. The face of a shelled egg can then be created with use of olive eyes or whole cloves and a cherry mouth. Place two chunks of shaped "feet" carrots in position as in directions for eggplant clown.

EGGPLANT HELICOPTER

Choose a large eggplant suitably shaped for the helicopter you will create. Preparing your helicopter will be somewhat familiar in procedure, as it is very similar to the preparation for a watermelon airplane. See diagram depicting the completed centerpiece, proceed accordingly: outline with pencil the pilot's windows. Cut out carefully but do not cut too deeply (as the seeds within will then be exposed, which would take away from the effect.)

To simulate wheels: Cut two slices of carrot ½" thick (see how to prepare scalloped carrots with use of lemon stripper in vegetable section). Place carrot wheels in appropriate position by securing into place with use of wood floral picks. Try not to expose pick's tip point through the other side of carrot wheel.

To create propellers:

Top front blades: Using a small chunk of carrot as a base, pierce top with cherry tomato or radish and two long pieces of string beans, all held together with club frill toothpick as in diagram.

These helicopters are very easy to make and are a big hit, as each child can take one home from the birthday party as a souvenir. As a centerpiece it can easily be suspended above the party table. Use dental floss or fishing line, which is less noticeable and is stronger.

To use helicopter as a mustard or relish holder: makes a big hit served with hot dogs at a party. Before outlining the window for the pilot compartment, cut out an oval shaped top of eggplant as illustrated. Scoop out all seeds and most of pulp within thus allowing more room for the mustard or relish. (Line eggplant with foil if desired before filling with relish.)

Continue as in procedure above placing the top propeller

blade and carrot stub into the cut out oval shaped cover. Keep cover on until ready to serve. Your little guests will love your airborne mustard holder.

Eggplant plane: you will need 2 oval shaped eggplants to create this. To create a plane use the same procedure for watermelon plane and apply to a more appropriately shaped eggplant. Use the stalk stem end for propeller end of plane and cut up the second eggplant to provide the other necessary wings to your airborne passenger liner.

CHEESE OR TOMATO ROSE

For tomato rose: Tomato must be very firm, but ripe.

Leaves: Will be simulated by using the block form cream cheese, as the whipped cream cheese will not hold up as well. Remove cheese from refrigerator at the last possible moment.

Stamen: Use hard cooked egg yolk crumbled and then color with dusting of paprika.

Hold tomato firmly between thumb and index finger. Take a teaspoon (preferably a grapefruit spoon, which is serrated on both sides and comes to a point on top) and scrape the top of the cream cheese block until cheese half fills spoon bowl. Starting first petal 1" from blossom top of tomato, transfer the "leaf" thus formed on spoon to tomato by holding against side of tomato and "wiping" in downward stroke. Continue same procedure and work around to complete the circle. Using same spoon method, start a new row of leaves by placing the first leaf of the second row just below and stagger it between the first two leaves of the first row. See diagram.

Work rows of leaves onto tomato until just above ½" from base. Push tomato rose onto a toothpick or skewer that is held in place atop a foil wrapped styrofoam piece which has been garnished with chicory. See diagram.

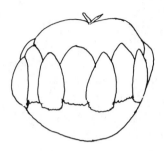

Using "poetic license" in the kitchen (use your finger), take a dab of the remaining block of cream cheese to cover the blossom end of the tomato and the remaining 1″ area exposed just above the first row of cheese leaves. Now press into this cream cheese center the crumbled hard cooked egg yolk to simulate the stamen. Dust with a little paprika for color.

The same principle can be applied to even a small cherry tomato. You would then use a demitasse spoon to press cream cheese on or use a pastry tube to decorate cherry tomatoes. To serve as is surround with other tidbits and hors d'oeuvres on a large tray or place on a bed of lettuce greens and complement with lox, onion and bagel for individual service for a luscious midnight snack. *TO CREATE A CHEESE ROSE:* using same procedure as above, merely substitute a firm hard cheese ball and proceed as above. Serve with crackers for spreading.

VIKING BOAT RELISH SERVER

It's a Viking boat fashioned from a cucumber, (OR to serve a larger group substitute an eggplant and line cavity with foil) sailing on waves of chicory. To make it you will need:
Large cucumber or appropriate sized eggplant
3 green or black pitless olives
Chicory
3 plastic straws cut into halves or 6 wooden cocktail forks
Frill toothpicks
Black oaktag
Small piece clear plastic wrap or scotch tape
Aluminum foil
Small 2″ thick styrofoam block about the same length as the
    cucumber or eggplant
    There is no need to stabilize vegetable as it will be secured to styrofoam block. Using the curve of a grapefruit knife blade, create a "widow's peak" at one end of the cucumber (like the top of a heart) and continue to other end, creating an oval shape at the other end opposite heart shape. Scoop out the seeds from the middle of the cucumber with a teaspoon or serrated grapefruit spoon. Cover the styrofoam (A) with aluminum foil and place chicory over the sides and top of the foil. This can be held in place effectively with the use of totem pole or philodendron pins (sometimes called greening pins) available at florist shop. Secure and position your cucumber on the top of the foil-covered styrofoam block by pushing a skewer, or 2 floral picks or orangewood stick (for eggplant) through the bottom of the scooped out cucumber (B and C), forcing it into the foam block. Cut a serpent's head shape from the black oaktag, following pattern given, and cover the bottom of its long neck with a small piece of clear plastic wrap held in place or piece of scotch tape. If for eggplant make larger head. Make a slit (D) with a

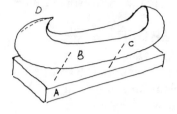

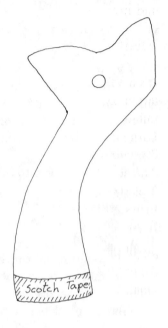

paring knife down the center of your point of the widow's peak and insert the head in place. The plastic wrap will prevent the oaktag from bleeding and becoming limp. Just below the long parallel sides of the cucumber insert the slices of olives and hold in place by piercing with frill toothpicks, approximately 3 or 4 per side, depending upon the size of the cucumber or eggplant being used. Slide on the plastic straws and you will find that they will hold easily in place on the cellophane frill of the toothpicks or cut off pointed fork end of cocktail fork and use remaining piece as it resembles an oar.

Place your entire creation on a tray and fill with mustard. An optional but nice touch is to place the boat on a larger size tray and to fill the balance of the open space with cold hors d'oeuvres such as cheese chunks, ham bits with pineapple wedges, peperoni, etc. Your Viking boat can also be used to hold seafood cocktail sauce, relish, dressings, etc., surrounded with appropriate combinations of accompanying food. E.g., for Lenten holiday: fish bites with tartar sauce; for Jewish Passover holiday: gefilte fish with horseradish, etc.

VEGETABLE MENAGERIE

VEGETABLE DUCKLING

To create a duckling using fresh garden vegetables instead of eggs, which are more fragile for handling and more perishable standing on a buffet table for long periods of time, one need only follow the same principle in miniature version as per the combined directions for creating the turnip swan and the directions to create the carrot feet base of the egg duckling and chickadee in chapter 5 on eggs.

Using directions for swan, choose a smaller turnip and outline wing areas. Follow procedure for swan and transform your little creature into a duck by merely reducing the length of the neck of your bird. Follow through with directions for the egg chickadee as for feet base made of carrot. see Chapter 5 on same.

VEGETABLE CHICKADEE

To transform an egg chickadee into a vegetable and more durable chick substitute a small turnip for the (egg) body and follow suit as for the body and wings of the turnip swan. Proceed then with directions to make head of chickadee from white icicle radish or pared red radish with proportionate neck size. Submerge head and neck and body sections into a yellow food bath for coloring properly. Let dry. With cotton bud apply undiluted yellow or red food coloring for beak area. Place whole cloves for eyes in proper position. Place on stabilized carrot feet base as per chickadee instructions in chapter 5 on eggs.

TURTLE

To create your turtle vegetable you will need:
1 scallop squash
1 green frying pepper
2 whole cloves
4 green frill toothpicks
(French) lemon stripper implement
food coloring and cotton bud

Depending on what size turtle you wish to form, choose an appropriately sized scallop squash. This will then become the hard shell (top) of your turtle. With this in hand, choose an appropriately long and curled tip shaped Italian hot frying green pepper. The bell shaped stem end of the pepper will then be long enough to extrude in front of the squash body and become the head of the turtle; the tip end of the same pepper will be long enough to extrude out the tail end of the squash body and become the exposed tail of the turtle.

With a lemon stripper, strip out pieces of the scallop squash, thus determining the age of your turtle (a turtle's age is judged by the number of shell boxes on its carapace). Optional: color in the strips with food coloring and cotton bud to emphasize same.

Undercut with a knife the underbase side of the scallop squash (shell) to custom fit the pepper into position across the bottom, leaving extruded both ends of the pepper to act as the head and tail of your animal. Secure into position on both sides of the turtle 4 green frill picks for its moving legs thereby simultaneously securing the pepper body into position.

For eyes: pre-hole and push into position on either side of green pepper head 2 whole cloves for eyes. Optional: With use of lemon stripper pull up but do *not cut out* 2 appropriate eyelids on pepper head. Lift gently and then place in the 2 whole cloves as eyes of turtle.

See springtime setting as centerpiece to make turtles feel right at home.

ONE GRACEFUL VEGETABLE SWAN

Turnip Body: Choose a medium size white oval turnip and pare skin. As per diagram place on side and cut to stabilize. Cut off green leaf top. With pencil or toothpick point design and outline on either side of turnip the wings of this graceful bird.

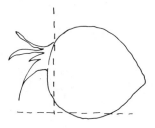

Following outline cut along outlined wing design with a sharp paring knife to depth of ¼″. After cutting in wing design start shaving out shaded areas as in diagram. Do *not* cut deeply, merely SHAVE turnip in layers until wing design stands out as in three dimensional art work. Using lemon stripper, pull *away but not off* little pieces on sides of wings *only* to provide wing with a feathered look to it. Place turnip in ice water bath to force wing cuts to open more for a nice feather effect to our bird.

Icicle radish head and neck section: Choose a long suitably shaped white icicle radish to act as the head and graceful neck

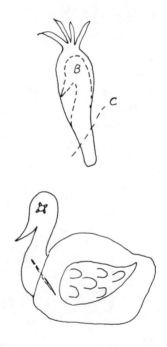

section for our swan. Pare skin. With sharp knife cut radish to outline form of head and neck for a swan. Use thickest part of radish top for head and beak. Use potato peeler to shape a more graceful neck by *shaving* layers of the radish off carefully. Cut off stabilizing slice at base of (radish) neck for angled placement against front of turnip body (see B and C). Push floral toothpick into turnip body at necessary angle leaving pick end exposed to receive the radish neck (and head section) of swan. Push base of radish neck onto exposed toothpick after first pre-holing neck for easier placement. Color in beak with yellow food coloring and cotton bud tip. Pre-hole and place in whole clove eyes on either side of head.

Pretty when displayed on a bridal table or set upon a lime gelatin lake amidst artichoke lily pads. (See this chapter for lily pads created from artichoke leaves and white icicle radishes.)

VEGETABLE BUTTERFLY

To create a beautiful, graceful and edible butterfly you can use any of the following vegetables. The size and diameter of our chosen vegetable will determine the size of your flying friend.

Vegetables suggested: Large black radish (NOTE: The actual pulp of a black radish is white), a turnip, carrot, and even a large common red radish take on the graceful and dainty wingspread of a butterfly very effectively.

Personally, I prefer using the Japanese white radish, called a

daikon. Daikons are obtainable in all sizes and grow up to even 4″ in diameter. The fibrous grain of this vegetable takes on a most beautiful shade of food coloring when immersed in a nice cold food dye and water solution.

Using the daikon as my model: Pare the vegetable and slice off a small thin stabilizing base. Following diagram carefully make the first slice ⅛ to ¼″ wide cutting to but *not* all the way down to the base. A second slice of equal width (⅛–¼″) will then be cut down and through the base thereby separating the workings of your butterfly from the rest of the daikon root. You can see that many more butterflies can be cut from the remaining piece of daikon.

Holding first and second slices together, follow the diagram and cut around one side of the butterfly simultaneously, thereby releasing two thin strips A & B. Be careful not to cut down to base or you will accidentally detach these strips; they are to serve as the antennae of your creature.

Cut out two small wedge shaped sections (as depicted in illustration) to add more design to the wings of your flying

creature. Cut out with a small paring knife, tiny V-shaped notches all along the intervening sections, as shown.

Proceed now to make one slash cut (dotted line in illustration) and holding this anterior section by its base, lift it up and push it into the opening of the remaining section of the butterfly placing it between the wings (the first and second ¼″ slices). It will give the appearance of a charging bull.

Be careful in placing the anterior section into the back end,

for it is at this point it is extremely fragile. If desired, immerse in ice cold food coloring solution. Your colorful butterfly will be emphasized more if it is simply set upon a bed of cut chicory or lettuce leaves off to the side of your main serving dish, as a garnish. It would also look most beautiful hovering above a chopped liver presentation of a beehive (see chapter 6) or above a floral arrangement of edible vegetable flowers.

SPRING SCENE

After learning how to present such vegetable figures as ducks, turtles, swans, etc., how can we put all that to use?

Of course, it would delight any child for a birthday party with a zoo as a theme setter, or use the swans for a wedding party, but let's have some fun and incorporate all our newly created animal figures into one grand setting—a picture of a refreshing springtime countryside scene.

Using a 3″ wide green styrofoam block form, cut out free form the piece desired for your setting and background. Please keep in mind the area allotted you on your serving table before outlining the size of foam for cutting.

To create our lake or pond *waterfront* area, outline with pencil and cut out to a depth of 1½″ a free form designed water area. Line only this *water* area with silver foil; it will later be filled with mashed lime jello to simulate the water hole of our country setting. Cover all the remaining "grass" area of the styrofoam with chicory greens. Hold greens in place with totem pole or greening pins.

To plant our garden: use floral picks to stabilize and hold our garden pieces in position on the styrofoam.

Logs: cut off all florets from broccoli stalks and lay only the stalks down horizontally onto styrofoam as if they were logs. Hold in place with (hidden) floral picks as aforementioned.

Small bushes: the large clumps of florets cut from the broccoli stalks (logs) can be separated and placed to act as little evergreen bushes.

Trees: the larger sized broccoli florets in larger clumps can serve as a tree here and there. To create a tree that appears to be swaying in the breeze merely use kohlrabi vegetable with leaves and flowers intact; stand up vertically. Stabilize into styrofoam with floral picks or the stronger orange wood sticks.

Flowers: choose any cut of vegetable flower you wish to "plant" amid your garden greenery. Use *fresh* stringbeans or pea pods as the large side leaves of each flower stalk stem.

Mushrooms: use fresh mushroom caps with base in tact to break up greenery.

Scallop squash: place in country setting to hold frog (egg); see Chapter 5.

Turtle: can be created from scallop squash and green frying pepper (see this chapter)

For waterfront area: fill foil lined lake or pond water area with blue or lime colored gelatin that has been set and then mashed to represent the water area of your setting; see Chapter 9 on gelatins.

Lily Pads: Place lily pad upon lake area; directions to follow.

Swan: see swan from white turnip and white icicle radish,

this chapter. Place upon lake water.

Duck: create duck from egg (see Chapter 5 on egg menagerie) or from vegetables (this chapter). Set upon (water) bank or in pond itself.

Choose any or all or a few of the above to combine and provide a refreshing spring time season setting and display of food presentation, all actually edible.

LILY PADS FOR SPRING OR LAKE DISPLAY

Its as simple as buying an artichoke and cutting a couple of white icicle radishes into flowers to create the lovely lily pad setting atop a lake or pond of lime jello.

Pare and cut white icicle radishes into flower forms. Pulling off several outside leaves of the artichoke (use remainder for cooking and serving the family another time) place 4-5 leaves together catching base end of each one and overlapping the leaves on the *same* floral pick. Spread out leaves and secure *white* radish flower onto remaining exposed pick end as per

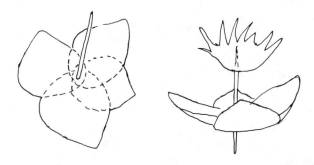

diagram. Several lily pads can be created from one artichoke. Set on lake of lime jello and float a swan or two nearby.

See spring scene for combining all these ideas into one food presentation.

AN OLD-FASHIONED VEGETABLE BOUQUET

It is lovely, although quite expensive nowadays, to set the party or dinner table with a centerpiece of fresh flowers delivered from your local florist. How much nicer and far less costly to create your own unique floral arrangement, one that is not only refreshing but *entirely edible.*

With the simple instructions to follow, you can cut and thereby create your own flowering blossoms using ordinary fresh vegetables from the local produce market or even vegetables from your own backyard or nearby farm. To hold and arrange your flowers into an old-fashioned nosegay bouquet you will need a small head of cabbage to be used as a "pincushion" base. The size of the cabbage selected depends upon how many you expect to feed. (See notes on vegetable bouquet as showpiece; to follow in context.)

I prefer using two 1 lb. cabbages as a base and placing them at both ends of the table rather than one 2 lb. cabbage head placed at the center of my entertainment table. The first reason being that you can just get so many pick ends or bamboo sticks (to hold your flowers) into the base; secondly, if you have that large a party for dinner, you want to break up the length of your serving table and keep your centerpieces low in height for better "visual" conversation of your guests. For a buffet dinner party, you would prefer directing your "table traffic pattern" in two directions so everyone has a chance to "gather" her own flowers.

Choose a well rounded 1 lb. cabbage, slice off a small piece to stabilize the base side. Wrap the cabbage with saran wrap to prevent the permeating of odors. On the day following the dinner party the cabbage can then be unwrapped and cut up for coleslaw or used to make a luscious cabbage soup. As you see your floral arrangement is really truly completely edible right down to and including the base.

Cut your flowers as per directions that follow. Using the cab-

— 318 —

bage head for a pincushion base, secure your heavier blossoms, the beet and turnip roses and dahlias onto orange wood sticks and force them into the cabbage base. These larger blooms need *not* be centered on the cabbage base but should be balanced so that the "pincushion" does not tip over before you have time to equalize the weight and fill in with other edible flowers. Use club and regular sized frill picks and wooden floral picks to hold and secure the lighter weights of flower shapes (e.g., radishes, scallion, carrots, olives, etc.). Cut bamboo skewers to various sizes to hold some of the flowers. The use of the varied lengths of bamboo sticks will also give your bouquet some height and dimension and thereby create more interest to your unique centerpiece. As filler for the floral arrangement and to provide edibility, fill in with whole cherry tomatoes, pickled onions, midget gherkin pickle fans, cut broccoli and cauliflower florets. Although the latter are *uncooked* they, as well as fresh uncooked mushrooms, are very tasty and retain even more vitamins. Fill in with sprigs of celery hearts, cucumber chunks, black olives, green pimento filled olives, etc. A nice variation to your vegetable creation would be the addition of small (serrated) cut chunks of different cheeses or even meats. For added color, use the various technicolor foil wrapped "Laughing Cow" tidbit cheese squares.

Garnish with fresh curly sprigs of American parsley and/or celery leaf tops. When all of your vegetables are pinned into position on the cabbage base, encompass the whole bouquet with (appropriate sized) paper doilies. The doilies will hold easily in place by pinning them through with totem pins. The area between the doilies and the vegetables on the cabbage may now be filled with chicory or some "greenery" leaves for extra nibbling and color contrast as well as filler.

Place your bouquet on an unobtrusive tray as the centerpiece for your dinner table and complement it with soft candlelight. Alternative: If you wish, you may place a small bouquet arrangement as the nibbling centerpiece at several smaller tables set up in cabaret style. Set your unique creation within the confines of a low curved wicker fireplace basket. Trim the handle appropriately with sprigs of lilies of the valley if it is for a wedding or engagement party. If you prefer you might also simply place the base of the cabbage inside and atop of a low round circular bamboo or rattan basket. If you are really enthusiatic you can bake your own basket from a bread dough (Fleischman's Yeast Company puts out a book on this) by forming rope like strands and shaping them into a bread basket, glazing and baking it. Use this to hold bouquet of vegetable flowers.

For those with a heavy working schedule, the bouquet need not necessarily be *overflowing* with *carved* fresh flowers to eat. Start, however, by encompassing the whole cabbage head in loads of chicory (pin greenery in with totem pins); plant amidst all that greenery, just a few well made *large* beet or turnip flowers. For those with less time to cut and shape the vegetables into flowers use more "filler" such as cherry tomatoes, mushrooms, broccoli, olives, and foil wrapped cheeses and serrated cut meat chunks.

If the nosegay bouquet is to be used as a centerpiece for a dinner show or a dance recital, pin in or paste onto the doily, a pretty bow with a flow of ribbon ends running onto the table. Attach an old fashioned program dance card to one of the ribbons recording the order of the dance performed or the show's musical score.

Lo and behold . . . you now have another avocation. You are no longer a housewife or even a domestic engineer. With a few turns of the knife, you have become a florist with the creative flair of making your own one-of-a-kind flower arrangements, be it for a large party, dinner show or even for a few friends in for a cocktail or two. Your small nosegay bouquet will look well set upon a cocktail or coffee table and accompanied by a small serving of hor d'oeuvres, before rushing off to the theater.

FLOWER FILLED POT OR VASE ARRANGEMENT

A nice variation of the floral bouquet is one created to resemble a flower filled pot or vase.

With so many pretty colorful flower pots (or vases) available, choose one that will pick up the color scheme of your party table. Line pot with a plastic bag. Fill base of pot with small rocks to prevent tipping over. In place of the usual styrofoam pincushion base, you will find it more advantageous to substitute a piece from a block of floral oasis. Available in floral houses or garden centers, the oasis can be more easily conformed to size and shape of the pot (or vase) and will act as an absorber for the melting ice water. Fill chipped or crushed ice in around sides and on top of oasis. Thus you now see the need for lining pot with a plastic bag. Use floral wooden picks and various size cuts of bamboo skewer lengths to stabilize and hold the carved vegetables flowers into the oasis base thus forming the blossoming flower part top to your "potted" floral arrangement.

Since we are looking for an overall vertical design, fill your flower pot holder with leafy topped celery stalks, escarole and chicory leaves, serrated carrots and cucumber sticks, etc. Fill in with fresh stalks of parsley. This vase or potted floral arrangement is especially nice as a table setting for a garden or springtime party. If invited for an Easter dinner, bring one or two fresh potted "vegetable plants" along for your hostess' table. It's much more unique and far less expensive than the usual floral bouquet or a potted geranium plant or Easter lily.

FOR A SMALLER INDIVIDUAL "FLOWER POT": Use a small eggplant or bell pepper as the vase (base) holder and fill with smaller cut vegetable flowers, escarole and leafy celery stalks. Pepper shells can also be used as holder to serve a dip, relishes and salad dressings. If preferred, bake minature bread baskets as per directions for previously described under: An Old Fashioned Vegetable Bouquet. Perch a vegetable carved butterfly hovering above. See: To create a Vegetable Butterfly, this chapter.

VEGETABLE GARDEN: A nice refreshing edible center-piece theme for a springtime garden party is to assemble an assortment of little wooden strawberry crate type baskets and fill them with different cut vegetables; e.g., a basket of cherry tomatoes, a basket of carrot sticks, a basket of red radishes . . . even a basket of sour pickles (if it goes better with your meal); just mark the latter "pickled cucumbers," for that's all they are. Fill in with fresh parsley. Using a cocktail wooden fork as a garden stick marker, paste on the little colorful pictured packets of real vegetable seeds respectively marked for each basket of vegetables "planted." Display your vegetable garden with little houseplant type garden tools such as a minature shovel, rake, etc. Each guest can use a garden tool close at hand to harvest his own vegetables from your garden box variety. Also see the following for mood setting edible centerpiece to accompany above garden vegetables.

A FLOWERING GARDEN WINDOW BOX: As per chapter 6 you may have already figured this cute variation out on your own. If not, try this party loaf filled bread version for a spring-time setting or Flower Garden Show.

Order loaf of pullman bread to be made up in desired color. Then remove crusts, leaving a colored box outside. Cut height

of loaf bread if necessary for overall proper look to your flower box. Empty some of the soft inside of the loaf to form the shape of a long flower window box leaving an 1" border all around. Prepare party loaf properly by coating inside of bread loaf with a butter spread or paste. Fill with egg salad or tuna or whatever. Cover entire top surface of filled in salad liberally with cut chopped fresh parsley "grass." "Plant" your window box with flowers every 2–3" apart.

TO CREATE FLOWERS FOR WINDOW BOX: Carrot sticks would make a nice sturdy stem topped off with a carved vegetable flower blossom in full bloom (opened properly in iced water). Cut green peppers up to act as leaves and place at each side of base of flower. Set window box as edible centerpiece on table. When ready to serve, cut into portions providing each guest with a section of the flowering window box.

To further set the mood and enhance the table setting, fill a water sprinkling can with ice chips. Use water can to hold

additional celery stalks, carrot and cucumber sticks, cherry tomatoes and olives, etc. Thus, your filled sprinkling can may provide more of a varied assortment of fresh garden vegetables to supplement your window box flowers and tuna salad. If large bowl of salad greens is being served with the tuna bread party loaf, then carry out your garden theme by providing a long nozzled smaller shallow watering pot to dispense your salad dressing for these greens. These pretty colored plastic type watering pots come in various designs and in assorted colors to perk up your table settings. Such water pots may be picked up at any 5 & 10¢ store.

TUNA BASKET: To serve a larger quantity of salad such as tuna or salmon or meat salad or chopped liver, form the basket shape itself from the selected main entree choice. Fill in top with carved vegetable flowers and assorted greens. For a more detailed account of the "How To" of same see chapter 8: Tuna Fish Salad; a Floral Basket Arrangement. Also see chicken salad.

FRESH VEGETABLES

Since this is a book primarily devoted to presentation of foods, we will concern ourselves with just those fresh vegetable varieties used for such display.

HOW TO CARVE AND CUT FANCIFUL VEGETABLE FLOWERS

A thing of beauty and a joy to eat: the fresh vegetable in its prime. Treated with deft hands and imagination, it offers an unexpected range of decorative possibilities. The equipment needed is simple and so are the techniques. At the beginning, you will need to read the directions several times over; this, as well as the actual workings of same, will take some time and patience on your part, but with patience, skill grows, likewise speed. It will then not be long before you find yourself composing your own freehand variations with these versatile techniques of cutting and carving vegetables for garnishing and display or just plain eating enjoyment. Rather than work with a firm cold carrot or any root vegetable that must be carved, leave them out to soften at room temperature overnight. You will find them much easier to slice and carve as they will be more pliable when slightly limp. Where sliced petals or leaves of a vegetable are cut, if left out *after* cutting for an hour, the petals will droop even more (as in red radish rose flowers or white radish tulip cuts.) Then when iced they will open to "bloom" even more.

If you wish to have your flowers bloom you must water them! After carving and shaping your vegetable flowers, immerse them in a tub filled with a tray of ice cubes and cold water. As the cubes melt, refill the tray with more cubes so the temperature of the cold water is always at its peak. With the *exception of soft vegetables* such as tomatoes and cucumbers, soak your vegetable carvings in this tray of ice cold water for at least one hour, overnight makes them open more fully. They will open into beautiful "fully bloomed" flowers to use as garnishes for your appetizer tray, and/or form into an old fashioned vegetable bouquet or other vegetable floral arrangements. *NOTE:* See onion mum for exception to above rule. Keep in iced bath until ready to use. Drain well and place on paper towelling for further absorbtion.

WHAT TO LOOK FOR

ONION FAMILY: ONION: Three varieties of onions grown in the states are globe and Spanish onions, similar to each other in their round to oval shape and the Granex-grano onion, shape ranging from somewhat flat to top-shaped. They all vary in color, and are available as white, yellow and red-skinned onions. Look for firm, dry onions with small necks, free from green sunburn spots and other blemishes. Some tend to taste very sharp, others sweet, but all have a strong odor, often leaving an aftertaste and smell to the user, as well as activating the tear ducts.

To help keep your eyes from tearing, I suggest the method I have found most reliable . . . before slicing, place onion in freezer for a short time (but not enough to freeze it). To rid yourself of the smell on your hands, rinse your hands with cold water and then rub with salt. To *disguise the odor* of the onion when using it as a garnish, soak finished cut flower in a solution of water to which a few drops of vanilla extract have been added. If kept in a cool and dry place (60°), onions will keep well for a month or so.

HOW TO CUT AN ONION MUM: Select firm and well shaped onion. Peel and place root end down. To create the flair of the mum flower, slice down leaving ½" base on bottom untouched. Cut into eighths as in a radial cut design.

Place your onion in a bowl of *warm* water. The bowl should be large enough to permit the spread of the cut petals. If you wish to alter the color of the onion, place it in a bowl to which a few drops of desired food coloring have been added. Let stand to equalize room temperature. When tip ends begin to curl and petals spread away from center core, remove the onion mum and then place it in a pan with ice cubes. When working with onions, radishes and turnips (strong odors) keep these vegetables in separate tray so the odors do not permeate the other iced flowers. If you are altering the color of any vegetable, needless to say, the same rule would apply to prevent the colors from running into the other iced flowers. Placed as is or placed inside a sawtoothed pepper cup, this onion mum looks especially beautiful as a garnish for a turkey, duck or lamb dish. To bring beautiful color to simple cut onion rings for salad service, immerse in pickled beets' juice for a few hours to absorb color.

SCALLIONS: Very similar in appearance and uses, the green

onion, shallot and leek are commonly called scallions. Tied and sold in small bunches, they taste refreshing raw but are frequently used to enhance flavor.

GREEN ONIONS: No bulb formation, with tubular tops, these are ordinary onions that were harvested while young.

SHALLOTS: Similar to green onions except they have no thickened bases. Shallots grow in clusters.

LEEKS: With a slight bulb formation but with flattened dark green leaf tops, they are larger than shallots. They make for a most delicious soup. Although bruised tops will not affect the eating quality if the tops are removed, they should possess white portions 2–3″ up from the root end. They should have fresh green tops as yellow wilted color is indicative of a fibrous condition of the bulb eating part.

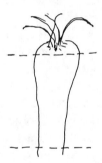

HOW TO CUT A SCALLION MUM: Another variation of a mum cut can be achieved in a somewhat similar fashion. Cut the desired 2–3″ length of the scallion's white bulb section, being sure to remove the yellowish membrane on the top of the bulb end. As per diagram, push into stalk end (approximately 1″) a green frill (stem) toothpick leaving cellophane covered tip of pick exposed to hold while cutting.

Holding exposed green frill pick end between fingers, proceed to cut white bulb end into narrow *pie shaped wedges,* being particularly careful not to cut through to bottom of scallion end. Having cut thusly, you have now exposed approximately ½" of wood pick tip in the center of the bulb. Force a

small slice of scalloped carrot onto the top of pick tip. (See how to cut scalloped slices in carrot section with the use of the lemon stripper.) Press carrot slice and surrounding scallion against cutting board or table to create the feathery effect and secure carrot piece firmly; or: a small melon baller can be used to make the center core out of a contrasting colored carrot or beet (use ¼–½" ball scoop). Substitute this round cut vegetable ball as center stamen of scallion mum. For larger effect, using same principle and club sized frill pick, apply method used above to a leek. Color if desired. Use to garnish large turkey roast or goose. (see chapter 10 on turkey presentation)

SCALLION BRUSH: White bulb section: cut off 2″ section of scallion root. Be sure to remove yellow membrane at bulb end. Cut bulb end in fan slices. (See directions to make fan pickles.) Now crosscut in opposite direction creating a mum effect to your vegetable. (See diagram.) To open, submerge in iced water. If desired, opposite green stalk end of scallion piece may be cut similarly. This scallion brush is very familiar to you as it is one that is always served with Peking duck at the better restaurants.

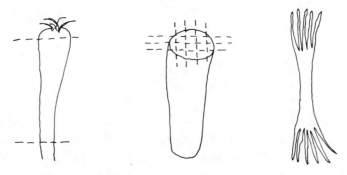

A slightly different feather effect can be achieved if, after the initial first fan cut, you spread out the fan and press the uncut end slightly with your thumb. After spreading the fan, cut the fanned slices crosswise. When iced, this will open into a more elaborate feathered effect.

CELERY: A popular vegetable and good source of roughage. It is most favored by those nibblers who are weight conscious, as the largest celery rib contains only five calories. Fresh and crunchy raw, it is a boon to meat, fish and green salads as well as enhancing the cooking of soups and stews. Look for crisp leafy vegetable stalks with branches that will snap easily. Look for a glossy shine. The fresh bunch of celery with thick branched green leaves is commonly called Pascal celery. Wrapped in plastic or kept in the new plastic containers, celery will keep in the refrigerator for one to two weeks. Leafy tops can be used as filler in vegetable floral arrangements and adds much to soups and salads when minced and mixed together. Celery hearts can also be cut and used as filler in floral vegetable arrangements. *Celery Fans:* The same method of fan cut and cross cut can be applied to 2–3″ sections of celery stalks. Fringe

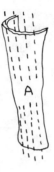

by cutting many slits in either or both ends being sure not to cut through the center area. (A) The ice water will cause the cut tip ends to curl in all directions. For variety cut a ½″ width section, pass the celery section through black ripe pitted olives before immersing in water to spread. Same principle can be applied with use of *carrot sticks,* pass through pitted olives.

CELERY STALK CURL: To add a very delicate type of celery curl to your bouquet arrangements of flowers, try your hand at this fragile looking version using the thin tubular branch stem ends of a celery leaf top or the top greenery stems of the daikon radish. Take narrow strip of celery and make deep angular slanted slices progressing from top to bottom as per diagram.

When placed in iced water it will curl very gracefully to give a very airy wispy effect to add to your potted plant or other vegetable flower arrangements.

INEDIBLE CELERY STEMS FOR YOUR FLOWERS: If centerpiece is strictly "show", then you might like to add some curves to your arrangement by substituting thin gauge floral wire in place of the usual bamboo skewers or wood picks. Using

a celery stem piece or watercress or thin (but limp) scallion green stalks, push floral wire up through center of each celery strand. Push wire from bottom up to and through top surface.

Push onto exposed wire tip point, a carved and opened vegetable flower blossom (your choice) with a bit of greenery tucked in between the two. With the insertion of the floral wire your stemmed flower can be curved and sent in any direction to add height and curvacious realism to your standing *in*edible arrangement.

PARSLEY: Available all year round, fresh parsley is used primarily for decorative purposes but actually should be considered a tasty food addition to one's diet since it is high in chlorophyll and vitamin A. *HELPFUL HINT:* If left with a distateful onion breath, chew a few fresh sprigs of parsley for relief. Look for crisp bright green leaves. If, however, some leaves become wilted, they can be freshened by cutting off stem end tips while they are submerged in cold water. The flat "Italian" parsley is used in preparation of spaghetti sauce; the curly variety is called American parsley. If growing your own home garden variety, and it is plentiful this season, chop parsley fine and store in freezer in covered container. Alternative is to wrap parsley as is, in tightly covering foil and grate only as needed. This same *freezing* process works equally well for storing scallions and chives for long periods of time. To keep parsley fresh for daily use, dry same and store in tightly covered jar in refrigerator for a period up to two weeks. Watercress and mint leaves can be similarly kept fresh in this manner.

CABBAGE: Available all year round, there are many varieties of this vegetable. A greener head of cabbage is more nutritious than white, so look for fresh green color when buying it. The green cabbage with smoother leaves is also less expensive than the others. Therefore, this is the one I choose to serve as my pincushion holders for my vegetable bouquets or for hors d'oeuvre service (see cabbage hibachi in chapter 6).

Choose a large firm head; stabilize and place core side down. The inner section can then be removed in almost all of its entirety leaving a thick shell all around thus forming a bowl or basket shape shell. Use this shell form as a holder for salads such as relishes, cole slaw, etc. Actual basket designs can be cut as per

watermelon shells (see directions for same in chapter 2 on baskets) to prettily hold and dispense same. See diagrams for suggested shapes for filling.

The red cabbage, being of a dark contrasting wine coloring would serve to add further color to your table display if cut similarly into basket shell to hold (contrasting colorful green and white) of coleslaw or salad mixture. Lastly, the texture of the savoy cabbage, possessing a more wrinkled leaf effect, would prove to be more beautiful as a shell holder if those textured outside leaves were to be spread out in a flouncy ruffled effect as a border.

BROCCOLI: Available all year round, broccoli is used in food sculpture designed pieces as trees and logs (see this chapter's Spring Scene) and is used extensively for its color, shape and texture as a filler for vegetable floral arrangements as in carved vegetable bouquets and potted "flower" plants. Look for dark firm floret clusters with no signs of yellowing, as yellow flowers and wilted outside leaves are signs of age. Although generally more common is the dark green member of the cauliflower family, there is also sage green broccoli and even a purple variety, to give you wide range of color variation for displays.

CAULIFLOWER: Used similarly as the broccoli florets this vegetable too is used as a filler for vegetable floral bouquet arrangements. This vegetable in its uncooked form adds a nice crunchy quality when used in salads and for dipping, as do the fresh broccoli florets. Look for firm compact curd with white or creamy white color. Same storing rules as for broccoli, keep cold and use as soon as possible.

GREENS: With so many varieties of leafy vegetables under this heading, one can easily pick up one or more for daily use any time of the year. The greener the leaf of the vegetable, the more chlorophyll content for good health. Greens are best kept wrapped in a Turkish towel to prevent browning of leaves. Used most widely with meat and fish and salads of all kinds is the top leader of salad greens—lettuce. Lettuce can be classified under four headings. Iceberg (the most popular), Butterhead, Romaine, and Leaf Greens. Other greens less commonly used but still classified under as greens for cooking and salad and food sculpture design would be spinach, turnip and beet greens, chicory (sometimes called *curly* endive,) and escarole. Other greens commonly used for cooking primarily are spinach (cooked or fresh, this is a winner combined with mushrooms and bamboo shoots), kale, collards, chard, mustard greens, Belgian endive, dandelion, watercress, and sorrel—and my favorite, Chinese cabbage which tastes just as good fresh in salads as it does cooked in soups or prepared as a side vegetable.

Look for compact bunches or firm heads and fresh healthy green coloring free of blemishes and bugs. If greens become wilted, some can be revitalized by dipping in hot water very quickly and then put in a bath of ice water to which vinegar or lemon juice has been added. Greens should never be cut with knives for successful salad making but should be torn by hand into small pieces. Large iceberg lettuce leaves can be used as cups to hold peas or minced carrots or such.

PEPPERS: Many kinds of peppers are available for use as fresh or cooked vegetables. There are bell shaped green and red peppers good for stuffing with chopped meat and rice combo and then baked to be served as a main entree. Bell peppers can be used as is, in fresh form to hold and serve dips, sauces, assorted fresh vegetables or antipasto or to serve a cold main entree such as tuna salad. Cut stem top off to fill and stabilize base if necessary *only*. Also very popular as an antipasto or for frying and pickeling are the thin elongated shaped peppers that come in sweet or hot form. Available throughout the year, they are most plentiful during late summer. Easy to grow in backyards, they may be harvested when plentiful and frozen for use another time. Look for firm "walled" peppers with glossy sheen and heaviness of weight. For a pretty addition to your plate, try cutting the tip end of a thin frying pepper in zig zag design and stuff with pimento filled or black olive. See diagram. Place large pieces skin side down and cut with serrator for leaf effect used in food sculpture.

TOMATOES: Probably the most useful of all vegetables, the red smooth skinned tomato, sometimes called the "love apple," is in reality a fruit. Used fresh in salads and primarily as sauces and pastes in cooking form, it is high in vitamin A and C. If purchased green, store to ripen in a brown bag away from light to attain red ripeness of color. Storing tomatoes on a window sill is a fallacy, as light will cause this fruit to wither and become pulpy. Once ripened, refrigerate with stems facing down as they will stay fresh longer if stored in such manner. Available and most recognized is the red roundish fruit shaped tomato. A smaller version of same, easy to pop into one's mouth is called the cherry tomato. Sweet, diminutive and very colorful, it is widely used in food sculpture presentations. (See Chapter 6.)

Another oval shaped elongated variety of this fruit is called a plum or egg tomato. It is also versatile and is used to create some of the menagerie figures discussed in sculptured food presentation. See tomato filled butterfly. The larger variety of the round tomato is called a beefsteak tomato and is primarily used for slices as in salad. This same larger tomato will yield more of a spiral cut skin to make a tomato rose. To make this variation of an attractive tomato rose, using only the *pared skin* of the large red fruit, follow procedure outlined to make a lemon rose as in chapter 4 on Citrus Fruits.

Tomatoes cut vertically instead of horizontally tend to bleed less. Any tomato, round, beefsteak, small cherry tomatoes, and oval plum tomatoes can be cut and used as hollow shell contain-

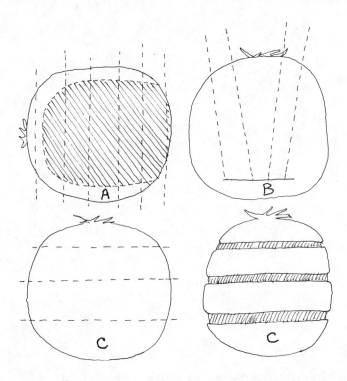

ers. Use the recommended grapefruit spoon with deep bowl and both sides serrated to clean and scoop out pulp and seeds thoroughly before filling. Turn upside down to drain. Try the pretty contrasting and yummy effect of filling shell with pastry tubed mashed potatoes and bake together. Dust with paprika and parsley. Also see eggs, chapter 5: Jack & Jill Boxes; also see chapter 6: Tomato filler-uppers.

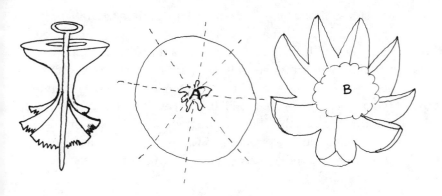

For cartwheel stuffed slices of filled tomatoes, (A) seeds and soft pulp must first be removed before filling with desired cheese or other filling. Slice vertically to serve. Tomatoes can be sliced vertically or horizontally in fan shape fashion (B) before adding stuffing. They can be sliced for pyramid effect, filled and then restacked as per diagram. (C)

Use fruit cutting tool (illustrated) to cut radial design providing a star sunburst type effect (A) which can then be stuffed with a scoopful of salad makings of your choice. (B) If preferred, simply cut with knife in radial arm sunburst effect and fill in each slash cut with a cucumber slice for the larger tomato or slices of water chestnuts for cherry tomato slashes. The same type of filler can be used to fill in a fan cut effect on a round or plum tomato whether the cuts be made horizontally or vertically. See diagrams. Optional: fill in between with cream cheese rosettes or egg yolk cream paste through pastry tube tip.

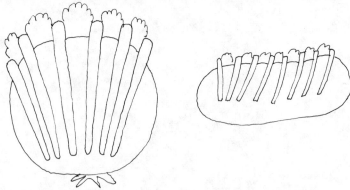

To provide a double petal effect to the tomato you must first loosen the tight skin of same. Dip larger fruit into boiling water for only five seconds to loosen skin covering. It will then release more easily for slicing into petal effect. Proceed then to cut through skin of fruit only. Cut into 6–8 parts (less if using cherry tomato) cut from stem end but not completely down through bottom of fruit. Keep petal cuts of skin in uniform size. Peel back only the skin, carefully leaving meat inside intact. Dust inner meat with parsley or pipe on cream cheese with fancy tip point or merely pull out stem piece and replace with a mint or parsley sprig.

For a single petal border flower effect on a smaller cherry tomato, cut tomato (this time skin and pulp inside together) into 4–6 petal shapes from stem end down leaving base intact. Pull petals outward and down. Remove inner seed and pulp care-

fully so as not to rip base. Fill pulp center, now void, with a black
or green pimento filled olive. Hold both sections, petal and
stamen together with a frill toothpick. Thus the outer tomato
cut section serves an encompassing flower petal border with the
olive filler acting as the flower's stamen. Any stamen of your
choosing can be substituted in place of the olive such as a firm
rolled parsley covered cheese ball, small floret of cauliflower or
broccoli, a cocktail onion, water chestnut, scallion cut mum
piece, etc. For a fuller more frilly petal effect on your cherry
tomato flower use a build-up of 2 or 3 small, medium, and large
cherry tomato skins together. Using the largest of the cherry
tomatoes as the base cut layer to build upon, cut this fruit into
8 petals. Remove pulp leaving just the skin (petals) intact. Cut
the smaller medium sized tomato into 6 petals; also cut the
smallest one the same way. Remove pulp and seeds from both.
Using the 8 petaled tomato as the base, place the larger 6 petal
tomato skin on top, staggering the petals in spoke fashion. Top

off with the smallest 6 petaled cherry fruit, placing same as to
stagger its petals in between the two bottom layered petal formations. Hold all three petal skins together with a frill picked
stamen on top using one of the above suggested stamen centers.
See diagram. Alternative: If petals cut are somewhat longer
they can be given a different effect by first pulling them outward and downward and then folding them over (if skin is not

too thick) toward center thus giving each petal a folded look. Place stamen center on top in center for a completely different look to this same petaled flower.

MUSHROOMS: Eaten raw or cooked, mushrooms are available all year round, with peak periods during November-April. Look for firm flesh that is thick and clean looking with white to creamy white coloring. Gills should not be brown, as this indicates age and means they will soon spoil. Since mushrooms bruise very easily, handle carefully and store *un*washed in a tall container with lots of breathing space about them. Use large caps sans stem for stuffing and baking or frost raw cap top with softened cheese spread and then dip in chopped parsley. Either one makes a nice hors d'oeuvres. Use lengthwise or crosswise cut slices of raw mushrooms in mixed green salads; they are especially tasty in combination with uncooked spinach and Chinese cabbage dressed with a mix of sesame oil, toasted sesame seed, soy sauce and other seasonings. Use whole raw stemmed mushrooms in Food Sculpture to set a garden and animal menagerie scene. See this chapter for "Spring Scene" and "Vegetable (animal) Menagerie." See chapter 5 on Eggs for egg (animal) menagerie. Raw mushrooms are excellent as filler when used in floral bouquet or flower pot carved vegetable arrangements. See this chapter for same. For fancier presentation of same, wipe mushroom clean and use the French (narrower, sharper) lemon stripper to "flute" any preferred pattern onto the cap section of a *very fresh* raw mushroom. As in diagram A, starting at center point strip out narrow pieces in a

curved spiral motion ending at the edge of the mushroom cap. As in diagram B, use spherical pinwheel design or as in diagram C, merely strip out in cross wedge shaped fashion. If preferred, rather than cut *out* the mushroom sections one might try for an entirely different look by merely *lifting up* the lemon strip edge tips. (Diagram D) similar to wing feathered effect on swan vegetable bird. In all cases, mushrooms may be enhanced by the placement of small piece of contrasting colored black olive head on center.

CUCUMBERS: Marketable all year round, these green refreshing vegetables reach peak distribution during May-August, when they are plentiful. A favorite of home growing backyard gardeners, cukes can be eaten fresh in salads or in salad dressings; they make for delicious, cold refreshing summertime soups such as schav (sour grass) or gazpacho; are good in gelatin mold forms, and are also used extensively in the cosmetic industry as a component in facial preparations. It is most used and more familiar to us fresh or marinated (pickle). A particularly overgrown or large in diameter cucumber, although a very good choice to use as a boat or basket holder would nonetheless make for poor eating, as it is likely to have hard seeds and taste bitter. Look for a good green rind on a firm, well shaped cuke. Store in cool place and use within 3–5 days. Some of the following suggestions for shell type holders can also be applied to the elongated zucchini vegetable as well as some eggplants or squash varieties. The option is yours as to sizes cut for formation of holders and cut designs.

TO SERVE A STUFFED WHOLE CUCUMBER: To stuff the whole cucumber as is, in its fresh form or in its smaller sweet or dill pickle form, cut off tip end. Use an apple corer to clean fresh cucucmber of its seed core. For the smaller diameter found on a gherkin pickle, use the pointed tip end of a potato peeler to do same. Fill removed center area of cuke or pickle with cheese or meat or fish paté. Refrigerate to chill. Slice into chunks or thin slices to use as an hors d'oeuvre or use as an edible garnish.

TO STUFF CUCUMBER SECTIONS: For this one, you may leave skin on in tact, use lemon stripper to make grooves or pare the skin completely off the cucumber . . . whatever suits your fancy. Cut crosswise into 1–2″ sections. Use ball scoop, grapefruit spoon or apple corer to remove only the top ⅔ of the seed center thus forming a well. Allow for a thick floor base when doing so. Dip surface cut top of cuke section into chopped parsley or dust with paprika. Fill center well with cheese or whatever. Serve as an hors d'oeuvres.

STUFFED CUCUMBER FLOWER CUP: Cut cuke crosswise

into 3″ sections. Outline and then cut off skin as per drawing. Carefully cut down and then cut out ¼″ of just the meat section from the top surface. This will allow the tip points of the skin

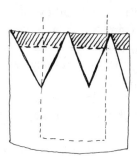

petals of the flower to stand aloft and above same. See shadowed area. To add a third dimension to cup, shave out cucumber meat. Leave a solid circumference of cucumber wall as shell bowl leaving a thick floor base. Fill with choice of filling. This same principle applied to a large eggplant would make for a deep serving holder for sauce or relish. Applied to smaller melons, it could serve as individual salad bowl holders; applied to the larger watermelon it can serve to hold chilled shrimp, fruit or liquid refreshment. Again, you see that whatever you learn for one vegetable can be easily applied to many other forms for food presentation.

STUFFED CUCUMBER PINWHEEL: For another different kind of stuffing effect using the cucumber vegetable, try this easy one which can serve as an hors d'oeuvre, a beautiful garnish or as a flower stamen center when it is superimposed on a larger flower stamped out design cut slice of carrot, thick cut slice of cheese or even a cracker. Cut pared cucumber crosswise into 3–4″ chunks. Put chunks into a quart of salted water. Let stand 20 minutes. (Do not cook this water at any time.) This process is used to soften this vegetable for easier spiral cutting. Cut (as per daikon mum to follow in more detail in this chapter) in spiraling effect in one long continuous 3–4″ wide strip. Keep width of cucumber spiral as thin as possible for rolling later. Cut spiral fashion down to the seed core. Discard core center. Pat with towel to dry cucumber well. Spread paté or finely chopped salad mix over entire length and width of cucumber spiral slice. Re-roll, starting from the (removed) core center toward the outside cut. Wrap well and refrigerate. Slice crosswise when chilled sufficiently. If you prefer your vegetable sans meat or fish salad stuffing, simply cut cuke into shorter spiral lengths. Cut into ½″ wide circle slices and use same to roll up and around carrot match sticks or turkey strips of meat. For a simple ring slice, leave rind in tact. Score rind if desired. Cut crosswise. Clean out center of seeded core and replace with matchstick strips of carrots or meat or celery fans. (See celery fans: olive filled.)

STUFFED CUCUMBER ACCORDION FANS: Cut unpared cucumber crosswise into 2–3″ lengths. Stabilize base side with very thin cut. Cut vertically into fan cut slices every ¼″ apart. Take care not to cut too far down to base, as this must be left intact as holder. As in tomato fan, slip in scalloped or scored carrot slices or whole red radish slices.

FANNED PICKLE CUT: A nice one to try on the small gherkin pickles has already been described in chapter 1 on Pineapples. See Deli-Doll. This same fan cut pickle can be used as a flower effect in the tuna basket (see chapter 8) or to top off an hors d'oeuvre canapé (see Chapter 6). Slice gherkin pickle into 3–4 fan cuts, starting from tip end cutting down toward but not cutting through stem end. Spread slices out to form fan effect and press down gently at stem base with thumb to conform to this postion. This same principle applied later on in this chapter to fan cut radishes will, when cross cut, make for a much more open frilly "mum flower."

CUCUMBER OUTRIGGER BOAT: Other than the Viking ship cucumber boat, a simple form of outrigger boat can be made from a cucumber in the following manner. With a grapefruit knife cut oval top section out of large cucumber. Remove seeded interior, leaving shell to form a canoe shaped boat. If boat is to be raised on chicory covered styrofoam, stabilize same

into foam with wood picks; if not, cut off a very thin slice to stabilize cucumber base. *PONTOONS:* Prepare 2 short equal-length carrot sticks and one length of carrot equal to or longer than the canoe shaped cuke boat. Butting the 2 shorter pieces into the pre-holed longer carrot piece, rounded sides up, you can thus create the pontoon outrigger for your boat. Pre-hole cucumber shell in two places to accept the pontoon as per diagram. To pre-hole, push picks in at upward angle. Fill boat shell with mustard or relish. Again, this same principle can be applied to a larger vegetable for quantity service. Use a large zucchini or properly shaped egg plant or squash. As in chapter 1, for a fish or meat salad filled pineapple boat (sans fronds) the same application of carrot pontoons would be most compatible as well as completely edible. Also see cucumber Viking Ship, this chapter.

CUCUMBER BASKET: By cutting an unpared cucumber crosswise into 2–3″ (or any desired) length sections it would be most easy to change it into a handled basket. See chapter 2 for various handle designed cuts from watermelon baskets. Scoop out seeds and some of the meat section to form basket shell. Use apple corer or grapefruit spoon to do this easily. Fill with assorted olives or carrot sticks and use as individual vegetable or relish baskets. To utilize simultaneously as a place setting, cut handle wide enough to write in each guest's name using writing tube gel.

SCALLOPED CUT EFFECT: Use French (narrower) lemon stripper to cut out thin strips of cucumber down the entire length of vegetable. Cut grooved cucumber crosswise into thin slices to create scalloped ring slices. For CARTWHEEL EFFECT: Slice each scalloped cucumber ring from center point to outer edge. Pull each outer edge point up and under in opposite directions to form a standing cartwheel affect. See chapter 4 for more embellished citrus cuts that can easily be applied to a cucumber round as well as lemons. For thicker cut strips to scalloped round slices use the lemon stripper end on the Kitchen Helper implement in place of the finer narrower French stripper. For different look, simply use the tines of a fork to dig deeply into the cucumber skin, going down the length of the pickle. Proceed as for lemon stripped with crosswise cuts.

SUNBURST HOLDER: A take-off on the above using the lemon stripper implement is to strip a large thick diametered cucumber skin ½ or ⅔ of the way down the length of the desired cut section of the cuke. Do not strip off the rind completely at that midway point. Instead, retrace your initial strip cut carefully and come up and off the top, thus releasing the stripped rind skin. It will automatically droop back down over the side. Repeat every ¼–½" around circumference of cuke.

Scoop out center and some of the meat pulp, leaving a ½″ cucumber wall all around to act as a holder. Optional: Dip surface of holder in paprika or chopped parsley. The half stripped down *(not* stripped *out)* rind will cascade gracefully outward appearing as the sunburst rays surrounding the vegetable. See drawing. Fill center. Using the same procedure but utlizing the wider mouthed stripper on the Kitchen Helper, you will achieve a different looking effect to same by stripping down every ½″ around circumference of cuke. The strips will be thicker and deeper when using the Kitchen Helper instead of the French implement.

PETAL FLOWER EFFECT: With skin on, cut crosswise a ⅓ end section off both sides of cucumber. Use knife to cut slices ¾ way down from *tapered* end thus forming dark green skin petals of flower. See diagram. Cut released skin with scissors to

form sharper points of petals if preferred. If fuller petal effect is desired, a second row of petals can be cut from meat closest to skin and in between first row of rind petals. Leave inside cucumber meat as is.

SCALLOP CUT EFFECT: Cut off optional desired length of cucumber. Leave skin intact. Stabilize base. To create scallop cut effect to rind, start at bottom and cut straight down using the flat side of the sharp edge of knife blade. Release a ½ round circle cut. Continue to work rows of scalloped cut slashes upward toward top. Stagger second row of cuts in between first scalloped row. Clean out seeds and some of the pulp lining to form shell like cup for filling. If smaller one is preferred use 2″ section cut chunks with only 2 rows of scallop cuts and eat vegetable as is, as a crudite. This same design can be rendered to a cucumber sans skin. Pare and then scallop rows of cuts as above. To emphasize the cut for contrast of color, slip in very thin rounds of carrots or red radish slices behind the row of scallop slices.

FORM CUT FLOWERS: Since the skin will come off when the cutter is used, there is no need to pare the cuke. Find a suitable vegetable or aspic cutter that will fit within the rind leaving a thick meat pulp border edge to the cucumber. Lay cucumber crosswise slice on cutting board and press cutter down to cut out shape. Many varied designs can result using this principle of cutting with formed tins. An aspic shaped cut slice can be overlaid with black olive or with cream cheese rosette. Superimpose it then, in its entirety on top of a larger aspic shaped cut carrot slice. Use frill pick to stabilize one through to the other or use unflavored gelatin paste.

This same principle of cutting vegetables with aspic or vegetable cutters can be applied to many other colorful vegetables to create various cuts of flowers. By overlaying or superimposing a smaller aspic cut vegetable slice onto a larger one, more color, design and texture-wise varied affects can be attained. To fasten one to the other for a 2 to 3-layer buildup of flower petals and stamen centers, use food pastes such as cream cheese or butter paste or colorless and unflavored gelatin. Or else, simply use wooden toothpicks, hidden method, or picks with colorful cellophane tops. Picture, then, two entirely different shaped

aspic cutters being used for top and bottom of the vegetable flower (as pictured) or utilize different sizes of the same shaped cutter, e.g., a most popular concept of the latter would be the use of two graduated sizes of potato daisy cutters. Cut and place potatoes in a staggered spoke wheel fashion. Do not limit yourself to potatoes or daisy potato cutters. Try this idea on larger daikon (Japanese radish) slices in combination with carrots or beet slices topped with a radish slice.

SERRATOR: Speaking of cutting brings to mind the various affects that can be featured by merely using the 7″ serrator implement in place of the usual knife to cut vegetables. Cucumber rind skins can be grooved with the use of the lemon stripper, a bar implement, or use the fork tine method. Use serrator to cut cuke crosswise thus giving you a crinkle faced, scalloped edged cucumber slice. Such cut slices would serve better to pick up and hold the vegetable dip. If cucumbers are preferred without skin, then merely cut pared cuke crosswise with serrator. Use aspic cutter to create a specific smaller design. Top serrated cucumber slice with aspic cut design thus adding a textured surface to the particular build up of a cucumber flower. You may also use the serrator to cut any of the chilled stuffed whole pickles into slices or use the implement to cut *un*-stuffed cucumbers lengthwise into sticks for just plain fresh vegetable nibbling.

If you really want to play a trick on your guests to keep them thinking how clever you are, try cutting the cuke in this manner with the serrator. They will never figure out how you cut one slice of the pickle or cucumber on one side into a vertical designed cut and the opposite side of the *same* pickle slice into a horizontal designed cut. Here's how. . . . Hold your cucumber up lengthwise to make the first serratored cut. Use the serrator vertically. Once cut, lay each vertical cut section down on its now flat cut base surface and recut the same slice horizontally.

This same cutting principle can be applied to other vegetables as well—carrots show up particularly well and when iced after being cut this way, tend to bend and curl.

CARROTS: Usually synonymous with bunny rabbits and good eyesight, this vegetable is actually a member of the parsley family. It is also true, however, that one would discard that same parsley green top stem and eat the leftover root. The first time this root was grown to be eaten as a food was by the early colonists in Virginia and Massachusetts. Were we to go further back into the history of this tuberous plant, back to ancient Rome and Greece, this same carrot would be prescribed purely as a drug to be used for medicinal purposes only. Rich in sugar and iron, it is now grown by many backyard enthusiasts as a combination of both . . . as a food, and medicinally for its high source of vitamin A, B, and C. Marketable all year round in plentiful supply, look for fresh green leafy tops indicating its young sweet fresh carrot roots on its bottom. Best kept in plastic bags, refrigerated after the tips and tops are cut off, they are best eaten raw or cooked, within 2 weeks. Many of the carvings and sliced cuttings of this vegetable can easily be applied to other root varieties such as beets, turnips, daikons, white icicle

radishes and red radishes. Therefore keep in mind that whatever is detailed to follow on carrot sculpting, can usually be
done just as well on carving and cutting of any of the other root
vegetables. We will therefore list many of these food sculpted
garnishments under this heading of carrots and will try not to
repeat when we go into the units on the turnip, beet, and
daikon and other radish vegetables.

Cut carrots with serrator to serve fresh or for cooking later.
Use cutting manner described above for the cucumbers.

Cut that same length of carrot, using a knife into narrower
and shorter pieces and the results would be referred to as carrot
sticks (long pieces) or matchsticks (shorter pieces). Use same as
is or to thread through cucumber spirals as detailed in last
section on cukes. Cut carrots as matchsticks for olives as described under heading of celery fans. To create a dumbbell
effect, using olives again, merely use one thick carrot stick as
the bar section and push tip ends into two small black olives.

Speaking of celery fans, the same procedure applied to the
latter can be done to a thinly cut ⅛" section of carrot. Slice
carrot into lengths of 3–4". When cut and placed in ice water
the slit ends will curl.

THE ICED WATER CURLING OF CARROTS: A nice nib-
bler to serve simply as a crudite is also the simplest one to make.
Pare carrot. Cut slice off large end to reveal thickness of core
center of root. Insert point tip of knife blade to make 4–5 cuts

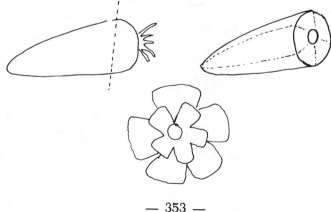

(just *slash* cuts *not* grooves) down the entire length of carrot cutting in depth up to just above core center. It is best to use a mandoline or a gyalu (special slicing implements) to slice the carrot crosswise, as slices must be absolutely paper thin for fine results. When chilled in ice water bath, the slashed petal sides will tend to curl. If multi-graduated sizes of the same or different thick rooted vegetables are thus sliced they can be reassembled to resemble a poppy-like flower using a black olive as its stamen center.

CURLED CARROTS: The thicker roots would make larger nicer and bigger width carrot curls. Thus also a large daikon would work most beautifully and be a little unique in this presentation in place of the usual carrot curls one always expects on a crudite plate. I prefer to work with the larger inner middle section of same, so I slice off the rounded outer side of the root vegetable. This cut off section can then be cut into matchstick pieces for service as nibblers for the same crudite plate providing you with different form and appearance and therefore variety, although it is the same vegetable. Hold the leftover carrot securely in the palm of your hand, flat side up. Holding the floating blade type of a potato peeler as flat as possible, press blade down hard against carrot's flat surface. Pare off a long

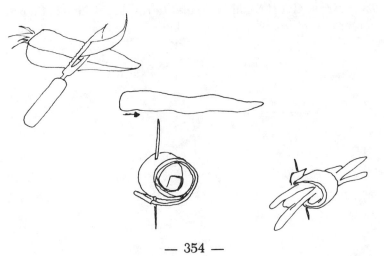

wafer-thin strip from surface of the root. Do several in succession, as one carrot will yield many strips for curling. When last flattened surface section of root remains and carrot strip curls are getting too narrow, merely slice reminder of carrot root into more matchstick pieces. Roll each carrot curl strip individually around your finger to attain a tighter curled effect. Secure in rolled position and fasten with a fine toothpick. Place pick held carrot curl in iced water bath. Remove pick before serving. Use as is or roll carrot curl around celery or cucumber matchsticks. If curls were formed from daikon, roll around the left over carrot matchsticks. Carrot curls may also be used as the center stamen on larger formed petal flowers such as the turnip or beet

slices. (See unit entitled turnips.) Using either round slice of beet or slashed turnip with petal effect, make small hole into which a carrot or radish curl can be snugly fit.

CARROT FLOWER: Assemble a flower using principle above. Follow directions above using a thick wide carrot which has been cut into a 4–6″ length (or however big you wish your flower to be). Place a few strips (3–4) in stack fashion and roll together as if one unit, around your finger. Secure toothpick through all four slices. Place in ice water. By stacking them together as one unit the curl will not be as tightly formed as the previously described individual rolled carrot slices. Remove

pick after chilling. Use frill toothpick as the focal center. Push pick end up through the bottom of the uncurled stacked carrots slices and up to and through the center point of the top. Maneuver or swivel each curl slice around so they lie staggered in crisscross fashion. Top with whole olive as stamen center atop pick.

At this point let me just interject a thought. Sometimes when presenting pretty vegetable flowers as I do, I am asked just what flower it is . . . a tulip. a daffodil, a dahlia? I am not a botanist. To me it's a flower—a thing of beauty made by God and emulated by my using poetic license in my kitchen. If you do not like the names of "my flowers," by all means rename them.

WATER LILY: Using this same principle of overlaying stacked curved petal slices and staggering them in crisscross fashion, see if you can graduate to this more difficult one. The petals of this flower are thicker and stiffer (after icing). When each petal slice is placed one atop the other, it forms a curved water lily (or whatever you like to name it). A large thick carrot or daikon must be used to make this one, along with a lot of patience and a very sharp knife. Be sure the daikon or the large thick soup carrot has been allowed to stand at room temperature at least overnight. Cut carrot or daikon crosswise into a thick 4" section and pare. Follow diagrams, carefully taking note of all views, as this one is sort of three dimensional. Cut

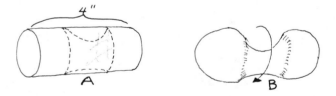

vegetable down to shape as in diagram A. To do so, cut out shallow wedge shapes from top surface and also off bottom. Round out with potato peeler. Be sure bottom base is narrower as in diagram B.

Using a very sharp knife, cut each petal in one continuous piece from top surface off one end down and across bottom and

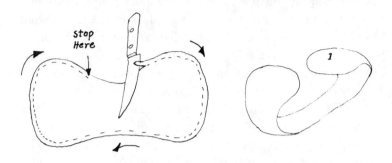

coming off opposite top surface of the other end. Follow diagram. Set this removed petal aside as this is one of the two base petals upon which the flower will be built up. Continue to cut second petal exactly as first. It will automatically be slightly smaller. Place on top of first cut petal in crosswise position as per diagram.

To decrease size of the future petals necessary to put our

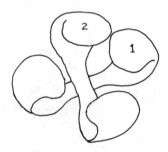

water lily together, you must continually cut down on the original working 4″ carrot section (A) being sure to duplicate exact same shape but in reduced smaller size. Remove wedges again and smooth out to rounded shape as per first original time around. This reduction process will be necessary to whittle the original shape down to acquire the *two* petals that must be cut from *each* reduced original flower section to make this water lily work. Continue to cut two more slices (3&4) from smaller original carrot as per 1 & 2 slices. Lay petals 3 & 4 crisscross fashion on top of petals 1 & 2.

It is because of the constant crisscrossing that the inside center width sections of the petal base must be kept narrow for easier stacking and assemblying.

TO MAKE WATER LILY STAMEN CENTER: Although the remaining carrot can be used, I prefer to use a contrasting color such as a crosswise cut thick round ½" slice from a daikon. Cut daikon stamen center round. See grooved stamen rounds detailed later in this chapter.

TO PUT LILY TOGETHER: Use hidden toothpick method to catch all layers of petals as well as stamen center. Insert pick up through bottom of assembled flower, Place in deep wide enough bowl to ice and firm up petals. Display on "greenery" foundation on serving tray. This one will take some practice but its uniqueness and beauty is most impressive. It is most colorful when formed from a daikon, which can then be dyed in food coloring to pick up your color scheme.

TO MAKE A GROOVED CENTER STAMEN FOR ANY FLOWER: Use any ½" round thick slice from a root type vegetable (carrot, beet, turnip, daikon, etc.) Optional: groove out or strip out depth sides of ½" round.

To groove top flat surface of round: starting at center section of the flat surface, working out to both edges, cut out 1/16" wedge or V-shaped groove strips horizontally.. To create the tic-tac-toe design, now cross cut similarly and remove cut out wedge strips vertically, creating a checkerboard or tic tac effect on surface of root vegetable round. Although it might remind you of the mum cut, the difference is that because it is not slash cut deeply (it is wedge cut), it therefore can not open any further than the cut 1/16" grooves in any direction.

Use as flower itself surrounded with greens. If preferred, use it as a stamen center atop a stamped out vegetable petal cut slice. If used as a stamen, reduce the width depth. Cut down slightly being sure not to cut off too much to upset the surface 1/16″ design already established. If preferred, after grooving out strips, then stamp out different aspic design (1) with metal form and use as smaller prettily edged stamen center. See illustration.(2)

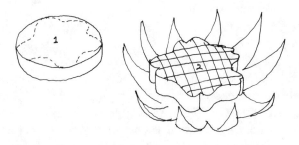

MARKING OUT CARROTS LENGTHWISE FOR VARIOUS SLICED AND CARVED EFFECTS: As mentioned in previous unit on cucumbers, pare any root vegetable of your choice, (carrot, daikon, icicle radish). Some of these will also work quite well on a cucumber possessing a small seeded core center. The manner in which you make your marking on a root vegetable lengthwise will determine the border edge cut you achieve later on when cutting same crosswise into slices or buttercup

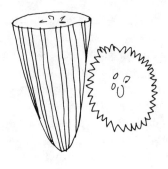

design flowers (to follow shortly). A simple example of this theory is the ICED WATER CURLING OF CARROTS previously detailed. Let us now delve into this theory, carrying it a step further for more intricate results. Strip out lengthwise, using the lemon stripper and cutting out strips down the entire sides of root at uniform intervals. If French stripper is used, a finer strip will be excised; if Kitchen Helper, wider mouthed stripper is used, a wider scallop effect will be achieved when cut crosswise. Cut crosswise after stripping out pieces. Use knife to cut crosswise for flat surface with a scalloped border edge; use serrator to slice crosswise for crinkled surface top with scalloped edge. Use tines of fork in place of either stripper for a more feathered effect; cut crosswise using knife or serrator to slice. A petal effect can be achieved by using the same principle and removing root pieces by wedging out grooves with a pointed tip of a knife inserted at angles. Replace stripper or fork tine method this time with a knife to cut out V-shaped notches or grooves lengthwise down the sides of the carrot or other root. Size of V groove cut out will determine the appearance of the petal effect when crosscut later. Keep the depth and width of each grove the same; keep the distance between each groove cut uniform. It is best to use a Mandoline or Gyalu for the

thinner the crosscut made from the root, the more the slice will curl when placed in iced water. However, it is your option to cut these crosscut slices as thin or thick as you wish. Once cut, use them as crudites or as layer stacked effect in floral designs. We will go into layering these flower slices together as one unit as we get deeper into this unit, covering circle slices from vegetable roots.

TRUMPET TYPE BUTTERCUP-LIKE FLOWERS: Using different ways of marking out or wedging out or lemon stripping out roots lengthwise can now be applied to making a trumpet type buttercup flower. Whatever root is chosen for your flower making, allow to stand to room temperature overnight or you will find the cutting difficult. Choose a large thick daikon or carrot. Cut out for version 1: V-shaped grooves; for version 2: strip out pieces with the French lemon stripper or for version 3: use fork tine method on vegetable root.

Each method used will yield a different bordered edge effect to the petal formation of your about-to-be-formed buttercup. Use knife to cut narrow tapered root end tip to a sharp cone-shaped bottom. Smooth out with potato peeler. Using this cone shaped tip end as the basic guide upon which to press your knife, use a sawing up and down motion of the knife to shave off a thin continuous layer all around the carrot root end tip. Once shaved layer is released, roll in cone shape around your finger tip as you would to form a cornucopia meat slice. Overlap ends and hold together by forcing a cellophane topped frill pick

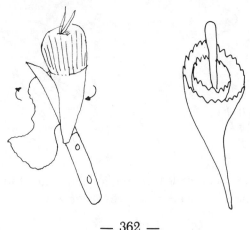

down center, catching end slices together. If preferred, before rolling to overlap ends, place a contrasting stamen matchstick or cylinder shaped cut vegetable into center of trumpet flower opening. With stamen in place, roll cornucopia style and secure same with unobtrusive pick. Different colored layered effects of trumpet like petals can be created by cutting cone shaped layers from different, graduated sized slices of root vegetables. When combining same, roll a white (daikon) cut cone shaped layer petal inside a much larger trumpet petal flower shaped carrot thus creating a two tone layered cone trumpet shaped flower buttercup design. A cylindrical cut stamen might still be incorporated if desired.

A variant of this buttercup type flower can be formed with a slightly thicker base and thicker flower cone shaped petals if in its preparation, it is *cut* rather than shaved off in sawing up and down motion. Follow preceeding unit to cut or strip or use tine fork approach on lengthwise outer coat of root vegetable. Prepare cone tapered base point. Instead of paring off thin layer of cone shaped carrot base in sawing up and down knife motion, this time insert point of knife into carrot base ⅛″ above border

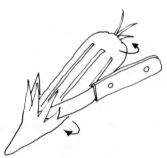

edge of carrot cone and cut all around. (See diagram.) To release this thicker buttercup end of carrot base, twist the larger carrot root section from side to side until cornucopia formed flower releases on its own. Contoured petals of buttercup will be thicker in appearance with a much thicker cone shaped pointed base bottom. Cutting in this manner and twisting off top will negate the need to overlap shaved edges as in previous unit and negate need to hold those overlapped edges together with picks.

If desired, stamen centers may still be used even in this version. Use a narrow cylindrical stamen from a contrasting colored root vegetable. As per stamen used in Mum Daikon Flower in this chapter, even if that stamen top is very small but is flat, it can be grooved out following the tic tac toe method used on large rounds (see how to make a Grooved Center Stamen). To assemble, however, push wood pick end of frill pick into cone shaped flower from bottom. Push cylindrical stamen into top exposed pick point in center of buttercup flower as shown in diagram.

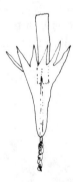

This same principle of cone shaped buttercup type flowers can be applied just as well to large turnip roots or beet roots. The result would be larger versions of the same type cutting. Also see turnip for take-off on this same principle.

CARROT TULIP: Using this same idea, let us go on with the natural tapered end of a long thin carrot (left out overnight for easier pliability when cutting). This one works beautifully on a pared white icicle radish. In fact, for your first attempt at this one I would try it on a more supple radish, as the roots of the latter are not as tuberous as that of the carrot. For a larger version of same, carve it from a daikon. Holding pared root vegetable, green stem end up, insert your knife for first petal cut as high or as low down from the tapered tip end, as you wish. This will determine the length or height size of the petals you will create. The thinness or thickness of that slice cut will then determine the rigidity of each petal or the fragility of same.

The thinner the slice the better chance of its petals opening up and curling outward more when placed in the iced bath

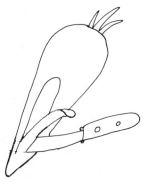

water. Always place side of knife blade in to cut at slight angle toward center core of vegetable. This will make for an easier release later when you will need to twist remaining top of root off (as in thick buttercup version). Again, you are not limited to thickness of slices nor how *many*, as the number of cuts you make will merely determine the number of petals your flower will have. The secret still remains in the actual separation of the cut flower formation from the remaining top section of vegetable root. Do not become impatient and break it off . . . merely hold flower cut sections in your left hand firmly and with your right hand, twist top root section from side to side until it will release its hold on the bottom cut flower held in your left hand. As per diagram, make the first slice cut above tapered carrot end in a downward cutting motion. If first cuts are kept shallow, there is still plenty of root left over with leeway to come around again and make a second row of staggered cuts just above the first, giving you a double petal effect when twisted apart. Need-

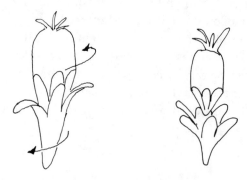

less to say, after removal of tulip flower you will still be left with a large root which will possess an already tapered cut end point. Simply continue the cutting method and cut more tulips from the same remaining leftover carrot. Depending on lengths (the height) of petal cuts one can usually get 1–2 tulips of a nice average size (1½"-2") from an average sized white icicle radish; a longer average sized carrot will yield 3–4 tulip carrots from one root. Centers of tulip cut flowers can be filled with contrasting colored stamens made from other vegetables. If large thick carrot is carved with *deep* thick cut petals you can actually use its center as a holder and fill with egg salad or such. The latter is very effective when incorporated into a tuna basket display (see chapter 8 in same).

VARIATIONS IN CROSSWISE ROUND SLICES. Once having sliced crosswise cuts from various sizes of different tuberous vegetables, the manner in which they are then assembled or put together will allow you much more variance in their design for food presentation. E.G.: a large wafer thin crosscut from a large thick daikon as a base can be topped with a smaller round cut wafer slice from a carrot, topped with a beet scoop ball to make a nice petal flower look. Don't ask me to tag a name on that one. Again, I feel if it's pretty to my eye it's a flower enough for me, with or without a Latin name. This time overlap the border outside edges for a different effect. Again the sizes of each petal and the number of thin wafer cuts put together will make for a varied appearance of a newly "born flower." Merely catch all the overlapping edge borders together with a covering

stamen center. Hold together with a pick. It need not be simple wafer thin cuts either. Slice off thicker cuts into rounds. Use the same aspic cutter to stamp out the particular design on each. Catch the overlapping border edges of these stamped out aspic cuts to make for another new flower. Thus you can easily see that such slices cut from a larger root such as a beet or turnip will, when assembled, look gigantic if possessing three slices, or more so if possessing five slices. A three petal flower or a five petal flower assembled however from cuts of a smaller root such as a carrot will also look quite differently. Look at all the fun you will have naming all these newly found flower formations. Thus, in summing up, the design of the outside edges used (aspic cut, fork tined, etc.) plus the number of sliced rounds put together, accounting for their circumference and the various stamen centers used, will create a different appearance to each flower every time one is assembled.

Now what of you gals who have not even one aspic or cookie cutter in your culinary kingdom? Throughout this book I have stressed the fact that tools of your trade are of utmost importance, but if you don't happen to own an aspic cutter to stamp out vegetable designs, then make do with your own ingenuity until you can acquire some. Aspic cutters are sold in single individual units such as daisy cutters of graduated sizes or in boxes of several metal forms, 6–12 in a box. I want to stress the importance of proper tools in your kitchen workshop. If need be, for one week, give up that manicure or whatever and treat yourself to some good aspic cutters that will truly show the beauty of your hands in *another* way, for the rest of your *cooking* life—which can be a long time! To cut simple flower like petal designs for garnishing or bouquets . . . cut off a round crosswise ⅛" thick slice from a root vegetable. Cut as per diagram into as many slices as you wish your flower to have petals; be sure to leave an uncut area in center as a base core to hold it all together. Use olive slice as stamen or a piped on rosette of cheese as center. Needless to add, any of these knife cut flowers can be stacked as per directions for those cut with aspic cutters.

For a fancier design using a knife instead of an aspic cutter try this one. . . . With knife cut into circle and cut out pieces so as to form a fat five pointed star. Top with stamen center. For a different aspect of the same principle take this flower one step further and use the cutting edge of a small ball scoop tool or use a clean tipped eraser sharp metal edge cup (remove eraser from end of pencil and use metal cup of same) or use plain end of

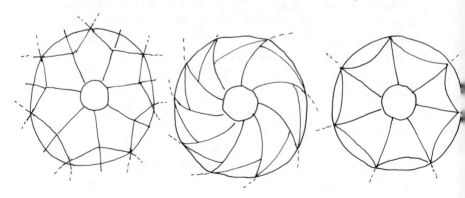

canvas bag decorator tip to cut out tip ends of each star's point. See some of the illustrated suggestions to make new flower designs without the use of aspic cutters. The final flower design would be the result of the cutouts used and size and color of root circle slices.

Now that you have gone the gamut of making flower stamped-out versions the hard way, using eraser tops, knives, ball scoops, etc., you realize how true is the adage that a carpenter is as good as his tools to get his (or your) job done better, faster, and more efficiently.

Speaking of knives, replacing implements to "make do" reminds me of an open spiral corkscrew fan cut that can be carved easily with a tool called a Spiral Slicer (picture below) but can be made nonetheless with a little more time and trouble by using a knife.

KNIFE SPIRAL CUT FOR CORKSCREW EFFECT: Insert tip of knife into a pared carrot or daikon (room temperature) at slight angle. By *rotating* the root vegetable, the knife can then be made to cut into but not through the center of root in spiraling effect. A corkscrew spiral of one continuous design will be the result. Place cut carrot to open in iced water. If it does not open fully then you will know your initial spiraling cut was not made deep enough. Repeat same and cut slightly deeper.

CARROT ROSE: Rose or dahlia shapes can be cut from a

large chunk end of a thick carrot as per directions for turnip roses. See same to follow under unit heading of turnips.

Many of these carrot flowers and garnish cuts should be listed

just as well under white radishes, daikons, turnips, beets, etc., so please consider them done so at this point. I left a few over for these aformentioned chapters so you don't think I have completely neglected any of the root vegetables . . . for what can be applied to one usually can be applied to all the other root vegetables. Experiment and see what flowers you can create on your own. Whatever mistakes you might make or whatever design you chance to come up with, no matter, all are edible. As I told you, this is one artisitic endeavor that will *never* end up in the wastebasket!

Turnips: To avoid confusion at the outset, let us differentiate between the turnip and the rutabaga. The turnip is the smaller vegetable with the white flesh and purplish tinting of outer skin. What most people refer to as the yellow turnip is actually a rutabaga, a relative of the white turnip which is extremely larger, harder, and is usually coated with paraffin to prevent loss of moisture and shriveling. Although some of the food presentation designs can be worked out from large round circle cuts of rutabaga, we will concern ourselves mostly with the carving of the more pliable, therefore more workable white turnip, a member of the mustard branch of the cabbage family and a very high source of vitamins A, B, and C. As with carrots, look for healthy green strong tops indicative of turnip roots that are smooth, firm, with few scars. Whatever cutting and carving that can be performed on a turnip can likewise be done to a beet. Although either can be eaten raw, it is preferable cooked. Therefore, if you wish to utilize turnips or beets as a garnish for a completely edible service, you must follow the basic C's of catering. Carve it! Cook it! Color it! Cleanse it! *in that order!!!*

CARVE: the design of your turnip or beet root. *COOK* it best by starting it in a pot of boiled salted water. Avoid overcooking, as this will ruin the design of the vegetable carvings if root becomes too soft. *COLOR* it: immerse all carved vegetables in color dyed water bath for at least one hour. A bright yellow tinted turnip is far more attractive than the resulting off-white cooked turnip. This holds true for beets also, as beets, when cooked, tend to bleed or lose their natural deep red coloring. Restore color to beets by revitalizing them in a bath of red food dyed water. The food dye bath should also be filled with ice cubes to firm up vegetables, at same time (taking into account color loss as cubes melt and dilute same.) *CLEANSE* it: allow dyed vegetables to sit in a bath of cool *running* water to allow all excess food dye to run off. Remove carved vegetable and set on paper toweling to absorb. Of course, if your vegetables are for displayed decoration only, nonedible, there is no need to cook them. Simply carve the vegetable, chill, (color it if desired). Set it upon your display tray after cleansing it properly. If using turnip or beet for display garnishing, I prefer to use 1–2 large root bulbs in the body cavity of a displayed carved turkey (see chapter 10) and 3–5 smaller sized bulbs for carved floral bouquet arrangements as detailed in this chapter. Avoid overly large carved flowers that will overpower the displayed centerpiece. Avoid those that are too heavy, causing imbalance and tipping over of floral arrangements, as in bouquet form or potted flowers featured in this chapter.

Allow all vegetables destined for carving to stand at room

temperature for at least 24 hours (or more if necessary) until soft and pliable enough for easily carving same.

CIRCLE ROUNDS: better for (raw) inedible presentations: Follow as per directions of other root vegetable cuts, with carrots. Here's a combination of 2 different cuts from previous unit. As per directions for sliced round root vegetable, cut center hole from round slice. Use eraser edge cup or plain edge of pastry tube tip, or scissors or knife to do so. Insert wound up carrot curl in center opening. Slash cut or use scissors to cut circle round to create any number of surrounding petals to your flower design. As per directions for carrot or other root bulb cuttings, use such sliced turnip and beet rounds for carved or stamped out cut designs and stack them in layers to create combinations offering different looking flowers.

Speaking of layered petals, some of whose designs are cut without the benefit of aspic cutters, here's a very nice one created with a homemade tool and made with the entire use of the root. This resulting flower design cut is made to look as if it was done by stacking aspic cut layers, but is actually created by cutting one whole turnip or beet a little differently, leaving vegetable with a connecting centerpiece penetrating through the entire length of the bulb root. For the woman whose husband is handy around the house, you might venture into his workshop and find a leftover small piece of metal called a Flash-

ing Metal Plate. It is a light, thin gauged weight of aluminum used for fixing roof joints. If not, it's so inexpensive—do go down to your local hardware store and treat yourself to a small piece of it. It is easily cut with scissors. Cut off a small piece to form into any width shape you wish, simply by folding or bending in any direction. Pare white turnip or beet. Hold tapered end up. Use the aluminum shaped sheet form to dig into the vegetable to form the first layer of cut petal shapes working from the outside edge of vegetable toward center, allowing for the connecting center to go untouched. See diagram.

Push pointed tip of knife into turnip just below petals grooved out with implement. Rotate turnip so layer of meat surrounding petal is cut away, as in shadowed area in illustration. Thus you have emphasized the petals by making them stand out more in raised fashion. Begin second row: groove out more petal formations, using the pointed shaped aluminum Flashing Plate form by staggering the second row of petals grooved out below and in between first row. Proceed to use knife and rotate turnip to cut away second row of attached turnip meat (shadowed area) under the second row of petals. Allow for center of turnip to remain intact. As each row of petals is cut in progression, the center left intact will become larger as the flower flares out more toward its thicker base. As you proceed to groove out the petals, stagger each petal under the preceding row of petals above. Undercut meat pulp of the row being cut, (shadowed area) as detailed before. You will find a most beautiful flower emerging. Food color the entire turnip by immersing in colored iced bath for at least one hour. If a more fragile, softer look is desired, chill in iced water and allow to dry somewhat. When root used is a turnip, then merely tip each petal point with desired shade of food coloring on a cotton bud to highlight points of each petal.

Thanks to turnips and carrots being available all year round. . . . *The CALLA LILIES ARE IN BLOOM:* Allow turnip to stand at room temperature for 24 hours or longer for softer workability. Pare. Slice thinly into rounds. Cut one side to trim

down to slight point. Place long carrot stamen stalk on top
of turnip slice with base end extruded beyond lower part of
lily and the top of carrot just short of pointed side of turnip.
Fold turnip slice over, cornucopia style overlapping base
edges. Use pick to catch all three pieces together. Insert extruded carrot stalk on bottom into a thick green scallion stalk

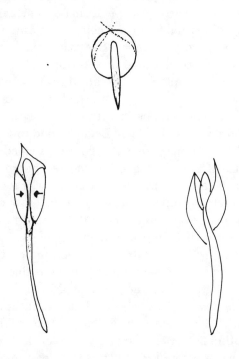

to act as stem of Calla Lily. For a pretty setting for a wedding table, have several green stalked Calla Lilies cascading
from the open end of a pretty cornucopia wicker basket,
garnish with lemon leaves, etc. For a fuller petal effect use 2
turnip slices to form flower. Cup each slice round so as to face
each other. Place carrot stamen. Overlap border edges of
cupped slices of turnip and catch all pieces together at base.

Attach green stem stalk as before.

VARIATIONS OF BUTTERCUP LIKE FLOWER: Look for a long tapering oval turnip or beet. Pare. Cut sides on tapered end to form a cone shaped beak bottom. Cut crosswise at round top section of cone form as per diagram. Use grapefruit knife to cut away inner center section in one bulk cone piece leaving

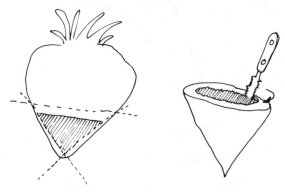

a ½" shell all around. Once inner cone is removed, use knife to cut out shallow V groove 1/16" wedged strips from outside beak tip end up to and over the border edge of trumpet shaped flower and down inside the horn of the flower itself for one version of this variety.

VERSION 2 OF SAME CUTTING: Using narrow French stripper tool, strip out pieces from top surface of border edge of flower and follow through down and around outside surface *only* of belled flower to its pointed peak bottom.

VERSION 3: Use wider lemon stripper end on Kitchen Helper to do same as in version 2.

Depending on implement used, Kitchen Helper stripper, French stripper or knife to form V-shaped grooved notches, your trumpet shaped flower will take on a different appearance. Add a new dimension now by simply adding a cylinder shaped stamen in center and/or attach a round of turnip or beet cut into petal formation at base as shown.

MORNING GLORY: Prepare and remove inside horn cen-

ter as for flower above. Proceed to cut *outer* sides of belled
flower with the curved *back* of the grapefruit knife blade in
concave fashion, giving flower a ribbed appearance so similar to
that of a Morning Glory.

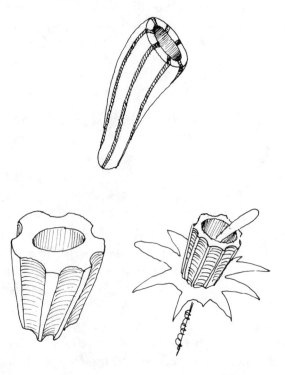

Doing a take-off on the above, a different look can be
achieved by the variance of the cuts made for these trumpet
like open flowers. Use long tapered turnip or beet. Follow diagram and outline in pencil the curved scallop petal cuts on the
thicker wider side of the root vegetable after the top leafy stalks
were removed. Cut following outline. This time, however, use
the front side of the curved grapefruit blade knife and dig in at
deep 45° angle toward center core of vegetable. Remove inside
area of same.

HELPFUL HINT: For easier removal of this center section, cross cut and take out in small pieces. Smooth out inside trumpet like surface of flower by rounding out concaved curves. Make deeper notches if necessary, at adjoining sides of scallop cut points. Using back side of grapefruit knife blade, remove the

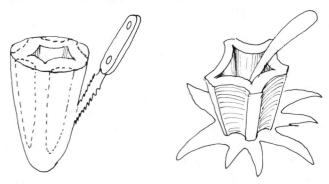

outside of the turnip or beet in convex shape following contour of the scalloped inner horn concaved shape. Carry same convex shape down to natural tapering bottom of vegetables.

Optional: If desired place stamen in center. Petal on base.

Thus, you see, it depends upon how you hold and use the *SAME* knife blade in making your designated curved cut, for this is what will determine the various flowers that can be formed.

14 SECTION CUT FLOWER USING APPLE SLICER: This next floral design is one that would work best on a turnip or beet that has been parboiled first, the *exception* to our standing rule. Parboil vegetable and then pare. *HELPFUL HINT:* The secret is to cook the vegetables in boiling water and then immerse immediately in iced water. The skins will literally burst off the beet. Stabilize base and position with tapered bulb end upward. Use the 14 section apple slicer according to directions and cut turnip into 14 section petaled flower. Reduce center stamen "core" by slicing off tip. If desired, cut each petal section off at angle giving a more angular point to your petal end. See diagram.

HERE'S ANOTHER PRETTY FLOWER: that looks just as pretty right side up as upside down . . . you'll see what I mean as we do it. Choose a large turnip. Pare. Hold wide side up and core out hole in center with apple corer or tip of potato peeler. Use pencil to design and outline 3 large curved graceful petals following roundish contour of turnip or beet (see petal 1 in diagram).

Use tip of knife, digging in point to depth of ⅛" to carve outlines of petals drawn on. With outline of petal shapes carved in, now remove remaining pulp, using the flat side of knife to shave off all the remaining (shadowed) area of vegetable. Thus, the 3 outlined petals will stand out as if raised in three dimensional effect. Turn vegetable upside down and undercut each petal form, thinning it so it stands away from body of turnip more, giving it a fragile appearance. Return to original position with wider base facing upward. Outline in pencil the next set of petals, 3 more graceful petals, staggering their position in between the petals of the first row (see petals #2 as in diagram).

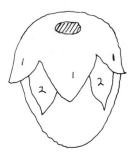

Carve petals outline to depth of ⅛″ with knife point again and proceed as before, repeating each step of the process. Continue working toward tapered turnip or beet root. Now, just for fun, turn your vegetable upside down and you will find an equally beautiful cut design automatically carved out of the underside too. This is one flower that looks good shown in any direction . . . right side up or down! If desired, use carrot stamen in carved center hole.

CALLA LILY: Following principle detailed previously for making the Three Petaled Flower, outline shape of Calla Lily in pencil on a turnip. Carve out core center as per diagram. Etch out, in depth, with point of knife, as per diagram, a fully formed lily. To do so, use a long tapered turnip, stalk end up, repeating the same theory of *shaving* remaining layers of turnip meat so etched outline remains raised. Shadowed area in diagram depicts area shaved off for three dimensional look. Fill entire core opening with carrot stamen.

Using this same theory of cutting or carving an outline to

depth of ⅛″ and then shaving layers of vegetable so that carved outline is raised up and emphasized, try this one as a foundation. We can then go on from there to bigger and more elaborate designs, using this premise. Hold turnip or beet tapered point up. Stabilize base. Outline 5 petals around base. Cut in with point of knife to depth of ⅛″ (or more if desired, depend-

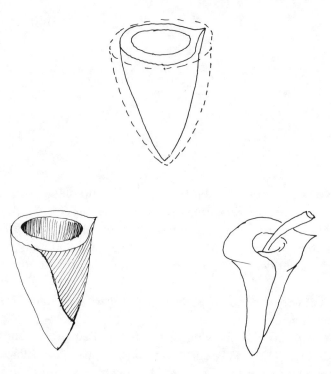

ing on just how thick you wish your petals to be); shave off all remaining meat of root to reduce shape over all. (as in shaded area in diagram). This will allow petals to stand out in raised position. If desired, tint just the border edge tips of each petal, coloring it with a cotton bud after cooking and icing; or immerse the whole root vegetable in food coloring and ice water bath if preferred.

Same effect can be accomplished by giving you various shapes if the cut shape of petal form is etched out differently. Try your hand at outlining in pencil a scalloped cut petal form as tall or shallow or curved or pointed as you wish. Continue as before to emphasize by outlining and shaving layers (shadowed area) of remaining meat pulp.

DAHLIA: Follow procedure in previous flower form above. Outline in pencil, cut to depth of ⅛″ and shave meat pulp in between petal formation. Start at thicker base side of tapered turnip or beet or thick carrot stub. Outline in pencil and then cut to depth of ⅛″ the first row of sawtooth shapes, as per diagram.

Place knife tip point above highest sawtooth point and shave out area in between two joining points all around first row as in shadowed area. Shave or shape up remaining turnip if necessary to keep to original smooth working shape. Follow diagram and outline and carve to depth of ⅛″ another row (#2 in diagram) of sawtoothed points. Stagger second row of teeth in between that of first row keeping points on even line. Clean out as per shadowed area, rounding out remaining turnip meat if conducive to retaining original contour of turnip. Continue repeating process until peak is reached at top. Each row (numbered in diagram) will therefore have fewer points than the previous one, as it diminishes in size toward top.

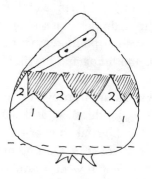

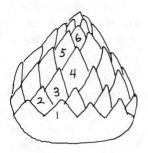

ROSE: Just as dahlia was formed, a scalloped rose design can be shaped similarly by merely changing your sawtooth points to that of pretty rounded scalloped half circles. The size of each scallop would be entirely up to you. So long as tops are kept alligned. The flare to each scallop circle outline and the distance set between each row of scallops will determine the overall finished look to your carved flower. Proceed as above, cutting out remaining shadowed area of diagram after each row of petals are carved in position. Reshape contour or form of remaining turnip to retain overall original shape of working root.

Smooth out before outlining in second row of petals. Stagger petals of second row in between that of first row outlining scallop circle at midway starting center of scallop below to midway point of successive scallop.

COMBINING ROSE AND DAHLIA INTO ONE FLOWER: Now that you have mastered both the scallop and the sawtooth

cut, combine the two for a variation of flower design. As per previous instructions, start first row at thicker base of beet or turnip. Outline and carve to create 2 rows of scalloped edges. Shave remaining meat of vegetable to shape for original working contour of root. Now continue outlining and carving using the sawtooth effect. Work to top of vegetable.

COMBINING SCALLOPED CUT WITH V SHAPED GROOVED STAMEN: Do *NOT* pare turnip. Carve out 5 scallop edges on wide based side of turnip after removing green stem base at top. Pare and clean out all areas above and in

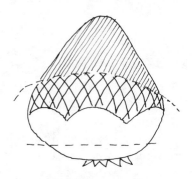

between scalloped design (shadowed area in illustration) on turnip. Now create the grooved center stamen section as detailed in carrot unit. Remove V shaped wedge strips of 1/16" widths in checkerboard design. To add that extra finishing touch, use French lemon stripper to strip *DOWN* and release but NOT CUT OFF the outside purplish skin on the scallop petal cuts, thus giving it a sunburst effect as in unit on cucumbers.

A different rose or scalloped affect can be achieved with the same basic starting point and using a slightly different follow through. Peel, shape and round turnip or beet. Outline and cut four equal sized petal slices around circumference of base. This time, however, merely cut out the turnip meat standing *just directly behind each sliced petal cut.* (Shadowed area.) The next carved set of 4 petals (#2 in diagram) will be staggered in

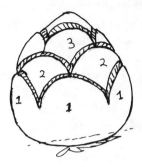

between first row of petals (#1). Cut meat out behind these petals *only* (shadowed area). Continue with third row, and so on. Color if desired.

More Fragile Rose Petal Cut: For a thinner, more fragile and beautiful carved petaled flower, try this more intricate one which can be performed on a turnip or beet or large red radish or roundish potato. Start, wide base side down, by completely slicing off thin flat cut from 4 sides of pared rounded root vegetable leaving a ½" space in between each sliced off area. This

is most important. All cuts removed will be depicted by shadowed area in illustration. Now make deep ⅛" thin cut slices (dotted line) behind each cut off area thus automatically forming a petal from these flat cut side slices, retaining the same ½" space in between. SECOND TIER LAYER: Second set of petals will begin to take shape when smaller ½″ area of turnip meat is removed from in between the adjoining scalloped edges that formed the first set of petals. (See shadowed sliced off area #2.) Now make cut down behind that piece (#2) thus forming petal for second set of flowers. THIRD TIERED LAYER: to form third set of petals, repeat process. Cut out shadowed area (#3); cut again behind this shadowed area to form scalloped circle. Continue process for making fourth set of petals working

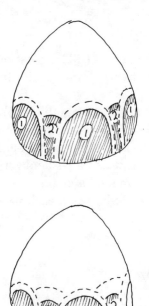

toward top, removing slices of meat pulp and cutting behind each slice to form scalloped petal. Needless to say, since these petal cuts are very thin and fragile, this is most beautiful when served in its *un*cooked form, fully bathed in pink or yellow food coloring. If preferred, merely top edge of each petal with food colored cotton bud instead.

HELPFUL HINT: Just a reminder to sum up: whatever can

be cut or carved on a turnip can usually be applied to a beet root. Allow all root vegetables to stand at room temperature before carving. Carve, cook, color and cleanse in that order. Be sure to immerse for at least one hour in ice bath to firm up vegetable. Keep coloring of vegetables to one color bath only. Immerse for at least one hour to absorb color. Allow carved vegetable to run off coloring and water and be absorbed with

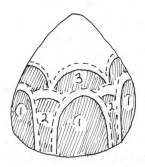

paper towelling before adding to display to prevent running of colors together. Practice, practice!

Beets: Usually sold in bunches all year round, the peak season for this root vegetable is June-October. As with carrots, look for fresh green leaf tops indicating young, sweet roots. Use greens for cooking as soon as possible, roots within a week or so. This vegetable, particularly good when cooked, is even more welcome as a refreshing side dish at any mealtime in its appetizing pickled version.

All good things that happen to turnips can also be applied to beets. Be sure, if they are prepared in cooked version, that they are revitalized (in appearance) by bathing in red food dye.

Daikon: A giant white sweet root vegetable more familiarly grown and featured in the cooking of the Orient, this radish is now also grown in western United States. Usually large in thickness and in length, it is sold by the piece primarily in gourmet fruit stores or in Chinese or Japanese food markets. One usually pays for it by weight.

Many of the carvings and cuts applied to other root vegetables can be similarly applied to the daikon. If you have never seen a daikon, picture if you will an Oriental counterpart of an enlarged gigantic state grown white icicle radish with green stemmed leaves on top, each root varying in diameter and length. Therefore, round slices can be treated as is or stamped out with aspic forms as one would treat a turnip round; long tapered daikon flowers can be made as one would the carrot carved tulip flowers. When crosscut, the inner pulp of this vegetable is sort of striated or tinged in circular appearance. It therefore takes vegetable food coloring well and absorbs same in flowing, intermingling striated shades of the particular color dye. Its meat is soft and pulpy, like the smaller white icicle radish, and more supple for carving *unlike* the carrot. It is white in color and sweeter than either the icicle or red radish. It can be eaten raw as well as cooked and is favored by the Oriental in pickled form. Try using such culinary implements as the narrower French lemon stripper or the wider mouthed Kitchen Helper stripper or the 14 section apple slicer on cut chunk sections of this root. Try any of the slices, carvings or cuts previously learned for carrots, beets or turnips on this most versatile winter radish.

Here's a new one to add, that works particularly well on the

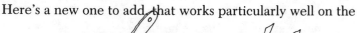
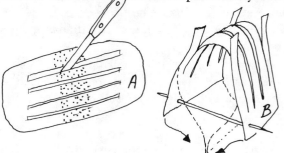

daikon and also on the carrot, but only if the latter is allowed to stand out to soften more. As per celery and carrot slit lengths for fan curled edges, let's try this variation of same on the daikon. Pare daikon as you would a carrot. Cut ⅛" thick slices of approximately 3–5" in length. This time, instead of slitting the tip *end* sections of the daikon lengths, merely slit the *center* area into ⅛" slash cuts as per diagram A. Leave the opposing end sections intact as well as the ½" widths on both lengthwise sides of the ⅛" vegetable slice. For folding crosswise more easily later, salt down the center area (see shadowed area in diagram). Fold daikon over crosswise, in half (diagram B). Cut ½" lengthwise sides in half. Join and hold ends together with toothpick as shown. Place three such treated sections (or more for fuller flower) together with picks. OPTIONAL: catch cylin-

drical carrot stamen or grooved carrot round in center with pick. See diagram. Immerse in iced bath of water to firm up and wash off salt. Color with food dye bath if desired.

For a take-off variation on the above concept, see Mum daikon to follow.

DAIKON OR (CARROT) MUM FLOWER

To create the very pretty soft petaled mum, use the Japanese white radish, the daikon, or a very large well rounded winter carrot (the large type used to make chicken soup). Cut off a 5-6″ portion. Pare or scrub clean. Hold a chef's knife flat against the full length of the vegetable and cut into one continuous thin long spiral.

Cut the daikon or carrot as thin as possible (almost to the

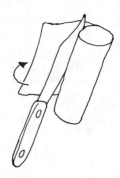

point of transparency), working the knife toward the center core.Detach the spiral length of vegetable when it is about 8″ long, leaving intact a remaining ½″ section of the vegetable core. Set this core aside to later shape and use as the center stamen of your mum.

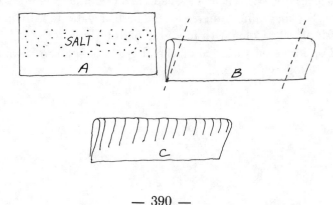

OPTIONAL: If carrot is used for the spiral cut then substitute a daikon core section for stamen center for contrast of color or vice versa: substitute a carrot stamen if a daikon spiral section is used. This will add a more dramatic look to your flower.

Lay your 8″ long spiral slice of vegetable flat on a cutting board. Rub the middle 2 to 3″ center area section of the daikon (lengthwise) with ordinary table salt. (A) The salt will soften the vegetable and so make it more pliable for folding. After "salting" for 10 to 15 minutes, fold down along center of the spiral. Match the cut edges evenly. Cut off end pieces on diagonal to even off pieces as shown in diagram B. Proceed to make diagonal slash line cuts across the folded edge keeping slashes ⅛″ apart. Start with very short slash cuts at one end of the spiral folded vegetable section and proceed to opposite end increasing the length size of the slashes accordingly (see diagram C).

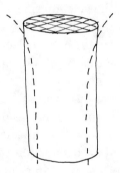

Remaining Center Core: Cut off a four inch chunk section. Shape as per diagram narrowing it down at the base. Cut crosswise design on the flat end of the cylindrical shaped stamen core as per diagram by removing narrow V-shaped strips.

Place core stub down on the shorter cut slashed end of the 8″ salted folded spiral section. Place narrowed base stub extended below spiral slashed strip. Hold stamen core firmly and roll core and spiral together toward opposite end. Hold last roll of spiral against the core stamen center tightly. Secure with two

toothpicks placed at right angles to each other.

The mum flower will appear to be very limp. Immerse in iced water to perk up and simultaneously remove salt. If desired, the white daikon mums can be immersed in food colored iced water of different lovely pastel shades and placed together to create a really beautiful "show" centerpiece. Hide the use of the toothpicks (to hold core stamen and spiral section together) with chicory or other greens before placing as individual garnish on presentation platter.

If desired a combined group of these mums of various pastel and vivid colors can be raised to various heights with floral wire or bamboo skewers and put together using floral oasis foam as pin cushion base. Fill in with lemon leaves from the florist to make a most beautiful (if even inedible) "show centerpiece" for your dinner table; one that would be more of a conversation piece than any floral arrangement sent by your best local flower shop.

Daikon iris: For the more daring sculptors, this one makes for a most beautiful flower in carrot or daikon form. I prefer the latter, for then I have more lattitude by food dying this vegetable. The food color dye of the petals is absorbed in blending striated shades since the petal cuts are thinner and will absorb dye in pastel hues; the thicker stamen center will appear to take

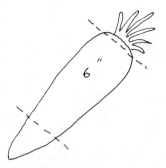

on a deeper shade of the same color lending more beauty to this fragile looking specimen.

Pare thick tapered daikon and cut crosswise leaving a 6″ long tapered stub section. Using center of daikon (or core of carrot)

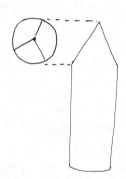

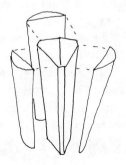

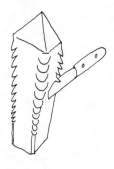

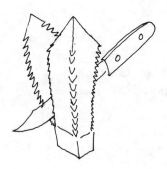

as apex point, cut off sharp angled wedge pieces from top surface (wide) end of root vegetable *only* in such a manner that
you are left with 3 flat equal cone shaped sides to the top as in
diagram.

Using the cone shaped cut of the top surface as a guide, start
at apex, follow it down the entire length of the root by slicing
off wide section strips of the daikon, thus flattening the 3 sides
of the daikon root stub. (diagram) Leave a ½" space *un*cut
lengthwise on the corner "turns" in between each one third
(flattened out) section of the root. See illustration for clear picture of this procedure.

Round off all points and edges so they are smooth. Using a
sharp paring knife, cut out uniform size notched steps, keeping

them absolutely parallel down the length of each uncut ½" corner side *only* as per diagram. Allow one inch on tapered bottom to remain *un*cut. Use flat side of blade of sharp knife and proceed to form daikon petals by cutting down from top apex in a thin slice. Cut each flat side catching horizontal ends of the opposing parallel notched side corners as per diagram. Do *NOT* cut through 1" base at tapered bottom of root. Use point of knife and cut inward at that base point toward core center. Each petal so cut (but not yet released) will then have step notched cuts (zigzag pattern) on *both* sides of *each* petal sliced. Cut inward into the solid 1" base at bottom. Hold root center firmly and gently twist slightly to release. Thus you now have a separately formed 3 petal flower with an attached solid base. (1) (To twist off top center root do so as per tulip cuts learned in carrot unit.) If base will not release easily, repeat by cutting in at deeper angle into 1" base area if necessary. Repeat entire process again to obtain second set of petals (2). When released, trim and taper base bottom section of the formed sec-

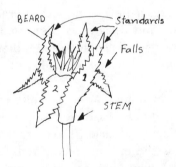

ond set of petals slightly so it can fit inside base of first set of petals. Push wood pick or bamboo stick up from bottom side of first released set of petals and up through second set leaving pick end extruded. Stagger petals between each other as in an Iris (1 and 2) in illustration.

Whittle down remaining root stub leftover from petal layers.

Push into extruded pick end in center of two joined sets of petals to simulate stamen center. Chill entire flower and/or bathe in food coloring.

For a more authentic looking Iris; proceed as above. Replace center with softer type brush stamen such as a short scallion cut mum. Proceed to join all together as previously detailed.

Your version would then possess a set of petals called the Falls, which would flare out and hang down. The second set of petals on an Iris stand up more rigidly and are called the Standards. The inner scallion mum brush would simulate the mat of soft fuzz found inside the flower and is called the Iris' beard. Since Irises are known to be cultivated in many shades, one may leave it white as is, or give any color you like.

If it is being used for display only, inedible, more curve to the Standards (petals) can be attained by inserting a fine gauged floral wire through center of petal which would not be visible on the surface. OPTIONAL: If stem like stalk is desired, impale base of Iris flower head on an orange wood stick or two joined bamboo skewers (for extra strength). Insert wood stick or skewers into green scallion tubular stalk. A most beautiful flower which requires care, patience and lots of practice but whose concept of cutting and design has been used in many other flowers carved in previous chapters, and is therefore really old hat to you who *practice* what you read!

Radishes: Grown in many varieties, white, red and heavily coated black skinned radishes, these roots, very low in calories, are used in appetizers and salads. The more familiar one to the home consumer is the entirely edible red skinned roundish global radish. The white skinned long tubular radish root, known as the icicle radish, must be pared as one does a carrot. The black coated, larger bulbous radish must also be shed of its heavy skin. In paring it, you find underneath the black coat a white, sharp tasting pulp. The red radish is a favorite of home gardeners, for they can be harvested in 4–5 weeks. The home gardener, planting a new seed crop every 10 days, can be sure of a continous supply, weather conditions permitting.

Many of the designs we will work out for the more roundish red radish can also be modified for use on the elongated icicle radish. Since we have dealt so much with the long tapered type of root similar to the white icicle radish, it will suffice to say you need only experiment and pattern your designs of all those familiar in shape to the icicle radish such as the cucumber, carrot and daikon.

A particularly pretty one that I know works beautifully on the icicle radish is the following. Pare a long white thick radish. Using the wider mouthed (Kitchen Helper) lemon stripper, pull down but *not off,* ½" lengthwise strips of the radish as in the sunburst design of the cucumber holder. Very gently, now twist off the center section on the white tubular radish as you did the core of the carrot tulip flower. When placed in water, the radish will open up and flare out more widely. Affix into a bouquet with a frill colored toothpick as the stamen center. Try the wider thicker cut petaled tulip flower shown previously on the carrot. You will find it is much easier to use the softer, more pliable white radish. If desired, after such carvings, immerse the white radish in a food dye bath, as they absorb color well. An entire bouquet of differently cut and color (dyed) white radishes can do nicely as a floral centerpiece for a luncheon table for a total cost of about a dollar. Icicle radishes are sold 10–12 radishes to a plastic bagged package for approximately 29 cents. Red radishes are sold similarly in 6 oz. plastic bags or are tied together in bunches with their leaf tops intact.

Many red radish cut designs can be made exactly as those already practiced using the turnip or beet. The red radish root flowers will be more beautiful, however, because of the natural contrast of their edible red skin covering and their white pulp beneath. Picture then, the fragile more intricate thin petaled rose cut flower or the simply cut mum. Speaking of the latter, here's a little extra twist (literally) to form that last one into a fanned-out mum cut, again combining 2 different designed cuttings. Prepare radish with horizontal slash cuts such as on the

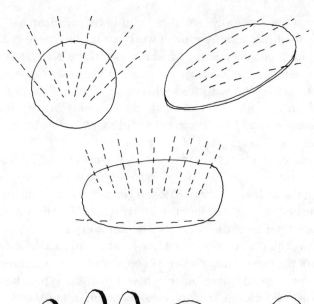

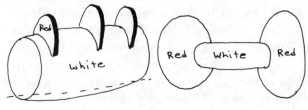

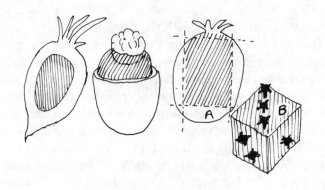

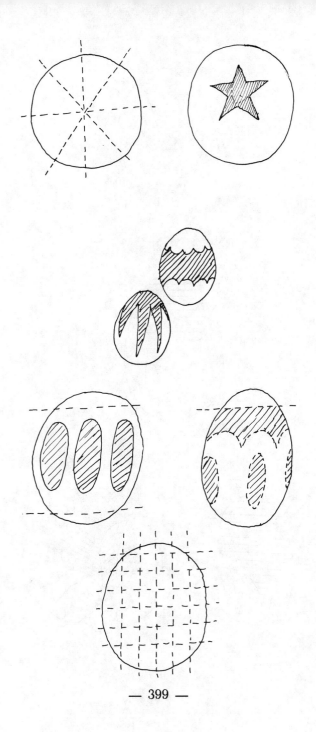

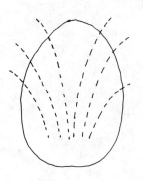

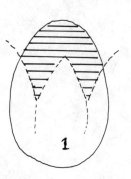

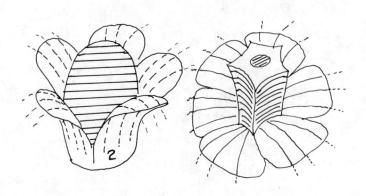

gherkin pickle in the cucumber unit and the Pineapple Deli-Doll (chapter 1). Spread out fan slices and press down with thumb at radish base. Hold in same position and now make the cross-cut vertically as for mum. When iced, it will open to bloom much more than the usual crisscross cut of the mum.

Other varieties of radishes can be made by the simple process of *slicing behind* the red skin thus releasing it from its white body or *removing* said red covering outer layer altogether. In all illustrated diagrams, the shadowed areas will represent red skin cut completely away or removed, thus leaving the white pulp showing. The dotted line indicates the actual knife cut. Using a few diagrams rather than many words, we can quickly set forth a few suggested designs merely using a paring knife.

Here are some more cuts or carvings of radishes, designed this time with the use of some culinary tools.

There is a simple plastic radish rose cutter selling in 5 & 10¢ stores for approximately 79¢. It will produce a radish cut as

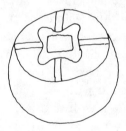

depicted in the diagram, shaped like that of the plastic gadget on which it was cut. I recommend and prefer the Wilesco 14 section apple slicer to "machine" or "quickly produce" my radish roses. Radishes, if they must be hurriedly produced, should be cut with the 14 section slicer, as these will open bigger and present a much more impressive display for the same time and motion involved. Place large red radish, stabilized green stem end down and press down with the apple slicer as per directions

with implement. The center stamen of the red skin radish (where the core of an apple would fall) may be left as is or a small slice may be taken off the enter of the red skin covered top. The red top surface can be completely removed or the "core" center can be reduced in vertical dimensional height. The tip ends of the 14 radish petals can then be cut as desired. Use knife to cut diagonally for a sharper petal point. The opened radish may also be colored with food dye; only the white meat pulp of the root will change color. The stamen center core of the (apple sliced) radish surface can be cut into 1/16" wedged grooves or it can be cross cut mum fashion. With so much variety provided with the Wilesco 14 section apple slicer, I could not bring myself to use the 79¢ gadget. At this point let me also make you aware of the fact that there are similar less expensive apple slicers on the culinary market, but the latter consist of only 8 (state produced) not too sharp sections and the 10-section slicer (made in Italy). The radishes cut with them will not have as nice a result as the aforementioned 14 section slicer with stainless steel sharp blades. The option of course is yours.

*LEMON STRIPPER:*The use of the narrower French lemon stripper again will vary in appearance with that of using the wider mouthed lemon stripper of the Kitchen Helper. For smaller radishes, I prefer the use of the narrower opening.

Vertically cut out the entire strip of red skin all around radish. Leave as is for one radish design. For another, proceed as before, but now slide a knife blade behind each *remaining* red skin strip left, in between the stripped out channels. Separate the red skin from white body pulp of the radish thus releasing same as a narrow petal. For variation, using the same implement, make stripped out spiral cuts or use stripper to cut out other designs. Here are some examples of stripped *out* cuts of radishes. For another different look using same implement and

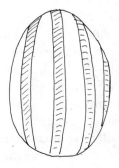 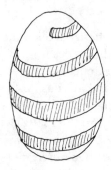

concept, pull strips vertically outward as far down as possible but not *off* to give sunburst effect as in cucumber holder.

Here are some which need some explanation. Before trying these new ones, apply to the red radish, the ones you've already learned on the other root vegetables: The thin petaled rose, the last one carved under the unit on turnips, is absolutely breathtaking when cut with the natural red skin left intact on a large red radish. Proceed then to food dye it yellow.

Speaking of large radishes: try this one which will look just as well when substituting a lemon as the base; so here's another two for one! For this one you will need a large red radish plus one medium and one smaller red radish. Starting at ½" above stabilized slice, make slashed diagonal downward gashes in staggered fashion, working from bottom to top. Optional: is to make a final diagonal slash cut to be filled later across face of top of radish (or lemon) or leave as is so that lemon rind or red skin

is emphasized. Slice the medium and smaller radish into cross-wise thin slices so they will fit snugly into the aforementioned slashed cuts on the larger "base" radish. Cut smaller radish slices in half. Push into slanted gashes. Place the larger halved slices near the base, working the smaller halved slices into cuts up toward the top. Place all halved radish slices, red skin (side) out, allowing the white meat of each half slice to remain slightly exposed. Do *not* immerse this one in iced water as slashes might widen and dislodge slices.

ANGLED PETAL CUTS: The angle used for cutting this one is what makes the difference. Heretofore, we have made petal cuts on radishes (or turnips) by slicing behind the red skin, placing the flat side of the knife blade against the radish. If you then wish, use scissors to cut and create the sharper points on

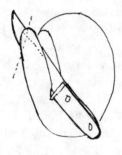

each petal. With the use of ice water, this version would open slightly since each petal is thick. Try this new version, holding that same knife differently to create this more opened effect. Starting at ¼" from the top of an elongated shaped radish, use just the *tip point* of the blade to cut in ¼" depth and cut down the length of the radish. Do *not* cut through the base.

Move point of your knife ¼" to the right and slice down again. Note diagram side view of cut petal separated from the white meat center of the radish; the difference between the above radish and this one being that each petal cut on this specimen has ¼" exposed side of the white pulp still at-

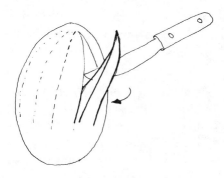

tached and showing on the red skin petal. This is due to the angular insertion point and cut of the knife blade in contrast to the flat blade slice made on the former radish which would release and reveal *only* a *full* red skin petal. This latter version opens most beautifully featuring very thin petals revealing a thick bulbous white meat stamen center. Place in ice water to open fully. If preferred, round out white meat stamen center of flower carefully or for contrast of color and variety, place lemon rind or olive slice on top surface of stamen center.

Here's another petal effect that will yield a different look and will be the basis for many other variations.

A tapering elongated radish would be a better working root than a round one for this beautiful flower. Start with (greens)

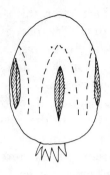

stem side down. Insert point of knife ¼″ up from base so as to carve out of the red skin (with part of the under meat attached) a wedge shape as per shadowed diagram. Now insert point tip of blade above removed apex and cut in around this convex wedge forming a border. Follow design and cut from top downward at 45° angle as per dotted line, applying separating pressure at top and half way down sides so the section is pulled away from the main body *as* you cut. It must remain attached at base, so note width of petal formed: narrow at top and gaining width as its cut reaches toward its base. Allow for space between the next *estimated border* edge to make the next cut out bordered petal. Repeat process. Remove red (and attached white meat) convex wedge and cut another border edge surrounding same. Pull petal away in process. It is important to leave that extra bit of red skin untouched in between each completely bordered petal cut.

Continue all around, cutting out wedged red convex area and bordering and pulling petals away from main body. Now for the variations, all off this same basic petal wedge convex cut.

1. Cut off slice from top.

2. Leave red center as is and use narrow French lemon stripper to strip and pull away (but not cut off) red skin left in between each convex petal cut. This will give you a longer thin sunburst petal strip effect because strip is started at apex of

radish not ¼" below as is the convex petal cut. Remove all remaining red skin on top area.

3. Starting ¼" above the apex tip point of the neighboring cut convex petal, make a crisscross sawtooth cut in the remaining red skin (*in between* the convex petal cuts). This cut is a take-off on the turnip dahlia cut (see turnip unit). Remove skin in between connecting each saw tooth cut as per dahlia. See diagram. Clean area above of remaining skin. These cuts may then be left as is or. . . .

4. Slide knife behind this new saw tooth cut to release it away from body of radish as another differently shaped petal.

5. This same effect can be elaborated on by limiting the petal cuts to only three sides of a large radish. Remove first red skin wedged area: cut border surrounding same, as in basic radish cut above. Now continue to follow *same contour* and cut and make another repeated border cut around the first petal one; add a third border cut around the second petal. Follow and repeat same procedure on two remaining sides of radish. Remove excess red skin left on tip and in between as before. When it is iced, you will have 9 stand away petals in sets of 3, a beautiful sight. *If* enough red skin is left in between, the 3 sides, cut into apex saw tooth fashion (dahlia) and then remove excess red skin on top. Any combination of the above with any of the previous diagramed ones can be made on one large radish. E.g. (as per #6) cut convex petals leaving a larger space in between. Incise 2 lemon stripped pieces sunburst fashion. If preferred, try this one (#7): make convex petals and in between make a thicker sliced cut of a red petal. Now slash that petal slice vertically into ⅛" slits as in diagram. Or try this one (#8): make convex cut and slice red skin facing off completely in between. Slide knife behind this sliced off cut to form a very *thin* roundish petal. This, when iced, will open outward, depending on thinness of cut; the thinner the sliced petal cut the more pliable it will be to open fuller.

Try this simple one (#9). Merely cut off outside red skin on 4 sides and slide knife behind to form thin petal leaving red skin

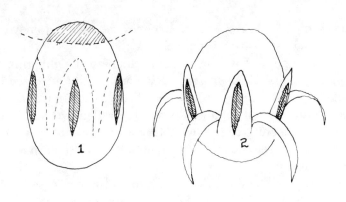

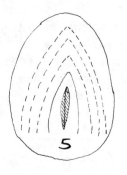

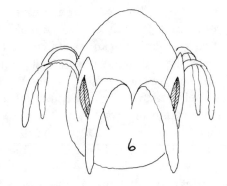

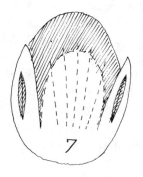

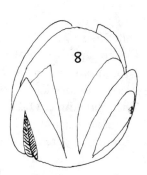

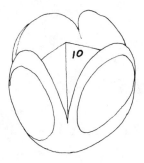

in between each slice. Cut that red skin in between as for saw toothed variation above (#3) and leave as is or: slide knife behind to release same into another petal. as in #4. Or . . . (#10) cut off red skin and slide knife behind to release *thin* petal. Clean out all remaining red skin from that point up. Shave to taper to point toward top.

By combining different designed cuts you can go on and on to make new variations of your own all the time.

The following is a take-off brought to my mind by the conical shape of the turnip bell-like flower. Using a red radish, remove top section as per diagram A. . . . Hold flat side of knife, pointing in at 60° angle toward center of white revealed top and rotate *radish*. This will give white surface of the radish a shallow conical shape, as per diagram. Now insert point of knife ⅛″

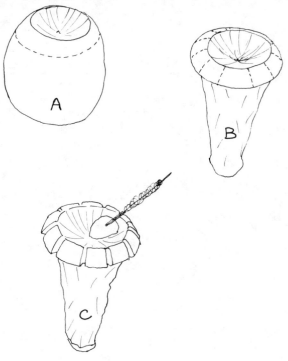

down from red outside surface edge and rotate *radish* again following contour *without* detaching same from its base B. Turn radish upside down and carve into cone shaped bottom. See diagram. Place white surface side of radish top (radish is again upside down) on cutting board and make slash cuts all around outside edge. Cut off side diagonal tips to reshape into a pointed petal if so desired. Return to upright position to chill as is, or place lemon slice or olive center or frill pick in top of conical center C.

HELPFUL HINTS: To sum up: any single cut or combinations of cuts can be used on the same radish. Choose the radish more conducively shaped for the cut planned for it; e.g., use accordion cut or convex wedged out petal cuts on elongated tapered radish. Use scallop rose cuts, etc. on round radishes. Use implements such as stripper for better uniformity when cutting designs. Use food dye to add more color to form a bouquet consisting of radishes only. Use crosswise cut slices for decorating canapes and salads. Be sure that whatever is cut or carved is given lots of room in a deep *ice cubed filled* bowl so it may open fully. Keep replacing ice cubes as they melt. The longer time allowed for carved flowers to be immersed in ice water, the more they will open. The *thinner* the slice, the more it will tend to open and curl or fan out. The *deeper* the cut, (without breaking piece off or cutting off base) the more it will pull away from body of radish, the more open it will become when iced. Try to keep vegetables as wet as possible for fresher appearance. Use atomized water spray bottle to refreshen bouquet from time to time. There is enough variation in red and white radish cuts and carved designs, to prepare a full floral arrangement using just radish roots. Add height to arrangement with the use of bamboo sticks. Use celery stalks with leaves attached as fillers for vertical designed bouquet; use curley parsley for lower section.

Experiment and practice and enjoy eating your mistakes as well as your triumphs. They will both taste the same . . . they're all good.

Also see Floral Basket Arrangements: Chapter 8 for utilizing all above vegetable carvings and cuts.

HOW AND WHERE TO GET IT

"All American Salad Favorites"; also "Western Iceberg Lettuce Makings": Western Iceberg Lettuce Inc., P.O.Box 9123, San Francisco, Calif. 94129

"Fresh Ideas for Fruits and Vegetables": Best Food Co., Division of CPC International, International Plaza, Sylvan Ave., Englewood Cliffs, N.J. 07632

"Selection and Care of Fresh Fruits and Vegetables": United Fresh Fruit & Vegetable Assoc., 777 14 St. N.W., Washington, D.C. 20005. Cost for handling, $1.00; also at no charge: "Publications & Materials for teachers, and "Supply Guide" featuring the average monthly availability of fresh fruits and vegetables broken down state wide in nation.

"How To Buy Fresh Vegetables," Bulletin #141, Dept. Of Agriculture, Washington, D.C. 20250.

8 MEAT & FISH

Have you ever had the girls for lunch and the word got around, "All she served was just tuna fish and salad" . . . ? Well, they could say the same thing about me. It's true, really! All *I* serve is tuna fish and salad too; but somehow they never say that! Because they never notice that "it's *just* tuna fish and salad."

The word's out and gotten around about me too, you know —"For lunch she had this beautiful fresh floral centerpiece, a wicker basket filled with fresh flowers." No, they're not talking about a freshly delivered floral centerpiece arrangement for the table; they're talking about the floral piece that WAS the lunch! It was a centerpiece all right—one that added a touch of creative elegance to my table, but one that we actually ate! The fresh floral arrangement consisted of a (tuna fish) wicker basket, with foliage (salad) greens and overflowing with fresh blooming (carved vegetable) flowers.

If tuna is not your cup of the sea, try the same arrangement substituting salmon or shrimp salad, or try a meat variation such as chicken salad or chopped liver (or whatever your preference might be). Not only is my flower arrangement unique and sure to be a conversation piece, but it isn't half as expensive as any real floral arrangement could be; the best part of all—they couldn't believe they ate the whole thing!

Tell you what, come join me for lunch . . . but all you'll get is tuna fish and salad! You see, it's the end of the week and the cupboard is just about bare. There are just a couple of cans from the sea left and we do have a few eggs but the vegetable garden is going strong and—anyway, who wants to eat heavily on a hot day? The table is set for lunch, so come on in.

TUNA FISH AND SALAD: A FLORAL BASKET ARRANGEMENT

TO CREATE THE BASKET: Prepare a large clear plastic tray; (so as not to detract from the setting, use a neutral background tray, preferably clear lucite. Or use a flat old mirror as tray). On the lower ⅓ section of tray, place the mixed tuna fish salad (liver, salmon, etc.) in the shape of a (horizontal) flat basket.

TO FILL BASKET: GREEN FOLIAGE: Fill in remaining top ⅔ section with foliage greens such as escarole leaves, iceberg lettuce, chicory leaves, spinach, etc. Supplement these with celery stalks, leaf tops, etc., full length cuts of serrated carrot sticks and white icicle radishes, strips of red and green pepper, cut cucumber sticks, cherry tomatoes and broccoli and cauliflower florets.

CARVED FLOWERS: Fill in greens with bouquet of iced carved flower blooms such as turnip and beet dahlias, icicle radish and carrot tulips, (apple sliced) red radishes and whole scallions with the bulb heads cut like mums, etc. (See How to Cut Vegetable Flowers in chapter 7.)

GARNISH: Top off with small sprigs of fresh parsley and fill in with an assortment of pimento filled green and black olives, cocktail onions and foil wrapped cheeses.

TO CREATE WICKER EFFECT (TO BASKET): Using the pastry tube method, outline the entire border of the basket by overlaying egg yolk cream paste by using the point star tube tip. To fill in wicker weave effect, overlay egg yolk cream paste onto the basket shaped tuna in a diagonal crisscross effect, using a small hole tube tip or a small leaf tube tip.

"And what did she have for lunch?"

"Well, it turned out it was just tuna fish and salad, but you wouldn't have believed it, unless you saw it! You see, she had this gorgeous fresh floral arrangement". . . .

You need not be limited to fish, however, for your floral arrangement basket. If there are some other salads you wish to replace for the tuna, by all means suit your family's taste. For instance, this same arrangement works most beautifully presented in a chicken salad variation. To give it an all over glazed and smooth coated appearance, I find *chicken salad basket* particularly looks its best when covered with the same type aspic glaze used to transform brown chopped liver into white igloos. Follow recipe for same in Chapter 6 under How to Make a Light Colored Covering Glaze; cover the chicken salad basket shape with the aspic coating then superimpose the wicker (egg yolk cream paste) effect atop the glaze. The overall look is that of a beautiful bouquet entrusted to the confines of a glossy ceramic basket. With this glaze in mind you can easily see that liver baskets can be worked out in similar fashion or whatever your family likes might be.

Although this aforementioned basket is a very impressive plate for the ladies, the small fry would much more appreciate one of the following for their get-to-gether luncheon:

FOR THE LITTLE ONES: A FISH Prepare a simple tuna or salmon fish mix. When having other children as guests, I find they usually prefer "plain old tuna fish" without the gourmet touches of added celery, chopped onions, pickle relish, etc. This high-protein lunch can be used as a main centerpiece, the mother hostess serving each child a portion of the large fish or it can be made as a scaled down version, giving each child a fish of his own. The little ones much prefer the latter, thinking they have each caught their own. For each platter: Free handshape a simple fish (see diagram). Use a pimento olive or a scalloped carrot round for eye. For gills, use cucumber circles, carrot sticks for dorsal fin, and sliced lettuce for ocean waves.

TO CREATE THE AIR BUBBLES: Place a few slices of a

whole hard cooked egg as in diagram. As a place setter for a seating plan for the party lunch, overlay each child's name onto his or her fish using egg yolk cream paste through a fine hole tube tip to do so.

TUNA FISH BOAT

As a take-off on the party loaf sailboat described in chapter 6, each child can own (and eat) his own fishing schooner. Prepare and place on each plate, tuna fish salad shaped like the oval hull of a boat. Stabilize a large stalk of celery (mast) in center and top off with an olive. Opt: use olive port holes and pepper halved rings for ropes off sides of schooner boat. Before mounting sails, write each child's name (use cake writing gel) on a slice of dark yellow American cheese (sails); e.g., . . . Steve's Sloop, Diane's Dinghy, etc. Set your tuna fish sailboat off on a sea of lettuce waves.

OTHER EDIBLE MAIN CENTERPIECE MOLDS

Prepare rooster, chicken or whatever free hand mold form you wish following procedure for making of same in chapter 6 under Chopped Liver. Displace the liver with your choice of fish salads, chicken or ham salads. As in chapter 6, any salad combination can be used to replace the liver in any of the detailed and described molds in that chapter as long as the salad prepared is of good binding and firm consistency and packed well. See: man's shirt, woman's bonnet, etc.

TO PREPARE A FISH OWL USING COMBINED SALAD MIXES

On a rectangular tray, hand mold the figure of an owl which can be made of either tuna or salmon or shrimp salad or whatever you choose. Follow directions described for the liver owl mold used as an hors d'oeuvre spread in chapter 6. Duplicate concept of same and decorate accordingly.

To combine and serve two salads such as tuna and salmon and present it as one main entree, use the salmon salad to make up the body and face of the owl. Use the tuna fish for the wings and tail area. *TO DECORATE:* Overlay flat anchovies vertically on the tuna to emphasize the tail feathers. Define and accentuate the outline of each area with egg yolk cream paste. For change of pace, use hard cooked whole egg slices as eyes and overlay wing area with red radish slices; continue to garnish accordingly. Thus, you have given your guests not only a uniquely presented display of fish foods but a choice of the sea to select from. The amount used and the finished size of the displayed motif designed figure created, depends solely on how many guests you are planning for. Since this is all done in free form method, using your hands as the mold, you are therefore not limited with a particular individual form's holding capacity. For reference guide and to coordinate a party theme, see this chapter and other chapters on owls. (chapters: 1, 2, 6).

COMBINED SALAD FISH MOLDS

Speaking of molds and combined fish platters brings to mind the straight vertical and curved fish molds which are so popularly marketed in aluminum and copper metal forms. See glossary: Tools of Your Workshop.

To provide a choice of colorful selection of combined fish salads in metal mold form: Brush mold form with mayonnaise or use the new designed aerated can sprays (of oil) used and recommended for Teflon pans. In the head section, lay in the tuna fish salad, salmon in the body area and egg salad in tail end or whatever combination and placement you wish. Pack in to mold firmly and refrigerate several hours. Release mold from pan onto tray to decorate and garnish; e.g., use olives for eyes, round slices of radishes for scales of fish (optional); lay on anchovy strips for vertical feather effect of tail, use whole sliced eggs or cherry tomatoes for air bubbles on tray etc.

This same mold can be used to hold and shape a mousse type of (gelatinized) fish mixture which can also be turned out for further garnishing or overlaid (use egg yolk cream) to emphasize some of the features of the fish mold. Just as this fish mold is packed, turned out and decorated, so can this same principle be applied to any other mold. For suggestions for displaying and garnishing see: *Butterfly Mold* as main entree in chapter 9 for presentation of tuna, chopped herring, salmon, etc.

SANTA'S SALMON

As a combined fish mold, butterfly mold or any other metal form mold can be turned out and then be garnished appropriately, as can a sandwich loaf be frosted after its making, so now let us combine these two theories of principle in our next presentation of a mousse type of fish mold. I found this recipe, called a *Salmon Party Salad in Better Homes & Gardens* (August 1968), in which it was recommended to be gelled, chilled and served using an ordinary 3 c. round mold. I found it, however, more versatile and exciting to customize it for the festive Christmas holiday season by using the following adaptation:

FOR CHRISTMAS TREE OR WREATH

The star of your holiday party table will be a salmon salad "frosted" with its own dressing—a blend of avocado and sour cream. You give it a holiday theme with the choice of mold you use, such as a rounded *ring* type mold which would resemble a Christmas wreath. For the copper mold ring form available in 12 c. size you will need to at least triple the recipe depending on how full you wish your finished wreath to stand. The alternative, a disposable aluminum bell form sold at this time of the year, can be given a push here and there to reshape it into a triangle or Christmas tree shape if you do not possess a regular tree mold form, the latter is marketed in copper form. The final garnishing will give each mold display used an unmistakable holiday look.

Recipe For Salmon Mold from *Better Homes & Gardens,* Aug. 1968
1 envelope (1 Tbs. unflavored gelatin)
¼ c. cold water
¾ c. boiling water
2 tbsp. sugar
1 tbsp. lemon juice
1 tbsp. vinegar
2 teas. grated *fresh* onion
½ teas. salt
½-1 teas. white horsereadish (depending on strength wished for taste)
1 lb. can salmon, drained and flaked
½ c. mayonnaise or salad dressing
⅓ c. sliced pitted black olives
¼ c. finely chopped celery

Soften gelatin in cold water. Add boiling water; stir till gelatin is dissolved. Add sugar, lemon juice, vinegar, onion, salt and horseradish.; chill until partially set. Stir in salmon, mayonnaise, olives and celery. Spoon into mold. Chill at least 5 hours, preferably overnight as for all type gelatin settings.

Avocado Dressing For Salmon Mold: Seed, peel and mash a large ripe avocado. Combine mashed avocado (about ⅔ c.) with ¼-½ c. sour cream (I prefer mine thicker so I only use the minimum amount of sour cream); add ½ teas. salt. Blend thoroughly. Cover dressing tightly and chill; (color of avocado dressing will darken on surface if not completely covered well while under refrigeration; just stir again). Unmold salmon mold onto a round serving plate (for wreath design); spread dressing mixture evenly over outside of salad mold. With tip of fork tines, "pick up" points of frosting to give green dressing the pine needle look of a wreath (or tree). *FOR WREATH DECORATION:* Place in clusters, some lemon leaves or flat Italian parsley with red cherry tomatoes or red radishes for garland and holly trim. Cut to form a pimento red bow at base. On remaining background of (round shaped) tray using writing gel, place your message: "Season's Greetings, 1975."

For Christmas Tree Decoration: If you had selected the tree-shaped mold, turn the salmon salad out onto the upper part of a rectangular tray. Insert a celery "trunk" stalk, rounded side up and cover bottom with slices of dark pumpernickel bread to form the shape of a pot. Frost and decorate as for wreath in the same manner, pine needles affect, etc. using Italian flat parsley stems and leaves. Use cherry tomato or red radishes and black olives and pickled cocktail onions as the colorful Christmas balls on the tree. Optional: write in Christmas message on tray.

A really unique and beautiful apropos holiday presentation. A 3 c. mold used for year round entertaining purposes, will serve four guests as a main entree (or it can be used as an hors d'oeuvre when served with crackers or bread rounds).

MORE FISH AND MEAT PRESENTATIONS

ICE MOLDS FOR SHRIMP SERVICE: Since shrimp are best served cold, use molds of ice to serve seafood while it simultaneously keeps it constantly chilled.

TO MAKE ICE RING MOLD: Place pretty colorful sea shells and fresh dillweed (to simulate seaweed) on bottom of a large ring mold. Fill mold with just enough "ocean" water (pre-color water with just a drop green food dye) to just about cover and submerge the shells.

HELPFUL HINT: When using water for ice molds (or to make iced tea) always use boiled cooled water. Ordinary tap water when used will yield a cloudy appearance. Freeze colored water in mold until underwater sea scene is set in position. Then fill to top of mold (form) with more of the lightly green tinted liquid ocean. This preparation can be done well in advance or freeze overnight.

TO SERVE: Cover a wire or plastic rack with heavy duty foil in which you have punched several air holes. This will provide you with a stabilized base to set your iced mold and seafood upon. The punched air holes will allow the melting ice water to run off down into the serving tray. (It is important that tray used has a lip on edges to contain the melting ice water.) If necessary to remove accumulated liquid from base of tray, use a meat basting bulb. By setting your tray in this manner, seafood will not be constantly left soaking in the melting ice water. Cover foil with cut up greens. Place ice ring mold on tray. Surround border edge of ice mold with cooked shrimp and/or cooked scallops. Fill empty ring center of mold with deep dish containing shrimp cocktail or tartar sauce. Garnish by hanging lemon slices over rim's edge of the sauce dish. A picturesque "all in one help yourself service" to set the mood for a buffet table.

ALTERNATIVE: Fill center of ring mold with a *gel formed* vegetable salad in place of the bowl to hold fish sauce. Use a deep bowl to act as form to *mold* salad. Serve vegetable salad as accompaniment for fish food.

FOR AN ICE FILLED CENTER MOLD: substitute water for gelatin mold and apply same principle as follows:

FOR GELATIN SALAD MOLD: Use a deep mixing bowl mold form that will fit inside center of mold ring. Prepare lime gelatin (cut down on water as per usual gelatin directions). To obtain a more desired lighter colored sea water, I prefer to use lemon gelatin with a dash of green food dye. Pour (either) gelatin into deep bowl mold to depth of 1″. Lay in "seaweed" and a few goldfish (carrot) figures. When partially set, (it will set quickly) top with second layer of (gelatin) "sea waters." Lay in some more goldfish, staggering them above and in between those already set in first layer below. If bowl is very deep and can accept same, set in a third layer. Allow to set overnight, Turn gelatin mold out onto tray. (Use rack for ice molded center only.) Place surrounding greens on tray. Lay shrimp or scallops all around. Place a Viking ship filled with tartar sauce or cocktail sauce nearby (see Chapter 7 to make Viking boat). To serve larger amount of sauce or to dispense dressing for gelled mold, use a smaller version of the cantaloupe or honeydew whale (see chapters 2 and 3 on watermelon whales and melons). Empty melon fruit from shell, line with foil and fill with dressing or sauce.

To serve a large crowd: a basket filled seafood holder: To serve even more guests lets combine several already learned lessons such as: (1) utilizing the iced ring mold this time in a completely different sense however with (2) the chilled shrimp on ice concept with (3) the watermelon basket we have mastered in chapter 2 of this book.

TO PREPARE ICE MOLD HANDLE: Using a ring mold of appropriate size for the melon basket we plan to prepare, place a double section of heavy duty foil midway on both sides of the ring mold. Thus you will be forming two halved ring mold sections. Do not fill mold too deeply with "ocean" water for these two halved forms must be faced together to form only one round handle for basket.

TO FORM SEE THROUGH BASKET HANDLE: Lay in dill-weed and pretty colorful seashells in the ocean green water. Freeze overnight or longer, as this can be prepared many days or weeks in advance.

WATERMELON BASKET: Prepare basket by cutting ⅓ section off top of melon. Ball out fruit from top and bottom of basket. Use melon meat for separate fruit dish. Optional: Score basket rind with basket weave design. Line watermelon shell with heavy foil and fill with chipped ice.

TO COMBINE FOR TABLE PRESENTATION: Unmold ice rings and place flat sides together. Measure base of combined ice handle and cut out exact fitting section on watermelon basket to accept base of handle, providing a snug fit for same. OPTIONAL: For a more secure stabilized interlocked foundation use a heated icepick to bore a hole in ice mold. Push orangewood stick into hole and exposed end of stick into watermelon basket base. Garnish top inside of ice filled melon basket with greens. Fill with boiled shrimp and scallops or clams. Garnish basket with lemon slices or leaves to cover border edge and hide insertion point of handle. Set on tray of greens and pretty sea shells or drape with fish net.

With this new concept of a *see through basket handle* you can easily see how it can be customized to fit *fruit presentations.* Simply fill mold with clear or pink or yellow tinted water to low depth and lay in rose petals, fancy lemon slices or leaves or fresh strawberries and peppermint leaves. Proceed as for ice ring handle used for seafood basket. Refill as basket cavity is depleted.

A HAM GROWN FLOWER GARDEN

For those who prefer carving their meat at the table (to carve properly meat must be cooked and allowed to cool to set before cutting) here are a few suggestions: To glaze a ham, I suggest this method as well as this special ham glaze:

To prepare glaze: sprinkle 3 envelopes of unflavored gelatin over a mixture of ¾ c. water and ¾ cup dry white wine in cooking vessel. Allow to stand to soften. Heat over low heat until crystals dissolve. Remove from heat and stir in 3 c. of mayonnaise until well blended and smooth. This will cover a cooked and cooled 10–12 lb. ham. Allow glaze to stand to thicken slightly. Place ham on wire rack over jelly pan and begin to spoon glaze over meat, as per usual glazing methods outlined in Chapter 6 on chopped liver. *For a rectangular long block type of canned ham:* cover meat with above glaze or use a white or brown aspic glaze. (See Chapter 6.) Before last coat of glaze is firmed set garden scene with Italian parsley as stems and leaves of flowers or use cut green pepper leaves for same. Top stems with carved flower blossoms such as scalloped carrot slices with olive centers, etc. Use writing tube gel to outline a picket fence along sides at bottom of glazed ham.

Alternative: cut thin crust slices of bread to resemble pickets in a fence. Press into glazed ham along sides at bottom of base.

Set on chicory grass bed of greens.

HAM BOAT

If ham is in an oval shaped tin, cover with brown aspic or white aspic glaze. Decorate ham as if it was the hull of a boat; complete with sails and pimento filled olives on sides as portholes.

See other suggestions and references to decorating boats in this chapter and in Chapter 6. Remove mast and sails to slice at table.

PEACOCK HAM

To present a nicely displayed ham, with bone in, for carving at the table, prepare ham duplicating concept of the pineapple

peacock in chapter 1. As per diagram, stabilize base of whole ham. Insert potato head with floral picks as in pineapple peacock, etc. Cover insertion area between head and ham body with canned pineapple slices topped with spiced apple rings or sprigs of fresh parsley.

Insert skewered bamboo sticks filled with cherry tomatoes, pineapple chunks, foil wrapped cheese bits, and black and green olives. Place in back portion of peacock as colorful fanned out tail spread of the proud bird.

And so, another take-off on an old theme proving once again —pineapple or ham, its what you do with what you've got that makes *your* table so different!

OWL—ASSORTED MEAT PLATTER

For bird lovers, or a springtime or graduation party, carry out your festivities by presenting cold cuts in the form of an owl for your buffet table.

To present your assortment of cold cuts, choose a large tray and, as per instructions, start laying upon it your own choice of meats, be they cooked and prepared at home by you or merely picked up presliced at the delicatessen store.

Picture your finished food presentation (see diagram).

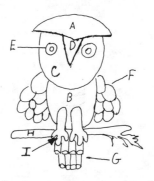

Since roast beef is a big favorite in our house and particularly similar to the coloring of an owl, I roast my own, slice it and use beef as the prime choice of my meat platter filling in with other selected meats such as turkey roll, boiled ham, etc.

(A) CAP ON OWL'S HEAD: Remove thick outside (well browned) cut of the roasted beef rump. Cut to shape like owl cap. Set aside. Slice down remaining meat to use as body of bird.

(B). OWL'S BODY: Start forming your roast beef body and build it high and rotund as befits an owl's front.

(C) FACE: Construct the face of the owl with a mound of round or oval shaped ham slices. Stack the meat up high on the sides and flat across the front of its face as an owl's face would tend to be. Set owl's cap of roast beef (A) atop head and face.

(D) BEAK: Set curved beak carved from large carrot chunk in proper position for owl's beak.

(E) EYES: Garnish with end tip slices of hard cooked egg white as background color of eyes. Cut out egg tip center and set in black olives for pupils of same. (Optional: pimento filled olives can be substituted.)

(F) WINGS: Cascading from neckline and down along both

sides of the (roast beef) body of your bird, place *folded* layers of chicken roll or turkey roll meat slices.

(G) TAIL: To improvise the tail affect for our feathered friend, lay out rolled-up slices of a catering breast of turkey in vertical placement design.

(H) TREE BRANCH: To simulate the tree branch for our owl to rest upon, set a large stalk of celery (leave celery leaves intact) horizontally across bottom of roast beef body.

(I) FEET: Pare skin of one large carrot and slice lengthwise in half. Place halved carrot feet slices rounded side up, in proper position descending from the body of the owl toward tree branch stalk of celery. From a one inch chunk of carrot, form 2 owl-like claws and attach with toothpicks to base of feet. Place leg and claw section over the celery branch to give our owl something to cling to.

What a nice old owl to sit upon his limb and hear the hoots and howls of your excited party guests.

After your buffet table is cleared of the main course and you're ready for dessert and coffee, carry out out your party theme by carrying in a pineapple owl (see chapter 1) raised as a styrofoam centerpiece; surround with fresh hand fruits, cheeses and nuts and some miniature Danish pieces to accompany your coffee and tea service.

HELPFUL HINTS: reminder: to prevent your styrofoam centerpiece from shifting position while it is being carried in for dessert, merely press a small dab of floral gum tape to the base of your styrofoam and it will stick to the tray securely. Don't forget to stabilize the pineapple owl's body into the foam with orange wood sticks or small dowels as is always necessary when presenting a raised styrofoam centerpiece.

SELECTIVE VARIETY OF OTHER MEAT PRESENTATIONS

As you can easily see now, once your creative juices are flowing, you can quickly create a flood of same as one thought quickly leads to another.

Now that you have created your first meat (owl) platter how much easier it will be to pursue the same idea and create other meat presentations in different shapes for many varieties and for attractive and specific centerpiece themes, e.g., to "lay" a duck in meat form: lay out white layers of rolled chicken or turkey meats so it appears to be a feathered layered effect to the body. Use carrot beak for mouth, olive for eye. To emphasize the feathered tail, fold each slice into cone shape placing point end up on tail area. Slice gherkin pickles into fan cuts (see Deli-Doll, chapter 1 on Pineapples) and interplay a fan cut pickle with the cone-shaped meat slices. Use carrot feet (cut shorter) for duck version. (See diagram.)

COMBINING COLD CUT MEATS AND SALADS

A nice way of displaying and serving a combined plate of cold cuts and salad is to use the roll-up method discussed in Chapter 6 on party breads.

Although hamburgers and hot dogs are usually associated with their respective bun holders, one needn't use it in that fashion exculsively; e.g., any of the aforementioned rollatinis in that chapter can be used in this fashion. Here is a really nice way to serve the youngsters an all-in-one, on paper plates: Using your choice of thinly sliced meats, turkey, ham or roast beef, overlap two slices so it may fully cover and enclose some potato salad or very well drained coleslaw when rolled. Refrigerate meat roll seam side down until ready to serve. On large center serving platter, place each (meat-potato salad) roll up inside a hot dog roll. *Optional:* Push two round circle slices of pickle into each end thus tucking in the salad. Serve lined up on a tray surrounded with potato chips or French fries. The kids love this "grab-your-own package" deal. Adults love this easy manner of serving as much, especially when the platter selection varies in choice of meats and fillings with some of the roll-ups being slices of overlapping cheeses in place of the sliced meat to enroll and hold a lengthwise chunk of ham or turkey inside.

ENTERTAINING THE DIET CONSCIOUS

A nice way of providing a protein meat and salad combination without the use of the aforementioned roll-up hot dog roll is this one:

If you own a large brandy sniffer glass (if not, borrow one from a neighbor) line the entire sides and bottom with layed out roast beef slices of meat (or turkey or whatever), being sure to drape the ends of the meat over the lip or rim of the brandy sniffer and partway down the outside of the glass. Fill in the sniffer center with fresh cut greens and salad (provide dressing separately for other guests to help themselves) Thread long metal skewers with assorted foil covered cheese bites, fresh cherry tomatoes, water chestnuts, pineapple chunks (packed in their own syrup), radish roses, broccoli florets, etc. Push the exposed unfilled skewer tip ends down into the fresh green salad leaving the skewered food tidbits of course in full view. Serve for eye appeal as well as diet appeal for those trying so hard to stay with it!

For another nice way of serving just meats and cheeses to these folk, review chapter 1 on the Pineapple Deli-Doll and the Bridal Doll, using only fresh vegetables as fill-in for her dress thus eliminating the olives which are so pretty but so high in calories and cholesterol.

HOW AND WHERE TO GET IT:

Tuna As You Like It
Tuna Research Foundation
Ferry Bldg., Terminal Island, California 90731

Mayonnaise Cookbook:
P.O. Box 307, Coventry, Conn. 06238

9 GELATINS AND ICE MOLDS

A gelatin can be very simple natural forms of food and juices combined with unflavored gelatin for an aspic form, or it can be as glamorous as a showgirl being starred in her first motion picture extravaganza.

To produce and direct this show for your particular theater (your family table) it is important to use a good base to unfold your movie's story. The effort you put into it and whom you get to star in the main role of your gelatin production is what will prove to be the fruits of your labor. This will be shipped out in that movie reel can (your mold form) sometimes even being forced to share it with other enthusiastic neighboring theater chains. Incorporate a good supporting cast . . . fruits, vegetables, chicken pieces etc. Add some extras to your cast if necessary to build up a part or enhance a good movie scene (garnish with other fruits, cocoanuts or accompany with dressings or whipped cream). Build up enthusiasm by keeping them waiting in line while you play it cool (keep it under refrigeration). You want that preview moment of unveiling to be just right to serve that hunger-ridden anticipating mad theater crowd. First-nighters sometimes prove to be a tough crowd, but I'm sure the critics will give you a standing ovation and favor your production with a four-star rating! Your epic production will always be tagged with a GP rating, as it is sure to be enjoyed by young and old theater-goers alike. It can never be cited as X rated or even R, for by using the proper understudies it can be relished and savored by even the diet conscious nowadays. Waiting in the wings to be called on are nature's own understudies, natural food forms ready to be mixed with a cast of unflavored gelatin to unite into one outstanding production on stage. There are also some company men on the payroll, kind of new to the movie lot, but key figures nonetheless, who have garnered certain roles in our filmmaking industry which take on the form of unsweetened gelatin powders to please those fans with special diet requirements to help keep them interested in the plot. In the wings, standing by, are also understudies for even those whipped cream rich laden roles played so well by those beautiful outstanding mousses and Bavarian fluffy models.

Discovered by that famed entrepreneur, the Knox Gelatin Company, her figure is kept lovely and thinner by using whipped instant nonfat dry milk for heavy cream as follows: beat ½ c. ice water with ½ c. of instant nonfat dry milk crystals until soft peaks form. Add 2 tbls. lemon juice and continue beating until firm peaks form. Fold into gelatin mixture in place of whipped cream. Her sister, usually featured as the star playing a salmon mousse, uses ⅓ c. of ice cold evaporated milk that has been whipped instead of the usually called for heavier whipped cream.

Keep in mind our overall budget for the film: amount of recipe needed to please your audience will determine which mold is chosen as its holder. These gelatin forms can be produced in more elaborate staged settings such as those marketed in aluminum or copper trappings in specific figures and designs. On the other hand, if you are a novice in this movie business, production costs can be kept down to a minimum by using such mundane equipment as easily found already on the (kitchen) lot such as: bowls, custard dishes, muffin tins for that crowd scene, cake pans, ice cube trays, paper drinking cups, and even used leftover empty food cans. As one director to another, let me tell you about this camera angle you might like to try next time you have to make a few rush scenes . . . less expensive in cost of time and extras, such as hiring extra bowls, strainer, spoons and pans. It's nice, for it features such big stars as peaches, grapes, pears, etc.

Make 2 holes in the top of a can of fruit cocktail as for pouring juice. Allow juice to run off into a large measuring cup. If needed add enough water to liquid syrup to equal 1 c. Heat liquid to boiling and sprinkle flavored gelatin powder of your choice over combination of liquids. Mix to dissolve. Use ice cubes method or add ice cold water equal to make 1 c. Chill to thicken. Open the can to add and mix fruit and gelatin together. Use can (if big enough) as mold or pour off into a decorative mold or dish to chill. Let fruit salad gelatin set to unmold before bringing to theater stage. The audience will love this one. You might say they will literally eat it up! Especially nice because cost production is kept to an absolute minimum. If molded in the original can, merely dip can in warm water, run knife around edge, and open opposite end of can with can opener. Push out onto stage setting just before curtain time. Can be decorated as if a log type cake.

THE PLAY ITSELF: As its producer, you may wish to present a dramatic "heavy" as your star or you may wish to simply fill out the theme of your play by featuring many lighter ingenue roles specifically tailored for a "filled" capacity audience. Try using a mousse or soufflé in the title roles and some of the lighter Bavarians, whips or snows to help bring down your curtain with a delightful finale. To costume your heavier starring roles you might try dressing them with a special sauce or salad dressing. If your play is a mystery, by all means mask her identity until the suspenseful end by completely disguising her in a cloak of mayonnaise and cream cheese frosting (if we know her to be a vegetable or salad type mystery) or try whipped cream or cream cheese and nuts if there be an accomplice to this "who-dun-it-dessert." I already know the ending to that one . . . the latter will prove to be the culprit who forced her to put on all that weight, but I bet you could have figured that one out by yourself! Sometimes you think the whole thing was worth it, but one must always pay in the end. Perhaps, with a show of good conduct and exercise she can be paroled or even get off scot free . . . but you know they always return to the scene of the crime sooner or later! The temptation is too much for them. Whatever thought and time given to your shimmering gelatin production will surely pay off, come Academy Award night, for you will surely garner an Oscar from the preview fans on opening night in your own hometown theater. I have known times when the movie is such an instant hit it is immediately sought out for shipment to nearby homes by some of the visiting movie magnates. So now let's quiet down on the set, the scene is the kitchen; we have many stars to present in our movie cast. We may have to edit it to overlay some parts, one upon the other at times to combine several roles to create just the dramatic scene we want. Let's get ready to produce this marvelous award-winning epic. Camera set? Ready to roll? Action!

The following is a *SHIMMERING GELATIN EPIC; filmed by technicolor PRODUCED BY:* THE MAGICIAN IN HER KITCHEN

STARRING ROLES PLAYED BY:

THE SIMPLETON: an ordinary gelatin but still holding box office appeal as the favorite star of the table featured in glorious assorted technicolors.

THE MIXED UP KID: a dual role played by the simpleton mixed up in personality by all those incorporated vegetables and/or fruits

THE SIAMESE TWINS: played by the simpleton whose character is split in half but remains held together although contrasting greatly in personality and outward appearance.

THE MASKED MARVEL: he covered the whole thing up and kept the secret hidden so no one could uncover the mystery until it was actually all brought out in the open when he was cut open on the operating table; played well by frostings and dressings.

SUPPORTING CAST OF PLAYERS:

A MOUSSE: a light mold of fish or meat combination sometimes dubbed in as the star of the film.

A SOUFFLE: sometimes starred as a souffle, it is better recoginized as Bavarian or cold mousse containing whipped cream and gelatin.

LIGHTER ROLES FOR INGENUES: Bavarians, whips, snows, chiffons.

FOR HEAVIER IMPORTANT WALK-ONS: Use chiffon pies, and Charlotte Russes to bring curtain down dramatically at end of show.

Director of show should give careful study to these characters so as to use their properties to best advantage.

WHIPPED GELATIN: when the gelatin is chilled and very thick, beat with an electric mixer at high speed, thereby incorporating air and making it light and feathery. Beat until double in volume and size. As you beat, the gelled whip will also change slightly in color to a lighter pastel shade of the original flavored gelatin. It is at this stage when it is light and double in volume you may add fruits well drained or fold in other flavored cubed gelatin pieces with miniature marshmallows for beautiful contrast of color and texture. Spoon into mold and return to refrigerator to set.

GELATIN SNOW: Prepare and chill gelatin until thickened stage. Add *unbeaten* egg whites to chilled mixture. Using one to two egg whites for a 3 oz. pkg. of flavored gelatin or two to three egg whites for a 6 oz. pkg.; continue as for above with similar fluffy dessert results.

MOUSSE: The gelatin is chilled til thickened. Pieces of poultry, meat or fish is then added. Finally, whipped cream is then folded in gently.

BAVARIAN CREAM: As above, the whipped gelatin is combined with folded in whipped cream to which eggs usually have been added.

CHIFFONS: Egg yolks are usually added and cooked together with the basic gelatin mixture. After chilling and allowing to partially set, the chilled mixture is folded into the beaten egg whites. It is *important to note* that the egg whites are already beaten for when combining beaten egg whites with any gelatin mixture, to have the final result stand up and be even fluffier, it is always best to *fold the gelatin mixture into* the bowl of already beaten *egg whites.*

CHIFFON CAKES OR PIES: recipe for above is then spooned into a baked or prepared (Graham crust) shell pie or combined with cookies (such as chocolate wafers for color constrast) to form cake; return to refrigerator to set before serving.

CHARLOTTE RUSSE: when a dessert type Bavarian whipped cream mix is served using a sponge cake or lady finger cake base for a light cake type repast.

(COLD) SOUFFLE: a gelatin puffed up airy mix similar to a Bavarian cream made in a high type collared souffle dish wherein egg yolks are cooked with the gelatin and then the chilled mixture is folded into beaten egg whites. (See note above under chiffons for folding properly.) After so doing, whipped cream is then folded in to the entire combination.

See also under Helpful Hints how to flake and mash gelatin for certain effects; also see how to cut with aspic cutters for decorative design.

HELPFUL HINTS

How to make gelatins: As noted in chapter 1 on pineapples, fresh or frozen pineapple meat or its fresh or frozen juice form cannot be incorporated into any gelatin mixture, as there is a certain enzyme in the fresh pineapple fruit called bromelin that prevents the gelatin liquid from ever gelling. This also holds true for the more exotic mango and papaya fruits and figs.

Canned pineapple fruit or juice does well, however, and adds much glamour to an ordinary mold in appearance (ring slices or spears) as well as taste (crushed pineapple and its juices). Never freeze a gelatin, with one exception noted under How To Gel.

To incorporate an unflavored gelatin there is no need to pre-soak gelatin. It will soften instantly when *sprinkled* over the cold liquid called for in the recipe (usually ¼ c. liquid to one tbsp. or pkg. of unflavored gelatin). To dissolve, mix with liquid and stir constantly while over low heat. It is best to use a rubber spatula to stir while simultaneously picking up any granules adhering to sides or bottom of cooking vessel. (Note: I have always used a rubber spatula for many things such as for puddings or making sauces, etc.)

TO PREPARE GELATIN: Be sure water has come to a full boil before pouring one 1 c. into a larger heatproof container as per directions on package of flavored gelatin. Now here is the mistake most of us make, thus creating a rubbery crystalized mass at the bottom of our gelatin, so please take note . . . Do NOT *pour* flavored gelatin crystals into the boiled water—rather, *sprinkle* them over the surface of the boiled water as you constantly stir to dissolve it. When granules are completely dissolved, add cold water. Cut down on the amount of *cold* water (never on the boiled water part) if gelatin is being prepared for a mold form or to be cubed later on. If being prepared to set family style in a bowl or small custard dessert cups and not for a mold shape, it is permissible to use quick setting ice cube method for setting (to follow in How to Gel).

When recipe calls for: SYRUPY CONSISTENCY: gelatin should be like thick running syrup used to glaze pies and such, taking about an hour to reach this stage.

UNBEATEN EGG WHITE CONSISTENCY: gelatin has reached slightly thickened appearance and will pour from spoon in thick but unbroken stream. This takes about an hour and a quarter to gel and is used at this stage to make a gelatin whip using ice bath method or to add the whipped cream for Bavarians and such.

SLIGHTLY THICKER THAN UNBEATEN EGG WHITES: gel mixture will drop unevenly in globs from spoon and be considered very thick. It will take about one and a half hours to reach this gelling stage, at which time it can be whipped for snow effect by adding unbeaten egg whites, or use as is to add fruits (well drained) or vegetables for salad gelatin.

In order to fold in beaten egg whites or whipped cream to form pie filling, as in chiffon cakes or pies, or to fold in for lady finger type cake, the gelatin must reach the stage of thickness whereby a spoon may be run through it and leave an impression. When using the spoon test, gelatin will fall from spoon and remain in mound on top of the remaining gelatin surface. Gelatin has reached the stage of being firm but not yet set enough for unmolding if finger is touched upon surface and it is sticky; mass of gelatin will move when bowl is tilted. It is at this point only that layers of other gelatins may be successfully added, being sure that such added on gelatin is also in a thickened and *cooled* stage. If added when even slightly liquefied or still warm it will penetrate through the first layer and melt into the underneath base thus spoiling the design of the layered look.

TO REACH UNMOLDING STAGE: before unmolding, test for both firmness and gelled stage or your mold will crumble upon release. When surface is touched there will be no sign whatever of stickiness and the mold, when tilted, will not leave the sides of the container.

SOME REASONS WHY GELATIN MOLDS FAIL: If successive gelatin layers are not added as directed above in cool stage atop a very thick firm first layer and while base underneath layer is still in sticky stage, the mold will separate, fall and slide off one layer from the other, whether they be two or three tiers high. That which could be a beautiful three-tiered molded bombe will be nothing but a gelatinized mass of mixed fallen layers; an untimely end for such a beautiful put-together skyscraper structure.

IF ADDING OTHER FOODS TO GELATIN MOLD: do so when gelatin is thickened or the added fruits (or whatever is added) will cause the gelatin to be lumpy. If added when gelatin is too thin the added lighter weight foods such as grapes and bananas will float to the top; if of heavier weight, such as carrot chunks or meat chunks, they will fall to bottom. In adding whipped cream to a too thin gelatin, the finished product will settle into clear and creamy layers; lumps will appear in finished turned out mold which will not offer a strong base and will therefore cause it to collapse.

While chilling a gelatin mix, stir once in a while to prevent too quick a gel from forming around the outside of the mixture and not in the center. By stirring you keep the gelling uniform and consistent. If you should forget a gelatin that is being chilled too long or it gels too quickly for needed consistency, simply reheat over double boiler or low heat to return to liquid stage and start over again. It is suggested to use a timer, if for no other reason than to remind you to check it once in a while in thickening stage.

TO ADD FRUIT OR VEGETABLES: add to incorporate by mixing gently into gelatin at very thick stage. To obtain a specific design, pour about 1 c. (when using a larger quart sized mold) into bottom of mold and allow to thicken. It will, of course, not take too long to do so as there is so much less in container. In the meantime, simultaneously place leftover gelatin mixture in separate bowl or container and refrigerate to chill and thicken also. When mold is thick enough to set in a fruit design or stand fruit vertically along sides as in tall bombe type tin, steep fruit (pears, pineapple spears, etc.) into position against sides and chill until almost set. Remove from refrigerator and add partially thickened and reserved gelatin from separate container; spoon reserve into molds. Return to chill and completely set before unmolding for an extraordinary beautiful production. If small specific design is needed for a gelatin mold, pour liquid gelatin into mold or use a loaf baking pan to depth of ¼"-½". Chill until slightly thick (check quickly as this process will not take too long.) Place in design (as in loaf pan a flower can be placed to appear as if in a vase) or use as described in chapter 8 on the seafood ring mold where cut out (carrot) fish were placed in layers as if swimming in an ocean effect or as in butterfly gelatin mold (this chapter) where slices of long strips of colored gelatin were pressed into thickening ¼" base to create the technicolored wing effect for same. Using aspic cut gelled designs (see how to cut aspics with cutters) various different colored aspic cut patterns can also be layered into base of mold as just described. Using ½" blocks of cream cheese (dust cutter with confectioner's sugar first), cut other cheeses or cooked whites of eggs with aspic cutters. Lay in cut design and top each aspic pattern cut with very thick gelatin to hold in position while design firmly sets in place. Spoon on remaining reserved thickened gelatin and fill to top of mold.

A GELATIN OVERLAY

In direct contrast to this theory set forth, of *interlaying* a garnish or simple design, one can create a more intricate design or even a complete scene by *overlaying* and using the gelatin itself as a cover. It may then be served as is without the need to unmold. By so overlaying and utilizing the gelatin as a cover, a more complicated picture or design can be created using cut-out pieces of fruits or vegetables to create same. For easier removal of serving portions, it is best to coat the pan lightly with the new aerated type can of oil spray. Use a deep jelly roll pan or large glass pan to hold your gelled scene while simultaneously providing a fruit dessert (or vegetable side dish). Prepare a light colored gelatin such as lemon or apricot; chill to slightly thickened stage or chill to syrupy stage and lay syrupy gel on tray or pan to depth of ¼". When sticky stage is reached, set your scene or intricate design on tray (or pan.) Spoon some thickened gelatin over the scene. Do so gently and carefully so as not to disturb or displace the picture scene desired. Spoon on remaining thickened gelatin after first layer has chilled a little to set the pieces more firmly in place. Shake pan slightly so as to settle any mounds that may be too high in spots on surface of pan. After setting properly place small dabs of floral gum tape all along the edge of the jelly pan or glass dish. Fasten lemon leaves as border effect to finish off your pictorial scene, as if presenting a painting. If you happen to have an old picture frame about that fits properly (I told you I save everything) use that to attach to the floral gum taped pan. If not, visit your nearest hardware store and invest in a picture framing kit and make up your own personal frame according to size and wood texture desired, thus framing out your culinary artwork. Didn't I tell you that in your own kitchen you can create "canvas" masterpieces as great as Leonardo da Vinci's—and eat them besides!

OTHER WAYS OF PRESENTING ASPICS: As there are Bavarian aspics, mouses, whips and snow forms of gelatin, so there are many other ways of utilizing aspic gels in presenting food displays. Since we have discussed mold forms at such length, at least let us give a fanfare to acknowledge some other means of showing aspic off to its best advantage.

As previously mentioned, I do sometimes like to set my scene presentation upon a framed mirror or tray (with slight lip). In so doing, a clear aspic can be made, as one envelope unflavored gelatin will gel two cups of any liquid such as water, apple juice, etc. Edible color dye can then be added thus creating a green ocean or body of water. (Avoid using blue vegetable dye, as it seems to negate the eye appeal, and what is not appealing to the eye is not truly tasty.) Apply a thin coat onto the (lipped) tray or framed mirror using a gelatin glaze while in its syrupy stage. Chill tray for short time and before it sets, place on (penguin or frog) figures or whatever (igloos, icebergs, etc.) thus automatically stabilizing them into position wherever you have placed them on the tray or mirror. To create other gelled forms of aspic that can be used as background or as a base or garnish for scenes (and or molds or mousse pieces) simply use gelled aspic in small or medium sized cubed form.

TO CUBE, FLAKE OR MASH GELATIN: Prepare gelatin for any of the above forms of presenting as if being prepared for a mold container. Cut down ¼ c.–½ c. on *cold* liquid portion for preparing aspic, depending upon desired firmness required. (For firmer more solid cubes or aspic cut out figures cut down ½ c. of cold water). Pour liquid into shallow ice cube trays or other shallow baking trays or dishes to desired depth. Let set overnight (a strict rule for aspic cuts and cubes) for firmer effect to gelatin. If using gelatin for flaked or mashed use, you need only chill for a few hours. Cut into cubes with knife dipped in hot water. Release from shallow tray mold by inverting onto cookie sheet and using hot wrung-out towel method for releasing (see How to Unmold). Mound these cut cube forms piled high in a dessert goblet dish or as foreground for fish display or whatever. For aspic cut-outs see later.

To flake or mash aspic: prepare as set forth in above directions. Use fork to break into pieces by flaking. To obtain a mashed appearance, chop on flat surface into finely or coarsely chopped pieces. For finer mashed effect simply put through a ricer. Use as ocean base or as background.

ASPIC CUTOUTS: Prepare gelatin as outlined above to make firmer aspic. Pour into shallow pan to depth of ⅓". Avoid air bubbles. Refrigerate overnight. Turn aspic sheet (use hot towel method) out onto flat surface. Cut out forms with aspic cutters or use larger cookie cutters if desired and more suitable for decoration and garnishes. Transfer easily by slipping a *wet* wide spatula beneath cut out design and move to desired position. There are variations as to color and use gone into in more depth in the culinary world. They are referred to as colored aspic sheets. They are made primarily of water, salt and unflavored gelatin to which is added a pureed form of pimento (to achieve red aspic sheets), boiled egg yolks (for yellow sheets), cooked spinach (for green sheets) and truffle peelings (for achieving black aspic sheets, etc.). Since truffles are grown as a delicacy in France for export and are quite expensive, let alone difficult to find (look for in specialty gourmet shops), for our housewifely purposes we will utilize the different shades of tasty flavored boxed gelatins or achieve our colors with the use of vegetable dye. Some specific effects can also be accomplished with the use of beef consommé aspics or mayonnaise combinations or gelatin syrup glazes. See aspics and glazes in chapters 6 and 8.

TO WHIP ASPIC FOR SPECIAL EFFECTS: To give a voluminous appearance to an ocean setting for a scene or centerpiece, first prepare a whipped gelatin. Prepare lime flavored box mix or for lighter colored ocean or water effect, use lemon or clear aspic (unflavored gelatin) to which a drop or two of green food dye has been added. Chill until very thick for whipping as per whipped gelatin (see directions for same under A Gelatin Epic Production in this chapter). Use as base or ocean floor to set watermelon ships or fish mousse upon, as it is also completely edible.

FOR SPECIALIZED WAVE AFFECT TO OCEAN WATERS: If using whipped lime gelatin (use mashed or finely chopped, if preferred) for realistic ocean bottom to set your watermelon whale or cucumber Viking ship upon or to set your watermelon frigate ship or sailing vessel upon, pile the lime gelatin high around the base of the watermelon centerpiece (as if boat is cutting through the waters). Prepare a white aspic sheet as follows; flake or mash with fork and pile upon the high crested waves as the sea foam breaking just below the hull of the whale or ship.

TO MAKE WHITE ASPIC SHEET FOR SEA FOAM OF OCEAN: Separate egg white from yolk. Bring egg white only to boil until gelled, use yolk elsewhere for cooking or baking. Blend together the cooked egg white with one cup of water and puree. Add pinch of salt and one package of unflavored gelatin and blend for one second. Pour into container and refrigerate. When set, it will tend to break down into layers: a foamy white top caused by the aerating of the blender blades, an opaque colored center from the unflavored gel and the base will consist of the whiter, stringy cooked egg white. Turn out to mash or flake and mix. In so doing the overall affect will be that of soft cloudy gelatin tufts. This will then act as the snowy whitecaps just breaking atop your crests of waves. For full effect to your ocean scene, place white gelatin (caps) just beneath the hull of the ship (centerpiece) and on top of the higher mounds of (green gelatin) ocean waves.

HOW TO SET GELATIN: Always prechill mold form to be used. Prepare, fill and refrigerate container filled with gelatin in the coldest part of your refrigerator for quicker setting. Never freeze gelatin except if pushed for time and forced to chill very quickly. In this case, place in freezer compartment for about ten minutes only. Stir gelatin occasionally for even setting throughout. Use a timer as a reminder if you are busy elsewhere in the kitchen. If it becomes solidified, melt over boiling water or over very low heat and start again. Refrigerate for quick setting by placing gelatin filled container into a larger receptacle filled with cold water and chipped ice. Place as is in refrigerator in the coldest spot possible (usually nearer the top of your box). Use metal containers rather than ceramic or plastic. Use smaller containers for quicker gelling. If adding fruits and/or vegetables, always prechill the ingredients to be added.

To prepare gelatin and hasten chilling stage use the *ICE CUBE METHOD:* Dissolve a 3 oz. pkg. of flavored powdered gelatin into 1 c. of boiling water.

In place of the usual added cold water, add six ice cubes immediately after dissolving crystals of gel powder form. Stir for about three minutes or until most of the ice cubes have melted and gelatin begins to thicken. Remove leftover small bits of ice. Refrigerate to chill and set. *IMPORTANT NOTE:* If making *mold form*, do *NOT* use ice cube method, as size and water content of ice cannot be measured or controlled.

HOW TO MAKE MOLD FORMS: Chill mold form of gelatin until firm and set. Less time for setting is required for the above methods used depending on size and shape of mold form or container. If mold is over three quarts or is a deep mold form in shape, refrigerate to set overnight or at least a minumum of five hours. Gelled Mold forms can be prepared several days and up to one week in advance if tightly covered, sealed with Saran wrap and kept under constant refrigeration. This will prevent evaporation and drying up of gelatin.

TO TEST FOR SETTING BEFORE UNMOLDING: Before releasing, tilt mold to one side. It should stick to sides of mold container and not sag toward center. Touch top surface with finger to be sure it is not sticky. To prepare molded forms of gelatin, I prefer to use a metal mold, as metal is the best conductor for cold (for gelling faster) as well as heat (warm water bath or hot towel method) to unmold faster. Metal pre-chills easily, retains and conducts cold faster to set mold more quickly.

WATER DECREASE FOR BETTER MOLDS: If decorative mold container is used or aspic cutters are to be used for pattern design cuts or gelatin is to be cubed, the cold water added in (gelatin) preparation must be cut down by ¼–½ c, amount cut down depending entirely on firmness desired. (E.g., cut down ¼ c. for flaking or ½ c. for firmer cubed gelatin). If ring mold or such is used I cut down *¼ c. water for every 3 oz. pkg.* of flavored gelatin used. If taller deeper type mold is used such as a three layer or bombe mold. I cut down by *½ c. water for every 3 oz. pkg. used,* thus giving extra stability and firmness for the extra height being utilized in forming this particular deep mold.

TO UNMOLD GELATINS: As simple as it is to create a beautiful mold, now that we know all the secrets and pitfalls, it will be just as easy to learn how to unmold it by following these directions. If prepared mold is one in which an unflavored gelatin is used but which consists primarily of tuna or salmon fish (mousse type mold) I find it best to spray the mold container before filling. Use the new aerated can of oil spray being advertised for use with Teflon pans. If preferred, a light coat of vegetable oil will also do the same job or brush out with a light coat of mayonnaise. Follow this procedure for all types of gelatin molds unless you specifically wish to feature and highlight the pure shimmer of the aspic. In this case do not use spray or any coating on the inside of the mold receptacle.

The only reason a gelatin will not release is that it is still caught in its molded vacuum. To release it, we must first break that seal tight hold the gelatin has on its container. Dip a metal knife or metal spatula in hot water. Use same to loosen edges of the molded gelatin all around the container form. Tilt to one side and then the other, thus allowing air to enter all around breaking the vacuum. Dip mold just to its rim edge in a bath of warm water for five to ten seconds. Do not allow the contained gelatin to start melting nor the water to make its way over the top and into the gelled mold itself. Do *not* use *hot* water. The extreme heat will quickly and easily loosen the gelatin from its container however it will do so by melting the gelatin, causing it to return to liquid form and run all over the plate. Rather, then, lift from warm water bath, tilt and rotate to shake to test for easy release. If necessary, dip again to repeat operation. Wet top of gelatin surface with cold water as well as wet the surface of the receiving plate or tray. Place wet surface of the receiving plate on top of mold and invert. By wetting the mold and tray surfaces, the gelatin shape can be slipped into desired position if it should drop off center when dislodging from container. If necessary to shift into proper place, do so by moving it with a *wet, wide* spatula. Garnish appropriately or overlay with whipped cream.

ALTERNATIVE FOR UNMOLDING: HOT TOWEL METHOD: A second method for unmolding gelatin is to loosen gelled form away from mold with wet hot knife as previously described. Allow air to reach under mold by tilting to side. Place receiving tray or plate on top and invert. Place *hot wrung-out* thick wet towels on top surface of container mold form. If unmolding a ring type mold do not neglect to also place a hot towel on the inside circle of the ring mold. Allow hot towels to set for 5–10 seconds. Carefully remove metal mold form by lifting straight up. If first effort to do so proves resistant, do not force but simply repeat the procedure of hot towel application. This method of releasing is particularly more efficient when working with large trays of gelatins to make cubes or flaked gelatin or aspic cut outs from same. It is also used when the mold container itself is very large and too cumbersome to dip into a basin filled with warm water.

If using the new plastic type of molds such as Tupperware, the vacuum is automatically broken when the covering seal of this particular three section mold is lifted off. The mold will automatically slip out onto the receiving tray or plate so be sure to have mold form in desired positioning (or liberally wet surfaces of gelatin and tray) before removing top seal of plastic mold container.

A GELATIN DESSERT—A BUTTERFLY MOLD

A DAY OR MORE BEFORE: Prepare three different flavored contrasting color gelatins. (e.g., raspberry, lime and orange) as per instruction, reducing cold water usually added down by ½ c. Pour into three shallow small containers such as ice trays and refrigerate. Let set overnight or at least 6 hours. When ready prepare a 6 oz. package of lemon gelatin according to directions, reducing cold water. Pour into butterfly mold to 1″ in depth. In another container set aside and refrigerate remaining lemon gelatin to thicken. Refrigerate butterfly mold.

Check butterfly mold in about 10 minutes for desired thickening; (it will set very quickly). Cut into appropriate size strips (for wing sections) the set lime, raspberry and orange gelatins. Press colored contrasting gelatin strips into thickened partially set lemon gelatin in mold; alternate the color strips. Push them down to bottom into the wing span section grooves of the mold. Press into the center core midsection groove of the butterfly's body, 2–3 pecan nuts, rounded side down. Proceed to cover strips and nuts with the remaining cooled and slightly thickened reserved lemon gelatin to set the design. Refrigerate. When mold is still sticky on top it is time to add second gelatin layer to your mold.

To accentuate the imbedded colors of the wings of the butterfly, layer it with any of your favorite white gelatins. A simple one would be to sprinkle 1 pkg. unflavored gelatin over ¼ c. water in cooking vessel. Add 3 tbls. sugar. Stir over heat to dissolve. Add to 16 oz. of sour cream and mix well. Allow to chill and thicken. *Spoon* over butterfly-lemon gelatin design. If preferred, use any of your own favorite recipes so long as it contains sour cream, whipped cream or cottage cheese; something that will emphasize the colored wing-layer of the dessert on its whitish background. If you must keep the cost of your creation down to a minimum and are calorie-wise, make the second covering layer a simple snow pudding. To make a snow pudding, prepare any desired flavored gelatin, chill until slightly thick. Add 2 unbeaten egg whites to thickened gelatin. Whip on high speed of electric mixer until double in volume; this will make for a pastel color to your gelatin. To create an almost white snow, use lemon flavored gelatin.

For those watching their calories, the entire creation can be prepared by using boxes of diet (Glimmer or D'Zerta) gelatins and a cottage or ricotta cheese recipe for second layer. Allow mold to set for at least 6 hours or (better) overnight. Unmold onto pretty plate. (I recommend the disposable aluminum cake mix sized pans will take this mold exactly and can then easily be given away as a gift.) Affix two red cherries in proper position with long frill red toothpicks. These will act as the antenna of your butterfly creation. Accentuate outline of your butterfly: border it with whipped cream forced through a pastry tube or use cool whip type squeezed container or aerosol canned whipped cream.

TO CREATE A MAIN ENTREE USING A BUTTERFLY MOLD

Prepare selected favorite recipe for main dish such as seafood salad, tuna or chicken mousse, chopped liver etc. It is suggested but not necessary that it contains a gelatin or salad dressing to bind it together. Prepare, put into slightly greased butterfly mold and chill for several hours. Unmold onto appropriate tray. See previous directions for frosting a cake (use of wax paper on plate) and use these directions to glaze with aspic, as in chapter 6. Cover the fish or meat salad with appropriately chosen glaze. Garnish attractively before last coat sets. The alternative is to use the overlay method. Proceed to overlay the design by decorating with egg yolks or deviled egg salad put through food mill. Force egg mayonnaise mixture through a canvas type cake decorating pastry tube. If more color is desired in displayed piece, mix portions of the egg yolk mixture with a few drops food coloring. Decorate top of the wing span of the butterfly with the varied colored egg yolk mixture. If you prefer merely garnish simply with radish slices, carrots slices or peppers instead. Short 1" scallion feathered "mums" (see chapter 7 on carved vegetables) can be used as antennae, or olives can be substituted. Hold in place with club frill toothpicks. Accentuate and decorate border outline of butterfly mold with small fresh curled parsley sprigs or use pastry tube method to edge design with egg yolk mixture.

VARIETIES OF BUTTERFLY MOLD

For Vegetable Salad: Using same procedure insert strips of green peppers and red radish slices (or whatever you choose) for garnishing. Push into the 1" depth of thickened lemon gelatin base. Continue as before, topping with preferred salad gelatin mixture containing shedded carrots or cabbage, etc. Unmold onto plate and use olives for antenna. Garnish with fresh parsley or use lettuce greens as "bedding."

For Other Dessert Type Gelatins: Prepare as recommended above, setting into 1" of thickened lemon gelatin mold, desired garnish such as pineapple spears and cherries or spiced apple rings or sliced peaches, etc. Continue as per directions above and fill with choice of a favorite gelatin dessert for top portion. Chill properly. Unmold and use cherries or grapes for antennae. Border with cottage cheese, or whipped cream.

ICE MOLDS

Using the mold forms we have already learned so much about and having worked with gelatin so successfully, we are now ready to fill those same forms with liquid to create ice molds. If you note, I did not specify water, I said *liquid* and therein lies some more tricks up this kitchen magician's sleeve to share with you.

With the realization one needn't be an ice sculptor with a walk-in freezer, let us, in our own kitchen workshop, use ordinary tools of our trade to create equally beautiful ice pieces to dress up our party tables. For that matter, whether they be small ice cubes or large pretty ice molds, iced forms play an important role in everyday kitchen living as well as entertaining. The most familiar form of ice mold is, of course, the ordinary ice cube made of clear water used as is, for chilling a cold drink of water, juice, tea, coffee, consommé or soda. The next time, replace that clear water with the very same liquid it's meant to chill. Fill the ice tray with its dividers in place, with the tea, coffee or punch in its full strength. Freeze. When these liquid cubes are used to chill the beverage refreshment, they will add to its flavor rather than dilute the drink as the cubes melt. Whether it is tea we have frozen or ordinary clear (boiled) water, make it decorative and different by slipping a garnish into each cubicle divider (such as a twist of lemon or lime, a cherry or strawberry or peppermint leaf, etc.). For that touch of the unusual, add some flavorful extract to the tray of cubes (that would blend with the liquid refreshment its meant for as it melts); e.g., peppermint extract within tea cubes or lemon extract with a grape drink, etc. *HELPFUL HINTS:* Use your ice cubes to even more advantage by making them from leftover soups or broth; an easy way of chilling consommé for service or for freezing leftovers, an easier way of defrosting just what you need when you need it. Soup cubes, as I call them, can easily be frozen with leftover bits and pieces of meat inside. If preferred, simply pour the while pot of leftover soup into an ice tray sans its dividers for a larger "when you need it" package. Unlike the green ocean ice molds suggested in chapter 8 for displaying seafood, I prefer to keep the iced cubed water clear (except for those bits of lemon or cherry garnish). If vegetable food dye is added for color affect to your freezing water, you must expect that likewise it will also discolor the beverage as it melts. (It will not affect its taste). Thus, a good Tom Collins or such changed into the green Nile might prove not to be so attractive nor appetizing. This iced form would have been better left as clear water with a twist of lime for garnish.

Therefore use food color in mold forms as a display centerpiece when it will not actually be eaten; then the added color lends to the overall beauty of the food displayed. There are other special moments where colored ice would lend to a better presentation; e.g., if presenting shrimp or fruits which are served in glass bowls on a bed of ice, it would be very festive, for entertaining, to serve your container on a bed of green (vegetable dyed chipped) ice. Add a drop of mint extract to send off lovely aromatic spirits of spearmint. Picture your green mint ice with yellow lemon wedges topped with large pink shrimp smothered in a deep red sea of cocktail sauce. A sight to first behold and smell and even better to eat! For a holiday theme try the same principle by presenting red (dyed) chipped ice, laden with honeydew balls or watermelon balls on a bed of green minted ice—either one garnished with a sprig of holly leaves, red (or green) cherries to add that festive Christmas look.

If you are not the owner of any fancy decorative mold and wish to make one anyhow, create your own. Use the oblong ice tray itself (sans cubed department) or use any cake pan. Lay in a decorative scene as you would a gelatin mold. Any decorative mold can be used to lay on designs using garnishes such as strawberries, peach and pineapple rings, peppermint leaves, rose petals, etc., to create a specific scene or design. Utilizing the ice tray as base proceed as for gelatin mold. Freezing 1″ of water in mold, lay in fruits or particular design. Wedding invitations or birth announcements may be frozen within the mold similarly. When announcement or card is frozen in place, add more water and fill to top of mold. Keep in mind that whatever design you lay on the *bottom of your mold, when inverted, will become the top of the design* to be viewed by all. That mold form or container must also be able to fit inside the punch bowl if that is the purpose for its existence. If necessary a few smaller ice molds may be used in place of one large form; e.g., use an 8 or 12 c. muffin tin. Treat each muffin cup as an individual mold. Garnish each one differently. Unmold to have many varied (and smaller) ice forms afloat in your punchbowl. Needless to add, *gelatin* forms can be made in like manner, giving you the opportunity to present a variety of gelatin molds all featuring different aspic designs or garnishments. If serving punch, use that same beverage punch to actually create your molded ice form; merely replace the clear water with the punch beverage, thereby adding natural color and flavor to your refreshment as it melts. By using an oblong ice tray without the dividers as a mold container form, a pretty flower design can be imbedded in the punch beverage (mold) itself, to float atop the bowl; e.g., lay in a cantaloupe (pot base) with peppermint plant (stalks and leaves) topped with a sunburst bloom of peach slices and a strawberry center. Using a heart shaped decorative cake pan or mold for gelatin, fill with a red beverage punch or a pastel pink grapefruit drink. For a wedding or anniversary party imbed a spray of orange blossoms or lilies of the valley. Being a large ice form, it is more likely the punch will be gone before the ice melts enough to free the flowers themselves. If you do not wish to concern yourself with this, use a more compatible and edible flower, such as the nasturtium, whose blossoms and leaves are frequently used in the gourmet world for cooking and baking. With decorative molds, ice cubes and simple trays you can, within the limits of your small kitchen, come up with some very pretty iced decor to add more beauty to your party table. You needn't be an ice sculptor at the Waldorf or in the employ of a fancy catering house or restaurant to produce a simple form of ice piece to highlight your party table. For instance: *SPECIAL EVENT PARTY ICE MOLDS:* Create an iced heart shaped mold: Imbed two plastic love birds as its center within a border of lilies of the valley or orange blossoms. When inverted, stand mold up on end leaning it against a cake cooling wire rack. Raise wire rack backing at slight angle for better viewing. To disguise and hide the wire rack backing simply face it with fresh green ferns and/or baby breath. Attach flowers or greens to rack backing with inconspicuous spots of floral gum tape. *ALTERNATIVE:* Tie greens or sprigs of baby breath to backing with dental floss or nylon thread to hold in place. Be sure there is a deep-lipped tray similarly masked with greens and baby breath to catch the ice drippings. When presenting this iced theme piece for the party I usually highlight it by adding and featuring it on a higher plane level of my table. Simply use long sturdy cartons covered decoratively with cloth and fern fronds, creating two tiers from one actual table. For further sentimental effect place next to your ice centerpiece another heart shape, one of styrofoam of equal size and shape and depth. Decorate border similarly as that of ice mold form by edging with lilies of the valley (use totem pins in foam). Fill center with shower umbrella (symbol) or picture of bridal couple.

HOW AND WHERE TO GET IT:

As with any good show, you always do best to feature your most famous star for your table, but unless we keep trying you might never unveil the other players just waiting to be discovered and brought out into the limelight. There are many producing companies who would like to have you meet some of these starlets waiting in the wings . . . give them a chance—at least an audition and let your family of critics be the judge. After a tryout, perhaps with a personal touch of your own Pygmalian hands, you might want to be her press agent and show her off to other houses, You will enjoy the plaudits of discovering her yourself.

Big Name Producing Companies and their starlets;

Knox Gelatin Co. % Lipton Tea Co., 800 Sylvan Ave., Englewood Cliffs, N.J. 07632:

Dishes that Fly

So Simple with Knox

Prize Winning Gel-Cookery Recipes

Delicious Dishes for Dieters

Knox Thin-down Kit for Dieters

General Foods Corporation; 250 North St. White Plains, N.Y. 10625

Make Someone Happy: Make Someone Jello

Joys of Jello (pamphlet) BOX 5070, Kankakee, Ill. 60901

New Joys of Jello (hard cover) Box 3070, Kankakee, Ill. 60901

Punches: Let Holland House add a little punch to your next party:c/o Holland House, BOX 566 Ridgefield, N.J. 07657

Gelatin & Ice Molds: Unusual old world and American recipes-(10¢ fee) Nordic Ware, Minneapolis, Minn. 55416

For gelatins also see:

Chapter 3: see melons filled with gelatin and frosted.

Chapter 4; see grapefruit filled with gelatin using Kitchen Helper.

Chapter 6: cottage cheese igloo mold spinach sea mold.

Aspics in chapters 6 and 8 for glazes.

Chapter 8: fish forms in seafood gelatin.

For ice molds see:

Chapter 8; fish presentation for shrimp ice ring.

10 AN APPLE TURKEY

A cute edible table decoration, seating arrangement and mood setter for Thanksgiving or any turkey dinnertime is the edible apple turkey.

Using a red Delicious apple (because of its shape) place apple on side with (removed) stem end as front. Thread dark colored raisins onto 4 club frill toothpicks. Following diagram, place 2 (raisin) toothpick points into each side of apple at angles so as to stabilize and balance your apple turkey properly. Using same procedure, thread 5–6 more club size frill picks. Push into back of apple fan-fashion to simulate tail spread of bird. Thread more black raisins onto two sandwich toothpicks (very long flat toothpicks used for sandwiches and French fries). Place together for extra wide looking neck of bird. Push into front end of apple. For head, push onto pick end point, a large pimento filled olive, red filling facing front and downward (see illustration). Use whole cloves as eyes. With a toothpick point, carefully pull out a long bit of the pimento to act as the turkey's wattle.

Use for individual edible party favors for the small fry's party or place one or two about as mood setters for a turkey buffet. When each guest's name (use contrasting cake writing gel) is written onto body of apple turkey, this captivating edible ani-

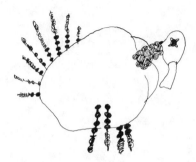

mal can also serve as a place setter for the annual turkey holiday family get-to-gether dinner.

CARVED TURKEY PRESENTATION

Well, it's that time of year again—Thanksgiving, so let's roast the traditional turkey.

When loads of company's coming and you wish not to be busy in the kitchen all evening, the best answer, of course, is roast a turkey.

If you want to do something easy and still have plenty of leftovers for a few extra meals, roast a turkey.

My, but our feathered friend gets around a lot!

At one time before freezers came into practically every home, we waited for a special holiday, a birthday party or a family get-together to purchase a fresh turkey from the poultry farm.

Poultry was very perishable, so one would wait for an occasion to invite a group of friends or the family over to help "polish off" the usually big bird. Who wanted to be stuck with leftover turkey to eat for three to four days in a row?

Now that we have freezers and convenience packaging of turkey breasts, drumstick and wing parts, rolled boneless roasts, etc., we can now easily provide turkey as family table fare any day of the year, purchasing same in any size suitable to the occasion or our family needs, weighing anywhere from 5 to 50 lbs; average size being 9–30 lbs. Although price is variable, turkey is usually equal to or only slightly higher than that of chicken. However, it would be less expensive to purchase turkey than chicken, since the larger fowl would provide more meat per inch of frame than the bonier, smaller chicken. A hen turkey would not only provide more edible meat but would provide more of the preferred juicy sweet white breast meat than is found in a Tom turkey of proportionate size. With the daily availability of frozen, eviscerated supermarket turkeys at equal or slightly higher than chicken prices, it would prove more econimical to purchase the larger bird.

Roast your larger turkey, cut into sections, and freeze. One can nowadays easily defrost a frozen fowl, cook it and then safely refreeze it for another day. If it is roasted and served as the main dinner meal one night, then freeze what is left, including the carcass frame, as provision for other light meals and/or sandwiches. The leftover carcass, if put to cook with greens and vegetables, makes an excellent stock base or even soup. One of my own family's favorite soups is based on just that, a leftover turkey frame. When, at a later dinner, one of our guests commented on my delicious soup, my youngest son announced that it was very easy to make. "Mother just takes a big pot, fills it with water and a couple of vegetables and then throws in whatever was left over in the 'frigator from all week." Well, it's not quite that, but I do use the turkey frame (broken up) and fill the pot with water flavored with some chicken bouillon; I do add a few soup greens, vegetables and seasonings as a base. When cooked, the poultry bits and pieces will very quickly fall off the frame. Give it a helping hand if need be. Remove the onion and other greens. While it simmers, I like to add some vermicelli (full length, not broken short) or, if you like, try adding a slightly beaten egg to the *simmering* soup liquid, mixing quickly to form egg drop effect. Throw in some leftover pork roast, devoid of fat, a few cut-up large shrimp, some water chestnuts or bamboo shoots and mushrooms. The easy way of assuring that some or all of the aforementioned are left around is to freeze all the little leftovers from pork roasts and chicken dinners or shrimp salad makings. It's economical, and if not used in soup, makes for a terrific home-prepared Chinese fried rice dinner. At the last minute, add some thyme and allow flavors to marry before adding some chopped chives. Pour from ladle into a deep soup bowl which contains a cut-up hard cooked egg. This is definitely a "taste as you do" recipe, tailoring your family's likes with whatever is left in the refrigerator (or freezer). My brother-in-law Jack teases me saying "For a gourmet food teacher, I've got the best *leftovers* in town!"

Just to prove to him and you, though, that I can still make something from scratch, let's prepare a nice big bird and dress him up fancy to go to a buffet dinner party. He should be dressed up as he's the guest of honor at the buffet table. I specify big because if you're having the get-to-gether *buffet* style chances are there is a larger than usual guest list; besides, a big bird is far easier to gussy up pretty and always looks so much nicer when presented on this cold type of buffet table. It can be roasted a day or even two before, *provided* it is cooked *without* the stuffing *inside* the poultry. On the second day, it can be carved and put back on the frame for serving that evening or the next day if it is saran wrapped well! There is also less work roasting a larger turkey than a smaller one, for the latter must be basted more often, as smaller fowls do not possess the fat natural to bigger sized birds.

Helpful Hints: Prepare and cook your bird in your own usual manner. Please just keep in mind that a "carved bird put back on the frame" must never be overcooked, as it would prove to be too dry and stringy to carve for this type of cold presentation. Although I could give you approximate time allotments for roasting a turkey, I won't for a lot depends entirely on the size and age of the bird, whether it is a self-basting fowl (usually so marked on the plastic casing), whether you use the open roasting method or use the foil-covered or brown bag method, and even how many times you will be opening the oven (cooling it) to check or baste the bird, and so on.

SERVING A CROWD: Knowing that a 10–12 lb. smaller turkey will do nicely for a family of five, providing them with a main meal plus two leftover fixings, allow ¾ lb.-1¼ lbs. of meat per person from a bird weighing 12 lbs. or more. The large variation of weight in meat per person depends on just who you have invited to feed. I kid you not!

My second and third planned left over fixings, at least planned in *my* mind, was once completely wiped out right before my eyes when I invited guests who, unbeknownst to me, had just started that "tomorrow diet" today! No problem except that the diet they chose was a "high protein only" diet wherein they were allowed nothing more than protein packed meat such as turkey, and so I was left with everything else I had prepared . . . and I do mean everything! Also beware of growing teenagers. On the common market of exchanges, one teenager is equal to two giant adults; ask any budget murdered teenage mother!

Now that we have gone to market looking particularly for a high full breasted bird to choose and having roasted and cooled same, let us carve it for the buffet party so it is the best dressed up "chick" in the room. Her admirers will crow of her elegance and will all flock to you to learn the know-how. I have had many students in my classes: restaurateur, gourmet cooking teacher and homemaker alike who may or may not be able to produce a decent soufflé, but I have *never* had anyone who could not get rave notices . . . *the first time out* . . . when displaying this "catered look" turkey on their party table.

I find the bigger the turkey, the easier it is to carve and present in this manner. If you'd like, however, make it a large capon bird and try a dry run.

You'll soon promote yourself onto bigger and better birds. No matter how big the mistake, you can always "cover it up," figuratively as well as literally with fresh chicory and parsley; you can always garnish it handsomely with carved vegetables and fruits. Remember, as in all of this food craft fun we've been having so far, unlike other crafts, no matter how it comes out it will still remain nutritiously edible and delicious and so it was just a practice run . . . and with more practice you'll find your turkey carving services much in demand. I warn you!

How To Carve a Turkey: There is of course the usual method of carving the turkey at the table which I personally leave to the man of my house when I'm serving the bird hot. Always allot a "setting" time of thirty minutes to allow the juices to be resorbed again by the meat. Carve in usual manner, that is, cut off the drumstick first and slice breast meat down horizontally. This way of carving the turkey hot can be found in any cookbook, so we will leave it right there in the cookbook for you to look up. Now for our Food Sculpture Cookbook version:

The second method of carving turkey is to remove the breast meat en totem by cutting along dotted line as shadowed in the diagram (see page 464).

Use a sharp boning knife to cut as close to the breast bone as possible *leaving the skin attached* and intact. Remove complete (skin-covered) breast section in one piece from both sides of breast bone. Lay each breast, meat side down; slice through skin. It is most important to keep the slices in the exact order in which they are cut for returning to the frame. Place the entire sliced breast back onto the respective side of breast bone from whence it was removed. At this time, if that is the manner you choose to serve it, cover just these complete breast sections with a white aspic covering glaze. Before final coating of glaze is applied, set specific design desired on breasts. There are other variations of presenting this carved turkey but let's take them each in turn. Therefore, if desired at this point, this carved and put back on the frame turkey would be placed on the serving tray and garnished as is. As has been previously stated, food always looks better when displayed at a slightly raised angle, so let's show off our dressed-up friend to his best advantage.

Using a bread socle, as outlined and to be discussed shortly, lay bird atop a chicory covered bread base called a socle. (see bread socle to follow in this chapter). Place turkey on bread base socle to back of serving tray or platter. Fill in surrounding area of platter with extra (cut) rolled turkey slices or sliced breast. A nice alternative to this is to fill in surrounding tray with turkey rollatinis filled with coleslaw or try turkey slices with French dressing wrapped around asparagus spears. Whatever you choose, decorate and garnish plate with kumquats which have been opened on top into trumpet flower blossoms; stand kumquats vertically and fill with cranberries or fill orange baskets with cranberry relish. If preferred garnish and decorate platter with the gelatin filled grapefruit (cut with the Kitchen Helper) or with quartered gelatin filled orange sections, as described in chapter 4. Fill in body cavity with chicory and carved vegetable flowers. (see how to: following in next variation).

For an easy but more dazzling presentation of a turkey, to be carved and sliced to be placed back on the frame, try your hand at this one, which is my favored version. Even better, invite a friend or neighbor to join you for a fun time in your kitchen workshop for a "learning to carve" practice dry run. Share the book, share the expenses of the food, share the fun, and then share the dinner as well as the applause from your families that will accompany it!

MY FAVORITE VERSION OF A CARVED (COLD) TURKEY

For This Carved Turkey Display You Will Need:
A large turkey with a high full breast
Plus other sliced meats to supplement bird if large group is
    expected
Large serving tray-very heavy in weight and sturdy enough to
    carry bird's weight

Pullman loaf of bread to act as socle to elevate and display turkey properly

For decorating and garnishing:

Chicory—approximately two large bunches

Fresh parsley

Wooden floral picks, regular frill picks, club frill picks, orange wood skewers

Carved vegetable flowers such as onion mums, leek, beets, turnips, red radishes all pre-cut and opened to full blossom in iced water day before

Canned pineapple slices, mandarin orange sections (one *large* can well drained) spiced apple rings and spiced crab apples, etc.

Place order for an unsliced Pullman loaf of white bread from your local bakery the day you begin defrosting the turkey. Pick up day before carving.

A day in advance: roast the turkey in your own preferred manner. Be sure it is not overcooked, as this will cause the meat to be dry and stringy and therefore difficult to carve and handle. Carve and ice vegetable flowers to open—color same.

TO PREPARE BREAD SOCLE: The purpose of using the bread socle is to physically lift the bird up to an angled presentation while simultaneously stabilizing it. Estimate length of cooked bird and accordingly cut Pullman loaf of bread to fit

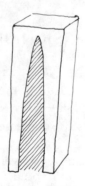

proper length. If any Pullman bread is left over one can always make delicious French toast, stuffing or croutons from same. Three inches from end of Pullman loaf cut out a large wedge as per shadow in diagram. Set aside.* This removed bread section will later be used as a fill-in substitute in place of the turkey meat removed from the right breast side of the bird.

Place socle on back section of a large serving tray. Choose a serving platter or tray large enough to hold displayed carved turkey and large enough to also allow enough room on front and sides of tray for additional meat and fruit accompaniments.

Slice as much of the dark meat as possible from back, thigh and side of drumstick areas for sandwich makings or plate service. Set this dark sliced meat aside in *hidden* secure recess of the refrigerator for refilling service tray later. Mothers of teenagers will know immediately why such emphasis was placed on this. May I relate a true story to bring home the importance of this rule for carving a turkey, which I learned the hard way.

As with all of food sculpture, carving a turkey, like all else, is just a matter of practice. However, on my first practice run at carving the big bird, I was at this very point and had, according to my directions, set aside all the dark meat on a separate plate. I then proceeded engrossed and excited with the carving of the turkey. When it was time, however, to place the dark, already sliced meat back on to the large turkey platter, I turned to retrieve same only to find a barren plate. Upon inquiry (translated to mother talk means a calm state of hysteria), I learned that my two boys had eaten all the dark meat I had diligently carved and set aside for use later. To this day, they cannot understand why I was so upset over a plate of meat. "After all, we were going to eat it for supper anyway!" . . . Come on, would you have laughed so easily if it was *your* first "carved and put-back-on-the-frame turkey" for company?

So . . . after hiding the dark sliced meat in the recesses of the refrigerator, with sign "eaten under penalty of death," let us go on to greater glory.

Place the bird on his back, the front of breast facing you, the body cavity vent to the back. Cut into skin of turkey along dotted line beginning on *YOUR* right side. To release skin, cut from point of body cavity down along and in between the inside

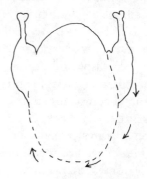 

breast and the drumstick, down along the breast, including the neck cavity skin; now cut down and around the front and continue up to front area of the opposing drumstick.

Starting again at the initial cutting area near the body cavity (right side) very carefully and gingerly insert your fingers under the skin. Gently lift up and push back the poultry skin separating it from the meat underneath. Retract those sharp or long nails of yours, for we want to detach the skin and lay it back without making any holes in same. This same skin covering (sans holes hopefully) will be used to recover the turkey breast once it has been sliced and put back on the frame. If at any point, the lifting back of the skin becomes resistant perhaps because a little piece of meat is clinging to the skin at one point, cut *under* and release that meat still attached to the skin rather than chance ripping the skin. Carefully lay the now released but still attached poultry skin back far enough to the left side of its turkey frame so as to fully expose the complete breasts on front of the turkey.

TO SLICE MEAT BREAST: With a boning knife, remove both left breast side of turkey in *one whole piece* as well as right side in one whole piece. The flexibility of the boning knife will enable you to get as close to the bone frame as possible. Any small pieces of meat left over on the breast frame will fall off when the carcass is cooked later to make soup. Make a mental note which breast was removed from which side, as once the meat is sliced down, breasts must fit back into their respective cavities. Gently place underside of turkey frame onto the top of the cut open bread socle; the bottom side of the breast area must be pressed into the opened crevice from whence cut wedge of bread was previously removed. This will now properly position your turkey for presentation at the raised angle desired. Use a few orangewood sticks, pushing same through back spine of turkey frame and down into bread to secure one to the other, stabilizing same.

*Shape and form the cut out wedge piece of previously removed bread to fit onto the right side of the boned out breast frame. *NOTE:* if extra breast of turkey or a boneless turkey roast is being used to supplement bird in order to feed a larger crowd, *only* then replace that right side with its respective sliced breast of meat for there will be ample enough extra meat and no need to use bread as mock filler. Use a sharp roast slicer knife to slice down the removed left breast of the bird keeping meat slices in the exact order of cutting. Replace meat back into respective left side of bird. Quickly but gently fully cover both meat and bread filled sides of bird with its own freed and pushed back poultry skin. As you can now see, the bread filler was used so as not to have the right side (fillet of meat) appear deflated in appearance. The turkey breast removed from the right side will be used as the cascading meat displayed on the outside front of that right breast. Use wooden floral picks to temporarily secure skin covering into the bread-filled right side section of the bird. On cutting board, slice down the removed right side of the breast meat. Cut *thinly on bias.* Replace all dark cut meat slices to fill around bottom front of tray. If large party is expected, supplement with other cut sliced meats from extra rolled boneless dark turkey roasts and white turkey breasts.

First time around ask your friend for her extra hand, as this is where you may need it until you get the swing of things. Prepare some wood floral picks at hand.

With a long spatula in hand, lift up the entire sliced down (right) breast of your bird and slide it off and on top of the *skin* covering on the right breast side of the turkey frame. Start by placing the first laid meat slice just below the body cavity, extend meat slices in fanned out cascade fashion working down and along the right side of drumstick, onto the breast and down and onto the tray front. The cascading breast sliced meat should cover the dark meat (slices) which had already been placed on the bottom front of the turkey platter. Quickly and deftly pin cascade of meat in approximate position with floral wood picks. Using one uniform color of club frill picks (all red *or* blue is a nice contrasting color) highlight this cascading array of bias-cut meat slices by bordering same with drained mandarin oranges. Use frill picks to pin in mandarin orange pieces individually, removing the (temporary holding) floral wood picks as you do so. Catch the mandarin orange and meat slices together and push frill club pick through both down into the bread simultaneously. As it would have been difficult pinning or holding anything into a meatless bony carcass, it was necessary to utilize the bread as filler.

TO GARNISH TURKEY: To pretty up our bird for his party, let's first fill that large void in his body cavity. Take a large handful of cleaned chicory in one piece. Wrap ¾" of its base in foil. Push this foil wrapped chicory base down into the well of the cavity opening. Allow the greenery of the chicory to remain frilly and fully exposed. Optional: Place little frilly paper booties on feet end tips of bird. Use orange wood sticks to secure into this chicory bed, an array of large beautiful carved vegetable flowers such as a large pink vegetable dyed onion mum, a red beet dahlia and a yellow dyed turnip carved rose or a large leek made up as scallion mum or whatever your choice to bring a touch of color to the greenery and beauty to your displayed edible centerpiece. See chapter 7 on carved vegetable flowers.

Cover exposed back and sides of raised bread socle with (totem pinned in) chicory. Garnish cascading breast of meat on front of turkey frame with sprigs of fresh parsley. Garnish and pretty up turkey with other strategically placed fresh cut vegetable flowers. Provide more edibility and beauty with the use of canned pineapple slices, whose centers can be topped with small spiced crab apples. If preferred, use your own creative flair to garnish and decorate turkey tray however it pleases your eye, teases your appetite and fits your pocketbook.

TO SERVE: When your guests have eaten most of the pre-cut exposed meat visibly displayed on the platter, slice the covering breast poultry skin down the mid-center of the turkey frame. Cutting the skin in this manner will not reveal the bread substitution trick you used as filler. Throw back the turkey skin on the remaining left covered breast to reveal more of the luscious white meat. At this point, one can begin to cut off drumsticks and wings if so desired, to serve to guests. If a large crowd is anticipated, refill serving platter whenever necessary with the extra cooked and reserved boneless dark and white sliced down turkey roasts.

VARIATION FOR A LARGE CROWD: If strictly white breast is your preferred meat, prepare an extra roasted breast or even two. Remove both sides of turkey breast as outlined previously from its bony framework. Slice meat and replace both meat sections back into their respective breastplates. Cover both sliced breasts with skin. Lay down the extra dark meat on front of plate for extra service. Overlay both sides of breast front with two cascading sides of bias cut extra meat. Decorate accordingly with parsley and fruit, as suggested above.

If serving a can of jelly strained cranberry sauce to complement your poultry dinner, cut the chilled cranberry sauce with a serrator. This accompanying side dish will look so much more elegant when cut and served in this manner.

Don't put off for tomorrow what you can do today. . . . Practice, practice, practice!

It's the name of the game . . . we're just having some fun with food.

HOW AND WHERE TO GET IT: As we near the conclusion of this book may I suggest several places to write to obtain booklets on how to complete your table presentations with beautifully folded napkins since we did not go into it extensively here.

"Fold a Pretty Napkin": The Belgian Linen Assoc., 280 Madison Ave. N.Y.C., N.Y. 10016

"Fascinate Your Family with Fancy Napkin Folds: Golem Press, Box 1342, Boulder, Col. 80302. $2.00 charge

Also: *send to P.O. Box 9400 St. Paul, Minn. 55177* for booklet: How the Shrewdest Shoppers Buy and Use Meat, Dairy Products and Eggs for poultry;

Send to Supt. of Documents; U.S. Gov't Printing Office, Washington D.C., 20402 for: Poultry in Family Meals—20¢ How to Buy Poultry—bulletin #157–10¢

11 HAVE YOU HAD FUN?

Well, I hope you've had fun. I'm sure your guests and family have enjoyed your newly learned sculpture skills as much as you have, so here's another surprise especially for you from me!

All along you've held the Mrs. degree *(summa cum laude,)* that of a domestic engineer . . . that's the title you found you *had* when you started reading my book. Now turn the page and see your *newly earned* sheepskin. It might even be fun to frame it and put it on the kitchen wall for it is a nice conversation piece. One of my gals, the wife of a very prominent doctor has her degree alongside his in the den, perhaps rightly so in their eyes. She feels she works and does just as fine a job in her role as a domestic engineer as he does as a doctor. In any case he is *very* proud of her culinary accomplishments. And so until we meet again, may I share my very favorite recipe given me to keep in mind always . . .

Actually, it's a recipe handed down through my family on Preserving . . . a Husband! Be careful of your selection. Do not choose too young. When once selected give your entire thought to preparation for domestic use. Some insist on keeping them in a pickle, others are constantly getting them into hot water. This makes them sour, hard and sometimes bitter. Even poor varieties may be made sweet, tender and good by garnishing them with patience, well sweetened with love and seasoned with kisses. Wrap them in a mantle of charity. Keep warm with a steady fire of domestic devotion and serve with peaches and cream. Thus prepared they will keep for years and years.

Fondly,

Florrie Paul